Camping
Northern California

Help Us Keep This Guide Up to Date

Every effort has been made by the author and editors to make this guide as accurate and useful as possible. However, many things can change after a guide is published—trails are rerouted, regulations change, techniques evolve, facilities come under new management, etc.

We would love to hear from you concerning your experiences with this guide and how you feel it could be improved and kept up to date. While we may not be able to respond to all comments and suggestions, we'll take them to heart and we'll also make certain to share them with the author. Please send your comments and suggestions to the following address:

The Globe Pequot Press
Reader Response/Editorial Department
P.O. Box 480
Guilford, CT 06437

Or you may e-mail us at:

editorial@GlobePequot.com

Thanks for your input, and happy travels!

Camping
Northern California

Richard McMahon

GUILFORD, CONNECTICUT
HELENA, MONTANA
AN IMPRINT OF THE GLOBE PEQUOT PRESS

FALCONGUIDES®

Copyright © 2001 Morris Book Publishing, LLC

FalconGuides is an imprint of The Globe Pequot Press.

Falcon and FalconGuides are registered trademarks of Morris Book Publishing, LLC.

Cover photo © Larry Prosor
All photos by Richard McMahon unless otherwise noted.

Library of Congress Cataloging-in-Publication Data
McMahon, Richard, 1928–
    Camping northern California / by Richard McMahon.—1st ed.
      p. cm.
    Includes index.
     ISBN 978-1-56044-895-2
      1. Camp sites, facilities, etc.—California, Northern—Guidebooks. 2. Camping—California, Northern—Guidebooks. 3. California, Northern—Guidebooks. I. Title.

GV191.42.C2 M34 2001
796.54'09794—dc21
                                  2001020511

Text pages printed on recycled paper
Manufactured in the United States of America
First Edition/Fourth Printing

Contents

To Susan and Nancy:

For bringing beauty, class,

and, most of all,

love to our family.

Acknowledgments

Many people assisted me in the writing of this book. They are too numerous to mention individually, but I would be remiss if I did not at least acknowledge the organizations they represented. I am indebted to the many rangers and administrative personnel of the national, state, and county parks of California who provided information and offered me assistance.

As I began my travels, I was aware of the minor controversy surrounding the Forest Service regarding public versus private use of national forest lands. I am happy to say that, wherever I went, I found Forest Service employees friendly, knowledgeable, and deeply committed to the recreational use of our national forests.

Whatever tax dollars are spent on the Division of Tourism of the California Trade and Commerce Agency, taxpayers are clearly getting their money's worth. Employees cheerfully answered a flood of questions, provided brochures, maps, and other publications, returned long distance calls, and generally worked to ensure that the wonderful features of their state were made known to me.

Finally, I would like to tip my hat to the many volunteers who are donating their time and energy in our national, state, and county parks and forests. Manning information desks, assisting with outdoor programs, building and maintaining trails, serving as campground hosts, and performing other tasks, these dedicated folks, many of them senior citizens, provide many services and perform many jobs that would not otherwise get done.

Welcome to California

Welcome to California, the Golden State, the most populous state in the Union and the third largest geographically. By far the richest state in terms of gross product, California is more appropriately compared to nations than to other states. In this context, California is the seventh largest "nation" in the world, its gross product exceeded only by that of the United States, Britain, Russia, Germany, France, and Japan.

Driving this economic dynamo is agriculture, where California's output far exceeds that of any other state. If the Midwest is the breadbasket of the United States, California is its fruit and vegetable basket, leading the nation in production of grapes, tomatoes, lettuce, and a host of other orchard and vegetable crops. In manufacturing, mineral extraction, and fishing, California ranks among the top four states.

Geographically, the state resembles a giant water trough. The coast ranges on the west and the Sierra Nevada to the east serve as sides to the trough, while Central Valley runs north-south through its bottom. Both the highest and the lowest points in the contiguous 48 states are found in California less than 100 miles apart. Mount Whitney soars to 14,495 feet, while Death Valley plunges to 282 feet below sea level.

The climate of California is as diverse as its landscape. The high reaches of the Sierra Nevada experience arctic winter temperatures, while the southeastern deserts bake in summer's heat. However, in the main, the state has dry summers and rainy winters, with regional variations. The coast from the Oregon border to just north of Los Angeles has cool summers and mild winters. South of Los Angeles, coastal residents enjoy some of the most pleasant year-round temperatures found anywhere. In the Central Valley a continental climate prevails, with hot summers and cool winters, and the mountainous regions are noted for short summers and cold winters.

Spanish navigator Juan Rodriguez Cabrillo was the first known European to sight California, in 1542. But it was not until 1769 that Franciscan friar Junipero Serra established the first mission at San Diego. Additional missions and the opening of an overland supply route from Mexico spurred colonization from the south, and following Mexico's independence from Spain in 1821, American settlers began to arrive. In 1846 a group of American settlers proclaimed the establishment of the California Republic, and in May of that year the United States declared war on Mexico. In the peace treaty that followed, Mexico ceded California to the United States, paving the way for California to become the 31st state in 1850.

With its diverse landscape, its relatively mild climate, and its magnificent scenery, California is a paradise for outdoor and sports enthusiasts. The state contains 8 national parks, 5 national monuments, nearly 400 state and county parks, 20 million acres of national forests, and numerous other recreational lands under federal, state, and local jurisdiction. There are more than 1,200 public campgrounds accessible by car. Stretching from the northern mountains to the southern deserts, they range from primitive sites for tents or self-contained RVs to plush resorts with pools, spas, tennis courts, and even golf courses. What they have in common is that they provide a memorable outdoor experience.

Camping in Northern California

Northern California has a campground for everyone. In addition to hundreds of standard family campgrounds, there are campgrounds designed for hikers, equestrians, boaters, anglers, and even off-road-vehicle drivers. Dozens of group campgrounds are set aside for organizations and other private groups.

This book describes more than 760 campgrounds accessible by conventional vehicles and managed by public agencies in Northern California. Together, the following agencies administer more than 95 percent of all the public campgrounds in the state.

The National Park Service manages campgrounds in all eight national parks; in Lava Beds, Devils Postpile, and Pinnacles National Monuments; and in Point Reyes and Whiskeytown-Shasta-Trinity National Recreation Areas. *Sunset Magazine* ranks Indian Well Campground in Lava Beds National Monument among its top 100 campgrounds in the western United States. It also lists two campgrounds administered jointly by the National Park Service and the California State Park system: Portola State Park and Gold Bluffs Beach in Prairie Creek Redwoods State Park. Some NPS campgrounds accept reservations, some require them, and others are available only on a first come, first served basis. This information is provided in the individual campground entries. NPS campgrounds do not have hookups. Most charge a fee, but some more remote sites with minimum facilities are free.

The USDA Forest Service manages by far the largest number of campgrounds in Northern California. They are found in all 13 national forests: Six Rivers, Klamath, Modoc, Shasta-Trinity, Lassen, Mendocino, Plumas, Tahoe, Eldorado, Toiyabe, Stanislaus, Inyo, and Sierra. *Sunset Magazine* has listed four Forest Service campgrounds among the top 100 campgrounds in the western United States: Almanor in Lassen National Forest, Lake Mary and Rock Creek Lake in Inyo, and Woods Lake in Eldorado. Although most Forest Service campsites are available on a first come, first served basis, reservations are accepted at the more popular locations, some of which have hookups. Most Forest Service campgrounds charge a fee, and many are operated by concessionaires. At many undeveloped sites, no fee is charged.

In the national forests you needn't restrict your stay to established campgrounds. You may camp anywhere unless specifically prohibited from doing so, as long as your campsite is at least 100 feet from bodies of water, trails, and roadsides. Check with the nearest Forest Service office or ranger station, where personnel can recommend the best areas for such open camping. A campfire permit is required outside developed campgrounds, even to cook with a camp stove or charcoal brazier. The permit is free at Forest Service facilities.

The California Department of Parks and Recreation manages campgrounds in some of the most scenic and recreational areas of the state. *Sunset Magazine* includes nine of these areas among the top 100 campgrounds in the west: Humboldt Redwoods, Castle Crags, D. L. Bliss, Grover Hot Springs, MacKerricher, McArthur-Burney Falls, Plumas-Eureka, and Salt Point State Parks and New Brighton State Beach. Many state park campgrounds accept

Campers in Northern California have a wealth of diversity from which to choose—from campgrounds sprawled across sunny coastal beaches to those tucked amid the alpine splendor of Yosemite National Park (shown here).

reservations, and during the summer months you'll most likely need them, especially on weekends or holidays. Many state park campgrounds offer hookups; of those that do not, many have flush toilets and hot showers. All state park campgrounds charge a fee.

Individual counties offer first-rate campgrounds in scenic areas that are often off the beaten path and sometimes overlooked by the traveling hordes of summer. If you are inclined to pass over county campgrounds, Del Valle Regional Park, near Livermore, made *Sunset's* top 100 list. About half of all county campgrounds accept reservations, and about half (not necessarily the same half) have hookups. All charge a fee.

The Bureau of Land Management administers campgrounds in the coast ranges, Cascades, and Sierra Nevada. BLM campgrounds do not accept reservations, and none have hookups. About half the campgrounds charge a fee; undeveloped campgrounds are usually free.

The U.S. Army Corps of Engineers has constructed a series of dams throughout California, and many of the reservoirs created by these dams offer a full range of water sports. The corps has constructed campgrounds at most of these reservoirs. Although none originally had hookups, some are now being upgraded to provide them. Corps campgrounds do offer most other amenities, including flush toilets and showers. These campgrounds do not accept reservations, and sites are available on a first come, first served basis. Fees are charged at all locations.

Special districts and municipalities also manage campgrounds throughout the state. Special district facilities are similar to Corps of Engineer sites in that they are usually associated with water reclamation projects, such as lakes. Cities and townships also manage campgrounds, normally in connection with a nearby point of interest or within a park. Most have hookups and accept reservations, and all charge fees.

Travel Tips

Reservations. If you are traveling in summer, on holidays, or on weekends, it is worthwhile making reservations wherever it is possible to do so—especially for longer stays. Beach, national park, state park, and many other campgrounds fill quickly during these periods, and campers who arrive late may find no vacancies.

Pets. In almost all public and private campgrounds where pets are permitted, they must be confined or leashed. In county, state, and national parks, pets are normally not permitted on hiking trails or beaches. In national forests pets are prohibited on some trails. Public campgrounds often charge additional fees for pets, ranging from $1 to $3 per night.

Wheelchair access. Many public campgrounds have wheelchair-accessible facilities, including restrooms. These campgrounds are indicated on the quick-reference tables in this book. Some have wheelchair-accessible trails. Because many public jurisdictions are making efforts to upgrade the accessibility of existing facilities, you should contact individual campgrounds for the latest information.

Fishing and hunting licenses. Licenses are required in California for both saltwater and freshwater fishing. Annual licenses for residents cost $27.05. There are three types of licenses for nonresidents: annual for $73.50, 10-day for $27.05, and 1-day for $9.70. Licenses are available for $4.25 for people over 65 years old, on reduced incomes or receiving financial aid, and to military veterans with 70 percent or higher disability.

To be eligible for a hunting license in California, you must take an approved hunter safety course, present a hunter safety certificate from another state or Canadian province, or present a valid hunting license from another state or province. Licenses cost $26.25 for residents and $92.25 for nonresidents.

Rules of the road. The speed limit on rural interstate highways is 65 miles per hour unless otherwise posted. Elsewhere, speed limits are as posted. Right turns at red lights are permitted after stopping unless posted otherwise. At least two people must be riding in a vehicle to use car-pool lanes. All passengers must wear seatbelts. Children up to 4 years of age or under 40 pounds must be in a child-restraint safety seat. Automobile liability insurance is mandatory.

Maps. Although it is possible to find most of the campgrounds in this book by using the maps and directions furnished with the entries, additional maps are required to find some of the more remote ones. For those who want more detail, I recommend the DeLorme Mapping Company's *Northern California Atlas and Gazetteer,* available in most large bookstores. For camping in the national forests, the appropriate Forest Service map is essential to locate the more remote campgrounds and is an invaluable guide, particularly if you intend to hike or explore by car, horseback, or bicycle. Maps are available at Forest Service visitor centers and most ranger stations. You can also order them from the Forest Service by mail (630 Sansome Street, San Francisco 94111). There is a map for each of the 13 national forests in Northern California. Cost per map is $4. A word of warning, though: campground information on Forest Service maps is not always up to date. This is particularly true with regard to fee status and availability of water. Some district offices have published separate pamphlets that update campground information. Finally, a good state road map is a good tool for getting an overall picture of an area and for finding nearby points of interest.

Rules for RVs. Passengers are not permitted to ride in trailers but may ride in fifth-wheelers if there is a way to communicate with the driver. Trailer brakes and safety chains are required for trailers weighing over 1,500 pounds; power-brake systems require breakaway switches. The maximum width for RVs driving on California roads is 102 inches, and the maximum combined length for two or three vehicles is 65 feet. Propane cylinders must be turned off while your vehicle is in motion. RVs are required to carry a fire extinguisher.

Off-season travel. One of the best times to travel in Northern California is the fall. After Labor Day, students and teachers go back to school and campgrounds are less crowded, as are beaches, hiking trails, and other points of interest. Travel is more enjoyable without the hassle of bucking large crowds on the road and at tourist attractions. Spring can also be an excellent time to hit the road, although the weather is not always as favorable. Snow may linger in the mountains, closing roads to certain campgrounds and scenic areas, and spring runoff can cause landslides, road blockages, and muddy conditions.

Avoiding the crowds. Unless you simply must have your TV or microwave, go to the more remote places, those without hookups and with a minimum of amenities. You will have more privacy, better scenery, more room between sites, and a better chance to see wildlife. This is particularly true for self-contained RVers, who do not need to rely on hookups.

How to Use This Guide

For the purposes of this book, I have defined Northern California as extending from the Oregon border to the southern borders of Santa Cruz, Santa Clara, Merced, Madera, and Mono Counties. For purposes of tourism and travel, the California Division of Tourism has divided the state into 12 tour regions. Of these, four fall completely within the borders of Northern California and two lie partially inside its boundary. I have grouped campgrounds using these same tour regions, usually in the order of their location along or near major highways.

This book is written primarily for campers who want to drive to campgrounds in conventional, two-wheel-drive vehicles. Thus, the campgrounds listed here vary from plush, amenity-rich locations to wilderness sites with no facilities except scenery and solitude. But there are also hundreds of back-country and trailside campgrounds that are accessible only to hikers and backpackers, and many of the campgrounds described here serve as excellent base camps from which to reach them. For information about these backcountry sites, consult offices and publications of the Forest Service, national and state parks, Bureau of Land Management, and similar organizations.

For each of the six tour regions covered in *Camping Northern California*, the following information is provided:

- A map of the tour region, as well as maps of smaller areas within the regions.

- A table listing all the campgrounds in the region and their most important attributes.

- A brief overview of the region and, in some cases, of areas within the region.

- A description of each of the public campgrounds within the region.

Maps of the tour regions. With the exception of the San Francisco Bay Area and the Central Valley, each of the six tour regions covered in this book has been divided into smaller areas. The regional maps indicate the boundaries of these areas. Each area map shows the location of the campgrounds located within it, with the number on the map corresponding to the number of the campground description within the text.

CALIFORNIA TOUR REGIONS

SHASTA CASCADE

NORTH COAST

NORTHERN CALIFORNIA

GOLD COUNTRY

CENTRAL

HIGH

SAN FRANCISCO BAY AREA

VALLEY

SIERRA

CENTRAL COAST

DESERTS

SOUTHERN CALIFORNIA

L.A. COUNTY

INLAND EMPIRE

ORANGE COUNTY

SAN DIEGO COUNTY

The maps in this book are not drawn to scale, and campground locations are approximate. However, by using the maps and the instructions in the "Finding the campground" section of each campground description, you should have no difficulty reaching many of the sites. You may need additional maps to find some of the more remote campgrounds, as noted previously.

Quick-reference tables. For quick reference, a table at the beginning of each section lists all the campgrounds in the area and highlights their most important attributes. If you are looking for specific amenities, such as fishing or wheelchair-accessibility, you can use these tables to narrow your selection of campgrounds.

Overview. Highlights and points of interest within the tour region are discussed briefly here. Overviews of smaller areas within the region are also included.

Campground descriptions. Each campground description is numbered to correspond with the campground's location on the map. For each campground, the following information is provided:

MAP LEGEND

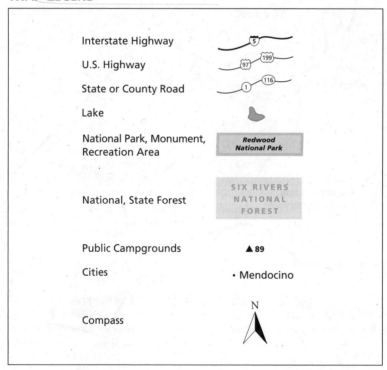

Interstate Highway	
U.S. Highway	
State or County Road	
Lake	
National Park, Monument, Recreation Area	Redwood National Park
National, State Forest	SIX RIVERS NATIONAL FOREST
Public Campgrounds	▲ 89
Cities	• Mendocino
Compass	N

- **Location.** This is the name of a city or town near the campground, the distance in miles from that city to the campground, and the general direction of travel to reach it.

- **Sites.** This information provides the number of campsites available and whether tents, RVs, or both are allowed. It also indicates whether hookups are available. An increasing number of public campgrounds are remodeling at least some of their sites to offer hookups. This is especially true of state and county parks.

Facilities. This describes the facilities and amenities provided, including any recreational facilities available at the campground.

- **Water.** Some public campgrounds do not provide drinking water, and this fact is indicated in this section. But a "no drinking water" notation does not necessarily mean there is no water at the site. Nonpotable water may be available at the campground or from a nearby stream or lake. In either case, the water should be filtered, boiled, or otherwise treated before use.

Fee per night. This is usually given as a price range for individual sites, allowing for differences between summer and winter rates, sites with or without hookups, and premium (such as waterfront) and average campsites. The fees shown here are current as of the date of this writing. Call the managing agency for updated information. Some campgrounds charge a daily fee for pets, and this is indicated where applicable.

- **Discounts.** Many public campgrounds offer discounts to senior citizens, which are noted in this section. The National Park Service, Forest Service, Bureau of Land Management, and U.S. Army Corps of Engineers offer 50-percent discounts to campers holding Golden Age Passports, and California state parks and recreation areas offer $2 discounts to campers 62 years of age and older.

- **Reservations.** Most public campgrounds do not accept reservations. For those that do, information about obtaining reservations is also provided. If the "Fee per night" section does not mention reservations, the campground does not accept them.

Management. The authority managing the campground is identified here, and contact information is provided. As indicated earlier, more than 95 percent of the public campgrounds in this book are controlled by one of the following entities: National, state, or county parks; Forest Service; Bureau of Land Management; U.S. Army Corps of Engineers; or various municipal and regional water authorities. See Camping in Northern California for a description of these agencies and the campgrounds they manage.

Key to Abbreviations

I have tried to minimize the use of abbreviations in this book. The few that have crept in are shown below, as well as some that may be encountered on maps or in other travel references.

AAA   American Automobile Association

ATV   all-terrain vehicle

BLM   Bureau of Land Management

FR   Forest Service Road. These letters precede numbers, as in FR 18S03, and designate roads in national forests maintained by the Forest Service. They always appear on Forest Service maps but they may not always be posted along the road.

NPS   National Park Service

OHV   off-highway vehicle. This usually refers to a campground or a trail for the primary use of those who wish to drive trail motorcycles, all-terrain vehicles, four-wheel-drive vehicles, and snowmobiles. It does not include mountain bicycles. In some publications the abbreviation ORV (off-road vehicle) may be used instead.

PG&E   Pacific Gas and Electric Company

SRA   State Recreation Area

SVRA   State Vehicle Recreation Area (for use of off-highway vehicles)

Activities. Recreational activities that can take place at or from the campground are listed here. For example, swimming may be possible at a lakeside campground, hiking trails may be within walking distance of a campground, or boats may be launched from a campground boat launch.

Finding the campground. Detailed instructions are furnished for driving to the campground from the nearest city, town, or major highway. Although it is possible to find most of the campgrounds in this book using these directions and the corresponding map, the task will be easier with the help of Forest Service maps and/or a good state road map.

About the campground. This is the information that differentiates this particular campground from others or highlights special features. For example, if a campground is located on the water (ocean, lake, river, or stream), that fact is noted.

- **Elevation.** This is provided if it is a significant factor, such as when the campground is at a high altitude in the mountains or at a location below sea level (Death Valley or the Salton Sea, for example).

- **Stay limits.** Most public campgrounds limit the number of days a camper may stay on site.

- **Season.** Many campgrounds are open year-round, while others are seasonal. The opening and closing dates of certain campgrounds are approximate and depend upon snowfall and other weather conditions.

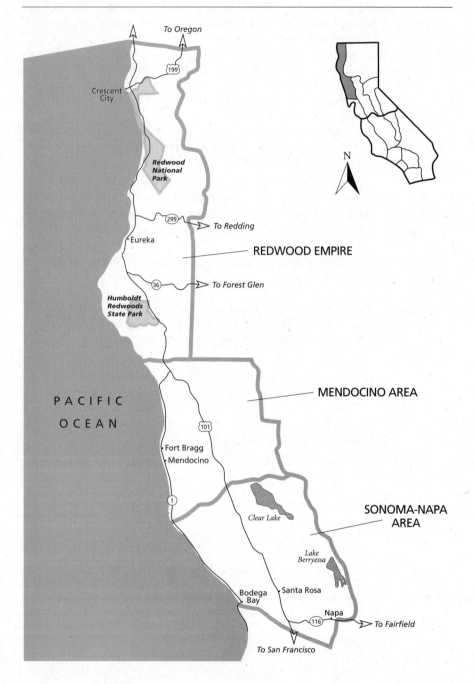

North Coast

Extending from the Oregon border to the southern borders of Sonoma and Napa Counties, the North Coast is a region of dramatic contrasts. From the majestic redwood forests of the north to the vineyards of the south, from the mountains of the coast ranges on the east to the rugged coastline on the west, the North Coast encompasses much of the best of California.

Most of the state's surviving ancient coastal redwoods lie within the borders of this region. They are protected by a national park and more than a dozen state parks and groves. From the Oregon border to Bodega Bay, almost 400 miles of Pacific shoreline lure beach goers, anglers, surfers, divers, whale watchers, and drivers eager to enjoy the spectacular coastal scenery. To the east, the 2 million acres of the Smith River and Mendocino National Forests provide a diverse woodland home for more than 300 species of wildlife, including black bears, deer, mountain lions, bald eagles, and wild turkeys. World-renowned vineyards line the Napa Valley, the heart of California's wine country. Only slightly less famous are some of the more than 100 wineries that line the Russian River north of Santa Rosa in Sonoma County, and both Mendocino and Lake Counties also produce fine wines.

The temperature of the North Coast varies relatively little and is moderate year-round. However, precipitation varies considerably with the seasons. Over most of the area more than 90 percent of the annual rainfall occurs from October through April. Rainfall is fairly heavy in the north, averaging 65 inches annually in Del Norte County. Precipitation decreases as you move southward, averaging 38 inches in Humboldt and Mendocino Counties and 30 inches in Sonoma County. Coastal areas are subject to morning fog. Average temperatures range from 42 to 54 degrees F in winter, 45 to 55 degrees F in spring, 52 to 60 degrees F in summer, and 48 to 60 degrees F in autumn. The average percentage of sunny days declines from a high of 55 percent in spring to 54 percent in summer, 49 percent in fall, and 43 percent in winter.

This guide divides the North Coast into three areas: Redwood Empire, Mendocino, and Sonoma-Napa.

REDWOOD EMPIRE

Sparsely populated but with a great natural endowment of beaches, forests, and fish-filled rivers and streams, the Redwood Empire attracts sports enthusiasts of all stripes. Overshadowing all are the huge and ancient coastal redwoods, which are preserved within Redwood National Park and almost a dozen state parks and groves. But the region also boasts many miles of sandy ocean beaches and hosts California's Lost Coast, created when rugged terrain forced the builders of U.S. Highway 1 to turn inland. Humboldt Bay offers saltwater fishing for salmon, halibut, and perch, while inland lie two of the nation's best salmon and steelhead rivers, the Smith and the Klamath.

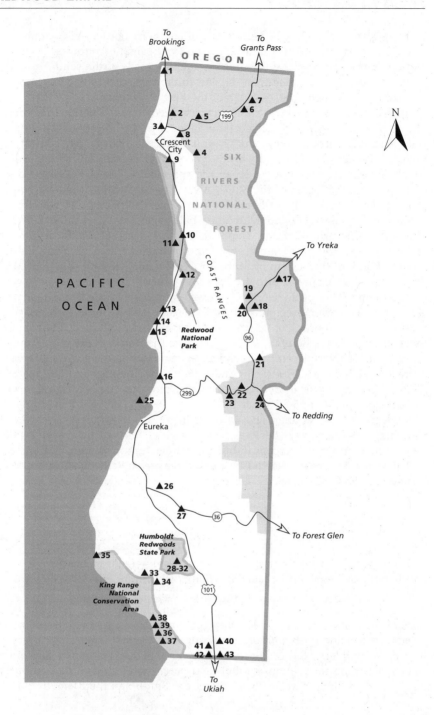

REDWOOD EMPIRE CAMPGROUNDS

		Group sites	RV sites	Total sites	Max. RV length	Hookups	Toilets	Showers	Drinking water	Dump station	Pets	Wheelchair	Recreation	Fee ($)	Season	Can reserve	Length of stay
1	Clifford Kamph Memorial County Park			8		WES	F		•		•		F	5		•	10
2	Ruby Van Devander County Park		•	18			F		•		•		SF	10		•	14
3	Florence Keller County Park		•	45			F		•		•		HF	10		•	14
4	Big Flat		•	28	22		V				•		HF	6	mid-May–October		14
5	Panther Flat		•	39	40		F	•	•		•	•	HF	12		•	14
6	Grassy Flat		•	19	30		V		•		•	•	F	8	May–mid-Sept.	•	14
7	Patrick Creek		•	13			F		•		•	•	HF	10	May–mid-Sept.	•	14
8	Jedediah Smith Redwoods State Park		•	107	36		F	•	•	•	•		HSF	12–1700		•	15/30
9	Del Norte Coast Redwoods State Park		•	145	31		F	•	•	•	•		H	12–17	April–October		15

Prairie Creek Redwoods State Park (10–11):

		Group sites	RV sites	Total sites	Max. RV length	Hookups	Toilets	Showers	Drinking water	Dump station	Pets	Wheelchair	Recreation	Fee ($)	Season	Can reserve	Length of stay
10	Elk Prairie		•	75	27		F	•	•	•	•	•	H	12–17		•	15/30
11	Gold Bluffs Beach		•	25	20		F	•	•		•	•	HF	12–17			15
12	Redwood National Park		•	open							•		HFB	5			15
13	Humboldt Lagoons State Park			6			F						HB	10–12			15
14	Big Lagoon County Park		•	22			F		•		•		SFBL	12			14
15	Patrick's Point State Park		•	124	31		F	•	•		•	Agate	HF	12–17			15/30
16	Clam Beach County Park		•	72			P		•		•		F	8			14
17	Pearch Creek		•	12	22		V		•		•		HSF	7	mid-May–mid-Nov.		14
18	E-Ne-Nuck		•	11	30		V		•		•		F	7	mid-July–mid-Nov.		14
19	Fish Lake		•	24	20		V		•		•		F	7	mid-May–mid-Sept.		14
20	Aikens Creek West		•	open	35		P		•		•		SF	5	May 22–Sept. 10		14
21	Tish Tang		•	40	30		V		•		•		SF	6			14
22	Boise Creek		•	17	35		V		•		•	•	HF	8	mid-May–mid-Sept.		14
23	East Fork		•	9	20		V				•	•	HF	6			14

	Group sites	RV sites	Total sites	Max. RV length	Hookups	Toilets	Showers	Drinking water	Dump station	Pets	Wheelchair	Recreation	Fee ($)	Season	Can reserve	Length of stay
24 Gray's Falls		•	33	35		F	•	•				HF	10	mid-May–mid-Sept.		14
25 Samoa Boat Launch County Park		•	50			F	•	•				SFBO	10		•	14
26 Van Duzen County Park		•	30			F	•	•		•		SF	12			14
27 Grizzly Creek Redwoods State Park		•	30	30		F	•	•		•	•	HSF	15–17		•	15/30

Humboldt Redwoods State Park (28–32)

	Group sites	RV sites	Total sites	Max. RV length	Hookups	Toilets	Showers	Drinking water	Dump station	Pets	Wheelchair	Recreation	Fee ($)	Season	Can reserve	Length of stay
28 Burlington		•	57	36		F	•	•	•	•	•	HSF	15–17		•	15/30
29 Hidden Springs		•	154	36		F	•	•		•		HSF	15–17	mid-May–mid-Oct.	•	15
30 Albee Creek		•	39	36		F	•	•		•		H	15–17	May–Sept.	•	15
31 Williams Grove Group Camp	•	•	2			F		•		•		HSF	60–90		•	15
32 Cuneo Creek Horse Camp	•	•	6			F		•		•		R	20–90		•	15
33 Honeydew		•	14			P				•	•		5			14
34 A.W. Way County Park		•	30			F	•	•		•		HFS	12			14

King Range National Conservation Area (35–39)

	Group sites	RV sites	Total sites	Max. RV length	Hookups	Toilets	Showers	Drinking water	Dump station	Pets	Wheelchair	Recreation	Fee ($)	Season	Can reserve	Length of stay
35 Mattole		•	14			P			•			HF	5			14
36 Nadelos			8			V		•		•	•	H	8			14
37 Wailaki		•	13			V		•		•		H	8			14
38 Tolkan		•	9			V		•		•	•	H	8			14
39 Horse Mountain		•	9			P		•				H	5			14
40 Benbow Lake State Recreation Area		•	75	30		F	•	•	•	•		SFBL	15–17	April–Oct.	•	14

Richardson Grove State Park (41–43)

	Group sites	RV sites	Total sites	Max. RV length	Hookups	Toilets	Showers	Drinking water	Dump station	Pets	Wheelchair	Recreation	Fee ($)	Season	Can reserve	Length of stay
41 Huckleberry		•	36	30		F	•	•	•	•	•	HSF	15–17		•	30
42 Madrone		•	40	30		F	•	•	•	•	•	HSF	15–17		•	30
43 Oak Flat		•	94	30		F	•	•		•	•	HSF	15–17	June–Sept.	•	15

Hookups: W = Water E = Electric S = Sewer
Toilets: F = Flush V = Vault P = Pit C = Chemical
Recreation: H = Hiking S = Swimming F = Fishing B = Boating L = Boat Launch O = Off-highway Driving R = Horseback Riding
Maximum Trailer/RV Length given in feet. Stay Limit given in days. Fee given in dollars.
If no entry under **Season,** campground is open all year. If no entry under Fee, camping is free.

In the east, Six Rivers National Forest encompasses 1,500 miles of rivers and streams, including 366 miles of designated Wild and Scenic Rivers. These beckon anglers, rafters, kayakers, and swimmers. Hikers, equestrians, and mountain bikers have 220 miles of trails and hundreds of miles of mining and logging roads to explore. The road-bound tourist can enjoy Smith River Scenic Byway (U.S. Highway 199) as it twists and turns through a granite gorge created by the Smith River. A portion of the Trinity Scenic Byway travels eastward from Blue Lake near Eureka along California 299, and the Avenue of the Giants brings motorists among the world's largest remaining redwoods. The towns of Eureka and Ferndale are noted for their beautiful Victorian homes.

1 Clifford Kamph Memorial County Park

Location: 3 miles south of the Oregon border, off U.S. Highway 101.
Sites: 8 sites for tents.
Facilities: Tables, grills, drinking water, flush toilets.
Fee per night: $5. Reservations accepted.
Management: Del Norte County Parks and Beaches, 707-464-7230.
Activities: Fishing, beachcombing.
Finding the campground: From the Oregon border, drive south on US 101 for about 3 miles to a sign for the park.

About the campground: With an oceanfront location on a wide, often windswept beach, the park offers one of the few accesses to the shoreline north of Crescent City. One campsite is directly on the sandy beach, while others are on a small hill above. Some pines provide partial shade. A private home bordering the park detracts somewhat from the isolated feeling of the beach. Anglers try for ling cod, cabezon, and rockfish but usually have to settle for surf perch. Stay limit 10 days. Open all year.

2 Ruby Van Devander County Park

Location: 13 miles northeast of Crescent City.
Sites: 18 sites for tents and RVs.
Facilities: Tables, grills, drinking water, flush toilets.
Fee per night: $10. Reservations accepted.
Management: Del Norte County Parks and Beaches, 707-464-7230.
Activities: Swimming, fishing.
Finding the campground: From the intersection of U.S. Highways 101 and 199 (about 5 miles northeast of Crescent City), drive east on US 199 for 4.3 miles, turn left onto California Highway 197, and drive 4 miles.

About the campground: The campground is attractively situated in a stand of redwood trees on the banks of the Smith River. The river is noted for large fish—salmon in the fall, steelhead in the winter, and cutthroat trout in the summer. It is also noted as a difficult place to catch them, and knowledgeable anglers use local guides, at least until they learn the technique of luring fish from this beautiful river. Stay limit 14 days. Open all year.

3 Florence Keller County Park

Location: 8 miles north of Crescent City.
Sites: 45 sites for tents and RVs.
Facilities: Tables, grills, drinking water, flush toilets.
Fee per night: $10. Reservations accepted.
Management: Del Norte County Parks and Beaches, 707-464-7230.
Activities: Hiking, fishing, kayaking.
Finding the campground: From the intersection of U.S. Highways 101 and 199 (about 5 miles northeast of Crescent City), drive north on US 101 for 0.5 mile, turn left onto Elk Valley Crossroad, and drive 2.5 miles to the park.

About the campground: Campsites are attractively located in a stand of mature redwood trees, and there are hiking trails through several parts of the forest. Nearby Lake Earl is shallow and provides only second-rate fishing, limited to flounder and trapped cutthroat trout that enter the lake from the ocean in winter. However, it is a good place for kayaks and canoes. Stay limit 14 days. Open all year.

4 Big Flat

Location: 22 miles southeast of Crescent City.
Sites: 28 sites for tents and RVs up to 22 feet long.
Facilities: Tables, fire rings, vault toilets. No drinking water.
Fee per night: $6.
Management: Six Rivers National Forest, 707-457-3131.
Activities: Fishing, hiking.
Finding the campground: From the intersection of U.S. Highways 101 and 199 (about 5 miles northeast of Crescent City), drive 6 miles east on US 199 to Hiouchi. Turn right just past Hiouchi onto South Fork Road and drive 15 miles. Turn left onto Big Flat Road and drive 0.5 mile.

About the campground: Located on the banks of Hurdygurdy Creek, these campsites are just a short walk away from winter fishing for steelhead. Several hiking trails explore the surrounding ridges and streambeds. Stay limit 14 days. Open mid-May through October.

5 Panther Flat

Location: 20 miles northeast of Crescent City.
Sites: 39 sites for tents and RVs up to 40 feet long.
Facilities: Tables, fire rings, drinking water, showers, flush toilets. The facilities are wheelchair accessible.
Fee per night: $12. For reservations call 800-280-CAMP. There is a one-time reservation fee of $8.65.
Management: Six Rivers National Forest, 707-457-3131.
Activities: Hiking, fishing.
Finding the campground: From the intersection of U.S. Highways 101 and

199 (about 5 miles northeast of Crescent City), drive east on US 199 for 15 miles.

About the campground: Situated on the banks of the Smith River, Panther Flat offers fishing for salmon in the fall and steelhead in the winter, but success is directly related to skill and experience when trying to land these wily fish. Stoney Creek Trail, which follows the creek to its junction with the North Fork of the Smith River, begins about 2 miles west of the campground, near Gasquet. A free hiking guide to this and other trails in the area is available by calling Six Rivers National Forest (see Management). Stay limit 14 days. Open all year.

6 Grassy Flat

Location: 27 miles northeast of Crescent City.
Sites: 19 sites for tents and RVs up to 30 feet long.
Facilities: Tables, fire rings, drinking water, vault toilets. The facilities are wheelchair accessible.
Fee per night: $8. For reservations call 800-280-CAMP. There is a one-time reservation fee of $8.65.
Management: Six Rivers National Forest, 707-457-3131.
Activities: Fishing, kayaking.
Finding the campground: From the intersection of U.S. Highways 101 and 199 (about 5 miles northeast of Crescent City), drive northeast 22 miles on US 199.

About the campground: Attractively situated on the banks of the Smith River, the campground would be a good location for steelhead anglers except that it is closed in fall and winter, the best fishing seasons. Stay limit 14 days. Open May through mid-September.

7 Patrick Creek

Location: 30 miles northeast of Crescent City.
Sites: 13 sites for tents and RVs.
Facilities: Tables, fire rings, drinking water, flush toilets. The facilities are wheelchair accessible.
Fee per night: $10. For reservations call 800-280-CAMP. There is a one-time reservation fee of $8.65.
Management: Six Rivers National Forest, 707-457-3131.
Activities: Fishing, hiking.
Finding the campground: From the intersection of U.S. Highways 101 and 199 (about 5 miles northeast of Crescent City), drive northeast 25 miles on US 199.

About the campground: Located in a grove of tall Douglas firs at the confluence of Patrick Creek and the Middle Fork of the Smith River, Patrick Creek Campground is a former Civilian Conservation Corps camp. Large steelhead are caught here, but only by expert anglers. And like nearby Grassy Flat Campground (number 6), it is closed during the best fishing season. Stay limit 14 days. Open May to mid-September.

8 Jedediah Smith Redwoods State Park

Location: 9 miles northeast of Crescent City.
Sites: 107 sites for tents and RVs up to 36 feet long.
Facilities: Tables, fire rings, drinking water, showers, flush toilets, dump station.
Fee per night: $12-$17, pets $1. For reservations call 800-444-7275. There is a one-time reservation fee of $7.50.
Management: California Department of Parks and Recreation, 707-464-9533.
Activities: Hiking, fishing, swimming, kayaking.
Finding the campground: From the intersection of U.S. Highways 101 and 199 (about 5 miles northeast of Crescent City), drive east on US 199 for 4 miles.

About the campground: Campsites are beautifully situated within an old-growth redwood forest and along the banks of the Smith River. Several trails lead from the campground, including a short walk to Stout Grove via a summer bridge over the Smith River. Longer hikes include the Mill Creek and Hatton-Hiouchi Trails. Salmon fishing takes place in the fall in the Smith River, followed by steelhead in the winter. Kayaking, canoeing, and rafting are also popular on the Smith, which is the last free-flowing major river in California. Howland Hill Road provides a 7-mile auto tour through some of the less-visited sections of the park. It is a narrow, gravel road, not recommended for trailers or large RVs. Stay limit 15 days from June through September, 30 days from October through May. Open all year.

9 Del Norte Coast Redwoods State Park

Location: 6 miles south of Crescent City.
Sites: 145 sites for tents and RVs up to 31 feet long.
Facilities: Tables, fire rings, drinking water, showers, flush toilets, dump station.
Fee per night: $12-$17, pets $1. For reservations call 800-444-7275. There is a one-time reservation fee of $7.50.
Management: California Department of Parks and Recreation, 707-464-9533.
Activities: Hiking.
Finding the campground: From park headquarters in Crescent City, drive south on U.S. Highway 101 for 5 miles, turn left at the campground sign, and drive 0.8 mile.

About the campground: Located in a mixed forest of mostly redwoods, the campground is deeply shaded and sites are well spaced in several loops. An excellent 6-mile loop hike through ancient and second-growth redwood stands is possible directly from the campground by combining the Mill Creek, Hobbs

Wall, and Saddler Skyline Trails. The popular Damnation Creek Trail begins about 3 miles south of the campground highway turnoff. This 5-mile round trip leads through a redwood and Sitka spruce forest, dropping 1,000 feet to the ocean. Stay limit 15 days. Open from April to October.

10 | Prairie Creek Redwoods State Park: Elk Prairie

Location: 8 miles north of Orick.
Sites: 75 sites for tents and RVs up to 27 feet long.
Facilities: Tables, fire rings, drinking water, showers, flush toilets, dump station, museum, visitor center. The facilities are wheelchair accessible.
Fee per night: $12-$17, pets $1. For reservations call 800-444-7275. There is a one-time reservation fee of $7.50.
Management: California Department of Parks and Recreation, 707-488-2171.
Activities: Hiking.
Finding the campground: From Orick, drive north on U.S. Highway 101 for 6 miles, turn left onto Newton B. Drury Scenic Parkway, and drive 2 miles.

About the campground: Elk Prairie is aptly named, as a herd of Roosevelt elk is almost always in residence, grazing in a large field between the campground and the highway. Revelation Trail (0.3 mile), which begins behind the visitor center, is designed to afford blind and wheelchair-bound people an opportunity to experience the redwood forest. Two trails lead from the campground to the coast: The James Irvine Trail (4.2 miles) leads to Fern Canyon, while the Miner's Ridge Trail (3.9 miles) leads to Gold Bluffs Beach. They can be combined with the connecting mile-long Clintonia Trail to form a loop. Stay limit 15 days from June through September, 30 days from October through May. Open all year.

11 | Prairie Creek Redwoods State Park: Gold Bluffs Beach

Location: 7 miles north of Orick.
Sites: 25 sites for tents and RVs up to 20 feet long.
Facilities: Tables, fire rings, drinking water, solar showers, flush toilets. The facilities are wheelchair accessible.
Fee per night: $12-$17, pets $1.
Management: California Department of Parks and Recreation, 707-488-2044.
Activities: Hiking, fishing.
Finding the campground: From Orick, drive north on U.S. Highway 101 for 3 miles, turn left onto Davison Road, and drive 4 miles. No trailers or vehicles wider than 7 feet are permitted on Davison Road.

About the campground: Gold Bluffs has been selected by *Sunset Magazine* as one of the 100 best campgrounds west of the Mississippi. It is an undeniably beautiful location: a wide, windswept, deserted beach backed by sandstone bluffs and forested hills. The beach got its name in 1851 from a gold rush that did not pan out. About 1.5 miles away, along the Coastal Trail, is the Fern Canyon Loop, which follows a stream through a narrow canyon lined with ferns. Stay limit 15 days. Open all year.

Redwood National and State Parks

One hundred fifty years ago, redwoods covered 2 million acres of coastal Northern California. Since then, intense logging has reduced this vast forest to no more than 300,000 acres, one third of which are protected in Redwood National and State Parks. The park complex consists of a partnership of federal and state lands, the state making the major contribution with three state parks in the northern portion of the complex. Redwood National Park proper encompasses the southern section of the complex and includes the Tall Trees Grove and Lady Bird Johnson Grove.

The coastal redwood is the tallest living thing on earth. Many trees stand taller than the Statue of Liberty and weigh up to 500 tons. The world's tallest tree, found in Tall Trees Grove, measured 367.8 feet when it was discovered in 1963. Incongruously, these trees sprout from a seed no larger than a tomato seed. Redwoods grow only along a narrow coastal strip of Northern California and southern Oregon. They can live up to 2,000 years.

The parks' woodlands and meadows host a variety of wildlife, including elk, black-tailed deer, black bears, mountain lions, and smaller animals such as coyotes, foxes, and gophers. Their streams shelter steelhead, cutthroat trout, and Chinook salmon. The park complex also includes many miles of coastline, some of it pristine and accessible only by trail. Four of the five vehicle-accessible campgrounds in the park complex are found in the state parks.

More than 270 separate groves of redwoods are preserved in 14,000-acre Prairie Creek Redwoods State Park, including many fine old-growth specimens. Seventy-five miles of trails help you visit them and also provide access to miles of wild, rugged coastline. The Newton B. Drury Scenic Parkway provides a 9-mile auto tour through the park, with pullouts along the route to attractions such as Big Tree and with opportunities to hike on several short trails or segments.

12 Redwood National Park: Freshwater Lagoon Spit

Location: 3 miles southwest of Orick.
Sites: Parallel parking for self-contained RVs on a mile-long segment on the ocean side of U.S. Highway 101 at Freshwater Lagoon. A tent area is located on the beach at the southern end of the spit.
Facilities: None.
Fee per night: None, but a donation of $5 is suggested.
Management: Redwood National and State Parks, 707-464-6101.
Activities: Fishing, swimming, boating.
Finding the campground: From Orick, drive south 2 or 3 miles on U.S. Highway 101 to Freshwater Lagoon Spit. Signs and bulletin boards identify the camping area, but the RVs parked alongside the road are the best guide.

About the campground: Although parking off a busy highway seems far from the ideal camping experience, the area is popular. With a sandy ocean beach on one side, a sheltered lagoon on the other, and the national park information center less than a mile away, Freshwater Lagoon has a lot to offer. Add the fact that the state stocks about 32,000 rainbow trout in the lagoon every year, and a camper need only cross the road to cast a line, and the place is a lazy angler's dream. Stay limit 15 days. Open all year.

13 Humboldt Lagoons State Park

Location: 13 miles north of Trinidad.
Sites: 6 sites for tents.
Facilities: Tables, fire rings, pit toilet. No drinking water.
Fee per night: $10-$12.
Management: California Department of Parks and Recreation, 707-488-2171.
Activities: Hiking, boating.
Finding the campground: From Trinidad, drive north 13 miles on U.S. Highway 101 to the entrance to the campground parking lot, halfway between mileposts 114 and 115. From the parking lot, it is about a 500-foot walk to the campground.

About the campground: Humboldt Lagoon is a wooded, usually secluded campground because of the walk necessary to reach it. It is close to beach access and to trout fishing at Stone Lagoon to the north and Big Lagoon to the south. No pets allowed. Stay limit 15 days. Open all year.

14 Big Lagoon County Park

Location: 10 miles north of Trinidad.
Sites: 22 sites for tents and RVs.
Facilities: Tables, fire rings, drinking water, flush toilets, boat ramp.
Fee per night: $12 per vehicle, pets $1.
Management: Humboldt County Parks Department, 707-445-7651.
Activities: Swimming, boating, fishing, hunting.
Finding the campground: From Trinidad, drive north 8 miles on U.S. Highway 101, turn left onto Big Lagoon Park Road, and drive 2 miles.

About the campground: Despite the narrowness of the spit which separates it from the ocean, Big Lagoon contains fresh water, and steelhead and rainbow trout fishing is popular, if only sometimes rewarding. Duck hunting is popular in winter. The boat ramp allows entry into Big Lagoon. Stay limit 14 days. Open all year.

15 Patrick's Point State Park: Agate, Abalone, Penn Creek

Location: 6 miles north of Trinidad.
Sites: 124 sites for tents and RVs up to 31 feet long, in 3 separate campgrounds less than a half-mile apart.
Facilities: Tables, fire rings, drinking water, showers, flush toilets.

Fee per night: $12-$17, pets $1.
Management: California Department of Parks and Recreation, 707-677-3570.
Activities: Hiking, fishing, surfing.
Finding the campground: From Trinidad, drive 5 miles north on U.S. Highway 101, turn left at Patrick's Point exit, and drive 0.5 mile.

About the campground: Patrick's Point encompasses a dramatic coastline of offshore rocks, sea stacks, secluded beaches, and tidepools. Its campsites are large and shaded, and most are protected from the wind. Agate Beach is one of Northern California's most beautiful beaches, reached by a 0.3-mile walk from Agate Campground. The best way to see the park is by hiking the Rim Trail and its six spurs, which descend to coves and tidepools and climb to vistas and lookouts. The park also includes a replica of a Yurok Indian village, "Sumeg," which is well worth a visit. Agate Campground has wheelchair-accessible facilities. Stay limit 15 days from June through September, 30 days from October through May. Open all year.

16 Clam Beach County Park

Location: 3.5 miles north of McKinleyville.
Sites: A large parking lot with space for 50 to 60 RVs, plus 12 sites for tents in a sandy dunes area.
Facilities: Tables and fire rings at tent sites only. Drinking water, pit toilets.
Fee per night: $8 per vehicle, pets $1.
Management: Humboldt County Parks Department, 707-445-7652.
Activities: Fishing, clamming.
Finding the campground: From McKinleyville, drive north 3.5 miles on U.S. Highway 101, take the Clam Beach exit, and drive west 2 blocks.

About the campground: Situated on a wide, long beach, the campground is exposed to windy conditions. It is noted as an excellent clamming spot, particularly at the north end of the beach at minus low tides. Fishing is fair, with perch the usual catch. Stay limit 14 days. Open all year.

17 Pearch Creek

Location: 2 miles northeast of Orleans.
Sites: 10 sites for tents, 2 sites for tents or RVs up to 22 feet long.
Facilities: Tables, fire rings, drinking water, vault toilets, fish smokers.
Fee per night: $7.
Management: Six Rivers National Forest, 530-627-3291.
Activities: Hiking, swimming, fishing, kayaking.
Finding the campground: From Orleans, drive 2 miles northeast on California Highway 96.

About the campground: The campground is located on the banks of Pearch Creek, about a quarter-mile from where it enters the Klamath River. Steelhead fishing can be good in the fall. Stay limit 14 days. Open from mid-May through mid-November.

18 E-Ne-Nuck

Location: 5 miles southwest of Orleans.
Sites: 11 sites for tents and RVs up to 30 feet long.
Facilities: Tables, fire rings, drinking water, vault toilets.
Fee per night: $7.
Management: Six Rivers National Forest, 530-627-3291.
Activities: Fishing.
Finding the campground: From Orleans, drive southwest 5 miles on California Highway 96.

About the campground: E-Ne-Nuck is situated on the banks of the Klamath River, which offers excellent steelhead fishing, especially in the fall. Stay limit 14 days. Open from mid-July through mid-November.

19 Fish Lake

Location: 12 miles north of Weitchpec.
Sites: 24 sites for tents and RVs up to 20 feet long.
Facilities: Tables, fire rings, drinking water, vault toilets.
Fee per night: $7.
Management: Six Rivers National Forest, 530-627-3291.
Activities: Fishing.
Finding the campground: From Weitchpec, at the intersection of California Highways 169 and 96, drive north 7 miles on CA 96, turn left onto Fish Lake Road, and drive 5 miles.

About the campground: This small lake is stocked annually with rainbow trout for the fishing season (Memorial Day to the end of July). The elevation is 1,800 feet. Stay limit 14 days. Open from mid-May through mid-September.

20 Aikens Creek West

Location: 5 miles northwest of Weitchpec.
Sites: Open camping for tents and RVs up to 35 feet long.
Facilities: Tables, fire rings, drinking water, pit toilets.
Fee per night: $5.
Management: Six Rivers National Forest, 530-627-3291.
Activities: Fishing, swimming, kayaking.
Finding the campground: From Weitchpec, at the intersection of California Highways 169 and 96, drive northwest 5 miles on CA 96.

About the campground: Across the highway from the banks of the Klamath River, the campground provides a good put-in for kayaks and rafts, and excellent steelhead fishing in the fall. Stay limit 14 days. Open from May 22 through September 10. (This campground replaces nearby Aikens Creek Campground, which has been permanently closed.)

21 Tish Tang

Location: 8 miles north of the community of Willow Creek.
Sites: 40 sites for tents and RVs up to 30 feet long.
Facilities: Tables, fire rings, drinking water (May through November), vault toilets.
Fee per night: $6.
Management: Hoopa Tribal Forestry Office, 530-625-0049.
Activities: Fishing, swimming, kayaking.
Finding the campground: From the intersection of California Highways 299 and 96 in Willow Creek, drive north on CA 96 for 8 miles.

About the campground: Located on a bend of the Klamath River, a large, flat gravel beach provides access to good kayaking in the spring, swimming in the summer, and steelhead fishing in the fall and winter. Stay limit 14 days. Open all year.

22 Boise Creek

Location: 2 miles west of the community of Willow Creek.
Sites: 17 sites for tents and RVs up to 35 feet long.
Facilities: Tables, fire rings, drinking water, vault toilets. The facilities are wheelchair accessible.
Fee per night: $8.
Management: Six Rivers National Forest, 530-627-3291.
Activities: Hiking, fishing.
Finding the campground: From Willow Creek, drive 2 miles west on California Highway 299.

About the campground: The campground is set above Boise Creek, and a trail leads down to its banks. Fishing for salmon in the fall and steelhead in the winter takes place along the Trinity River, beginning about 2 miles from the camp. Stay limit 14 days. Open from mid-May through mid-September.

23 East Fork

Location: 6 miles southwest of the community of Willow Creek.
Sites: 9 sites for tents and RVs up to 20 feet long.
Facilities: Tables, fire rings, vault toilets. No drinking water. The facilities are wheelchair accessible.
Fee per night: $6.
Management: Six Rivers National Forest, 530-629-2118.
Activities: Hiking, fishing.
Finding the campground: From Willow Creek, drive southwest on California Highway 299 for 6 miles.

About the campground: Fishing is fair for native trout in Willow Creek. Stay limit 14 days. Open all year.

24 Gray's Falls

Location: 12 miles southeast of Willow Creek.
Sites: 33 sites for tents and RVs up to 35 feet long.
Facilities: Tables, fire rings, drinking water, flush toilets.
Fee per night: $10.
Management: Six Rivers National Forest, 530-627-3291.
Activities: Hiking, fishing, kayaking.
Finding the campground: From Willow Creek, drive southeast on California Highway 299 for 12 miles.

About the campground: On the banks of the Trinity River, the campground is a good base for salmon fishing from July through September. The same would be true for steelhead, except that the campground is closed during the steelhead runs in the late fall. Stay limit 14 days. Open from mid-May through mid-September.

25 Samoa Boat Launch County Park

Location: 7 miles southwest of Eureka.
Sites: 50 sites for tents and RVs.
Facilities: Tables, fire rings, drinking water, flush toilets, boat ramp.
Fee per night: $11, pets $1. Reservations accepted; call number below.
Management: Humboldt County Parks Department, 707-445-7652.
Activities: Swimming, fishing, boating, clamming, bird watching, OHV driving.
Finding the campground: From the intersection of U.S. Highway 101 and California Highway 255 in Eureka, drive 2 miles northwest on CA 255, turn left (south) onto New Navy Base Road, and drive 5 miles.

About the campground: The park is situated on Humboldt Bay at the south end of the Samoa Peninsula. Perch and halibut are the main catches in the bay, with some salmon taken during the fall run. The Samoa Dunes Recreation Area, operated by the BLM, is just south of the campground. It has an OHV driving area and a hiking trail through a protected wetland that is closed to vehicles. The Samoa Cookhouse and Museum, 5 miles north on New Navy Base Road, is known for its family-style service, large portions, and reasonable prices. It is well worth a visit and a dining stop if you have a large appetite. Stay limit 14 days. Open all year.

26 Van Duzen County Park

Location: 33 miles southeast of Eureka.
Sites: 30 sites for tents and RVs.
Facilities: Tables, fire rings, drinking water, flush toilets, showers.
Fee per night: $12, pets $1.
Management: Humboldt County Parks Department, 707-445-7652.
Activities: Fishing, swimming, rafting, paddling.

Finding the campground: From the intersection of California Highway 255 and U.S. Highway 101 in Eureka, drive south on US 101 for 21 miles, turn left (east) onto California Highway 36, and drive 12 miles.

About the campground: The park is situated on the Van Duzen River, which can provide seasonally good fishing for salmon and steelhead. Check regulations carefully, as the river is subject to closures and restrictions. The Van Duzen offers good rafting and paddling in the spring, a popular course being the 6-mile downstream run to Grizzly Creek Redwoods State Park. Stay limit 14 days. Open all year.

27 Grizzly Creek Redwoods State Park

Location: 38 miles southeast of Eureka.
Sites: 30 sites for tents and RVs up to 30 feet long.
Facilities: Tables, fire rings, drinking water, flush toilets, showers. The facilities are wheelchair accessible.
Fee per night: $15-$17, pets $1. For reservations call 800-444-7275. There is a one-time reservation fee of $7.50.
Management: California Department of Parks and Recreation, 707-777-3683.
Activities: Hiking, swimming, fishing.
Finding the campground: From the intersection of California Highway 255 and U.S. Highway 101 in Eureka, drive south on US 101 for 21 miles, turn left (east) onto California Highway 36, and drive 17 miles.

About the campground: Situated near the confluence of Grizzly Creek and the Van Duzen River, the campground is only minutes from several fine redwood groves. The best of these is Cheatham Grove (4 miles west of camp), which has a mile-long trail to explore. Two other groves are within easy walking distance of the campground. For information on fishing the Van Duzen River, see Van Duzen County Park (number 26). Stay limit 15 days from June through September, 30 days from October through May. Open all year.

28 Humboldt Redwoods State Park: Burlington

Location: 51 miles south of Eureka.
Sites: 57 sites for tents and RVs up to 36 feet long.
Facilities: Tables, fire rings, drinking water, flush toilets, showers, dump station.
Fee per night: $15-$17, pets $1. For reservations call 800-444-7275. There is a one-time reservation fee of $7.50.
Management: California Department of Parks and Recreation, 707-946-2409.
Activities: Hiking, fishing, swimming.
Finding the campground: From Eureka, drive south 50 miles on U.S. Highway 101 to the Weott-Newton Road exit, which is signed for the visitor center. The campground is adjacent to the visitor center.

Humboldt Redwoods State Park

This largest of the state's redwood parks encompasses 52,000 acres, 17,000 of which are covered with old-growth coast redwoods. Rockefeller Forest, in the northeast section of the park, is the world's largest coast redwood grove. The average age of redwoods in the park ranges from 500 to 1,200 years; the oldest known tree is more than 2,000 years old. Many trees are more than 300 feet high, and some top 360 feet. More than 100 miles of hiking, mountain biking, and equestrian trails traverse through the park's many groves of ancient trees. An inexpensive trail guide describes 50 of the more popular trails. It is available at the visitor center, located just off U.S. Highway 101 on Avenue of the Giants, 1.3 miles south of the small town of Weott.

A feature of the park is Avenue of the Giants, a 32-mile scenic auto tour with a series of stops at points of interest along the route, where you may park and enjoy short walks. The South Fork of the Eel River flows through the park, offering fishing and swimming. Fishing for salmon and steelhead is permitted during the fall and winter. You may fish for squawfish at any time. The park offers three developed family camps, a group camp, and a horse camp.

About the campground: This campground is situated in a relatively open grove of second-growth redwoods, with stumps of the old-growth trees scattered throughout. It is sobering to compare the size of these giant stumps with the newer trees. A short trail leads from the campground to the Eel River for swimming and fishing. A summer bridge across the river allows access to extensive hiking trails. Stay limit 15 days from June through September, 30 days from October through May. Open all year.

29 Humboldt Redwoods State Park: Hidden Springs

Location: 56 miles south of Eureka.
Sites: 154 sites for tents and RVs up to 36 feet long.
Facilities: Tables, fire rings, drinking water, flush toilets, showers.
Fee per night: $15-$17, pets $1. For reservations call 800-444-7275. There is a one-time reservation fee of $7.50.
Management: California Department of Parks and Recreation, 707-946-2409.
Activities: Hiking, fishing, swimming.
Finding the campground: From the visitor center, 1.3 miles south of Weott, drive south 5 miles on Avenue of the Giants.

About the campground: Situated on a hillside in a mixed forest, this campground has a short trail that leads to the Eel River for swimming and fishing. Another trail, accessible from campsites 133 and 75, leads to Williams Grove via a footbridge. Stay limit 15 days. Open from mid-May through mid-October.

30 Humboldt Redwoods State Park: Albee Creek

Location: 56 miles south of Eureka.
Sites: 39 sites for tents and RVs up to 36 feet long.
Facilities: Tables, fire rings, drinking water, flush toilets, showers.
Fee per night: $15-$17, pets $1. For reservations call 800-444-7275. There is a one-time reservation fee of $7.50.
Management: California Department of Parks and Recreation, 707-946-2409.
Activities: Hiking.
Finding the campground: From the visitor center, 1.3 miles south of Weott, drive north 4 miles on Avenue of the Giants, turn left onto Mattole Road, and drive 5 miles.

About the campground: Situated on the grounds of an old homestead, campsites are either shaded by second-growth redwoods or sprawled across open meadows. Hiking and mountain biking trails are easily accessible from the campground, and Rockefeller Forest is only a short hike away. *Sunset Magazine* has listed Albee Creek as one of the 100 best campgrounds west of the Mississippi. Stay limit 15 days. Open from May through September.

31 Humboldt Redwoods State Park: Williams Grove Group Camp

Location: 54 miles south of Eureka.
Sites: 2 sites for tents and RVs; site A accommodates 60 people, site B 40.
Facilities: Tables, fire rings, drinking water, flush toilets.
Fee per night: Site A $90, site B $60, pets $1. Reservations are required; call 800-444-7275. There is a one-time reservation fee of $15.
Management: California Department of Parks and Recreation, 707-946-2409.
Activities: Hiking, fishing, swimming.
Finding the campground: From the visitor center, 1.3 miles south of Weott, drive south 3 miles on Avenue of the Giants.

About the campground: This group camp is situated in a redwood grove along the South Fork of the Eel River. The River Trail runs from north to south alongside the campground. Stay limit 15 days. Open all year.

32 Humboldt Redwoods State Park: Cuneo Creek Horse Camp

Location: 58 miles south of Eureka.
Sites: 5 individual sites for tents and RVs, plus 1 group site for up to 60 people.
Facilities: Tables, fire rings, drinking water, flush toilets, showers, corrals, water troughs.
Fee per night: $20 for individual sites, $90 for group site, pets $1. Reservations may be made (required for the group site) by calling 800-444-7275. There is a one-time reservation fee of $7.50.

Management: California Department of Parks and Recreation, 707-946-2409.
Activities: Horseback riding.
Finding the campground: From the visitor center, 1.3 miles south of Weott, drive north 4 miles on Avenue of the Giants, turn left onto Mattole Road, and drive about 7 miles.

About the campground: Situated just off Mattole Road, the camp provides access to numerous roads and trails for riding. It is reserved for equestrian use. Stay limit 15 days. Open all year.

33 Honeydew

Location: 41 miles south of Fortuna.
Sites: 14 sites for tents and RVs.
Facilities: Tables, fire rings, pit toilets. No drinking water. The facilities are wheelchair accessible.
Fee per night: $5.
Management: Bureau of Land Management, 707-825-2300.
Activities: None.
Finding the campground: From Fortuna, drive south 22 miles on U.S. Highway 101, turn right (west) onto Mattole Road, and drive 17 miles to Honeydew. Turn left onto Wilder Ridge Road (toward Ettersburg) and drive 2 miles.

About the campground: There is little to recommend this campground except an isolated location near a pretty creek. A better alternative would be to stay at A. W. Way County Park (number 34). Stay limit 14 days. Open all year.

34 A. W. Way County Park

Location: 44 miles south of Fortuna.
Sites: 30 sites for tents and RVs.
Facilities: Tables, fire rings, drinking water, flush toilets, showers, playground.
Fee per night: $12, pets $1.
Management: Humboldt County Parks Department, 707-445-7652.
Activities: Fishing, swimming, hiking.
Finding the campground: From Fortuna, drive south 22 miles on U.S. Highway 101, turn right (west) onto Mattole Road, and drive 22 miles.

About the campground: The park is situated on the bank of the Mattole River, which can offer good salmon and steelhead fishing from mid-November through February. The campground is a good alternative for those who would like to explore the Mattole portion of the King Range National Conservation Area (number 35) but would like more amenities than offered by the BLM campgrounds there. Stay limit 14 days. Open all year.

King Range National Conservation Area

Encompassing some 63,000 acres of Northern California's "Lost Coast," the conservation area extends 35 miles from the Mattole River to Whale Gulch Creek and up to 6 miles inland from the Pacific Ocean. The King Range rises from sea level to more than 4,000 feet in less than 3 miles, creating a spectacular meeting of land and sea, isolated beaches, mountain streams, and virgin forests. The area enjoys a mild but wet climate (between 100 and 200 inches of rainfall annually) and frequent dense morning fog.

Three major trails run generally north to south through the region. The longest, the Lost Coast Trail, follows the shoreline from Mattole Campground south for 24 miles to Black Sand Beach. Combining with the Chemise Mountain Trail, it continues (inland) from Hidden Valley to Whale Gulch Creek (8 miles) and on into the Sinkyone Wilderness. The King Crest Trail System provides 16 miles of hiking and equestrian trails along the main coastal ridge north of Shelter Cove, with excellent views of the ocean and the Mattole River Valley. Shore fishing takes place for perch and cod, and salmon and steelhead are taken by boaters near Shelter Cove, where boat launch facilities and rentals are available. The Mattole River is open to salmon and steelhead fishing from the campground to Honeydew from mid-November through February. An OHV use area has been established along the coast from Black Sand Beach to Gitchell Creek, about 3.5 miles long.

Roads to and within the area are a combination of pavement, gravel, and dirt. Many are steep, winding, and narrow; some are impassable during wet weather. Large trailers and RVs are not recommended. Five vehicle-accessible public campgrounds are located in the conservation area.

35 King Range National Conservation Area: Mattole

Location: 55 miles south of Fortuna.
Sites: 14 sites for tents and RVs.
Facilities: Tables, fire rings, pit toilets. No drinking water.
Fee per night: $5 donation requested.
Management: Bureau of Land Management, 707-825-2300.
Activities: Hiking, fishing.
Finding the campground: From Fortuna, drive south 22 miles on U.S. Highway 101 and turn right (west) onto Mattole Road. Drive 28 miles toward Honeydew\Petrolia, turn left onto Lighthouse Road (before Petrolia), and drive 5 miles.

About the campground: This campground is situated on an isolated, attractive beach at the mouth of the Mattole River. The Lost Coast Trail begins here and runs south 24 miles to Black Sands Beach. A good introduction to the trail is a 6-mile round-trip hike to the abandoned Punta Gorda Lighthouse. Perch fishing can be good at the mouth of the river. Stay limit 14 days. Open all year.

36 King Range National Conservation Area: Nadelos

Location: 63 miles south of Fortuna.
Sites: 8 sites for tents.
Facilities: Tables, fire rings, drinking water, vault toilets. The facilities are wheelchair accessible.
Fee per night: $8.
Management: Bureau of Land Management, 707-825-2300.
Activities: Hiking.
Finding the campground: From Fortuna, drive south 45 miles on U.S. Highway 101 to Redway, turn right (west) onto Briceland/Shelter Cove Road, and drive 16.5 miles. Turn left (south) onto Chemise Mountain Road and drive 1 mile.

About the campground: A trail leaves camp and leads to the summit of Chemise Mountain (2,598 feet), and the southern section of the Lost Coast Trail passes by en route to the Sinkyone Wilderness. The camp is at an elevation of 1,850 feet. Stay limit 14 days. Open all year.

37 King Range National Conservation Area: Wailaki

Location: 64 miles south of Fortuna.
Sites: 13 sites for tents and RVs.
Facilities: Tables, fire rings, drinking water, vault toilets.
Fee per night: $8.
Management: Bureau of Land Management, 707-825-2300.
Activities: Hiking.
Finding the campground: From Fortuna, drive south 45 miles on U.S. Highway 101 to Redway, turn right (west) onto Briceland/Shelter Cove Road, and drive 16.5 miles. Turn left (south) onto Chemise Mountain Road and drive 1.5 miles.

About the campground: See Nadelos Campground (number 36).

38 King Range National Conservation Area: Tolkan

Location: 66 miles south of Fortuna.
Sites: 9 sites for tents and RVs.
Facilities: Tables, fire rings, drinking water, vault toilets. The facilities are wheelchair accessible.
Fee per night: $8.
Management: Bureau of Land Management, 707-825-2300.
Activities: Hiking.
Finding the campground: From Fortuna, drive south 45 miles on U.S. Highway 101 to Redway, turn right (west) onto Briceland/Shelter Cove Road, and drive 17 miles. Turn right (north) onto Kings Peak (Horse Mountain) Road and drive 3.5 miles.

About the campground: The King Crest Trailhead is 4 miles north of the camp. Elevation 1,840 feet. Stay limit 14 days. Open all year.

39 King Range National Conservation Area: Horse Mountain

Location: 68 miles south of Fortuna.
Sites: 9 sites for tents and RVs.
Facilities: Tables, fire rings, drinking water, pit toilets.
Fee per night: $5.
Management: Bureau of Land Management, 707-825-2300.
Activities: Hiking.
Finding the campground: From Fortuna, drive south 45 miles on U.S. Highway 101 to Redway, turn right (west) onto Briceland/Shelter Cove Road, then drive 17 miles. Turn right (north) onto Kings Peak (Horse Mountain) Road and drive 6 miles.

About the campground: The King Crest Trailhead is 2 miles north of the camp. Also at this trailhead is the beginning of the 3-mile Buck Creek Trail, which leads to the coast. Elevation 2,000 feet. Stay limit 14 days. Open all year.

40 Benbow Lake State Recreation Area

Location: 4 miles south of Garberville.
Sites: 75 sites for tents and RVs up to 30 feet long.
Facilities: Tables, fire rings, drinking water, flush toilets, showers, dump station, boat ramp and rentals.
Fee per night: $15-$17, pets $1. For reservations call 800-444-7275. There is a one-time reservation fee of $7.50.
Management: California Department of Parks and Recreation, 707-947-3318.
Activities: Swimming, boating, fishing.
Finding the campground: From Garberville, drive 2 miles south on U.S. Highway 101. Take the Benbow Drive exit and drive east 1.5 miles.

About the campground: Benbow Lake only exists in the summer months when the Eel River is temporarily dammed. No motorized boats are permitted on the lake. Fishing is poor in the lake itself but can be good for salmon and steelhead in the Eel River in the fall and winter. Stay limit 14 days. Open from April through October.

41 Richardson Grove State Park: Huckleberry

Location: 7 miles south of Garberville.
Sites: 36 sites for tents and RVs up to 30 feet long.
Facilities: Tables, fire rings, drinking water, flush toilets, showers, dump station, store. The facilities are wheelchair accessible.
Fee per night: $15-$17, pets $1. For reservations call 800-444-7275. There is a one-time reservation fee of $7.50.

Richardson Grove State Park

This park covers 1,500 acres and protects an old-growth redwood forest. Many of the trees are over 300 feet tall and more than 1,000 years old. A visitor center and a nature trail featuring a walk-through tree are located near the park entrance. Longer trails lead to the most prominent groves, and the South Fork of the Eel River bisects the park from north to south, providing good swimming holes in summer and salmon and steelhead fishing in late fall and winter.

Management: California Department of Parks and Recreation, 707-247-3318.
Activities: Hiking, swimming, fishing.
Finding the campground: From Garberville, drive south for 7 miles on U.S. Highway 101.

About the campground: Huckleberry is near the park visitor center on the west side of US 101, only a short walk away from the South Fork of the Eel River. The Woodland Loop Trail (1.3 miles) leads from the campground through a mixed forest, and the 2-mile Toumey Trail (accessed by a footbridge over the river) visits an impressive redwood grove and extends southward to Oak Flat. Stay limit 30 days. Open all year.

42 Richardson Grove State Park: Madrone

Location: 7 miles south of Garberville.
Sites: 40 sites for tents and RVs up to 30 feet long.
Facilities: Tables, fire rings, drinking water, flush toilets, showers, dump station, store. The facilities are wheelchair accessible.
Fee per night: $15-$17, pets $1. For reservations call 800-444-7275. There is a one-time reservation fee of $7.50.
Management: California Department of Parks and Recreation, 707-247-3318.
Activities: Hiking, swimming, fishing.
Finding the campground: From Garberville, drive south for 7 miles on U.S. Highway 101.

About the campground: Madrone is near the park visitor center on the west side of US 101, only a short walk away from the South Fork of the Eel River. The Tanoak Spring-Durphy Creek Loop Trail (4.6 miles) can be accessed between campsites 58 and 60. It offers a 1,200-foot climb through a forest of large trees, including redwoods, Douglas firs, and tanoaks. Stay limit 30 days. Open all year.

43 Richardson Grove State Park: Oak Flat

Location: 7 miles south of Garberville.
Sites: 94 sites for tents and RVs up to 30 feet long.

Facilities: Tables, fire rings, drinking water, flush toilets, showers. The facilities are wheelchair accessible.
Fee per night: $15-$17, pets $1. For reservations call 800-444-7275. There is a one-time reservation fee of $7.50.
Management: California Department of Parks and Recreation, 707-247-3318.
Activities: Hiking, swimming, fishing.
Finding the campground: From Garberville, drive south for 7 miles on U.S. Highway 101.

About the campground: Situated half a mile from the park visitor center on the east side of US 101, Oak Flat offers easy access to the South Fork of the Eel River. The Toumey Trail and Settlers Trail are close by. Stay limit 15 days. Open from June through September.

MENDOCINO AREA

The Mendocino area enjoys some of the most dramatic coastal scenery found anywhere. While much of it is private and inaccessible, much more is open to the public as marvelous state and county parks and public beaches. The towns in this area are as varied and scenic as the coast itself. The entire town of Mendocino, which was founded by New England whalers, is on the National Register of Historic Places.

Inland, a major wine-producing region centers around Ukiah, which has 35 wineries within its city limits. To the east, the Mendocino National Forest offers a million acres of trails, rivers, streams, and lakes for outdoor enjoyment.

1 Standish-Hickey State Recreation Area: Hickey

Location: 22 miles south of Garberville.
Sites: 65 sites for tents and RVs up to 27 feet long.
Facilities: Tables, fire rings, drinking water, flush toilets, showers. The facilities are wheelchair accessible.
Fee per night: $15-$17, pets $1. For reservations call 800-444-7275. There is a one-time reservation fee of $7.50.
Management: California Department of Parks and Recreation, 707-925-6482.
Activities: Hiking, swimming, fishing.
Finding the campground: From Garberville, drive south 22 miles on U.S. Highway 101.

About the campground: This 1,070-acre park, bisected by the highway and the South Fork of the Eel River, consists mainly of a mixed forest, with second-growth redwoods, and some small pockets of old-growth trees, including Douglas fir. A trail leads from the picnic area south of the campground to a good swimming hole, and here a summer bridge provides access to the 2.1 mile Big Tree Loop and the Miles Standish Tree. The 1.7-mile Grove Trail begins off US 101, a short distance south of the campground. Fishing in the river is for salmon and steelhead in late fall and winter. Stay limit 15 days from June through September, 30 days from October through May. Open all year.

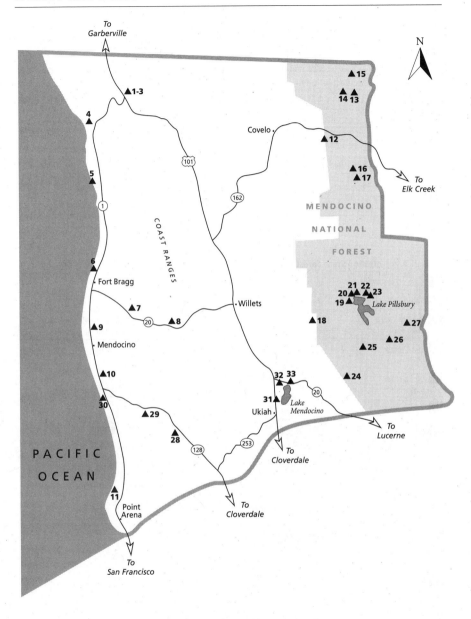

MENDOCINO AREA CAMPGROUNDS

	Group sites	RV sites	Total sites	Max. RV length	Hookups	Toilets	Showers	Drinking water	Dump station	Pets	Wheelchair	Recreation	Fee ($)	Season	Can reserve	Length of stay
Standish-Hickey State Recreation Area (1–3)																
1 Hickey		•	65	27		F	•	•		•	•	HSF	15–17		•	15/30
2 Rock Creek		•	36	27		F	•	•		•	•	HSF	15–17		•	15
3 Redwood		•	63	18		F	•	•		•	•	HSF	15–17	Mem. Day–Labor Day	•	15
4 Sinkyone Wilderness State Park			15			V				•		HF	6			14
5 Westport-Union Landing State Beach		•	130			V		•		•	•	HF	10			15
6 Mackerricher State Park		•	142	35		F	•	•	•	•	•	HFR	15–17		•	15/30
Jackson Demonstration State Forest (7-8)																
7 Camp One Area	•	•	34			P				•		HSR			•	14
8 Camp 20 Area	•	•	22			P				•		HSR			•	14
9 Russian Gulch State Park	•	•	30	27		F	•	•	•	•	•	HSF	15–17	mid-March–mid-Oct.	•	30
10 Van Damme State Park	•	•	75	27		F	•	•	•	•	•	HSF	15–17		•	15/30
11 Manchester State Beach		•	48	30		C	•	•				HF	10–12		•	15
12 Eel River		•	16			V		•		•		F	6	May–Sept.		14
13 Little Doe		•	13			V				•		HF		June 15–Sept.		14
14 Howard Meadows and Lake		•	6			V				•		FSBL		June 15–Sept.		14
15 Hammerhorn Lake		•	9			V		•		•	•	HF BL	6	June–Sept.		14
Plaskett Lakes Recreation Area (16–17)																
16 Plaskett Meadows		•	32			V		•		•		HFB	5	mid-June–mid-Oct.		14
17 Masterson Group Camp	•	•	1			V		•		•		HFB	20	mid-June–mid-Oct.	•	14
18 Trout Creek		•	15			V		•		•		F	15	May–October		14

	Group sites	RV sites	Total sites	Max. RV length	Hookups	Toilets	Showers	Drinking water	Dump station	Pets	Wheelchair	Recreation	Fee ($)	Season	Can reserve	Length of stay
Lake Pillsbury Recreation Area (19–23)																
19 Fuller Grove	•	•	31	22		V		•		•		HSF BL	10-100		•	14
20 Pogie Point		•	50			V		•		•		HSF BL	10			14
21 Navy Camp		•	20			V		•		•		HS FB	8			4
22 Oak Flat		•	12							•		HS FB		weekends		14
23 Sunset		•	54			V		•		•		HS FB	10			14
24 Middle Creek	•	•	23			V		•		•		F	4			14
25 Deer Valley		•	13			V				•						14
26 Bear Creek		•	16			V				•		F				14
27 Lower Nye		•	6			V				•		H				14
28 Hendy Woods State Park		•	92	30		F	•	•	•	•	•	H	15–17		•	15/30
Navarro River Redwoods State Park (29–30)																
29 Paul M. Dimmick Wayside Campground		•	28	30		V				•		SF	10–12			15
30 Navarro Beach		•	10	30		C				•		SF	5			15
Lake Mendocino (31–33)																
31 Che-Ka-Ka		•	22	35		V		•		•		HSF BL	8	April– Sept.		14
32 Ky-en		•	103	35		F	•	•	•	•	•	HS FB	14–16			14
33 Bu-Shay	•	•	167	35		F	•	•	•	•	•	HS FB	14–120	April– Sept.		14

Hookups: W = Water E = Electric S = Sewer
Toilets: F = Flush V = Vault P = Pit C = Chemical
Recreation: H = Hiking S = Swimming F = Fishing B = Boating L = Boat Launch O = Off-highway Driving R = Horseback Riding
Maximum Trailer/RV Length given in feet. Stay Limit given in days. Fee given in dollars.
If no entry under **Season,** campground is open all year. If no entry under **Fee,** camping is free.

2 | Standish-Hickey State Recreation Area: Rock Creek

Location: 22 miles south of Garberville.
Sites: 36 sites for tents and RVs up to 27 feet long.
Facilities: Tables, fire rings, drinking water, flush toilets, showers. The facilities are wheelchair accessible.
Fee per night: $15-$17, pets $1. For reservations call 800-444-7275. There is a one-time reservation fee of $7.50.
Management: California Department of Parks and Recreation, 707-925-6482.
Activities: Hiking, swimming, fishing.
Finding the campground: From Garberville, drive south 22 miles on U.S. Highway 101.

About the campground: See Hickey Campground (number 1).

3 | Standish-Hickey State Recreation Area: Redwood

Location: 22 miles south of Garberville.
Sites: 63 sites for tents and RVs up to 18 feet long.
Facilities: Tables, fire rings, drinking water, flush toilets, showers. The facilities are wheelchair accessible.
Fee per night: $15-$17, pets $1. For reservations call 800-444-7275. There is a one-time reservation fee of $7.50.
Management: California Department of Parks and Recreation, 707-925-6482.
Activities: Hiking, swimming, fishing.
Finding the campground: From Garberville, drive south 22 miles on U.S. Highway 101.

About the campground: See Hickey Campground (number 1). This campground is situated in an attractive spot on the bank of the Eel River and is accessible via a temporary summer bridge. The Big Tree Loop (2.1 miles) and the Lookout Point Trail (3.5 miles) are convenient to the campground. Stay limit 15 days. Open from Memorial Day through Labor Day.

4 | Sinkyone Wilderness State Park: Usal Beach

Location: 20 miles southwest of Leggett.
Sites: 15 sites for tents.
Facilities: Tables, fire rings, vault toilets. No drinking water.
Fee per night: $6.
Management: California Department of Parks and Recreation, 707-986-7711.
Activities: Hiking, fishing.
Finding the campground: From the intersection of U.S. Highway 101 and California Highway 1 at Leggett, drive southwest 14 miles on CA 1, turn right (north) onto County Road 431 (Usal Road), and drive 6 miles. The road is not advised for large vehicles.

About the campground: The campground is near an isolated black-sand beach at the south end of the 7,000-acre Sinkyone Wilderness on Northern

At Westport-Union Landing State Beach, trails and stairways lead from campsites to the dramatic surfswept shore.

California's "Lost Coast." See the sidebar on King Range National Conservation Area, page 32, for more information about the area. The Lost Coast Trail runs north and south at the campground. Stay limit 14 days. Open all year.

5 Westport-Union Landing State Beach

Location: 18 miles north of Fort Bragg.
Sites: 130 sites for tents and RVs.
Facilities: Tables, fire rings, drinking water, vault toilets. The facilities are wheelchair accessible.
Fee per night: $10 ($7 when there is no water), pets $1.
Agency: California Department of Parks and Recreation, 707-937-5804.
Activities: Fishing, hiking, whale watching.
Finding the campground: From Fort Bragg, drive north on California Highway 1 for 17 miles to the town of Westport. The park has several entrances between 1 and 3 miles north of the town.

About the campground: The park is divided into four segments of bluff and beach, separated by creek gulches, extending along a 2-mile stretch of coastline. There are several campgrounds, all above the beach on the open, almost treeless bluffs, with stairs and trails down to the narrow, surfswept beaches. Offshore rocks and islands, wave-pounded cliffs, and distant mountains provide a dramatic setting and excellent ocean and mountain views. The park is a good place to whale watch from November through January. Stay limit 15 days. Open all year.

6 Mackerricher State Park

Location: 3 miles north of Fort Bragg.
Sites: 142 sites for tents and RVs up 35 feet long.
Facilities: Tables, fire rings, drinking water, flush toilets, showers, dump station. The facilities are wheelchair accessible.
Fee per night: $15-$17, pets $1. For reservations call 800-444-7275. There is a one-time reservation fee of $7.50.
Agency: California Department of Parks and Recreation, 707-937-5804.
Activities: Fishing, hiking, horseback riding, whale watching.
Finding the campground: From Fort Bragg, drive north 3 miles on California Highway 1.

About the campground: Mackerricher's 1,600 acres contain an 8-mile-long, wide, sandy beach, a coastal forest, a 13-acre fresh water lake, a boardwalk leading to a promontory for viewing whales and sea lions, hiking/jogging trails, and a shoreline equestrian trail. The spacious campground, chosen by *Sunset Magazine* as one of the 100 best in the western United States, is spread over several loops, shaded by coastal pines, and adjacent to the beach. Cleone Lake, near the campground, contains a resident population of bluegill, bass, and bullhead, and is stocked annually with rainbow trout. Horses may be rented just outside the park. Stay limit 15 days from June through September, 30 days from October through May. Open all year.

7 Jackson Demonstration State Forest: Camp One Area

Location: 7 miles southeast of Fort Bragg.
Sites: 34 sites in 14 campgrounds, including 1 equestrian and 2 group camps.
Facilities: Picnic tables, fire rings, pit toilets.
Fee per night: None, but a permit is required; call number below.
Management: Jackson Demonstration State Forest, 707-964-5674.
Activities: Hiking, swimming, mountain biking, horseback riding, hunting.
Finding the campground: From Fort Bragg, drive south 1.3 miles on California Highway 1, turn left (east) onto California Highway 20, and drive 5.7 miles. Turn left onto Road 350 and drive 1.5 miles to the day use area and check in with the campground host.

About the campgrounds: Jackson is a working forest with the goal of demonstrating sustained timber production, while maintaining soil, water, scenic, wildlife, and recreational values. Timber production has been continuous in the forest since the 1850s. The campgrounds are located along the North Fork of the South Fork of the Noyo River. A map issued by the State Forestry Office is essential for finding them, and can be obtained when applying for the permit. A series of trails lead through this isolated redwood and fir forest, including one to 50-foot high Chamberlain Creek Falls, in a virgin old-growth redwood grove. Fishing is not permitted in the forest. Stay limit 14 days. Open all year, but some campgrounds are seasonal.

8 Jackson Demonstration State Forest: Camp 20 Area

Location: 18 miles southeast of Fort Bragg.
Sites: 22 sites in 3 campgrounds, including 1 for equestrian and group use.
Facilities: Picnic tables, fire rings, pit toilets.
Fee per night: None, but a permit is required; call number below.
Management: Jackson Demonstration State Forest, 707-964-5674.
Activities: Hiking, swimming, mountain biking, horseback riding, hunting.
Finding the campground: From Fort Bragg, drive south 1.3 miles on California Highway 1, turn left (east) onto California Highway 20 and drive about 17 miles. Turn left and drive 300 yards to the day use area and check in with the campground host.

About the campground: See Camp One Area (number 7).

9 Russian Gulch State Park

Location: 2 miles north of Mendocino.
Sites: 30 sites for tents and RVs up to 27 feet long, plus 1 group site for tents only.
Facilities: Tables, fire rings, drinking water, flush toilets, showers. The facilities are wheelchair accessible.
Fee per night: $15-$17, pets $1. Group site $60. Reservations may be made (required for group site) by calling 800-444-7275. There is a one-time reservation fee of $7.50.
Management: California Department of Parks and Recreation, 707-937-5804.
Activities: Fishing, hiking, mountain biking, swimming, scuba diving.
Finding the campground: From Mendocino, drive north 2 miles on California Highway 1.

About the campground: The park includes both coastal sections and an inland forest of second growth redwoods, alder, and western hemlock. The campground is located along a pretty, wooded stretch of Russian Gulch Creek, close to the shore. A protecting cove shelters an attractive beach, and trails lead north and south along the coast to a blow hole and a collapsed sea cave. Inland, another trail through Russian Gulch makes a 6-mile round trip to Russian Gulch Falls, accessible part way by mountain bike. Stay limit 30 days. Open from mid-March to mid-October.

10 Van Damme State Park

Location: 3 miles south of Mendocino.
Sites: 74 sites for tents and RVs up to 27 feet long, plus 1 group site for up to 50 people.
Facilities: Tables, fire rings, drinking water, flush toilets, showers, dump station. The facilities are wheelchair accessible.

Fee per night: $15-$17, pets $1. Group site $75. Reservations may be made (required for group site) by calling 800-444-7275. There is a one-time $7.50 reservation fee ($15 for the group site).
Agency: California Department of Parks and Recreation, 707-937-5804.
Activities: Fishing, hiking, swimming, mountain biking, scuba diving.
Finding the campground: From Mendocino, drive 3 miles south on California Highway 1.

About the campground: The park contains both coastal and inland sections, including an attractive beach on a scenic coastal bay, a 10-mile round-trip trail through a fern-lined canyon, and a boardwalk through a pygmy pine grove and cypress trees. The campground is well laid out and nicely wooded, with a stream running through the lower level, and mixed wooded and open meadow sites at its upper level. Stay limit 15 days from June through September, 30 days from October through May. Open all year.

11 Manchester State Beach

Location: 28 miles south of Mendocino.
Sites: 48 sites for tents and RVs up to 30 feet long.
Facilities: Tables, fire rings, drinking water, chemical toilets, dump station.
Fee per night: $10-$12. For reservations call 800-444-7275. There is a one-time reservation fee of $7.50.
Management: California Department of Parks and Recreation, 707-937-5804.
Activities: Fishing, hiking, bird watching, scuba diving.
Finding the campground: From Mendocino, drive south 28 miles on California Highway 1 (2 miles north of Point Arena). Three separate roads lead to different sections of the park. The campground entrance is Kinney Road, and it is signed.

About the campground: The park's 1,419 acres comprise a 5-mile-long brown-sand beach backed by grass-covered dunes. Two creeks, a pretty lagoon, and a saltwater marsh complete the picture. The area can be windy, especially in summer. Located on a wide, attractive, grassy plateau with some trees, the campground has an excellent view of mountains to the west, but no view of the ocean. A trail leads to the beach, about ten minutes away. Shore casting is reputedly good along the beach all year, and Alder Creek offers steelhead runs in the winter. A 5-mile loop trail, beginning near the campground, offers a fine sampling of beach and inland hiking, and includes a stretch of Alder Creek and its attractive lagoon. Stay limit 15 days. Open all year. No pets allowed.

12 Eel River

Location: 13 miles east of Covelo.
Sites: 16 sites for tents and RVs.
Facilities: Tables, stoves, drinking water, vault toilets.
Fee per night: $6.
Management: Mendocino National Forest, 530-938-6118.

Activities: Fishing.
Finding the campground: From Covelo, drive east 13 miles on California Highway 162.

About the campground: The camp is adjacent to the Eel River Work Center and has good river access. The elevation is 1,500 feet. Stay limit 14 days. Open from May through September.

13 Little Doe

Location: 25 miles northeast of Covelo.
Sites: 13 sites for tents and RVs.
Facilities: Tables, fire rings, stoves, vault toilets. No drinking water.
Fee per night: None.
Management: Mendocino National Forest, 530-938-6118.
Activities: Fishing, hiking.
Finding the campground: From Covelo, drive east 13 miles on California Highway 162 to Eel River Work Center. Turn left (north) onto Forest Road M1 (Indian Dick Road) and drive 12 miles.

About the campground: Little Doe is situated in a mixed-conifer forest at 3,600-feet elevation. Stay limit 14 days. Open from June 15 through September.

14 Howard Meadows and Lake

Location: 29 miles northeast of Covelo.
Sites: 6 sites for tents and RVs up to 16 feet long.
Facilities: Tables, fire rings, vault toilets, small boat ramp. No drinking water.
Fee per night: None.
Management: Mendocino National Forest, 530-938-6118.
Activities: Fishing, hiking, boating, swimming.
Finding the campground: From Covelo, drive east 13 miles on California Highway 162 to Eel River Work Center. Turn left (north) onto Forest Road M1 (Indian Dick Road) and drive 12 miles. Turn left onto Forest Road 23N37 and drive about 3 miles. The access road is unimproved, so a vehicle with good clearance is recommended.

About the campground: Situated in a mixed-conifer forest with a large meadow. The campground is a short walk to 12-acre Howard Lake, which is stocked annually with foot-long rainbow trout. No motors are allowed on the lake. The elevation is 3,700 feet. Stay limit 14 days. Open from June 15 through September.

15 Hammerhorn Lake

Location: 31 miles northeast of Covelo.
Sites: 9 sites for tents and RVs up to 16 feet long.
Facilities: Tables, fire rings, stoves, drinking water, vault toilets, small boat ramp, fishing piers. The facilities are wheelchair accessible.

Fee per night: $6.
Management: Mendocino National Forest, 530-938-6118.
Activities: Fishing, hiking, boating.
Finding the campground: From Covelo, drive east 13 miles on California Highway 162 to Eel River Work Center. Turn left (north) onto Forest Road M1 (Indian Dick Road) and drive 18 miles.

About the campground: Situated in a mixed-conifer forest on the shore of a 5-acre lake. Hammerhorn is stocked annually with a surprising number of 10,000 ten- to twelve-inch rainbow trout, which makes for good fishing in early summer. No motorized boats are allowed on the lake. The Smoke House Trail begins 2 miles northeast of the campground and leads north into the Yolla Bolly-Middle Eel Wilderness. Elevation 3,500 feet. Stay limit 14 days. Open from June through September.

16 Plaskett Lakes Recreation Area: Plaskett Meadows

Location: 28 miles southeast of Covelo.
Sites: 32 sites for tents and RVs up to 16 feet long.
Facilities: Tables, fire rings, drinking water, vault toilets.
Fee per night: $5.
Management: Mendocino National Forest, 530-963-3128.
Activities: Fishing, boating, hiking.
Finding the campground: From Covelo, drive east 13 miles on California Highway 162 to Eel River Work Center. Turn right (southeast) onto Forest Road M7 and drive 15 miles.

About the campground: Situated in an area of mixed pine and fir, the campground is adjacent to two small lakes, one 3 acres, and the other 4 acres. No motorized boats are allowed. Swimming is not recommended. Fishing for up to 12-inch rainbow trout can be good in early summer. Elevation 6,000 feet. Stay limit 14 days. Open from mid-June to mid-October.

17 Plaskett Lakes Recreation Area: Masterson Group Camp

Location: 28 miles southeast of Covelo.
Sites: 1 group site for tents and RVs up to 16 feet long; accommodates up to 90 people.
Facilities: Tables, fire rings, drinking water, vault toilets.
Fee per night: $20. Reservations are required; call 800-444-7275. There is a one-time reservation fee of $15.
Management: Mendocino National Forest, 530-963-3128.
Activities: Fishing, boating, hiking.
Finding the campground: From Covelo, drive east 13 miles on California Highway 162 to Eel River Work Center. Turn right (southeast) onto Forest Road M7 and drive 15 miles.

About the campground: Situated in a mixed-pine forest about half a mile from the Plaskett Lakes. See Plaskett Meadows Campground (number 16).

18 Trout Creek

Location: 25 miles northeast of Ukiah.
Sites: 15 sites for tents and RVs, including 1 double site.
Facilities: Tables, fire rings, drinking water, vault toilets.
Fee per night: $15, pets $1.
Management: PG&E, 530-386-5164.
Activities: Fishing.
Finding the campground: From Ukiah, drive north 6 miles on U.S. Highway 101, turn right (east) onto California Highway 20, and drive 5 miles. Turn left onto County Road 240 (Potter Valley-Lake Pillsbury Road) and drive 14 miles (2 miles past the Eel River bridge).

About the campground: Situated near the confluence of Trout Creek and Eel River. Trout Creek offers fair fishing for small, native trout. Stay limit 14 days. Elevation 1,500 feet. Open from May through October.

19 Lake Pillsbury Recreation Area: Fuller Grove

Location: 38 miles northeast of Ukiah.
Sites: 30 sites for tents and RVs up to 22 feet long, plus 1 group site for up to 60 people.
Facilities: Tables, fire rings, drinking water, vault toilets, boat ramp.
Fee per night: $10, pets $1. Group site $50 up to 29 people, $100 for 30 to 60 people. Reservations required for group site; call number below.
Management: PG&E, 530-386-5164.
Activities: Fishing, swimming, boating, waterskiing, hiking.
Finding the campground: From Ukiah, drive 6 miles north on U.S. Highway 101, turn right (east) onto California Highway 20, and drive 5 miles. Turn left onto County Road 240 (Potter Valley-Lake Pillsbury Road) and drive 26 miles to the Eel River Information Kiosk at Lake Pillsbury. Continue north around the lake for 1.5 miles.

About the campground: Lake Pillsbury encompasses 2,000 acres of surface area, its shore lined with meadows, several beaches, and stands of oaks and conifers. It is subject to water drawdowns in summer and fall, which can affect the appearance and use of the shoreline. Its waters are stocked annually with 20,000 rainbow trout, and the lake also contains bluegill, sunfish, and bass. Elevation 1,800 feet. Stay limit 14 days. Open all year.

20 Lake Pillsbury Recreation Area: Pogie Point

Location: 39 miles northeast of Ukiah.
Sites: 50 sites for tents and RVs.
Facilities: Tables, fire rings, drinking water (except in winter), vault toilets, boat ramp.
Fee per night: $10, pets $1.
Management: Mendocino National Forest, 530-824-5196.

Activities: Fishing, swimming, boating, waterskiing, hiking.

Finding the campground: Adjacent to Fuller Grove Campground (number 19).

About the campground: Situated in an attractive cove on the northwest shore of the lake. See Fuller Grove Campground (number 19).

21 Lake Pillsbury Recreation Area: Navy Camp

Location: 40 miles northeast of Ukiah.
Sites: 20 sites for tents and RVs.
Facilities: Tables, fire rings, drinking water (except in winter), vault toilets. Boat ramp 0.5 mile south.
Fee per night: $8, pets $1.
Management: PG&E, 530-386-5164.
Activities: Fishing, swimming, boating, waterskiing, hiking.
Finding the campground: From Ukiah, drive 6 miles north on U.S. Highway 101, turn right (east) onto California Highway 20, and drive 5 miles. Turn left onto County Road 240 (Potter Valley-Lake Pillsbury Road) and drive 26 miles to the Eel River Information Kiosk at Lake Pillsbury. Continue north around the lake for 3.5 miles.

About the campground: Situated in a pretty, wooded cove on the north shore of the lake. See Fuller Grove Campground (number 19).

22 Lake Pillsbury Recreation Area: Oak Flat

Location: 40 miles northeast of Ukiah.
Sites: 12 sites for tents and RVs.
Facilities: Tables, stoves. No drinking water or toilets. Boat ramp 1 mile southeast.
Fee per night: None.
Management: Mendocino National Forest, 530-824-5196.
Activities: Fishing, swimming, boating, waterskiing. hiking.
Finding the campground: From Ukiah, drive 6 miles north on U.S. Highway 101, turn right (east) onto California Highway 20, and drive 5 miles. Turn left onto County Road 240 (Potter Valley-Lake Pillsbury Road) and drive 26 miles to the Eel River Information Kiosk at Lake Pillsbury. Continue north around the lake for 3.5 miles. Oak Flat is just past Navy Camp (number 21).

About the campground: Used as an overflow area on weekends when other campgrounds are full. See Fuller Grove Campground (number 19).

23 Lake Pillsbury Recreation Area: Sunset

Location: 42 miles northeast of Ukiah.
Sites: 54 sites for tents and RVs.
Facilities: Tables, fire rings, drinking water (except in winter), vault toilets. Boat ramp nearby.

Fee per night: $10, pets $1.
Management: Mendocino National Forest, 707-275-2361.
Activities: Fishing, swimming, boating, waterskiing, hiking.
Finding the campground: From Ukiah, drive 6 miles north on U.S. Highway 101, turn right (east) onto California Highway 20, and drive 5 miles. Turn left onto County Road 240 (Potter Valley-Lake Pillsbury Road) and drive 26 miles to the Eel River Information Kiosk at Lake Pillsbury. Continue north around the lake for 5 miles.

About the campground: Situated in an attractive wooded area on the north shore of the lake. There is a nature loop trail directly across from the campground. See Fuller Grove Campground (number 19).

24 Middle Creek

Location: 8 miles north of the community of Upper Lake.
Sites: 23 sites, including 2 for small groups, for tents and RVs.
Facilities: Tables, fire rings, stoves, drinking water, vault toilets.
Fee per night: $4.
Management: Mendocino National Forest, 707-275-2361.
Activities: Fishing.
Finding the campground: From Upper Lake, drive 8 miles north on County Road 301 (Forest Road M1).

About the campground: Situated near the confluence of the East and West Forks of Middle Creek. Elevation 2,000 feet. Stay limit 14 days. Open all year.

25 Deer Valley

Location: 16 miles north of the community of Upper Lake.
Sites: 13 sites for tents and RVs.
Facilities: Tables, fire rings, vault toilets. No drinking water.
Fee per night: None.
Management: Mendocino National Forest, 707-275-2361.
Activities: None.
Finding the campground: From Upper Lake, drive 12 miles north on County Road 301 (Forest Road M1), turn right onto Forest Road 16N01, and drive 4 miles.

About the campground: Other than for fall hunting, there is little reason to stay at this campground. Elevation 3,700 feet. Stay limit 14 days. Open all year. Please call the national forest for winter road conditions.

26 Bear Creek

Location: 25 miles north of the community of Upper Lake.
Sites: 16 sites for tents and RVs.
Facilities: Tables, fire rings, vault toilets. No drinking water.
Fee per night: None.

Management: Mendocino National Forest, 707-275-2361.
Activities: Fishing.
Finding the campground: From Upper Lake, drive 17 miles north on County Road 301 (Forest Road M1), turn right (east) onto Forest Road 18N01, and drive 8 miles.

About the campground: Situated near the confluence of two small creeks. Elevation 2,000 feet. Stay limit 14 days. Open all year. Please call the national forest for winter road conditions.

27 Lower Nye

Location: 38 miles north of the community of Upper Lake.
Sites: 6 sites for tents and RVs.
Facilities: Tables, fire rings, vault toilets. No drinking water.
Fee per night: None.
Management: Mendocino National Forest, 707-275-2361.
Activities: Hiking.
Finding the campground: From Upper Lake, drive north 17 miles on County Road 301 (Forest Road M1), turn right (east) onto Forest Road 18N01, and drive 7 miles. Turn left (north) onto Forest Road 18N04 and drive 14 miles.

About the campground: Situated on the northwest border of the Snow Mountain Wilderness, the campground is used primarily by backpackers. Elevation 3,300 feet. Stay limit 14 days. Open all year. Please call the national forest for winter road conditions.

28 Hendy Woods State Park

Location: 28 miles west of Ukiah.
Sites: 92 sites for tents and RVs up to 30 feet long.
Facilities: Tables, fire rings, drinking water, flush toilets, showers, dump station. The facilities are wheelchair accessible.
Fee per night: $15-$17, pets $1. For reservations call 800-444-7275. There is a one-time reservation fee of $7.50.
Management: California Department of Parks and Recreation, 707-937-5804.
Activities: Hiking, kayaking, canoeing, mountain biking.
Finding the campground: From the intersection of U.S. Highway 101 and California Highway 253 in Ukiah, drive southwest on CA 253 for 16 miles, turn right (north) onto California Highway 128, and drive about 12 miles.

About the campground: The park protects 128 acres of virgin and second-growth redwoods in several groves. Providing fine views of the trees are excellent short trails, including the Gentle Giants All Access Trail (1.5-mile loop), and the Hermit Hut Trail (0.3-mile round trip). Kayaking and canoeing in the Navarro River is best in the winter and spring. Fishing is not permitted in the river within the park. The Husch Vineyards and Navarro Vineyards are located along the highway, within a few miles of the campground. They offer tours, tasting, sales, and picnicking. Stay limit 15 days from June through September, 30 days from October through May. Open all year.

29 Navarro River Redwoods State Park: Paul M. Dimmick Wayside Campground

Location: 42 miles west of Ukiah.
Sites: 28 sites for tents and RVs up to 30 feet long.
Facilities: Tables, fire rings, drinking water (summer only), vault toilets.
Fee per night: $10-$12, pets $1.
Management: California Department of Parks and Recreation, 707-937-5804.
Activities: Kayaking, canoeing, hiking, fishing, swimming.
Finding the campground: From the intersection of U.S. Highway 101 and California Highway 253 in Ukiah, drive southwest on CA 253 for 16 miles, turn right (north) onto California Highway 128, and drive about 26 miles.

About the campground: This narrow, 674-acre park follows the Navarro River (and CA 128) from the ocean to a point about 12 miles inland. The forest is mainly second-growth redwoods, with huge stumps attesting to the logging of former giants. The 11-mile Navarro River Redwoods Car Tour along CA 128 has turnouts for exploring short sections of the forest. The river provides steelhead fishing in the winter. The park is a good put-in for kayaks and canoes during the winter and spring paddling season. Stay limit 15 days. Open all year.

30 Navarro River Redwoods State Park: Navarro Beach

Location: 50 miles west of Ukiah.
Sites: 10 sites for tents and RVs up to 30 feet long.
Facilities: Tables, fire rings, chemical toilets. No drinking water.
Fee per night: $5, pets $1.
Management: California Department of Parks and Recreation, 707-937-5804.
Activities: Kayaking, canoeing, fishing, swimming.
Finding the campground: On the coast near the intersection of California Highways 1 and 128.

About the campground: Situated on the beach, just south of the bridge across the Navarro River. See Paul M. Dimmick Campground (number 29) for a description of the park. Stay limit 15 days. Open all year.

31 Lake Mendocino: Che-Ka-Ka

Location: 4 miles northeast of Ukiah.
Sites: 22 sites for tents and RVs up to 35 feet long.
Facilities: Tables, fire rings, drinking water, vault toilets, playground, boat ramp.
Fee per night: $8.
Management: U.S. Army Corps of Engineers, 707-462-7581.
Activities: Swimming, fishing, boating, waterskiing, hiking.
Finding the campground: From Ukiah, drive north on U.S. Highway 101 about 2 miles, take the Lake Mendocino Drive exit, and drive east about 2 miles.

About the campground: Lake Mendocino provides 1,822 acres for virtually all water sports. You can launch your boat from one of two six-lane boat ramps located at either end of the lake, and sailing is popular. Boat slips and boat rentals are available at the marina, near the north end. Fish catches include striped, large-, and small-mouth bass; bluegill; crappie; and three types of catfish. A hiking trail circles the lake (except for the north end), beginning at either end of Coyote Dam. The lake is subject to water drawdowns during the summer and fall. Four wineries are located near the lake, Cresta Blanca and Parducci in Ukiah, Olson Winery on California Highway 20 near the north end of the lake, and Frey Vineyards, 6 miles north on Tomki Road. They offer tours, tastings, and purchase. Che-Ka-Ka Campground is at the north end of the dam near the park office. Stay limit 14 days. Open from April through September.

32 Lake Mendocino: Ky-En

Location: 8 miles northeast of Ukiah.
Sites: 103 sites for tents and RVs up to 35 feet long.
Facilities: Tables, fire rings, drinking water, flush toilets, showers, dump station, playground. Boat ramp nearby. The facilities are wheelchair accessible.
Fee per night: Regular sites $14, waterfront $16.
Management: U.S. Army Corps of Engineers, 707-462-7581.
Activities: Swimming, fishing, boating, waterskiing, hiking.
Finding the campground: From Ukiah, drive north on U.S. Highway 101 about 6 miles, take the California Highway 20 exit, and drive east about 1.5 miles. Turn right onto Marina Drive and drive half a mile.

About the campground: See Che-Ka-Ka Campground (number 31). Open all year.

33 Lake Mendocino: Bu-Shay

Location: 8 miles northeast of Ukiah.
Sites: 164 individual sites, plus 3 group sites for up to 120 people each, for tents and RVs up to 35 feet long.
Facilities: Tables, fire rings, drinking water, flush toilets, showers, dump station, playground. Boat ramp 2 miles west. The facilities are wheelchair accessible.
Fee per night: $14, group sites $80-$120. Group sites must be reserved; call number below.
Management: U.S. Army Corps of Engineers, 707-462-7581.
Activities: Swimming, fishing, boating, waterskiing, hiking.
Finding the campground: From Ukiah, drive north on U.S. Highway 101 about 6 miles, take the California Highway 20 exit, and drive east about 2 miles. Turn right after the small bridge and drive half a mile.

About the campground: See Che-Ka-Ka Campground (number 31).

SONOMA-NAPA AREA

The vineyards of the Sonoma-Napa area are world famous. Many of California's premium wines are born in Napa Valley, and tours of the wineries here are a growing part of the tourism industry. If you want to avoid the crowded roads of the Napa tour and are willing to see the vineyards from a different perspective, you can canoe or kayak on the Russian River north of Santa Rosa, passing nearly 100 wineries between Guerneville and Cloverdale.

But wineries are not the only attraction of Sonoma-Napa. The coastline from Jenner north to Point Arena is wild and glorious. The ocean pounds furiously against the headlands. Along the coast are fine beaches and Fort Ross, a restored Russian outpost established in 1812.

1 Gualala Point Regional Park

Location: 43 miles north of the community of Bodega Bay.
Sites: 25 sites for tents and RVs up to 30 feet long.
Facilities: Tables, fire rings, drinking water, flush toilets, dump station. The facilities are wheelchair accessible.
Fee per night: $15.
Agency: Sonoma County Parks Department, 707-785-2377.
Activities: Hiking, fishing.
Finding the campground: From Bodega Bay, drive north 43 miles on California Highway 1.

About the campground: Situated within a majestic redwood grove along the banks of the Gualala River, and close to the coast. Sites are relatively close together. A trail leads along the bluff for good coastal views, and steelhead fishing in the river is good, but crowded, in early winter. Stay limit 14 days. Open all year.

2 Salt Point State Park: Woodside

Location: 28 miles north of the community of Bodega Bay.
Sites: 110 sites for tents and RVs up to 31 feet long, including 1 group site for up to 40 people.
Facilities: Tables, fire rings, drinking water, vault toilets, dump station.
Fee per night: $16, pets $1.
Agency: California Department of Parks and Recreation, 707-865-2391.
Activities: Hiking, scuba diving, mountain biking, horseback riding.
Finding the campground: From Bodega Bay, drive about 28 miles north on California Highway 1.

About the campground: Salt Point Park has been chosen by *Sunset Magazine* as one of the 100 best places to camp in the western United States. It encompasses almost 6,000 acres, and includes 6 miles of rocky shoreline, hard sand beach coves, an underwater preserve, a redwood grove, a pygmy forest,

Sonoma-Napa Area

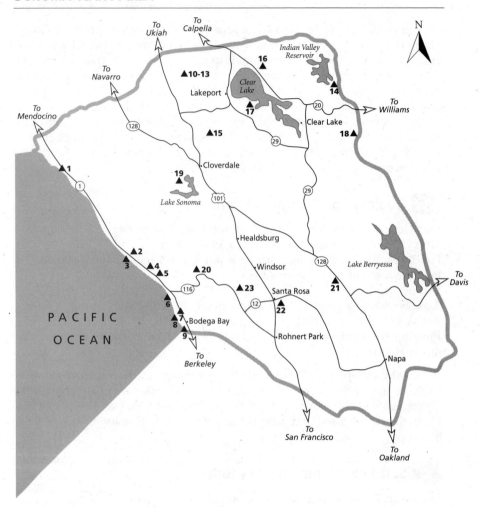

several scenic trails for hikers, equestrians, and mountain bikers, and a small visitor center. There is a primitive boat launch for scuba divers but the coast is too rough to launch pleasure boats. The waters offshore are a protected marine reserve; no fishing or collecting is permitted. The 2-mile Stump Beach Trail leads along the bluff to a beautiful cove beach lined with driftwood. Adjacent to the park is the Kruse Rhododendron State Reserve, which comes alive with color in April and May. Woodside Campground is located on the east side of the highway in a mixed, mostly pine forest. Stay limit 10 days. Open all year.

3 Salt Point State Park: Gerstle Cove

Location: 28 miles north of the community of Bodega Bay.
Sites: 30 sites for tents and RVs up to 31 feet long.

SONOMA-NAPA AREA CAMPGROUNDS

	Group sites	RV sites	Total sites	Max. RV length	Hookups	Toilets	Showers	Drinking water	Dump station	Pets	Wheelchair	Recreation	Fee ($)	Season	Can reserve	Length of stay
1 Gualala Point Regional Park		•	25	30		F	•	•	•		•	HF	15			14
Salt Point State Park (2–3)																
2 Woodside	•	•	110	31		V	•	•		•		HR	16			10
3 Gerstle Cove		•	30	31		V		•		•		HLR	16			10
4 Stillwater Cove Regional Park		•	22	35		F	•	•	•	•		HF	15			14
5 Fort Ross State Historic Park		•	20			V		•		•		H	12	mid-March–Nov.		14
Sonoma Coast State Beach (6–7)																
6 Wright's Beach		•	30	27		F		•		•	•	HFR	20		•	10/30
7 Bodega Dunes		•	98	31		F	•	•	•	•	•	HFR	16		•	10/30
8 Westside Regional Park		•	47			F	•	•	•	•	•	FBL	15			14
9 Doran Regional Park		•	138			F	•	•	•	•	•	FBL	15			14
Cow Mountain Recreational Area (10–13)																
10 Red Mountain			10			V		•		•		O				14
11 Mayacmas			9			V		•		•		HFR				14
12 Bushy			1					•		•		O				14
13 Buckhorn			1			V		•				O				14
14 Blue Oak		•	5			V		•		•		SFB				14
15 Sheldon Creek			6			V		•		•						14
16 Lakeview		•	9			V				•		H				14
17 Clear Lake State Park		•	147			F	•	•	•	•	•	HSF BL	17–22		•	15/30
18 Lower Hunting Creek		•	5			V		•		•		O				14
19 Lake Sonoma	•	•	115			F	•	•	•	•		HS FB	16–75		•	14
20 Austin Creek State Recreational Area		•	24	20		F		•		•		HR	10–12			15
21 Bothe-Napa Valley State Park		•	51	31		F	•	•	•	•	•	HSR	15–17		•	15
22 Spring Lake Regional Park		•	30			F	•	•	•	•		HF BL	14		•	14
23 Sugarloaf Ridge State Park	•	•	51	27		F		•		•		HR	15–75		•	15/30

Hookups: W = Water E = Electric S = Sewer
Toilets: F = Flush V = Vault P = Pit C = Chemical
Recreation: H = Hiking S = Swimming F = Fishing B = Boating L = Boat Launch O = Off-highway Driving R = Horseback Riding
Maximum Trailer/RV Length given in feet. Stay Limit given in days. Fee given in dollars.
If no entry under **Season**, campground is open all year. If no entry under **Fee**, camping is free.

ables, fire rings, drinking water, vault toilets.
ht: $16, pets $1.
ifornia Department of Parks and Recreation, 707-865-2391.
Activities: Hiking, scuba diving, mountain biking, horseback riding.
Finding the campground: From Bodega Bay, drive about 28 miles north on California Highway 1.

About the campground: Situated on the ocean side of the highway, Gerstle Cove is close to the shoreline, but still suffers from the aftermath of a fire in 1992, which has left blackened trees in the area. See Woodside Campground (number 2).

4 Stillwater Cove Regional Park

Location: 25 miles north of the community of Bodega Bay.
Sites: 22 sites for tents and RVs up to 35 feet long.
Facilities: Tables, fire rings, drinking water, flush toilets, showers, dump station.
Fee per night: $15, pets $1.
Agency: Sonoma County Regional Parks, 707-527-2041.
Activities: Fishing, hiking.
Finding the campground: From Bodega Bay, drive north 25 miles on California Highway 1.

About the campground: An attractive campground shaded by tall trees, Stillwater Cove bears the name of the dramatic cove which is across the highway, and not visible from the campsites. The mile-long Stockoff Creek Loop Trail begins at the campground and travels through a mixed redwood/Douglas fir forest to a cove used by abalone divers. Stay limit 14 days. Open all year.

5 Fort Ross State Historic Park: Reef

Location: 21 miles north of the community of Bodega Bay.
Sites: 20 sites for tents and RVs.
Facilities: Tables, fire rings, drinking water, vault toilets.
Fee per night: $12.
Agency: California Department of Parks and Recreation, 707-847-3286.
Activities: Hiking, scuba diving.
Finding the campground: From Bodega Bay, drive north about 21 miles on California Highway 1. Watch for the campground sign.

About the campground: Fort Ross is the site of a Russian fort built in 1812 to protect the Russian fur trade in California. The Russians withdrew from the area in 1841, due to the decline of the sea otter population. The reconstructed fort consists of several buildings surrounded by a log stockade, including the commandant's house, officers' quarters, and a church. The park includes more than 3,000 upland acres containing some of the world's oldest second-growth redwoods. Although there are no formal trails, hikers are welcome to use the old Russian logging roads which lead through the area.

A Russian fort, built in 1812 to protect the Russian fur trade in California, is the centerpiece of Fort Ross State Historic Park.

Reef Campground, in a coastal canyon, is 3 miles south of the fort on the west side of the highway on a separate entry road. A trail leads from the campground to Fort Ross Cove, a small beach with an underwater park offshore. The trail continues uphill to the fort. Stay limit 14 days. The park is open all year; the campground is open from mid-March through November.

6 Sonoma Coast State Beach: Wright's Beach

Location: 6 miles north of the community of Bodega Bay.
Sites: 30 sites for tents and RVs up to 27 feet long.
Facilities: Tables, fire rings, drinking water, flush toilets. The facilities are wheelchair accessible.
Fee per night: $20, pets $1. For reservations call 800-444-7275. There is a one-time reservation fee of $7.50.
Agency: California State Parks, 707-875-3483.
Activities: Hiking, fishing, scuba diving, whale watching, horseback riding.
Finding the campgrounds: From Bodega Bay, drive north 6 miles on California Highway 1.

About the campground: Situated directly on the beach, without the wind protection of Bodega Dunes Campground, but with a wider vista and some trees for shade. See Bodega Dunes (number 7).

7 Sonoma Coast State Beach: Bodega Dunes

Location: 1 mile north of the community of Bodega Bay.
Sites: 98 sites for tents and RVs up to 31 feet long.
Facilities: Tables, fire rings, drinking water, flush toilets, showers, dump station. The facilities are wheelchair accessible.
Fee per night: $16, pets $1. For reservations call 800-444-7275. There is a one-time reservation fee of $7.50.
Agency: California State Parks, 707-875-3483.
Activities: Hiking, fishing, scuba diving, whale watching, horseback riding.
Finding the campground: From Bodega Bay, drive north 1 mile on California Highway 1.

About the campground: This park of 5,000 acres runs more than 16 miles along the dramatic Sonoma coastline from Bodega Bay to just north of Jenner. At least 13 separate, isolated beaches lie within its borders, most of them reachable by trails from the highway. A visitor center is located in Jenner.

The campground is situated in an attractive pine grove behind high dunes, which hide the beach. A boardwalk crosses the dunes, leading to 3-mile-long South Salmon Creek Beach. The Bodega Head Trail is a good place to watch for whales from December through April. Stay limit 10 days from June through September, 30 days from October through May. Open all year.

8 Westside Regional Park

Location: 2 miles northwest of the community of Bodega Bay.
Sites: 47 sites for tents and RVs.
Facilities: Tables, fire rings, drinking water, flush toilets, showers, dump station, fish-cleaning station, boat ramp. The facilities are wheelchair accessible.
Fee per night: $15, pets $1.
Management: Sonoma County Regional Parks, 707-875-3540.
Activities: Fishing, boating.
Finding the campground: From Bodega Bay, drive north a short distance on California Highway 1, turn left onto West Shore Road, and drive 2 miles.

About the campground: Situated on the west shore of Bodega Bay. Noted for good salmon fishing in early summer, and rockfish year-round; ling cod, flounder, and perch are also taken. Stay limit 14 days. Open all year.

9 Doran Regional Park

Location: On Bodega Bay.
Sites: 138 sites for tents or RVs.
Facilities: Tables, grills, drinking water, flush toilets, showers, dump station, fish-cleaning station, boat ramp. The facilities are wheelchair accessible.
Fee per night: $15, pets $1.
Agency: Sonoma County Regional Parks, 707-875-3540.
Activities: Fishing, boating.

Finding the campground: From the community of Bodega Bay, drive 1 mile south on California Highway 1 and turn right at the campground sign.

About the campground: Located on an attractive spit of land dividing Bodega Bay and Bodega Harbor, the campground has water on both sides. Ice plant is the predominant vegetation, but there are some shrubs and small trees, but little shade. Fishing by boat yields salmon in early summer, and rockfish and ling cod year-round. Perch and flounder can be taken from shore. Stay limit 14 days. Open all year.

10 Cow Mountain Recreation Area: Red Mountain

Location: 11 miles southeast of Ukiah.
Sites: 10 sites for tents.
Facilities: Tables, fire rings, drinking water, vault toilets.
Fee per night: None.
Management: Bureau of Land Management, 707-468-4000.
Activities: OHV driving.
Finding the campground: From the intersection of U.S. Highway 101 and Talmadge Road in Ukiah, drive east 1.5 miles on Talmadge, turn right onto East Side Road, and drive 0.3 mile. Turn left onto Mill Creek Road (which becomes Mendo Lake Road) and drive 9 miles.

About the campground: This south section of the recreation area contains 23,000 acres of rugged terrain set aside primarily for OHV use. There are 25 trails and roads graded by difficulty and type of vehicles (motorcycles, ATVs, four by four short base, four by four long base). Stay limit 14 days. Open all year.

11 Cow Mountain Recreation Area: Mayacmus

Location: 12 miles southeast of Ukiah.
Sites: 9 sites for tents.
Facilities: Tables, fire rings, drinking water, vault toilets.
Fee per night: None.
Management: Bureau of Land Management, 707-468-4000.
Activities: Hiking, fishing, horseback riding, hunting.
Finding the campground: From the intersection of U.S. Highway 101 and Talmadge Road in Ukiah, drive east 1.5 miles on Talmadge, turn right onto East Side Road, and drive 0.3 mile. Turn left onto Mill Creek Road and drive 3.5 miles, then turn left onto Mendo Rock Road and drive 7 miles.

About the campground: This north section of the recreation area contains 27,000 acres of rugged terrain, hot in summer and rainy in winter. Hunting is the major activity, and a rifle range is located off Mendo Rock Road, coming into the area. Rainbow trout can be found in the colder streams, and some of the small reservoirs have been stocked with sunfish. Trails and roads are open to hikers and equestrians, but OHV driving is prohibited. See Red Mountain Campground (number 10) for OHV use. Stay limit 14 days. Open all year.

12 Cow Mountain Recreation Area: Bushy

Location: 15 miles southeast of Ukiah.
Sites: 1 site for tents.
Facilities: Tables, fire rings, drinking water. No toilet.
Fee per night: None.
Management: Bureau of Land Management, 707-468-4000.
Activities: OHV driving.
Finding the campground: From the intersection of U.S. Highway 101 and Talmadge Road in Ukiah, drive east 1.5 miles on Talmadge, turn right onto East Side Road, and drive 0.3 mile. Turn left onto Mill Creek Road (which becomes Mendo Lake Road) and drive about 13 miles. Watch for the camp on the left.

About the campground: See Red Mountain Campground (number 10).

13 Cow Mountain Recreation Area: Buckhorn

Location: 17 miles southeast of Ukiah.
Sites: 1 site for tents.
Facilities: Tables, fire rings, vault toilet. No drinking water.
Fee per night: None.
Management: Bureau of Land Management, 707-468-4000.
Activities: OHV driving.
Finding the campground: From the intersection of U.S. Highway 101 and Talmadge Road in Ukiah, drive east 1.5 miles on Talmadge, turn right onto East Side Road, and drive 0.3 mile. Turn left onto Mill Creek Road (which becomes Mendo Lake Road) and drive about 14 miles. Turn right onto Buckhorn Road and drive 1.5 miles.

About the campground: See Red Mountain Campground (number 10).

14 Blue Oak

Location: 28 miles west of Williams, near Indian Valley Reservoir.
Sites: 5 sites for tents and RVs.
Facilities: Tables, fire rings, drinking water, vault toilets. Boat ramp nearby.
Fee per night: None.
Management: Bureau of Land Management, 707-468-4000.
Activities: Swimming, fishing, boating (at nearby Indian Valley Reservoir).
Finding the campground: From the intersection of Interstate 5 and California Highway 20 in Williams, drive southwest 21 miles, turn right (north) onto Walker Ridge Road, and follow the signs for the campground for 7 miles.

About the campground: The primary attraction of this campground is its location 1.5 miles from the south end of Indian Valley Reservoir. While the lake is not much to look at, it offers excellent bass fishing from mid-March through the first week in June, and the lake is well stocked annually with Eagle Lake trout, best fished for from late winter to early spring. A boat ramp is located at the south end of the lake. There is a boat speed limit of 10 miles per hour. Stay limit 14 days. Open all year.

15 Sheldon Creek

Location: 26 miles north of Cloverdale.
Sites: 6 sites for tents.
Facilities: Tables, fire rings, drinking water, vault toilets. Boat ramp nearby.
Fee per night: None.
Management: Bureau of Land Management, 707-468-4000.
Activities: Hunting.
Finding the campground: From Cloverdale, drive north about 15 miles on U.S. Highway 101, turn right (east) onto California Highway 175, and drive 3 miles. Turn right (south) onto Old Toll Road and drive 8 miles.

About the campground: Situated on a small creek in rolling grassland, which is green in spring and brown the rest of the time. Stay limit 14 days. Open all year.

16 Lakeview

Location: 10 miles east of Lucerne (2 miles by trail), near Clear Lake.
Sites: 9 sites for tents and RVs.
Facilities: Tables, fire rings, vault toilets. No drinking water.
Fee per night: None.
Management: Mendocino National Forest, 707-275-2361.
Activities: Hiking.
Finding the campground: From Lucerne, on the east shore of Clear Lake, drive 2 miles north on California Highway 20, turn right (east) onto County Road 303 (Forest Road M8), and drive 5 miles. Turn right (southeast) onto Forest Road 15N09 and drive 3 miles.

About the campground: Situated high above Clear Lake and the town of Lucerne. A 2-mile trail leads down to the town, with a 2,000-foot elevation drop. Elevation 3,400 feet. Stay limit 14 days. Open all year. Please call the national forest for winter road conditions.

17 Clear Lake State Park

Location: 11 miles southeast of Lakeport.
Sites: 147 sites for tents and RVs in 4 campgrounds.
Facilities: Tables, fire rings, drinking water, flush toilets, showers, dump station, boat ramp, swimming beach. The facilities are wheelchair accessible.
Fee per night: $17-$22. For reservations call 800-444-7275. There is a one-time reservation fee of $7.50.
Management: California Department of Parks and Recreation, 707-279-4293.
Activities: Hiking, swimming, fishing, boating, waterskiing.
Finding the campground: From Lakeport, drive south 3 miles on California Highway 29, turn left (east) onto Soda Bay Road, and drive 8 miles.

About the campground: Clear Lake is the largest natural freshwater lake within the borders of California. It is 19 miles long, covers 40,000 acres, and has 100 miles of shoreline. Fishing is good for largemouth bass, black crappie, channel catfish, bluegill, and Sacramento perch. The water warms up sufficiently in summer for comfortable swimming and waterskiing. A half-mile nature trail and a 1.5-mile wooded loop begin near the four campgrounds: Kelsey Creek, Lakeside Premium, Lower and Upper Bayview, and Cole Creek. Elevation 2,000 feet. Stay limit 15 days from June through September, 30 days from October through May. Open all year.

18 Lower Hunting Creek

Location: 20 miles southeast of the town of Clearlake.
Sites: 5 sites for tents and RVs.
Facilities: Tables, fire rings, drinking water, vault toilets, ramadas.
Fee per night: None.
Management: Bureau of Land Management, 707-468-4000.
Activities: Mountain biking, OHV driving.
Finding the campground: From the intersection of Olympic Drive and California Highway 29 in Clearlake, drive south 3 miles to Lower Lake, turn left onto Morgan Valley Road, and drive 15 miles. Turn right (south) onto a dirt road and drive 2 miles.

About the campground: There are 25 miles of trails for OHV driving, plus miles of existing dirt roads for mountain bikes. Stay limit 14 days. Open all year.

19 Lake Sonoma: Liberty Glen

Location: 13 miles northwest of Healdsburg.
Sites: 115 sites for tents and RVs, including 2 group sites for up to 80 people each.
Facilities: Tables, fire rings, drinking water, flush toilets, showers, dump station. Boat ramp 2.5 miles away.
Fee per night: $16, group fee $75. For reservations call 877-444-6777.
Management: U.S. Army Corps of Engineers, 707-433-9483.
Activities: Hiking, swimming, fishing, boating, waterskiing.
Finding the campground: From Healdsburg, drive northwest on Dry Creek Road for 11 miles, continue over the bridge across Lake Sonoma, and drive an additional 2 miles.

About the campground: Lake Sonoma is a 9-mile-long lake covering 2,700 acres, in the coastal foothills of Sonoma County. Largemouth bass, channel catfish, Sacramento perch, and red ear sunfish are the normal catches. The lake has divided areas for fishing and waterskiing. A dozen wineries lie within a 6-mile radius of the campground, most offering tastings and sales. A marina is located on the western side of the bridge, offering boat rentals and other services. A visitor center is nearby. For campers with boats who want to escape their vehicles, nine attractive boat-in campsites are located on various arms of the lake. More than 40 miles of hiking and equestrian trails lead through redwood groves and oak woodlands.

Liberty Glen Campground is about 2.5 miles from the lake, requiring driving for boat access. A half-mile foot trail leads downhill from the campground to the lakeshore. Stay limit 14 days. Open all year.

20 Austin Creek State Recreation Area: Bullfrog Pond

Location: 22 miles northwest of Santa Rosa.
Sites: 24 sites for tents and RVs up to 20 feet long. No trailers.
Facilities: Tables, fire rings, drinking water, flush toilets.
Fee per night: $10-$12, pets $1.
Management: California Department of Parks and Recreation, 707-869-2015.
Activities: Hiking, mountain biking, horseback riding.
Finding the campground: From the intersection of U.S. Highway 101 and Guerneville Road in Santa Rosa, take the Guerneville Road exit and drive west 8 miles to where the road turns north and becomes California Highway 116. Continue to Guerneville, additional 9 miles, then drive straight north 2.2 miles on Armstrong Woods Road to Armstrong Redwoods State Reserve. Continue through the reserve for another 2.5 miles. Trailers and RVs over 20 feet long are not permitted on the winding, narrow road to the campground.

About the campground: Austin Creek State Recreation Area and Armstrong Redwoods State Reserve are adjoining parks. The campground (Bullfrog Pond) is located in Austin Creek, while most of the redwoods are found in Armstrong. A mile-long loop tours the heart of the Armstrong Reserve, visiting its most famous trees, and a strenuous 9-mile loop for hikers and equestrians begins at the campground. A riding concession operates adjacent to the camp, offering rides and pack trips. Mountain bikers have access to service roads. Half a dozen wineries are located within a 10-mile radius of the campground, most offering tastings and sales. Fishing is not permitted in the streams within either park. Stay limit 15 days. Open all year.

21 Bothe-Napa Valley State Park

Location: 5 miles northwest of St. Helena.
Sites: 51 sites for tents and RVs up to 31 feet long.
Facilities: Tables, fire rings, drinking water, flush toilets, showers, dump station, pool (summer only). The facilities are wheelchair accessible.
Fee per night: $15-$17, pets $1. For reservations call 800-444-7275. There is a one-time reservation fee of $7.50.
Management: California Department of Parks and Recreation, 707-963-2236.
Activities: Hiking, swimming, horseback riding.
Finding the campground: From St. Helena, drive northwest 5 miles on California Highway 29.

About the campground: Located in the heart of Napa Valley, with two dozen of the nation's most famous wineries within a radius of 18 miles, this 1,900-acre park offers a surprisingly rugged and varied terrain, ranging from creek-lined redwoods, to dry, chaparral-covered hillsides. A feature of the park is a 1.2-mile trail to Bale Grist Mill, a restored and functioning grinding mill, which docents in period dress operate on weekends. The ground flour and products made from it are available for sale. Another excursion, the Redwood Trail-Coyote Peak Loop, offers a 4.7-mile tour of the park, including a view from atop Coyote Peak (1,170 feet).

Calistoga, 5 miles west of the campground, is noted for its hot springs and mud baths, and for Old Faithful Geyser, which spouts 60 feet in the air every 40 minutes. Stay limit 15 days. Open all year.

22 Spring Lake Regional Park

Location: In Santa Rosa.
Sites: 30 sites for tents and RVs.
Facilities: Tables, fire rings, drinking water, flush toilets, showers, dump station, boat ramp and rentals.
Fee per night: $14, pets $1. Reservations accepted; call number below.
Management: Sonoma County Regional Parks, 707-527-2041.
Activities: Hiking, fishing, boating.
Finding the campground: From the intersection of U.S. Highway 101 and California Highway 12 in Santa Rosa, drive east on CA 12 about 5 miles, turn right (south) onto Newanga Avenue, and drive about 1.5 miles to its end at the park.

About the campground: This 75-acre lake, within the city limits of Santa Rosa, is stocked annually with more than 20,000 rainbow trout and has a small bass and bluegill population. No motor boats are permitted. A short trail from the campground leads south to the dam. Stay limit 14 days. Open from mid-May through mid-September, weekends only for the rest of the year.

23 Sugarloaf Ridge State Park

Location: 14 miles east of Santa Rosa.
Sites: 51 sites for tents and RVs up to 27 feet long, including 1 group site for up to 50 people.
Facilities: Tables, fire rings, drinking water, flush toilets.
Fee per night: $15-16, pets $1, group site $75. Reservations required for group site; call 800-444-7275. There is a one-time reservation fee of $15.
Management: California Department of Parks and Recreation, 707-833-5712.
Activities: Hiking, mountain biking, horseback riding.
Finding the campground: From the intersection of U.S. Highway 101 and California Highway 12 in Santa Rosa, drive east 11 miles on CA 12, turn left (north) onto Adobe Canyon Road, and drive 3.3 miles.

About the campground: Situated in the rugged coastal mountains, on the edge of a meadow shaded by oak trees, this campground features trails. Miles of well-marked trails and service roads weave through its 2,700 acres, including a 0.75-mile nature trail, and a 1.6-mile loop that visits a 25-foot waterfall. A map is available at the small visitor center to plan itineraries. Coastal redwoods and large Douglas fir trees can be found in some of the drainages. Stay limit 15 days from June through September, 30 days from October through May. Open all year.

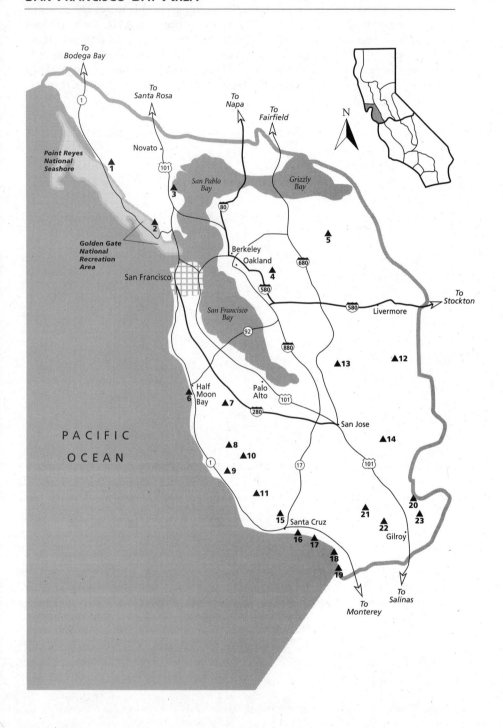

San Francisco Bay Area

Ocean access, marvelous views, and temperate weather—these define the San Francisco Bay Area. Add the human contributions—the Golden Gate Bridge, Chinatown, cable cars, Fisherman's Wharf, the Embarcadero, and much more—and you have what makes San Francisco such a special city. But the Bay Area is far more than the city on the hills. Its borders extend from Point Reyes National Seashore in the north to Santa Cruz in the south, and they encompass a variety of natural settings for outdoor recreation.

The 74,000-acre Golden Gate Recreation Area spans several counties and is the world's largest urban park. Point Reyes, only an hour's drive from the city, offers many miles of isolated beaches, hiking and riding trails, and walk-in campsites. Muir Woods, a beautiful redwood grove, is even closer. To the south, 18,000-acre Big Basin State Park preserves more of these giant, ancient trees and offers 80 miles of trails from which to view them. A long string of beaches reaches from Daly City to south of Santa Cruz, while to the east, wooded parks such as Mount Diablo and Henry Coe offer sylvan settings close to the urban sprawl.

The temperature of the San Francisco Bay Area is moderate year-round and varies little from spring through fall. Rainfall is light, averaging from 4.2 inches in January to virtually zero in June, July, and August. Morning fog is common in the coastal areas during the summer months. Average winter temperatures range from 58 to 46 degrees F, spring temperatures from 63 to 49, summer from 69 to 55, and fall from 69 to 53. The average percentage of sunny days is a steady 69 percent from spring through fall but drops to 57 percent in winter.

1 Samuel P. Taylor State Park: Devil's Gulch, Madrone

Location: 5 miles east of Olema.

Sites: 60 sites for tents and RVs up to 18 feet long, plus a group camp for up to 50 people and a horse camp.

Facilities: Tables, fire rings, drinking water, flush toilets, showers. The facilities are wheelchair accessible.

Fee per night: $12, pets $1. Group camp $75. For reservations call 800-444-7275. There is a one-time reservation fee of $7.50.

Management: California Department of Parks and Recreation, 415-488-9897.

Activities: Hiking, cycling, mountain biking, horseback riding.

Finding the campground: From the intersection of California Highway 1 and Sir Francis Drake Boulevard in Olema, drive east 5 miles on Drake Highway to the horse camp, 5.7 miles to the group camp (Madrone), and 6 miles to the family camp.

About the campground: The sites at the family camp are within a large redwood grove and deeply shaded. The Pioneer Tree Trail makes a 2.5-mile loop through both ancient and second growth redwoods, and a 9-mile loop trail beginning from the group camp ascends Barnabe Peak. The Cross Marin Bike-

SAN FRANCISCO BAY AREA CAMPGROUNDS

	Group sites	RV sites	Total sites	Max. RV length	Hookups	Toilets	Showers	Drinking water	Dump station	Pets	Wheelchair	Recreation	Fee ($)	Season	Can reserve	Length of stay
1 Samuel P. Taylor State Park	•	•	62	18		F	•	•		•	•	HR	12–75		•	7
2 Mount Tamalpais State Park		•	21			F	•			•		HFR	15–17			15
3 China Camp State Park		•	30			V	•					HSF	9			15
4 Anthony Chabot Regional Park		•	75	40	WES	F	•	•	•	•	•	HF	15–20		•	14
5 Mount Diablo State Park		•	60	25		F	•		•	•		HR	15–17		•	30
6 Half Moon Bay State Beach		•	55			F	•	•	•	•	•	HS FR	16			15
7 Huddart Park Group Camp	•		3			F	•		•			H	100		•	14
8 Memorial County Park	•	•	135	35		F	•	•	•			HR	15–200		•	14
9 Butano State Park		•	39			V	•					H	17		•	15
10 Portola State Park		•	52	24		F	•	•		•		H	14–18		•	15/30
11 Big Basin Redwoods State Park		•	100			FV	•	•	•	•		HR	17		•	30
12 Del Valle County Park		•	150	40	WE	F	•	•	•	•		HFB	14–16		•	14
13 Sunol Regional Wilderness			4			V		•				H	11			14
14 Joseph D. Grant County Park		•	22	30		F	•	•	•	•		HR	8	April–Nov.		14
15 Henry Cowell Redwoods State Park		•	112			F	•	•	•	•		HF	17–18		•	7/15
16 New Brighton State Beach		•	112	36		F	•	•	•	•		SF	14–19		•	7/15
17 Seacliff State Beach		•	26	40	WES	F	•	•		•	•	SF	26–29		•	7
18 Manresa State Beach			64			F	•	•		•		SF	14–19			7/15
19 Sunset State Beach		•	90	31		F	•	•		•		SF	14–19		•	7/15
20 Henry W. Coe State Park		•	28	26		P	•		•			HFR	8			14
21 Uvas Canyon County Park		•	30	28		F	•		•	•		HFB	10			14
22 Mount Madonna County Park		•	117		WE	F	•	•	•	•		HR	8–20			14
23 Coyote Lake County Park		•	74			F	•		•			FBL	10			14

Hookups: W = Water E = Electric S = Sewer
Toilets: F = Flush V = Vault P = Pit C = Chemical
Recreation: H = Hiking S = Swimming F = Fishing B = Boating L = Boat Launch O = Off-highway Driving R = Horseback Riding
Maximum Trailer/RV Length given in feet. Stay Limit given in days. Fee given in dollars.
If no entry under **Season**, campground is open all year. If no entry under **Fee**, camping is free.

Golden Gate Recreation Area encompasses 74,000 acres, making it the largest urban park in the world.

Trail passes through the park, and fire roads provide challenging ups and downs for mountain bikers. Stay limit 7 days. Open all year.

2 Mount Tamalpais State Park: Pantoll

Location: 10 miles northwest of Sausalito.

Sites: 16 sites for tents (100 feet from parking area), en-route lot for up to 4 self-contained RVs, environmental camp with 6 walk-in sites and 10 primitive cabins, horse camp, which can accommodate 25 people and 12 horses. Horse camp by reservation only, 2 weeks in advance.

Facilities: Tables, fire rings/grills, drinking water, flush toilets.

Fee per night: $15-$17, pets $1.

Management: California Department of Parks and Recreation, 415-388-2070.

Activities: Hiking, fishing, mountain biking, horseback riding.

Finding the campground: From the intersection of U.S. Highway 101 and California Highway 1 northwest of Sausalito, drive 3.5 miles west on CA 1 toward Stinson Beach. Turn right onto Panoramic Highway and drive 5 miles. The road is winding and steep and not recommended for trailers or RVs over 25 feet long.

About the campground: Mount Tamalpais is noted for its scenic vistas of San Francisco Bay and the Pacific coast. The Verna Dunshee Trail circles East Peak (2,571 feet), providing views of such landmarks as the Golden Gate Bridge, Alcatraz, and Mount Diablo. The Steep Ravine Trail (4 miles round trip) leads into a beautiful gorge with tall redwoods and a rushing stream. The Stapleveldt-Alpine Trail Loop, a forested 4.4-mile hike through impressive redwoods, begins at the Pantoll Ranger Station, near the campground. The Matt Davis Trail also begins at the ranger station and traverses the park's coastal slopes for a little over 4 miles. Stay limit 15 days. Open all year.

3 China Camp State Park

Location: 6 miles northeast of San Rafael.
Sites: 30 sites for tents (short walk in); self-contained RVs may overnight in the parking lot.
Facilities: Tables, grills, drinking water, vault toilets.
Fee per night: $9.
Management: California Department of Parks and Recreation, 415-456-0766.
Activities: Hiking, swimming, fishing, sailboarding, mountain biking.
Finding the campground: From San Rafael, drive northeast on North San Pedro Road for 6 miles.

About the campground: A historic Chinese fishing village is the centerpiece of the park, which is situated along the southwestern shore of San Pablo Bay. Abandoned in the late 19th century as a result of anti-Chinese legislation, the site now contains wooden structures that served as dwellings, a small museum, a Chinese fishing boat, and artifacts and exhibits. A trail leads to the shoreline, and another climbs the ridge behind the park, for scenic views over the water. The campground is located in a wooded area, with a meadow and a marsh between it and the bay. Stay limit 15 days. Open all year. No pets.

4 Anthony Chabot Regional Park

Location: On the eastern outskirts of Oakland.
Sites: 75 sites for tents and RVs up to 40 feet long, 10 with full hookups. The facilities are wheelchair accessible.
Facilities: Tables, fire rings, drinking water, flush toilets, showers, dump station.
Fee per night: $15-$20, pets $1. Reservations accepted, and there is a one-time reservation fee of $5.
Management: East Bay Regional Parks District, 510-635-0135.
Activities: Hiking, fishing, cycling.
Finding the campground: From Interstate 580 in Oakland, exit east on 35th Avenue (which becomes Redwood Road) and drive 7.5 miles.

About the campground: The campground is in a eucalyptus grove on a hilltop. Fishing and boating are available at Lake Chabot, about a half-mile away, and a trail leads to the lake from the campground. Private boats are not permitted on the lake, but boat rentals are available. Fishing from shore is allowed. The lake is stocked with more than 70,000 trout annually and is also a source of largemouth bass, bluegill, and crappie. A bike path circles the lake. Stay limit 14 days. Open all year.

5 | Mount Diablo State Park

Location: 6 miles northeast of Danville.
Sites: 60 sites for tents and RVs up to 25 feet long.
Facilities: Tables, fire rings, drinking water, flush toilets. The facilities are wheelchair accessible.
Fee per night: $15-$17, pets $1. For reservations call 800-444-7275. There is a one-time reservation fee of $7.50.
Management: California Department of Parks and Recreation, 510-687-1800.
Activities: Hiking, mountain biking, horseback riding.
Finding the campground: From Interstate 680 in Danville, take the Diablo Road exit and drive northeast for 6 miles on Diablo Road. The park is also accessible from Walnut Creek via North Gate Road.

About the campground: Although only 3,849 feet high, Mount Diablo affords one of the most sweeping views found anywhere in the United States. On clear days the vista extends from Mount Lassen to the Sierra Nevada to the Farallon Islands. An observation tower on the summit provides a 360-degree view, and contains a small museum and interpretive center. A 0.7-mile long trail circles the peak, and a series of trails combine to make the Grand Loop, a 6-mile trip around the mountain for hikers, horses, and mountain bikes. Stay limit 30 days. Open all year.

6 | Half Moon Bay State Beach

Location: In the community of Half Moon Bay.
Sites: 55 sites for tents and RVs.
Facilities: Tables, fire rings, drinking water, flush toilets, showers, dump station. The facilities are wheelchair accessible.
Fee per night: $16, pets $1.
Management: California Department of Parks and Recreation, 415-726-8820.
Activities: Swimming, fishing, surfing, hiking, cycling, horseback riding.
Finding the campground: From the intersection of California Highways 92 and 1 in the community of Half Moon Bay, drive south 0.3 mile on CA 1 and turn right onto Kelly Road to reach the entrance on the right.

About the campground: Four beaches comprise the Half Moon Bay State Beach complex. The campground is located in an attractive, grassy area directly behind the fine sandy stretch known as Francis Beach. Some of the sites are directly on the beach, but most RV sites are standard back-in pads 50 to 100 feet behind the beach. Shoreline fishing for perch can be very good right after the beginning of an incoming tide, and striped bass runs occur occasionally during the summer. A 2.3-mile trail for hikers and cyclists runs north from Francis Beach to Dunes Beach. Stay limit 15 days. Open all year.

7 Huddart Park Group Camp

Location: 5 miles southwest of Redwood City.
Sites: 3 group tent sites for up to 50 people each.
Facilities: Tables, barbecue grills, drinking water, flush toilets.
Fee per night: $100 per site. Reservations required; call the number below.
Management: San Mateo County Parks and Recreation, 650-363-4021.
Activities: Hiking.
Finding the campground: From the intersection of Interstate 280 and California Highway 84 in Redwood City, drive west on CA 84 for 1.8 miles, turn right onto Kings Mountain Road, and drive 3.5 miles.

About the campground: Suited for groups who want to get away and enjoy their own activities while remaining close to Palo Alto and Redwood City. Stay limit 14 days. Open all year.

8 Memorial County Park

Location: 14 miles southwest of Redwood City.
Sites: 132 sites for tents and RVs up to 35 feet long, plus group camp with two group sites, and horse camp. The group sites accommodate up to 75 and 100 people respectively, and adjacent Sam McDonald County Park has several sites with corrals for horse camping, the smallest accommodating up to 9 horses.
Facilities: Tables, barbecue pits, drinking water, showers, flush toilets, dump station.
Fee per night: $15 for 8 people, extra vehicle $5. Group sites $100, horse sites $20-$200. No reservations for family camping; reservations required for group and horse camps.
Management: San Mateo County Parks and Recreation, 650-363-4021.
Activities: Hiking, horseback riding.
Finding the campground: From the intersection of Interstate 280 and California Highway 84 in Redwood City, drive west and then south on CA 84 for 11 miles, turn left onto Pescadero Road, and continue about 3 miles to the campground entrance.

About the campground: Located in an attractive redwood grove, the campground has hiking and riding trails leading to nearby Portola State Park. Stay limit 14 days. Open all year on a reduced basis. No showers or dump station from November to May, and family camp is reduced to 30 sites during that period. No pets are allowed.

9 Butano State Park

Location: 20 miles south of the community of Half Moon Bay.
Sites: 20 sites for tents and RVs, plus 19 walk-in sites.
Facilities: Tables, fire rings, drinking water, vault toilets, nature center.
Fee per night: $17, pets $1. For reservations call 800-444-7275. There is a one-time reservation fee of $7.50.

Management: California Department of Parks and Recreation, 650-879-0173.
Activities: Hiking, mountain biking.
Finding the campground: From the intersection of California Highways 92 and 1 in the community of Half Moon Bay, drive south 14.5 miles on CA 1, turn left onto Pescadero Road, and drive 2.5 miles. Turn right onto Cloverdale Road and drive 3 miles.

About the campground: Butano State Park encompasses a 3,200-acre rain forest of old-and new-growth redwoods and large Douglas fir. A stand of tall, mature redwoods gives the campground a dark, cathedral-like aura. Excellent hiking opportunities in the park include Ano Nuevo Lookout, 2.7 miles round trip; the 1.6-mile Little Butano Creek Loop; and the 1.9-mile Jackson Flats/Six Bridges Trail Loop. Longer hikes include Mill Ox Loop (5 miles) and Butano Rim Loop (11 miles). Work is under way to extend the trail system to Big Basin Redwoods State Park (number 11). Stay limit 15 days. Open all year.

10 Portola State Park

Location: 17 miles south of Palo Alto.
Sites: 52 sites for tents and RVs up to 24 feet long.
Facilities: Tables, barbecue grills, drinking water, showers, flush toilets, visitor center.
Fee per night: $14-$18, pets $1. For reservations call 800-444-7275. There is a one-time reservation fee of $7.50.
Management: California Department of Parks and Recreation, 650-948-9098.
Activities: Hiking, mountain biking.
Finding the campground: From Interstate 280 about 3 miles south of Palo Alto, take the Page Mill Road exit and drive south about 7 miles to California Highway 35 (Skyline Boulevard). Page Mill Road now becomes increasingly narrow and winding. Cross CA 35, where the route becomes known as Alpine Road, and drive about 4 miles. Turn left onto Portola Road and drive about 3 miles.

About the campground: Portola is included in *Sunset Magazine*'s 100 best campgrounds in the west. The narrow, winding access results in fewer visitors than at less isolated redwood parks. The campground is located in a grove of tall, second-growth redwoods. Short hikes include the 0.7-mile Sequoia Nature Trail and the 0.4-mile Old Tree Trail. Longer trails are the 2.7-mile-loop Iverson Trail visiting the ruins of an old pioneer cabin, and the Slate Creek Trail to Page Mill, about 8 miles round trip. Stay limit 15 days from June through September, 30 days from October through May. Open all year.

11 Big Basin Redwoods State Park

Location: 20 miles northwest of Santa Cruz.
Sites: 100 sites for tents and RVs.
Facilities: Tables, fire rings, drinking water, flush and vault toilets, showers, visitor center, snack bar, dump station. The facilities are wheelchair accessible.

The ancient redwood known as "Father of the Forest" is located in Big Basin Redwoods State Park, the oldest and one of the largest state parks in California.

Fee per night: $17, pets $1. For reservations call 800-444-7275. There is a one-time reservation fee of $7.50.

Management: California Department of Parks and Recreation, 408-338-8860.

Activities: Hiking, horseback riding, mountain biking.

Finding the campground: From the intersection of California Highways 1 and 9 in Santa Cruz, take CA 9 north for 11 miles to Boulder Creek, turn left onto California Highway 236, and drive 9 miles.

About the campground: Big Basin is California's oldest state park, and its 18,000 acres also make it one of the largest. *Sunset Magazine* has listed the campground as one of the ten best in the western United States. A highlight of the park is the Skyline to the Sea Trail, a 37.5-mile equestrian and hiking trail, which runs through the park connecting Castle Rock State Park, high in the Santa Cruz Mountains, and Waddell Beach on the coast. From the visitor center, the Redwood Nature Trail makes a 0.6-mile loop through a grove of ancient redwoods, including Mother of the Forest, the tallest tree in the park at 329 feet. Another short trail (1.2 miles) goes to small, but pretty Sempervirens Falls. Stay limit 30 days. Open all year.

12 | Del Valle County Park

Location: 10 miles southeast of Livermore.

Sites: 150 sites for tents and RVs up to 40 feet long, 21 with water and electric hookups.

Facilities: Tables, grills, drinking water, showers, flush toilets, dump station. The facilities are wheelchair accessible.

Fee per night: $14-$16, pets $1. Reservations required; call 510-635-0135. There is a one-time reservation fee of $4.

Management: East Bay Regional Park District, 510-373-0332.

Activities: Hiking, fishing, boating.

Finding the campground: From the intersection of Interstate 580 and South Vasco Road in Livermore, drive south on South Vasco for 3 miles, turn right onto Tesla Road, and drive 1 mile. Turn left onto Mines Road and drive 3 miles, then bear right onto Del Valle Road and drive 3 miles.

About the campground: *Sunset Magazine* includes the campground at Del Valle Park among the 100 best in the western United States. The campsites are located in open grassland, without shade, on the shore of Del Valle Reservoir, which provides good fishing for trout, bluegill, and to a lesser extent, catfish and smallmouth bass. Among the trails accessible from the campground is a steep climb to 100-foot Murietta Falls. Three wineries (Concannon, Wente Brothers, and Livermore Valley Cellars) are located between Livermore and the campground. They offer tastings, tours, sales, and picnicking. Stay limit 14 days. Open all year. This park was formerly known as Del Valle State Recreation Area.

13 | Sunol Regional Wilderness

Location: 13 miles south of Pleasanton.
Sites: 4 sites for tents.
Facilities: Tables, grills, drinking water, vault toilets. The facilities are wheelchair accessible.
Fee per night: $11, pets $1. Reservations required; call 510-635-0135. There is a one-time reservation fee of $4.
Management: East Bay Regional Park District, 510-373-0332.
Activities: Hiking.
Finding the campground: From the intersection of Interstates 580 and 680 north of Pleasanton, drive south on I-680 for 7 miles to the Sunol exit. Continue south on Calaveras Road for 4 miles, turn left onto Welch Creek Road, and drive 2 miles.

About the campground: Set in rolling grasslands, the campground is quiet and secluded and is a good place to see spring wildflowers. Stay limit 14 days. Open all year, except that closures may occur in late summer due to fire danger.

14 | Joseph D. Grant County Park

Location: 12 miles east of San Jose.
Sites: 22 sites for tents and RVs up to 30 feet long.
Facilities: Tables, grills, drinking water, showers, flush toilets, dump station. The facilities are wheelchair accessible.
Fee per night: $8, pets $1.
Management: Santa Clara County Parks, 408-274-6121.
Activities: Hiking, mountain biking, horseback riding.
Finding the campground: From the intersection of U.S. Highway 101 and Interstate 680 in San Jose, drive 2 miles northeast on I-680 to the Alum Rock Avenue exit. Drive east on Alum Rock Avenue for 2.4 miles, turn right onto Mount Hamilton Road (California Highway 130), and drive 8 miles.

About the campground: Shaded by oak trees, the campground provides access to 40 miles of hiking and horse trails, and 20 miles of dirt roads for mountain biking. The park is a former ranch, and Hall's Valley Loop (5.5 miles) offers a good hiking introduction to its landscape. Stay limit 14 days. Open from April through November, weekends only in March.

15 | Henry Cowell Redwoods State Park

Location: 4 miles north of Santa Cruz.
Sites: 112 sites for tents and RVs.
Facilities: Tables, fire rings, drinking water, flush toilets, showers, dump station. The facilities are wheelchair accessible.
Fee per night: $17-$18, pets $1. For reservations call 800-444-7275. There is a one-time reservation fee of $7.50.

Management: California Department of Parks and Recreation, 408-335-4598.
Activities: Hiking, fishing.
Finding the campground: From the intersection of California Highway 1 and Graham Hill Road in Santa Cruz, drive north on Graham Hill Road for 4 miles to the campground entrance on the left.

About the campground: The park consists of 1,800 acres of diverse forest, including ancient redwoods, pine, and oak. Chaparral covers the ridges, and sycamore, cottonwood, and willow line the banks of the San Lorenzo River, which flows through the park. Silver salmon and steelhead are caught in the river during the winter fishing season.

The campground is located in a well-shaded grove of medium and large trees. While the site doesn't include redwoods, they're not far away. The Eagle Creek Trail leads from the campground to Redwood Loop, park headquarters, and a nature center (1.8 miles). The Pine Trail leads from the campground to an observation deck (0.6 miles round trip). The park provides access to the San Lorenzo River for steelhead fishing in the winter months. Stay limit 7 days from June through September, 15 days from October through May. Open all year, but subject to occasional winter closures.

16 New Brighton State Beach

Location: 5 miles east of Santa Cruz.
Sites: 112 sites for tents and RVs up to 36 feet long.
Facilities: Tables, fire rings, drinking water, showers, flush toilets, dump station. The facilities are wheelchair accessible.
Fee per night: $14-$19, pets $1. For reservations call 800-444-7275. There is a one-time reservation fee of $7.50.
Management: California Department of Parks and Recreation, 408-475-4850.
Activities: Swimming, fishing, surfing.
Finding the campground: From Santa Cruz, drive about 4 miles east on California Highway 1 to the Capitola/Brighton Beach exit. Take the exit road and drive 1 mile south toward the beach.

About the campground: *Sunset Magazine* lists it as one of the 100 best campgrounds west of the Mississippi. Situated on a low bluff overlooking the beach, the campground is shaded by pine and cypress trees. A 0.2-mile path leads to the beach, which is sheltered from the brisk winds that blow along the Santa Cruz coastline. Fishing is mediocre and usually limited to small surf perch. Two wineries (Bargetto's Santa Cruz Winery and Devlin Wine Cellars) are located in Soquet, less than 3 miles from the campground. Both offer tastings, tours, sales, and picnicking. Stay limit 7 days from June through September, 15 days from October through May. Open all year.

17 Seacliff State Beach

Location: 5 miles east of Santa Cruz.
Sites: 26 sites for RVs up to 40 feet long, with full hookups.

Facilities: Tables, grills, drinking water, showers, flush toilets. The facilities are wheelchair accessible.
Fee per night: $26-$29, pets $1. For reservations call 800-444-7275. There is a one-time reservation fee of $7.50.
Management: California Department of Parks and Recreation, 408-688-3222.
Activities: Swimming, fishing, surfing.
Finding the campground: From Santa Cruz, drive about 5 miles east on California Highway 1 to the Seacliff Beach/Aptos exit and then drive south for 0.4 mile.

About the campground: Seacliff is classified as a "premium beachfront" campground, hence the higher than usual fees. Its beach is a mile long, and adjoins New Brighton Beach to the west. The park boasts a unique pier—a standard wooden-plank fishing pier, lengthened by the *Palo Alto*, a World War I supply ship that had a brief reincarnation as a shoreline dining and dancing facility until it broke up in a storm. It was subsequently incorporated into the pier. Fishing from the pier is better than from almost any other shore location on Monterey Bay. The catch is usually perch and kingfish, but striped bass and even halibut are taken occasionally in summer, while winter high tides can bring in mackerel. Stay limit 7 days. Open all year.

18 Manresa State Beach: Manresa Uplands

Location: 6 miles southeast of Aptos.
Sites: 64 sites for tents.
Facilities: Tables, fire rings, drinking water, showers, flush toilets. The facilities are wheelchair accessible.
Fee per night: $14-$19, pets $1. For reservations call 800-444-7275. There is a one-time reservation fee of $7.50.
Management: California Department of Parks and Recreation, 408-761-1795.
Activities: Swimming, fishing, surfing.
Finding the campground: From Aptos, drive southeast 2.5 miles on California Highway 1, turn right onto San Andreas Road, and drive 3 miles. Turn right onto Sand Dollar Road and drive half a mile.

About the campground: For those willing to lug their camping gear about half a mile, Manresa offers a relatively isolated retreat. The campground sits on a bluff overlooking the beach, with limited shade from young trees and a small, well-established pine grove. Beach access is via a 170-step staircase. Fishing is fair for surf perch. Stay limit 7 days from June through September, 15 days from October through May. Open all year.

19 Sunset State Beach

Location: 8 miles southeast of Aptos.
Sites: 90 sites for tents and RVs up to 31 feet long.
Facilities: Tables, grills, drinking water, showers, flush toilets. The facilities are wheelchair accessible.

Fee per night: $14-$19, pets $1. For reservations call 800-444-7275. There is a one-time reservation fee of $7.50.
Management: California Department of Parks and Recreation, 408-763-7062.
Activities: Swimming, fishing, surfing.
Finding the campground: From Aptos, drive southeast 2.5 miles on California Highway 1, turn right onto San Andreas Road, and drive 5 miles. Turn right onto Sunset Beach Road and drive half a mile.

About the campground: The campground is located on a bluff back from the beach, shaded by pines, and connected to the shore by steep trails. The beach itself is one of the most scenic in the state, but swimming can be dangerous due to surf conditions. As at Manresa Beach, fishing here is fair, surf perch being the main catch. Stay limit 7 days from June through September, 15 days from October through May. Open all year.

20 Henry W. Coe State Park

Location: 13 miles northeast of the community of Morgan Hill.
Sites: 20 sites for tents and RVs up to 26 feet long (trailers up to 18 feet), plus 8 equestrian sites.
Facilities: Tables, grills, drinking water, pit toilets, visitor center.
Fee per night: $8, pets $1. Horse sites can be reserved; call number below for information.
Management: California Department of Parks and Recreation, 408-779-2728.
Activities: Hiking, fishing, horseback riding.
Finding the campground: From U.S. Highway 101 in Morgan Hill, take the East Dunne Avenue exit and drive northeast for 13 miles on East Dunne. The road becomes narrow and winding shortly after leaving town.

About the campground: A former ranch, the park covers 79,500 acres of rugged grassland and forest, including oak, pine, and chaparral. The campground is located on an open rise with a fine view of the surrounding countryside. The original Coe homestead ranch buildings stand adjacent to the visitor center, which houses a small museum devoted to Coe family memorabilia. Hiking trails range from the 1.6-mile Monument Trail to 9.3-mile China Hole Loop. Equestrians will find many trails of varying difficulty. Mountain bikers can use the open terrain of the park, as well as former ranch roads. The park contains more than 100 lakes and ponds, about two dozen offering good fishing. The best fishing is in backcountry lakes, such as Mississippi, Coit, and Paradise, which you must backpack to reach. Stay limit 14 days. Open all year.

21 Uvas Canyon County Park

Location: 18 miles southwest of the community of Morgan Hill.
Sites: 30 sites for tents and RVs up to 28 feet long.
Facilities: Tables, grills, drinking water, flush toilets. Boat ramp nearby. The facilities are wheelchair accessible.
Fee per night: $10, pets $1.

Management: Santa Clara County Parks, 408-779-9232.
Activities: Hiking; fishing and boating 5 miles away.
Finding the campground: From the intersection of U.S. Highway 101 and East Dunne Avenue in Morgan Hill, drive 0.9 mile west on East Dunne, turn left onto Monterey Highway, and drive 2 miles. Turn right onto Watsonville Road and drive 4 miles. Turn right onto Uvas Road and drive 6 miles, then turn left onto Croy Road and drive 5 miles.

About the campground: Chesbro and Uvas Reservoirs, about 5 miles east of the campground offer fishing for bass, trout, and crappie. Both have boat ramps. Fishing can be good but is dependent upon high water, and the reservoirs are often drawn down for irrigation purposes. Powerboats are not permitted on either lake, but electric motors are allowed. Swimming is prohibited. Four wineries (Summerhill, Thomas Kruse, Fortino, and Hecker Pass) are located in Gilroy, 12 miles southeast of the campground. They offer tastings, tours, retail sales, and picnicking. Stay limit 14 days. Open all year.

22 Mount Madonna County Park

Location: 7 miles west of Gilroy.
Sites: 117 sites for tents and RVs, 17 with water and electric hookups.
Facilities: Tables, grills, drinking water, flush toilets, dump station. The facilities are wheelchair accessible.
Fee per night: $8-$20, pets $1.
Management: Santa Clara County Parks, 408-842-2341.
Activities: Hiking, horseback riding.
Finding the campground: From the intersection of U.S. Highway 101 and California Highway 152 (Hecker Pass Highway) in Gilroy, take CA 152 west for 7 miles. Once it begins climbing Mount Madonna, the road becomes narrow and winding.

About the campground: Mount Madonna is a park of considerable beauty, and it provides sweeping views of Monterey and the Santa Clara Valley. More than 18 miles of trails, many of them short and interconnecting, wind through the park. A good introduction is the 2.5-mile Bay View Loop, a combination of short trails beginning at the park entrance station, where a free trail map can be obtained. Horse rentals are available. Four wineries (Summerhill, Thomas Kruse, Fortino, and Hecker Pass) are located within a mile of each other on Hecker Pass Highway, about midway between the campground and Gilroy. They offer tastings, tours, sales, and picnicking. Elevation 1,400 feet. Stay limit 14 days. Open all year.

23 Coyote Lake County Park

Location: 6 miles northeast of Gilroy.
Sites: 74 sites for tents or RVs.
Facilities: Tables, fire rings, drinking water, flush toilets, boat ramp.
Fee per night: $10, pets $1, $5 boat launch fee.

Management: Santa Clara County Parks, 408-842-7800.

Activities: Fishing, boating.

Finding the campground: From the intersection of U.S. Highway 101 and Leavesley Road in Gilroy, drive east on Leavesley for 3 miles, turn left onto New Avenue, and drive 0.7 mile. Turn right onto Roop Road (which becomes Gilroy Hot Springs Road) and drive 4 miles. Turn left onto Coyote Reservoir Road and drive about 1 mile.

About the campground: Coyote Reservoir can provide good trout fishing in the spring and bass fishing in the summer, depending on the water level. The lake is stocked with both kinds of fish annually. Stay limit 14 days. Open all year.

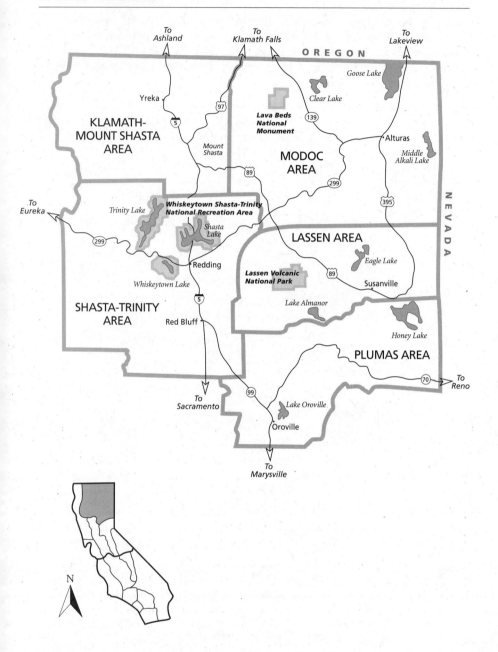

Shasta Cascade

Crossing from Oregon to California on Interstate 5, you enter a vast, spectacular outdoor domain. Shasta Cascade boasts within its borders five national forests, a national park, a national monument, a national recreation area, and more than two dozen state and county parks. There is something here for everyone. Soaring mountains, large lakes, rushing streams, deep forests, lava fields, and scenic drives all combine to provide a perfect outdoor experience.

Near the center of this superb scenic region stands awesome Mount Shasta, second highest of the Cascade Range volcanoes after Rainier. Farther south, Shasta Lake provides almost 30,000 acres of paradise for water sports. Other large lakes, such as Eagle, Trinity, and Almanor, offer similar pleasures, while dozens of smaller lakes appeal to those seeking a quieter, more isolated experience. The Trinity Alps provide a dramatic backdrop for hikers, equestrians, and anglers. Lassen Volcanic National Park and Lava Beds National Monument offer a chance to explore both dormant and active volcanic terrain. Feather Falls, near Lake Oroville, is the sixth highest waterfall in the United States.

Temperatures in the Shasta Cascade region vary considerably between the mountains and the lowlands of the Sacramento River valley. Precipitation is heaviest in the winter months, and rain lasting several days is not uncommon. Average winter temperatures range from 44 to 26 degrees F, spring from 60 to 35 degrees, summer from 82 to 48, and fall from 65 to 38. The average percentage of sunny days increases from a low of 50 percent in the winter to 62 percent in the spring and 88 percent in the summer. It then declines to 72 percent in the fall.

This guidebook divides Shasta Cascade into five areas: Klamath-Mount Shasta, Shasta-Trinity, Modoc, Lassen, and Plumas.

KLAMATH-MOUNT SHASTA AREA

The centerpiece of the Klamath-Mount Shasta area is the snow-covered cone of Mount Shasta itself. It rises to an elevation of 14,162 feet and is visible on clear days from more than 100 miles away. Most of the remainder of the area lies within the Klamath National Forest. This 1.7-million-acre woodland provides a host of outdoor opportunities. Excellent trout, salmon, and steelhead fishing is available in the Klamath, Salmon, and Smith Rivers and their tributary streams, as well as in the many small lakes that dot the area.

The Marble Mountain Wilderness provides hikers and backpackers with almost a quarter-million acres of pristine terrain and 89 lakes stocked with trout. A section of the Pacific Crest Trail passes through the wilderness. For rafting and kayaking enthusiasts, the forest has 200 miles of whitewater, mostly on the Klamath and Salmon Rivers. If you prefer to tour by car, the State of Jefferson Scenic Byway follows the upper Klamath westward from Interstate 5 just north of Yreka to California Highway 199.

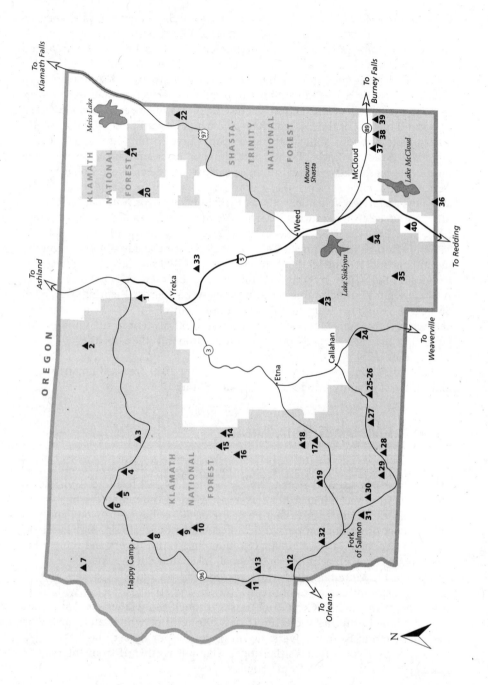

KLAMATH-MOUNT SHASTA AREA CAMPGROUNDS

	Group sites	RV sites	Total sites	Max. RV length	Hookups	Toilets	Showers	Drinking water	Dump station	Pets	Wheelchair	Recreation	Fee ($)	Season	Can reserve	Length of stay
1 Trees of Heaven		•	21	34		V		•		•		HF	8			14
2 Beaver Creek		•	8	30		V				•		F		May–October		14
3 Sarah Totten	•	•	10			V				•		SF	6–50	May–November	•	14
4 O'Neil Creek		•	18	16		V				•			3	May–October		14
5 Grider Creek		•	10	24		V				•		HF		May–October		14
6 Fort Goff			5			V				•		HF		May–October		14
7 West Branch		•	15			V		•		•		F	3	May–October		14
8 Curly Jack	•	•	19			V		•		•	•	SF	6–20	April–October	•	14
9 Sulphur Springs			7			V				•		HS		May–October		14
10 Norcross		•	6			V				•	•	HFR		May–October		14
11 Dillon Creek		•	21			V		•		•		HSF	8–15	May–October		14
12 Oak Bottom		•	26			V		•		•	•	HSF	8	May–October		14
13 Ti-bar Flat		•	5			V				•		SFL		May-October		14
14 Indian Scotty	•	•	29	30		V		•		•		SF	6–30	May–October	•	14
15 Bridge Flat		•	4	30		V				•		HFS		May–October		14
16 Lovers Camp			8			V				•		HR		May–October		14
17 Idlewild		•	18			V		•		•		HSF	6	May–October		14
18 Mule Bridge		•	5			V				•		HS	FR	May–October		14
19 Red Bank		•	5			V				•		SF		May–October		14
20 Martin's Dairy		•	12			V		•		•		HFR	6			14
21 Juanita Lake	•	•	25			V		•		•	•	HFB	6–20	May–October	•	14
22 Shafter		•	10			V		•		•		HF	4			14
23 Kangaroo Lake			18			V		•		•		HS	8 FB	May–October		14

#	Name	Group sites	RV sites	Total sites	Max. RV length	Hookups	Toilets	Showers	Drinking water	Dump station	Pets	Wheelchair	Recreation	Fee ($)	Season	Can reserve	Length of stay
24	Scott Mountain		•	5			V				•		H		May–October		14
25	Carter Meadows Group Horse Camp	•	•	1			V		•		•		R	30	May–October	•	14
26	Hidden Horse			6			V		•		•		R	8	May–October		14
27	Trail Creek		•	12			V		•		•		HF	6	May–October		14
28	Shadow Creek		•	6	16		V				•				May–October		14
29	East Fork		•	9	16		V				•		HSF		May–October		14
30	Matthews Creek		•	12	24		V		•		•		HSF	6	May–October		14
31	Hotelling		•	5	16		V				•		HSF		May–October		14
32	Nordheimer Flat	•	•	12			V		•		•		HF	8–30	May–October	•	14
33	McBride Springs		•	9	10		V		•		•		H	10	May 15–October		14
34	Castle Lake		•	6	16		V			•	•		HSF		June–October		14
35	Gumboot Lake		•	4	10		V				•		HF		June–October		14
36	Ah-Di-Na			16			F		•		•		HF	8	April 15–Nov. 15		14
37	Fowlers Camp		•	39	30		V		•		•	•	HSF	12	April 15–October		14
38	Cattle Camp		•	30			V		•		•		SF	12	April 15–Sept. 15		14
39	Algoma		•	8			V				•		F		April 15–October		14
40	Castle Crags State Park		•	64	27		F	•	•		•		HSF	15–17		•	15/30

Hookups: W = Water E = Electric S = Sewer
Toilets: F = Flush V = Vault P = Pit C = Chemical
Recreation: H = Hiking S = Swimming F = Fishing B = Boating L = Boat Launch O = Off-highway Driving R = Horseback Riding
Maximum Trailer/RV Length given in feet. Stay Limit given in days. Fee given in dollars.
If no entry under **Season**, campground is open all year. If no entry under **Fee**, camping is free.

1 Trees of Heaven

Location: 13 miles north of Yreka.
Sites: 21 sites for tents and RVs up to 34 feet long.
Facilities: Tables, fire rings, drinking water, vault toilets.
Fee per night: $8.
Management: Klamath National Forest, 530-468-5351.
Activities: Hiking, fishing, rafting, kayaking.
Finding the campground: From Yreka, drive north 8 miles on California Highway 263, turn left (west) onto California Highway 96, and drive 5 miles.

About the campground: On the banks of the Klamath River, with excellent river access. Steelhead and salmon fishing is good in the winter months. A trail from the campground follows the river. A large day use area offers horseshoe pits, volleyball, and an open-pit barbecue. Stay limit 14 days. Open all year. Elevation 2,100 feet.

2 Beaver Creek

Location: 26 miles northwest of Yreka.
Sites: 8 sites for tents and RVs up to 30 feet long.
Facilities: Tables, fire rings, vault toilets. No drinking water.
Fee per night: None.
Management: Klamath National Forest, 530-468-5351.
Activities: Fishing, rafting, wading, hunting.
Finding the campground: From Yreka, drive north 8 miles on California Highway 263, turn left (west) onto California Highway 96, and drive 14 miles. Turn right (north) onto Beaver Creek Road (Forest Road 11) and drive 4 miles.

About the campground: Beaver Creek offers good trout fishing and tube rafting and is a base for fall hunting. Elevation 2,400 feet. Stay limit 14 days. Open from May through October.

3 Sarah Totten

Location: 39 miles northwest of Yreka.
Sites: 8 sites for tents and RVs, plus 2 group sites, one for up to 20 people and the other for 20 or more.
Facilities: Tables, fire rings, vault toilets. No drinking water.
Fee per night: $6. Group sites $20 and $50 respectively. Reservations required for group sites; call 800-280-CAMP. There is a one-time reservation fee of $15.
Management: Klamath National Forest, 530-493-2243.
Activities: Fishing, rafting, swimming, kayaking, canoeing.
Finding the campground: From Yreka, drive north 8 miles on California Highway 263, turn left (west) onto California Highway 96, and drive 31 miles.

About the campground: Situated on the bank of the Klamath River, with excellent river access. The river offers good salmon fishing in the fall, and steelhead fishing in the winter. Elevation 1,400 feet. Stay limit 14 days. Open from May through November.

4 O'Neil Creek

Location: 44 miles northwest of Yreka.
Sites: 18 sites for tents and RVs up to 16 feet.
Facilities: Tables, fire rings, vault toilets. No drinking water.
Fee per night: $3.
Management: Klamath National Forest, 530-493-2243.
Activities: River activities nearby, hunting.
Finding the campground: From Yreka, drive north 8 miles on California Highway 263, turn left (west) onto California Highway 96, and drive 35.5 miles.

About the campground: Situated in an old-growth forest near the Klamath River, but with no access to it. The campground is used as a hunting base in the fall. Elevation 1,500 feet. Stay limit 14 days. Open from May through October.

5 Grider Creek

Location: 52 miles northwest of Yreka.
Sites: 10 sites for tents and RVs up to 24 feet long.
Facilities: Tables, fire rings, vault toilets. No drinking water.
Fee per night: None.
Management: Klamath National Forest, 530-493-2243.
Activities: Hiking, fishing.
Finding the campground: From Yreka, drive north 8 miles on California Highway 263, turn left (west) onto California Highway 96, and drive 42 miles. Turn left (south) onto Forest Road 46N66 and drive 2.2 miles.

About the campground: The Pacific Crest Trail passes the campground, which is on the banks of Grider Creek. Elevation 1,400 feet. Stay limit 14 days. Open from May through October.

6 Fort Goff

Location: 53 miles northwest of Yreka.
Sites: 5 sites for tents.
Facilities: Tables, fire rings, vault toilets. No drinking water.
Fee per night: None.
Management: Klamath National Forest, 530-493-2243.
Activities: Hiking, fishing, rafting, kayaking.
Finding the campground: From Yreka, drive north 8 miles on California Highway 263, turn left (west) onto California Highway 96, and drive 45 miles.

About the campground: Situated on the banks of the Klamath River, with trout and salmon fishing in late summer and steelhead fishing in winter. A trail runs northwest from the campground along Fort Goff Creek to the Boundary National Recreation Trail. Elevation 1,300 feet. Stay limit 14 days. Open from May through October.

7 West Branch

Location: 12 miles northwest of the community of Happy Camp.
Sites: 15 sites for tents and RVs.
Facilities: Tables, fire rings, drinking water, vault toilets.
Fee per night: $3.
Management: Klamath National Forest, 530-493-2243.
Activities: Fishing, gold panning.
Finding the campground: From Happy Camp (65 miles west of Yreka on California Highway 96), drive 12 miles north on Indian Creek Road.

About the campground: A quiet and secluded campground in a canyon near Indian Creek. Elevation 2,200 feet. Stay limit 14 days. Open May through October.

8 Curly Jack

Location: In the community of Happy Camp, on Curly Jack Road.
Sites: 17 sites for tents and RVs, plus 2 group sites.
Facilities: Tables, fire rings, drinking water, vault toilets. The facilities are wheelchair accessible.
Fee per night: $6. Group sites $20. Reservations required for group sites; call 800-280-CAMP. There is a one-time reservation fee of $15.
Management: Klamath National Forest, 530-493-2243.
Activities: Fishing, swimming, rafting, kayaking.
Finding the campground: From Happy Camp (65 miles west of Yreka on California Highway 96), drive 1 mile southwest on Curly Jack Road.

About the campground: On the banks of the Klamath, the campground provides excellent access to the river. The swimming location is among the best on the river. Fishing is good for trout in the late spring and early summer, and steelhead in late fall, early winter. Salmon catches are possible in late fall. Elevation 1,100 feet. Stay limit 14 days. Open from April through October.

9 Sulphur Springs

Location: 15 miles south of the community of Happy Camp.
Sites: 7 sites for tents.
Facilities: Tables, fire rings, vault toilets. No drinking water.
Fee per night: None.
Management: Klamath National Forest, 530-493-2243.
Activities: Hiking, swimming.
Finding the campground: From Happy Camp (65 miles west of Yreka on California Highway 96), drive 15 miles south on Elk Creek Road.

About the campground: Situated on the banks of Elk Creek, the campground is a 50-yard walk from parking. It is the starting point for the Elk Creek Trail, a main route into the beautiful Marble Mountain Wilderness. One of the main attractions of Sulphur Springs Campground is a warm springs located along Elk Creek. The temperature of the springs is approximately 75 degrees, and it can accommodate five or six people at one time. Elevation 3,100 feet. Stay limit 14 days. Open from May through October.

10 Norcross

Location: 17 miles south of the community of Happy Camp.
Sites: 6 sites for tents and RVs.
Facilities: Tables, fire rings, vault toilets. The facilities are wheelchair accessible. No drinking water, but water for livestock is available.
Fee per night: None.
Management: Klamath National Forest, 530-493-2243.
Activities: Hiking, fishing, horseback riding.
Finding the campground: From Happy Camp (65 miles west of Yreka on California Highway 96), drive 16.5 miles south on Elk Creek Road.

About the campground: This campground serves as a staging area for various trails that provide access into the Marble Mountain Wilderness. Elevation 2,400 feet. Stay limit 14 days. Open from May through October.

11 Dillon Creek

Location: 24 miles north of Orleans.
Sites: 21 sites for tents and RVs, including some double sites.
Facilities: Tables, fire rings, drinking water, vault toilets.
Fee per night: $8, double sites $15.
Management: Klamath National Forest, 530-627-3291.
Activities: Hiking, swimming, fishing, rafting.
Finding the campground: From Orleans, drive 24 miles north on California Highway 96.

About the campground: Situated on the Klamath River at the site of a spring cascading down Dillon Creek, this campground enjoys a scenic setting. The campsites, carved into the mountain slopes, are sheltered, shaded, and offer privacy. A path leads to one of the most scenic natural swimming holes in northern California. River access is adjacent to the camp, with good seasonal fishing for trout, steelhead, and occasional salmon. Excellent rafting and kayaking opportunities exist from the campground south to several take-outs before Somes Bar. Stay limit 14 days. Open from May through October.

12 Oak Bottom

Location: 9 miles northeast of Orleans.
Sites: 26 sites for tents and RVs.

Facilities: Tables, fire rings, drinking water, vault toilets. The facilities are wheelchair accessible.
Fee per night: $8.
Agency: Klamath National Forest, 530-627-3291.
Activities: Hiking, fishing, swimming.
Finding the campground: From Orleans, drive north on California Highway 96 for 6 miles, turn right (east) onto Salmon River Road, and drive 3 miles.

About the campground: Situated across the road from the Salmon River, which offers a few swimming holes and steelhead fishing in the fall. The Oak Bottom River Access, located directly across from the campground, provides access to the Salmon River, which is renowned for its class 3-5 whitewater (upriver from the campground). The lower portion of the Salmon offers excellent swimming and tubing opportunities. Two unnamed trails lead off the road about 2 and 3 miles east of the campground. Stay limit 14 days. Open from May through October.

13 Ti-bar Flat

Location: 19 miles north of Orleans.
Sites: 5 sites for tents and RVs.
Facilities: Tables, fire rings, vault toilets, boat launch. Potable water can be found at Ti-bar Fire Station, just east of the campground.
Fee per night: None.
Management: Klamath National Forest, 530-627-3291.
Activities: Fishing, swimming, rafting.
Finding the campground: From Orleans, drive 19 miles north on California Highway 96.

About the campground: Situated on a large flat on the banks of the Klamath River, the campground has several sites with trees to provide shade from the summer sun. Tents and RVs can disperse over a wide area. There is a boat launch for drift boats and rafts. Elevation 900 feet. Stay limit 14 days. Open from May through October.

14 Indian Scotty

Location: 31 miles southwest of Yreka.
Sites: 28 sites for tents and RVs up to 30 feet long, plus 1 group site.
Facilities: Tables, fire rings, drinking water, vault toilets.
Fee per night: $6. Group site $30. Reservations required for group site; call number below.
Management: Klamath National Forest, 530-468-5351.
Activities: Fishing, swimming.
Finding the campground: From Yreka, drive southwest 17 miles on California Highway 3 to Fort Jones, turn right onto Scott River Road, and drive 14 miles.

About the campground: Indian Scotty is situated on the bank of the Scott River, with river access for fishing and swimming. Elevation 2,400 feet. Stay limit 14 days. Open from May through October.

15 Bridge Flat

Location: 34 miles southwest of Yreka.
Sites: 4 sites for tents and RVs up to 30 feet long.
Facilities: Tables, fire rings, vault toilets. No drinking water.
Fee per night: None.
Management: Klamath National Forest, 530-468-5351.
Activities: Fishing, hiking, rafting, swimming, kayaking.
Finding the campground: From Yreka, drive southwest 17 miles on California Highway 3 to Fort Jones, turn right onto Scott River Road, and drive 17 miles.

About the campground: Situated on the bank of the Scott River, Bridge Flat offers easy access to kayaking and whitewater rafting on the river in the spring. Fishing is available throughout the season. The Kelsey National Recreation Trail begins across the road from the campground. This historic route offers excellent scenic day hikes or backpack trips into the Marble Mountain Wilderness. It connects with the Pacific Crest Trail approximately 8 miles from the campground at Paradise Lake. Elevation 2,000 feet. Stay limit 14 days. Open from May through October.

16 Lovers Camp

Location: 39 miles west of Yreka.
Sites: 8 sites for tents.
Facilities: Tables, fire rings, vault toilets, watering and unloading ramp for horses, corral. No drinking water.
Fee per night: None.
Management: Klamath National Forest, 530-468-5351.
Activities: Hiking, horseback riding, hunting.
Finding the campground: From Yreka, drive southwest 17 miles on California Highway 3 to Fort Jones, turn right onto Scott River Road, and drive 14 miles. Turn left (south) onto Forest Road 44N45 and drive 8 miles.

About the campground: Lovers Camp is shaded and has a good view of the Marble Mountains. It serves as a staging area for backpacking and equestrian trips into the Marble Mountain Wilderness and is the starting point for day hikes to the Sky High Lakes, Deep Lake, and Marble Valley. The campground is very busy during holiday weekends and on the opening weekend of hunting season. Elevation 4,300 feet. Stay limit 14 days. Open from May through October.

17 Idlewild

Location: 20 miles southwest of Etna.
Sites: 18 sites for tents and RVs.
Facilities: Tables, fire rings, drinking water, vault toilets.
Fee per night: $6.
Management: Klamath National Forest, 530-468-5351.
Activities: Hiking, fishing, swimming.
Finding the campground: From Etna (27 miles southwest of Yreka on California Highway 3), drive southwest 20 miles on Sawyers Bar Road.

About the campground: Situated in an open conifer and oak grove on the North Fork of the Salmon River, which offers steelhead fishing and swimming. Trailheads to both the Marble Mountain Wilderness (2 miles north) and Russian Wilderness (3 miles east) are within a short drive. Elevation 2,600 feet. Stay limit 14 days. Open from May through October.

18 Mule Bridge

Location: 22 miles southwest of Etna.
Sites: 5 sites for tents and RVs.
Facilities: Tables, fire rings, water for stock (not potable), vault toilets, corrals.
Fee per night: None.
Management: Klamath National Forest, 530-468-5351.
Activities: Hiking, fishing, swimming, horseback riding, mountain biking.
Finding the campground: From Etna (27 miles southwest of Yreka on California Highway 3), drive southwest 20 miles on Sawyers Bar Road, turn right (north) onto Forest Road 41N37, and drive 2 miles.

About the campground: Mule Bridge is the trailhead for the North Fork Trail into the Marble Mountain Wilderness. Elevation 2,800 feet. Stay limit 14 days. Open from May through October.

19 Red Bank

Location: 32 miles southwest of Etna.
Sites: 5 sites for tents and RVs.
Facilities: Tables, fire rings, vault toilets. No drinking water.
Fee per night: None.
Management: Klamath National Forest, 530-468-5351.
Activities: Fishing, swimming.
Finding the campground: From Etna (27 miles southwest of Yreka on California Highway 3), drive southwest 32 miles on Sawyers Bar Road.

About the campground: A shady location next to the North Fork of the Salmon River, with adjacent river access. Elevation 1,760 feet. Stay limit 14 days. Open from May through October.

20 Martin's Dairy

Location: 42 miles northeast of Weed.
Sites: 8 sites for tents and RVs, plus a 4-unit horse camp.
Facilities: Tables, fire rings, drinking water, vault toilets, corrals.
Fee per night: $6.
Management: Klamath National Forest, 530-398-4391.
Activities: Hiking, fishing, horseback riding, mountain biking, bird watching, hunting.
Finding the campground: From the intersection of Interstate 5 and U.S. Highway 97 in Weed, drive northeast 30 miles on US 97, turn left onto Forest Road 70, and drive 10 miles. Bear left onto Forest Road 46N12 and drive 2 miles.

About the campground: Martin's Dairy is adjacent to a pretty mountain meadow and the Little Shasta River. You can see Mount Shasta in the distance. The river is regularly stocked with rainbow and brown trout. Periwinkles are abundant in the stream and make good trout bait. There are numerous gated logging roads in the area that can be used as trails for hikers, mountain bikers, and equestrians. Elevation 6,000 feet. Stay limit 14 days. Open all year.

21 Juanita Lake

Location: 45 miles northeast of Weed.
Sites: 24 sites for tents and RVs up to 34 feet long, plus 1 group site for up to 50 people.
Facilities: Tables, fire rings, drinking water, vault toilets. The facilities are wheelchair accessible.
Fee per night: $6-$8. Group fee $20. Reservations required for group site; call number below.
Management: Klamath National Forest, 530-398-4391.
Activities: Hiking, fishing, boating, mountain biking, bird watching.
Finding the campground: From the intersection of Interstate 5 and U.S. Highway 97 in Weed, drive northeast 38 miles on US 97, turn left onto Ball Mountain Road, and drive 3 miles. Bear right on Forest Road 46N04 and drive 3.5 miles.

About the campground: Situated on the shoreline of 55-acre Juanita Lake, which is regularly stocked with modest numbers of rainbow and brown trout and has a bass and catfish population. No motorized boats are allowed on the lake. Two fishing jetties provide easy, barrier-free access. A 1.5-mile paved, barrier-free trail circles the lake, and a 6-mile trail climbs 2,700 feet to Ball Mountain Lookout. Elevation 5,100 feet. Stay limit 14 days. Open from May through October.

22 Shafter

Location: 46 miles northeast of Weed.
Sites: 10 sites for tents and RVs.
Facilities: Tables, fire rings, drinking water, vault toilets.
Fee per night: $4.
Management: Klamath National Forest, 530-398-4391.
Activities: Hiking, fishing.
Finding the campground: From the intersection of Interstate 5 and U.S. Highway 97 in Weed, drive northeast 38 miles on US 97, turn right (east) onto Ball Mountain Road, and drive 2.2 miles. Bear right for 0.4 mile and then right again (south) onto County Road 8Q01 and drive 5.5 miles.

About the campground: Situated on the banks of Butte Creek, which is regularly stocked with rainbow and brown trout and offers good fishing for small trout early in the season. Shafter is a tranquil campground next to meadows that bloom with wildflowers early in the spring. During the fall hunting season, the campground fills up quickly. Orr Mountain Lookout, 6 miles south of the campground (last 2 miles by foot or four-wheel-drive vehicle) has fine views of Mount Shasta. Elevation 4,300 feet. Stay limit 14 days. Open all year.

23 Kangaroo Lake

Location: 39 miles southwest of Weed.
Sites: 18 sites for tents.
Facilities: Tables, fire rings, drinking water, vault toilets, fishing pier. The facilities are wheelchair accessible.
Fee per night: $8.
Management: Klamath National Forest, 530-468-5351.
Activities: Hiking, fishing, swimming, boating.
Finding the campground: From Weed, drive 11 miles north on Interstate 5 to the Edgewood/Gazelle exit, turn left (southwest), and drive 6 miles to Gazelle. From Gazelle, continue southwest on the Gazelle-Callahan Road for about 15 miles to the Kangaroo Lake turnoff. There, turn south onto Forest Road 41N08 and follow the signs for about 7 miles to the campground.

About the campground: The lake is within a five-minute walk of the campsites, and a paved trail leads to the accessible fishing pier. Covering 25 acres, and 110 feet deep, the lake is regularly stocked with catchable rainbow and brown trout. Motorized boats are not allowed. A self-guided interpretive trail connects to the Pacific Crest Trail at the top of the ridge. Elevation 6,500 feet. Stay limit 14 days. Open from May through October.

24 Scott Mountain

Location: 8 miles southeast of Callahan.
Sites: 5 sites for tents and RVs.
Facilities: Tables, fire rings, vault toilets. No drinking water.

Fee per night: None.
Management: Klamath National Forest, 530-468-5351.
Activities: Hiking.
Finding the campground: From Callahan, drive east and south on California Highway 3 for 8 miles.

About the campground: The Pacific Crest Trail passes the campground. Elevation 5,300 feet. Stay limit 14 days. Open from May through October.

25 Carter Meadows Group Horse Camp

Location: 11 miles southwest of Callahan.
Sites: 1 group site for tents and RVs, for use by equestrians.
Facilities: Tables, fire rings, drinking water, vault toilets, 3 large corrals.
Fee per night: $30. Reservations required; call number below.
Management: Klamath National Forest, 530-468-5351.
Activities: Horseback riding.
Finding the campground: From Callahan, take the Callahan-Cecilville Road and drive southwest for 11 miles.

About the campground: A network of interconnecting trails lead to Long Gulch, Trail Gulch, and the Pacific Crest Trail. The latter leads into the Trinity Alps Wilderness. Elevation 6,000 feet. Stay limit 14 days. Open from May through October.

26 Hidden Horse

Location: 11 miles southwest of Callahan.
Sites: 6 sites for tents.
Facilities: Tables, fire rings, drinking water, vault toilets.
Fee per night: $8.
Management: Klamath National Forest, 530-468-5351.
Activities: Horseback riding.
Finding the campground: From Callahan, take the Callahan-Cecilville Road and drive southwest for 11 miles. This campground is adjacent to Carter Meadows Group Camp (number 25).

About the campground: Each campsite is designed for a small group and has a pull-through driveway, four 12-by-12-foot corral stalls, drinking water, and a tent site. There are no stock watering troughs or feed bunks. You must bring your own buckets and hay nets or feed on the ground. A network of interconnecting trails lead to Long Gulch, Trail Gulch, and the Pacific Crest Trail. The latter leads into the Trinity Alps Wilderness. Elevation 6,000 feet. Stay limit 14 days. Open from May through October.

27 Trail Creek

Location: 15 miles southwest of Callahan.
Sites: 12 sites for tents and RVs.

Facilities: Tables, fire rings, drinking water, vault toilets.
Fee per night: $6.
Management: Klamath National Forest, 530-468-5351.
Activities: Hiking, fishing.
Finding the campground: From Callahan, drive 15 miles southwest on the Callahan-Cecilville Road.

About the campground: Situated near the banks of Trail Creek, the campground offers day hikes to Fish Lake and Long Gulch Lake in the Trinity Alps Wilderness. Access to the Pacific Crest Trail is nearby. Elevation 4,700 feet. Stay limit 14 days. Open from May through October.

28 Shadow Creek

Location: 20 miles southwest of Callahan.
Sites: 6 sites for tents and RVs up to 16 feet long.
Facilities: Tables, fire rings, vault toilets. No drinking water.
Fee per night: None.
Management: Klamath National Forest, 530-468-5351.
Activities: None.
Finding the campground: From Callahan, drive 20 miles southwest on the Callahan-Cecilville Road.

About the campground: A secluded site at the confluence of Shadow Creek and the East Fork of the Salmon River. Fishing is prohibited, as the river at this location is a spawning ground for steelhead. When the Forest Service decided to close the campground a few years ago due to lack of funding, local residents volunteered to maintain it. It is still open for public camping, though services are reduced. Elevation 2,900 feet. Stay limit 14 days. Open from May through October.

29 East Fork

Location: 24 miles southwest of Callahan.
Sites: 9 sites for tents and RVs up to 16 feet long.
Facilities: Tables, fire rings, vault toilets. No drinking water.
Fee per night: None.
Management: Klamath National Forest, 530-468-5351.
Activities: Hiking, fishing, swimming.
Finding the campground: From Callahan, drive southwest 24 miles on the Callahan-Cecilville Road.

About the campground: Situated on the banks of the Salmon, which offers seasonal steelhead and salmon fishing and has some deep, cold swimming holes. Hiking from the campground provides access to the lakes in the Caribou Basin, Rush Creek, and Little South Fork drainages. Elevation 2,600 feet. Stay limit 14 days. Open from May through October.

30 Matthews Creek

Location: 8 miles southeast of the community of Forks of Salmon.
Sites: 12 sites for tents and RVs up to 24 feet long.
Facilities: Tables, fire rings, drinking water, vault toilets.
Fee per night: $6.
Management: Klamath National Forest, 530-468-5351.
Activities: Fishing, swimming, hiking.
Finding the campground: From Forks of Salmon, drive 8 miles southeast on the Cecilville Road (Forest Road 93).

About the campground: Dramatically situated in a canyonlike setting along the South Fork of the Salmon River, the campground has a good swimming hole. Fishing here for steelhead and salmon requires skill. A 4-mile trail from the campground leads to the abandoned King Solomon Mine. Elevation 1,760 feet. Stay limit 14 days. Open from May through October.

31 Hotelling

Location: 3 miles southeast of the community of Forks of Salmon.
Sites: 5 sites for tents and RVs up to 16 feet long.
Facilities: Tables, fire rings, vault toilets. No drinking water.
Fee per night: None.
Management: Klamath National Forest, 530-468-5351.
Activities: Fishing, swimming, hiking, mountain biking.
Finding the campground: From Forks of Salmon, drive 3 miles southeast on the Cecilville Road (Forest Road 93).

About the campground: Situated between the highway and the banks of the South Fork of the Salmon River, which offers seasonal steelhead and salmon fishing. Elevation 1,500 feet. Stay limit 14 days. Open from May through October.

32 Nordheimer Flat

Location: 4 miles northwest of the community of Forks of Salmon.
Sites: 8 family sites and 4 group sites for tents and RVs.
Facilities: Tables, fire rings, drinking water, vault toilets.
Fee per night: $8. Group sites $30. Reservations required for group sites; call number below.
Management: Klamath National Forest, 530-468-5351.
Activities: Fishing, rafting, hiking.
Finding the campground: From Forks of Salmon, drive northwest 4 miles on the Salmon River Road.

About the campground: Beautiful and secluded, Nordheimer Flat is located in the center of the Salmon River whitewater area. Rafting activities begin in the spring and continue until the water levels drop in early summer. River access is adjacent to the campground. Remnants from historic mining operations can still be seen in this remote but beautiful camping area. A few fruit trees remain from past homesteading activities. Elevation 900 feet. Stay limit 14 days. Open from May through October.

33 McBride Springs

Location: 5 miles northeast of the community of Mount Shasta.
Sites: 9 sites for tents and RVs up to 10 feet long.
Facilities: Tables, fire rings, drinking water, vault toilets.
Fee per night: $10.
Management: Shasta-Trinity National Forest, 530-926-4511.
Activities: Hiking.
Finding the campground: From Interstate 5 in Mount Shasta, take the Central Mount Shasta exit, turn right onto Lake Street (which becomes Everett Memorial Highway), and drive 5 miles.

About the campground: Situated on the southwest slope of Mount Shasta at an elevation of 4,900 feet, the campground serves as a base for hiking on and around the mountain. Stay limit 14 days. Open from May 15 through October 31.

34 Castle Lake

Location: 8 miles southwest of the community of Mount Shasta.
Sites: 6 sites for tents and RVs up to 16 feet long.
Facilities: Tables, fire rings, vault toilets. No drinking water.
Fee per night: None.
Management: Shasta-Trinity National Forest, 530-926-4511.
Activities: Hiking, fishing, swimming.
Finding the campground: From Interstate 5 in Mount Shasta, take the Central Mount Shasta exit, turn left at a stop sign, cross back over the highway, and drive 0.4 mile. Turn left at a stop sign onto Barr Road (County Road 2MO20) and drive 7.5 miles.

About the campground: Located at the end of the road, the campground sits about 200 feet from the lakeshore. Tents pitch off the road; RVs must camp off the road on the shoulder. A lookout about half a mile back down the road from the campground offers a marvelous view of Mount Shasta. Castle Lake is stocked with modest numbers of rainbow trout, and fishing is fair. A 3-mile round-trip trail leads from the lake to tiny Heart Lake, where you can get an even better view of Mount Shasta. Elevation 5,280 feet. Stay limit 14 days. Open from June through October.

35 Gumboot Lake

Location: 16 miles southwest of the community of Mount Shasta.
Sites: 4 sites for tents and RVs up to 10 feet long.
Facilities: Tables, fire rings, vault toilets. No drinking water.
Fee per night: None.

Management: Shasta-Trinity National Forest, 530-926-4511.
Activities: Fishing, hiking.
Finding the campground: From Interstate 5 in Mount Shasta, take the Central Mount Shasta exit, turn left at a stop sign (crossing the highway) and drive 0.4 mile. Turn left at a stop sign onto Barr Road (County Road 2MO20) and drive 3 miles. Turn right onto Forest Road 26 at Lake Siskiyou and drive 13 miles.

About the campground: Gumboot is a small but very pretty mountain lake with decent fishing for small to midsize rainbow trout. No motorized boats are permitted. A poorly defined trail leads uphill from the campground to a junction with the Pacific Crest Trail. Elevation 6,080 feet. Stay limit 14 days. Open from June through October.

36 Ah-Di-Na

Location: 15 miles south of McCloud.
Sites: 16 sites for tents.
Facilities: Tables, fire rings, drinking water, flush toilets.
Fee per night: $8.
Management: Shasta-Trinity National Forest, 530-964-2184.
Activities: Fishing, hiking.
Finding the campground: From McCloud, drive south 11 miles on Squaw Valley Road (Forest Road 11), following the west shore of Lake McCloud. Turn right (west) onto FR 38N53 and drive 4 miles.

About the campground: Situated on the scenic banks of the McCloud River. Check fishing regulations, as catch-and-release rules are in effect downstream of the campground. A nature trail follows the river in a Nature Conservancy preserve nearby. Elevation 2,300 feet. Stay limit 14 days. Open from April 15 through November 15.

37 Fowlers Camp

Location: 6 miles east of McCloud.
Sites: 39 sites for tents and RVs up to 30 feet long.
Facilities: Tables, fire rings, drinking water, vault toilets. The facilities are wheelchair accessible.
Fee per night: $12.
Management: Shasta-Trinity National Forest, 530-964-2184.
Activities: Hiking, swimming, fishing.
Finding the campground: From McCloud, drive 5 miles east on California Highway 89, turn right (south) onto Forest Road 40N44, and drive about 1 mile.

About the campground: Located on the banks of scenic McCloud River, with only mediocre fishing for native trout but good swimming holes in summer. Two fine waterfalls, one upstream and the other downstream, are within easy hiking distance of the campground. Elevation 3,600 feet. Stay limit 14 days. Open from April 15 through October 31.

38 Cattle Camp

Location: 10 miles east of McCloud.
Sites: 30 sites for tents and RVs.
Facilities: Tables, fire rings, drinking water, vault toilets.
Fee per night: $12.
Management: Shasta-Trinity National Forest, 530-964-2184.
Activities: Fishing, swimming.
Finding the campground: From McCloud, drive 10 miles east on California Highway 89.

About the campground: Situated near the McCloud River, which offers fair fishing. There is a good swimming hole nearby. Elevation 3,800 feet. Stay limit 14 days. Open from April 15 through September 15.

39 Algoma

Location: 14 miles east of McCloud.
Sites: 8 sites for tents and RVs.
Facilities: Tables, fire rings, vault toilets. No drinking water.
Fee per night: None.
Management: Shasta-Trinity National Forest, 530-964-2184.
Activities: Fishing.
Finding the campground: From McCloud, drive east 13 miles on California Highway 89, turn right (south) onto Forest Road 39N06, and drive about 1 mile.

About the campground: Situated on the McCloud River in an area of fair trout fishing. Elevation 3,800 feet. Stay limit 14 days. Open from April 15 through October 31.

40 Castle Crags State Park

Location: 12 miles south of the community of Mount Shasta.
Sites: 64 sites for tents and RVs up to 27 feet long (52 sites in main campground, 12 along the Sacramento River).
Facilities: Tables, fire rings, drinking water, showers, flush toilets.
Fee per night: $15-$17. For reservations call 800-444-7275. There is a one-time reservation fee of $7.50.
Management: California Department of Parks and Recreation, 530-235-2684.
Activities: Hiking, fishing, swimming.
Finding the campground: From Mount Shasta, drive south 12 miles on Interstate 5 and take the Castle Crags exit. To reach the main campground, turn right toward the crags. For the river campground, turn left, go under the freeway, and follow the signs to the picnic area.

Campgrounds in Castle Crags State Park offer dramatic views of the massive granite sentinels for which the park was named.

About the campground: Castle Crags features dramatic granite spires that can be seen from Interstate 5. The campground complex has been listed by *Sunset Magazine* as one of the 100 best in the western United States. Campsites are divided between two campgrounds. If you are interested in hiking the trails to the crags, you should use the main campground. If you are interested in swimming, fishing, and hiking along the Sacramento River, use the river campground. A trail connects the two.

A short trail from the end of the access road leads to a great viewpoint with fine views of the crags and Mount Shasta. A 6-mile round-trip trail to the base of the crags also begins here. Trailers and large RVs should not continue on the access road past the campground, because it becomes steep, curving, and only one lane wide.

The Indian Creek Interpretive Trail begins at the ranger station and makes a 1-mile loop. From the river campground, a 1.5-mile trail leads upstream along the river, passing fishing spots and swimming holes. Fishing in this section of the river is catch and release. Soda Springs, a bubbling mineral pool, is a short distance from the river campground. Stay limit 15 days from June through September, 30 days from October through May. Open all year.

SHASTA-TRINITY AREA

The core of this area is the Whiskeytown-Shasta-Trinity National Recreation Area, a huge, water-oriented outdoor resource that encompasses three large lakes: Shasta, Trinity, and Whiskeytown. More than three dozen public campgrounds are located throughout the area, most of them on the water. You can enjoy water sports of almost every description, including fishing, waterskiing, and sailing. Boats, canoes, kayaks, sailboards, and personal watercraft are available for rent. Each of the three units comprising the recreation area is described separately below.

Much of the northern and western portions of the Shasta-Trinity Area is covered by the Shasta-Trinity National Forest, 3,280 square miles of public land. Outstanding features of the forest include the 513,000-acre Trinity Alps Wilderness, with its granite peaks, 55 lakes and streams, and many miles of trails.

The Pacific Crest Trail traverses the forest in a north-south direction. From it, you can get fine views of Mount Shasta, Castle Crags, and the Trinity Alps. The South Fork National Recreation Trail begins at Forest Glen and climbs gradually along the South Fork of the Trinity River to Smokey Creek, and the Sisson-Callahan National Recreation Trail traces a historic route from the town of Sisson to the old mining town of Callahan.

More than 105 miles of Wild and Scenic River have been designated in the forest, many of them along the Trinity. The Trinity Scenic Byway follows the course of the Trinity along California Highway 299 from the town of Shasta west to Blue Lake. The Trinity Heritage Scenic Byway follows California Highway 3 along the west bank of Trinity Lake from Weaverville to the town of Mount Shasta, passing through historic towns and mountain landscapes.

1 Iron Canyon Reservoir: Hawkins Landing

Location: 56 miles northeast of Redding.
Sites: 10 sites for tents and RVs up to 19 feet long.
Facilities: Tables, fire rings, drinking water, vault toilets, boat ramp.
Fee per night: $15, pets $1.
Management: PG&E, 530-686-5164.
Activities: Fishing, swimming, boating.
Finding the campground: From the intersection of Interstate 5 and California Highway 299 in Redding, take CA 299 northeast for 36 miles, turn left (north) onto Big Bend Road, and drive 16 miles to a T junction 1 mile north of Big Bend. Bear left onto Forest Road 11 and drive 4 miles.

About the campground: Situated on the shore of a reservoir subject to heavy drawdowns in summer, the campground is best visited in midspring, when the water is high and the trout fishing reasonably good. The lake is stocked with 8,000 rainbow and brook trout in the 10- to 12-inch range. Elevation 2,700 feet. Stay limit 14 days. Open from mid-April through October.

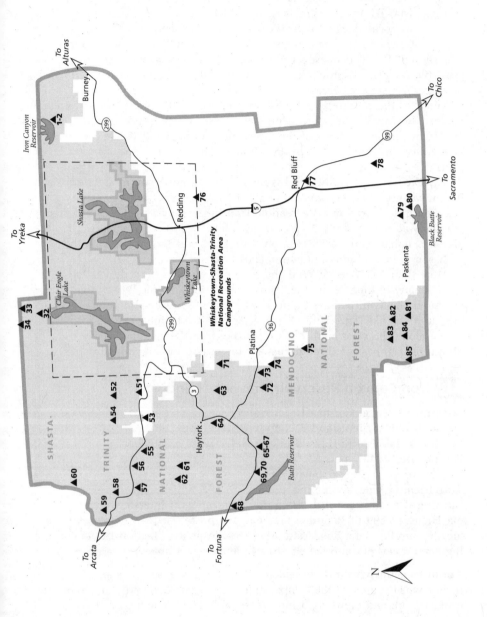

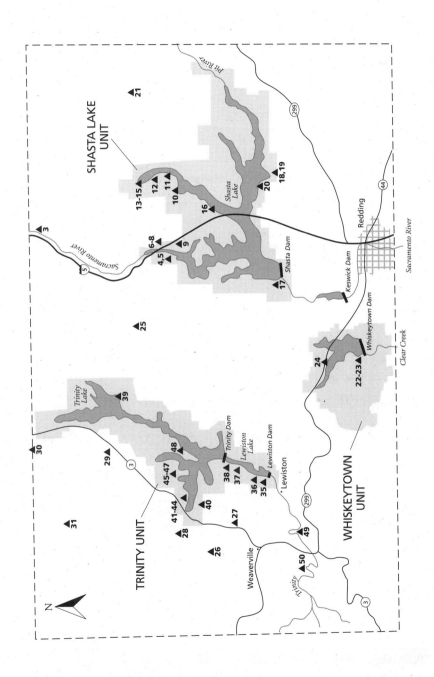

SHASTA-TRINITY AREA CAMPGROUNDS

		Group sites	RV sites	Total sites	Max. RV length	Hookups	Toilets	Showers	Drinking water	Dump station	Pets	Wheelchair	Recreation	Fee ($)	Season	Can reserve	Length of stay
Iron Canyon Reservoir (1–2)																	
1	Hawkins Landing		•	10	19	V	•		•				SFB	15	mid-April–Oct.		14
2	Deadlun		•	30	24	V				•			SFB		May–September		14
3	Sims Flat		•	20	24	F	•		•	•	•		HS FB	12	April 15–Nov. 15		14

Whiskeytown-Shasta-Trinity National Recreation Area

		Group sites	RV sites	Total sites	Max. RV length	Hookups	Toilets	Showers	Drinking water	Dump station	Pets	Wheelchair	Recreation	Fee ($)	Season	Can reserve	Length of stay
Shasta Unit (4–20)																	
4	Lakeshore		•	26	30	F	•		•	•	•		SFB	15–25	April–October	•	14
5	Beehive Point		•	open	30	V			•				SFB	6			14
6	Antlers		•	59	30	F	•		•				SFB	15–25		•	14
7	Gregory Beach		•	open	30	V			•				SF	6			14
8	Gregory Creek		•	18	16	F	•		•				SF	12	mid-May–Labor Day		14
9	Nelson Point	•	•	9	16	V			•				SFB	8–65	April–Labor Day	•	14
10	Hirz Bay	•	•	50	30	F	•		•		•		SFB	15–90			14
11	Dekkas Rock Group Camp	•	•	4	16	V	•		•				SF	90	April–October	•	14
12	Moore Creek	•	•	12	16	V	•		•				SFB	12–90	summer weekends	•	14
13	Ellery Creek		•	19	30	V	•		•	•	•		SFB	12	mid-May–Labor Day	•	14
14	Pine Point		•	14	24	V	•		•				SFB	12	mid-May–Labor Day		14
15	McCloud Bridge		•	20	16	F	•		•				F	12	April–September		14
16	Bailey Cove		•	7	30	F	•		•				SF BL	15–25	May–October	•	14
17	Shasta		•	22	30	V	•		•				HFO	9			14
18	Upper and Lower Jones Valley		•	27	16	V	•		•				FB	12			14
19	Jones Inlet		•	open	30	V	•		•				HS FB	6	March–October		14
20	Mariners Point		•	open	16	V	•		•				SFB	8	March–October		14
21	Madrone		•	10	16	V			•				HF		May–September		14

Whiskeytown Unit (22–24)

	Group sites	RV sites	Total sites	Max. RV length	Hookups	Toilets	Showers	Drinking water	Dump station	Pets	Wheelchair	Recreation	Fee ($)	Season	Can reserve	Length of stay
22 Brandy Creek		•	46	25				•	•	•		HS FB	7–14			14/30
23 Dry Creek Group Camp	•		2			V		•		•		HS FB	60		•	14/30
24 Oak Bottom		•	150			F	•	•	•	•	•	HSF BL	7–18		•	14/30
25 Clear Creek		•	22	22		V				•						14
26 East Weaver		•	15	16		V		•		•		HF	8			14
27 Rush Creek		•	10	16		V				•			5	April–mid-Sept.		14
28 Bridge Camp		•	10	12		V		•		•		HR	8			14
29 Preacher Meadow		•	45	32		V		•		•			8	mid-May–mid-Oct.		14
30 Goldfield		•	6	16		V				•		H				14
31 Big Flat		•	5	16		V				•		H				14
32 Trinity River		•	7	32		V		•		•		F	8			14
33 Eagle Creek		•	17	27		V		•		•		F	8			14
34 Horse Flat		•	16	16		V				•		HR		mid-May–October		14

Trinity Unit (35–48)

	Group sites	RV sites	Total sites	Max. RV length	Hookups	Toilets	Showers	Drinking water	Dump station	Pets	Wheelchair	Recreation	Fee ($)	Season	Can reserve	Length of stay
35 Mary Smith			18			F		•		•		F	9	May–October		14
36 Cooper Gulch		•	5	16		V		•		•	•	F	10	April–November		14
37 Tunnel Rock		•	6	15		V				•		F	5			14
38 Ackerman		•	66	40		F	•	•	•	•		F	10			14
39 Jackass Springs		•	21	32		V				•		FS				14
40 Tannery Gulch		•	87	40		F		•		•		HSF BL	12–18	May–September	•	14
41 Stoney Point Group Camp			22			F		•		•		SFB	10			14
42 Stoney Creek Group Camp	•		1			F		•		•	•	SFB	50	May–September	•	14
43 Fawn Group Camp	•	•	1	37		F		•		•		SFB	60	May–September	•	14
44 Bushy Tail Group Camp	•	•	30	20		F		•		•		SFB	30	May–September	•	14
45 Minersville		•	21	18		F		•		•		SFBL	10–17			14
46 Clark Springs		•	21	20		F		•		•		SFB	8	April–mid-Sept.		14

#	Name	Group sites	RV sites	Total sites	Max. RV length	Hookups	Toilets	Showers	Drinking water	Dump station	Pets	Wheelchair	Recreation	Fee ($)	Season	Can reserve	Length of stay
47	Hayward Flat		•	98	40		F	•	•				SFB	12–18	mid-May–mid-Sept.	•	14
48	Alpine View		•	66	32		F	•	•				SFB	12–18	mid-May–mid-Sept.		14
49	Steelbridge		•	9			V		•				SF				14
50	Douglas City		•	18			F	•	•				SF	8	May–October		14
51	Junction City		•	22			V	•	•				SF	7	May–October		14
52	Ripstein			10			V		•				H				14
53	Pigeon Point		•	35	25		V		•			•	SF	6	May–October		14
54	Hobo Gulch		•	10			V		•				H				14
55	Big Flat		•	10	25		V	•	•				SF	8			14
56	Skunk Point Group Camp	•		2			V	•	•				SF	20		•	14
57	Big Bar			3			V		•				SF				14
58	Hayden Flat		•	35	25		V	•	•		•	•	SF	8–10			14
59	Burnt Ranch		•	16	25		V	•	•		•	•	SF	8			14
60	Denny		•	16	25		V	•	•		•		HF				14
61	Big Slide		•	8			V		•				F				14
62	Slide Creek		•	5			V		•				F				14
63	Shiell Gulch		•	5			V		•								14
64	Philpot		•	6			V		•								14
65	Hell Gate		•	17	15		V	•	•			•	HSF	6			14
66	Scotts Flat		•	10	20		V		•				HSF				14
67	Forest Glen		•	15	15		V	•	•				SF	6			14
68	Mad River		•	40	30		V	•	•				F	10			14

Ruth Lake (69–70)

#	Name	Group sites	RV sites	Total sites	Max. RV length	Hookups	Toilets	Showers	Drinking water	Dump station	Pets	Wheelchair	Recreation	Fee ($)	Season	Can reserve	Length of stay
69	Fir Cove	•	•	22			V	•	•				SFB	10–45	May 22–Sept. 13	•	14
70	Bailey Canyon		•	25	22		V	•	•				SFB	10	May 22–Sept.13		14
71	Deer Lick Springs		•	13			V		•				HF				14
72	White Rock			3			V		•								14
73	Basin Gulch		•	13	20		V		•								14
74	Beegum Gorge		•	2			V		•				H				14
75	Tomhead Saddle	•	•	5			V		•				HR				14

	Group sites	RV sites	Total sites	Max. RV length	Hookups	Toilets	Showers	Drinking water	Dump station	Pets	Wheelchair	Recreation	Fee ($)	Season	Can reserve	Length of stay
76 Reading Island		•	9	30		V	•		•	•		SFB	5			14
77 Lake Red Bluff		•	25			F	•	•		•	•	SFBL	10			14
78 Woodson Bridge State Recreation Area	•	•	46	31		F	•	•	•	•	•	HS FB	14–60		•	15/30

Black Butte Lake (79–80)

	Group sites	RV sites	Total sites	Max. RV length	Hookups	Toilets	Showers	Drinking water	Dump station	Pets	Wheelchair	Recreation	Fee ($)	Season	Can reserve	Length of stay
79 Buckhorn	•	•	86	35		F	•	•	•	•		HSF BL	10–75		•	14
80 Orland Buttes	•	•	36	35		F	•	•	•	•		HSF BL	12–50	April–September	•	14
81 Whitlock		•	3			V	•		•			H		June–October		14
82 Rocky Cabin		•	3			V			•			H		June–October		14
83 Three Prong		•	6			V	•		•			H		June–October		14
84 Kingsley Glade		•	6			V	•		•			HR		June–October		14
85 Wells Cabin			25			V	•		•			H		July–October		14

Hookups: W = Water E = Electric S = Sewer
Toilets: F = Flush V = Vault P = Pit C = Chemical
Recreation: H = Hiking S = Swimming F = Fishing B = Boating L = Boat Launch O = Off-highway Driving R = Horseback Riding
Maximum Trailer/RV Length given in feet. Stay Limit given in days. Fee given in dollars.
If no entry under **Season,** campground is open all year. If no entry under Fee, camping is free.

2 Iron Canyon Reservoir: Deadlun

Location: 57 miles northeast of Redding.
Sites: 30 sites for tents and RVs up to 24 feet long.
Facilities: Tables, fire rings, vault toilets. No drinking water.
Fee per night: None.
Management: Shasta-Trinity National Forest, 530-275-1587.
Activities: Fishing, swimming, boating.
Finding the campground: From the intersection of Interstate 5 and California Highway 299 in Redding, take CA 299 northeast for 36 miles, turn left (north) onto Big Bend Road, and drive 16 miles to a T junction 1 mile north of Big Bend. Bear left onto Forest Road 11 and drive 5 miles.

About the campground: See Hawkins Landing Campground (number 1). A boat ramp is located 1 mile south at Hawkins Landing. Elevation 2,700 feet. Stay limit 14 days. Open from May through September.

3 Sims Flat

Location: 21 miles south of the community of Mount Shasta.
Sites: 20 sites for tents and RVs up to 24 feet long.
Facilities: Tables, fire rings, drinking water, flush and vault toilets. The facilities are wheelchair accessible.
Fee per night: $12.
Management: Shasta-Trinity National Forest, 530-926-4511.
Activities: Hiking, fishing, swimming, kayaking, canoeing.
Finding the campground: From the community of Mount Shasta, drive south 20 miles on Interstate 5, take the Sims Road exit, and drive east about 1 mile on an unmarked road.

About the campground: Situated on the banks of the Sacramento River, with good access to it. The river is stocked annually with more than 25,000 catchable-sized rainbow trout. A trail leads east from the campground to the summit of Tombstone Mountain (5,613 feet). Elevation 3,600 feet. Stay limit 14 days. Open from April 15 through November 15.

4 Shasta Unit: Lakeshore

Location: 26 miles north of Redding.
Sites: 20 single and 6 double sites for tents and RVs up to 30 feet long.
Facilities: Tables, fire rings, drinking water, flush toilets. Boat ramp 1 mile south. The facilities are wheelchair accessible.
Fee per night: $15 single, $25 double site. For reservations call 800-280-CAMP. There is a one-time reservation fee of $8.65.
Management: Shasta-Trinity National Forest, 530-275-1587.
Activities: Swimming, fishing, boating.
Finding the campground: From the intersection of California Highway 44 and Interstate 5 in Redding, drive north 24 miles on I-5, take the Antlers Road

exit, and turn left at the stop sign. Go under the freeway, turn left onto Lakeshore Drive, and go 2 miles.

About the campground: Situated on the west shore of the Sacramento River Arm of the lake. Stay limit 14 days. Open from April through October.

5 Shasta Unit: Beehive Point

Location: 28 miles north of Redding.
Sites: Open shoreline camping for tents and RVs up to 30 feet long.
Facilities: Vault toilets. No drinking water. Boat ramp 1 mile north.
Fee per night: $6.
Management: Shasta-Trinity National Forest, 530-275-1587.
Activities: Swimming, fishing, boating.
Finding the campground: From the intersection of California Highway 44 and Interstate 5 in Redding, drive north 24 miles on I-5, take the Antlers Road exit, and turn left at the stop sign. Go under the freeway, turn left onto Lakeshore Drive, and go 4 miles.

About the campground: Situated on the upper Sacramento River Arm of the lake, campsites are undesignated in a semiwooded shoreline area. Stay limit 14 days. Open all year.

6 Shasta Unit: Antlers

Location: 25 miles north of Redding.
Sites: 41 single and 18 double sites for tents and RVs up to 30 feet long.
Facilities: Tables, fire rings, drinking water, flush and vault toilets. Boat ramp half-mile south.
Fee per night: $15 single, $25 double site. For reservations call 800-280-CAMP. There is a one-time reservation fee of $8.65.
Management: Shasta-Trinity National Forest, 530-275-1587.
Activities: Swimming, fishing, boating, waterskiing.
Finding the campground: From the intersection of California Highway 44 and Interstate 5 in Redding, drive north 24 miles on I-5, take the Antlers Road exit, and turn right at the stop sign. Turn right onto Antlers Road and drive about 1 mile.

About the campground: Situated on the upper Sacramento River Arm of the lake. Stay limit 14 days. Open all year.

7 Shasta Unit: Gregory Beach

Location: 24 miles north of Redding.
Sites: Open shoreline camping for tents and RVs up to 30 feet long.
Facilities: Vault toilets. No drinking water.
Fee per night: $6.
Management: Shasta-Trinity National Forest, 530-275-1587.
Activities: Swimming, fishing.

Whiskeytown-Shasta-Trinity National Recreation Area: Shasta Unit

Shasta Lake, with its 29,500-acre surface area and 370 miles of shoreline, gets large numbers of visitors, especially during the summer months. Yet its numerous arms, inlets, and coves can provide privacy for those willing to seek it. Much of the shoreline is accessible only by boat, providing opportunities for exploration. Interstate 5, which runs north-south, bisects the lake neatly, facilitating access to many campgrounds, resorts, and marinas. Shasta Dam is the tallest dam in the United States and the second largest in volume. It is open to tours.

The lake supports 21 varieties of fish and is stocked annually with a mix of almost 200,000 rainbow and Eagle Lake trout (10 to 12 inches long) and 50,000 king salmon. There are 14 boat ramps on the lake, half of them public. They all charge a fee. You can rent a boat at 11 commercial marinas around the lake; houseboats are especially popular. There are no developed shoreline swimming areas, but many people swim at their campgrounds and from boats.

The Forest Service maintains four boat-in campgrounds on Shasta Lake. They all have vault toilets, no drinking water, no fee, and are open all year. Arbuckle Flat (Pit River Arm) has 11 sites; Ski Island (Pit River Arm) has 23 sites; Greens Creek (McCloud River Arm) has 8 sites; and Gooseneck Cove (Sacramento River Arm) offers 11 sites.

Hiking trails at Packers Bay, Bailey Cove, Hirz Bay, and Jones Valley offer moderate hiking and good shoreline fishing access. Mountain biking is permitted on most of the trails. Packers Bay is also a good place to view bald eagles. The Chappie-Shasta Off Highway Vehicle Area provides trails and roads for adventurous off-road driving, as well as a nearby campground. Shasta Caverns (commercially operated) and Samwel Cave (no charge) are open to visitors year-round. A definite plus for campfire enthusiasts is that dead wood may be gathered freely and without a permit.

Two visitor centers provide brochures, maps, exhibits, campfire permits, and general information:

Shasta Lake Visitor Information Center
Mountain Gate/Wonderland Boulevard exit from Interstate 5
530-275-1589

Shasta Dam Visitor Information Center
Shasta Dam Boulevard exit from Interstate 5
530-275-4463

Finding the campground: From the intersection of California Highway 44 and Interstate 5 in Redding, drive north 20 miles on I-5, take the Salt Creek exit, and drive 4 miles north on Gregory Creek Road.

About the campground: Situated on the upper eastern shore of the Sacramento River Arm of the lake, campsites are undesignated in an attractive shoreline area. Stay limit 14 days. Open all year.

8 Shasta Unit: Gregory Creek

Location: 25 miles north of Redding.
Sites: 18 sites for tents and RVs up to 16 feet long.
Facilities: Tables, fire rings, drinking water, flush toilets.
Fee per night: $12.
Management: Shasta-Trinity National Forest, 530-275-1587.
Activities: Swimming, fishing.
Finding the campground: From the intersection of California Highway 44 and Interstate 5 in Redding, drive north 20 miles on I-5, take the Salt Creek exit, and drive 4.5 miles north on Gregory Creek Road.

About the campground: Situated on the eastern shore of the Sacramento River Arm of the lake, above the lakeshore. Stay limit 14 days. Open from mid-May through Labor Day.

9 Shasta Unit: Nelson Point

Location: 21 miles north of Redding.
Sites: 9 sites for tents and RVs up to 16 feet long. May be reserved as a group camp.
Facilities: Tables, fire rings, vault toilets. No drinking water.
Fee per night: $8, $65 for group camp. To reserve group camp, call 800-280-CAMP.
Management: Shasta-Trinity National Forest, 530-275-1587.
Activities: Swimming, fishing, boating, waterskiing.
Finding the campground: From the intersection of California Highway 44 and Interstate 5 in Redding, drive north 20 miles on I-5, take the Salt Creek exit, turn left, and drive 1 mile west.

About the campground: Situated on the shore of Salt Creek Inlet. Stay limit 14 days. Open from April through Labor Day.

10 Shasta Unit: Hirz Bay

Location: 29 miles north of Redding.
Sites: 37 single sites, 11 double sites, plus 2 group sites for tents and RVs up to 30 feet long.
Facilities: Tables, fire rings, drinking water, flush toilets (vault toilets at group sites). Boat ramp half a mile south. The facilities are wheelchair accessible.
Fee per night: $15 single, $25 double sites. Group sites $65, $90.

Management: Shasta-Trinity National Forest, 530-275-1587.
Activities: Swimming, fishing, boating, waterskiing.
Finding the campground: From the intersection of California Highway 44 and Interstate 5 in Redding, drive north 20 miles on I-5, take the Gilman exit, and drive 9 miles northeast on Gilman Road (County Road 7H009).

About the campground: Situated on the McCloud River Arm of Shasta Lake. The scenic Hirz Bay Trail begins at the campground and follows the shoreline for 2 miles to Dekkas Rock Group Camp (number 11). Stay limit 14 days. Open all year (group sites open from April through October).

11 Shasta Unit: Dekkas Rock Group Camp

Location: 30 miles north of Redding.
Sites: 4 group sites for tents and RVs up to 16 feet long.
Facilities: Tables, fire rings, drinking water, vault toilets. Boat ramp 1.5 miles south.
Fee per night: $90. For reservations call 800-280-CAMP. There is a one-time reservation fee of $15.
Management: Shasta-Trinity National Forest, 530-275-1587.
Activities: Swimming, fishing.
Finding the campground: From the intersection of California Highway 44 and Interstate 5 in Redding, drive north 20 miles on I-5, take the Gilman exit, and drive 10 miles northeast on Gilman Road (County Road 7H009).

About the campground: Situated on an oak-shaded flat above Shasta Lake on the McCloud River Arm. Stay limit 14 days. Open from April through October.

12 Shasta Unit: Moore Creek

Location: 31 miles north of Redding.
Sites: 12 sites for tents and RVs up to 16 feet long. May be reserved as a group camp.
Facilities: Tables, fire rings, drinking water, vault toilets.
Fee per night: $12, group fee $90.
Management: Shasta-Trinity National Forest, 530-275-1587.
Activities: Swimming, fishing, boating, waterskiing.
Finding the campground: From the intersection of California Highway 44 and Interstate 5 in Redding, drive north 20 miles on I-5, take the Gilman exit, and drive 11 miles northeast on Gilman Road (County Road 7H009).

About the campground: Situated on the McCloud River Arm of the lake. Open summer weekends and holidays.

13 Shasta Unit: Ellery Creek

Location: 34 miles north of Redding.
Sites: 19 sites for tents and RVs up to 30 feet long.

Facilities: Tables, fire rings, drinking water, vault toilets. The facilities are wheelchair accessible.
Fee per night: $12. For reservations call 800-280-CAMP. There is a one-time reservation fee of $8.65.
Management: Shasta-Trinity National Forest, 530-275-1587.
Activities: Swimming, fishing, boating, waterskiing.
Finding the campground: From the intersection of California Highway 44 and Interstate 5 in Redding, drive north 20 miles on I-5, take the Gilman exit, and drive 13.5 miles northeast on Gilman Road (County Road 7H009).

About the campground: Situated on the McCloud River Arm of the lake. Stay limit 14 days. Open from mid-May through Labor Day.

14 Shasta Unit: Pine Point

Location: 35 miles north of Redding.
Sites: 14 sites for tents and RVs up to 24 feet long.
Facilities: Tables, fire rings, drinking water, vault toilets.
Fee per night: $12.
Management: Shasta-Trinity National Forest, 530-275-1587.
Activities: Swimming, fishing, boating, waterskiing.
Finding the campground: From the intersection of California Highway 44 and Interstate 5 in Redding, drive north 20 miles on I-5, take the Gilman exit, and drive 14 miles northeast on Gilman Road (County Road 7H009).

About the campground: Situated on the McCloud River Arm of the lake. Stay limit 14 days. Open from mid-May through Labor Day.

15 Shasta Unit: McCloud Bridge

Location: 36 miles north of Redding.
Sites: 20 sites for tents and RVs up to 16 feet long.
Facilities: Tables, fire rings, drinking water, flush and vault toilets.
Fee per night: $12.
Management: Shasta-Trinity National Forest, 530-275-1587.
Activities: Fishing.
Finding the campground: From the intersection of California Highway 44 and Interstate 5 in Redding, drive north 20 miles on I-5, take the Gilman exit, and drive 14 miles northeast on Gilman Road (County Road 7H009).

About the campground: Situated on the McCloud River Arm of the lake. Stay limit 14 days. The mile-long Samwel Cave Nature Trail begins just south of the campground, runs along the shoreline, and ends at Samwel Cave. Only the first room of the cave is open to visitors without a permit. A permit for further entry (and a key to the gate) may be obtained at the Shasta Lake Ranger District Headquarters in Mountain Gate. It is a good idea to reserve the key in advance, as only one key is available for issue. To do so, call 530-275-1589. Stay limit 14 days. Open from April through September.

16 Shasta Unit: Bailey Cove

Location: 18 miles north of Redding.
Sites: 5 single and 2 double sites for tents and RVs up to 30 feet long.
Facilities: Tables, fire rings, drinking water, flush toilets, boat ramp.
Fee per night: $15 single, $25 double site. For reservations call 800-280-CAMP. There is a one-time reservation fee of $8.65.
Management: Shasta-Trinity National Forest, 530-275-1587.
Activities: Swimming, fishing, boating, waterskiing, bird watching.
Finding the campground: From the intersection of California Highway 44 and Interstate 5 in Redding, drive north 17 miles on I-5, take the Lake Shasta Caverns exit, and drive 1 mile east.

About the campground: Situated on the lower McCloud River Arm of the lake. Packers Bay, 3 miles southwest of the campground, offers four short trails, the longest being the scenic Waters Gulch Loop (3.2 miles). Packers Bay is also a good place for watching birds, including bald eagles, ospreys, and migratory birds. Stay limit 14 days. Open all year. The ferry to Lake Shasta Caverns is half a mile east of the campground. The caverns began forming 250 million years ago, and interesting limestone formations are accessible via paved walkways, staircases, and indirect lighting. A fee is charged for the tour. The caverns are open from May through October.

17 Shasta Unit: Shasta

Location: 13 miles north of Redding.
Sites: 22 sites for tents and RVs up to 30 feet long.
Facilities: Tables, fire rings, drinking water, vault toilets. Boat ramp 1.5 miles east.
Fee per night: $9.
Management: Shasta-Trinity National Forest, 530-275-1587.
Activities: OHV driving, fishing, hiking.
Finding the campground: From the intersection of California Highway 44 and Interstate 5 in Redding, drive north 6.5 miles on I-5, take the California Highway 151 exit (Shasta Dam Boulevard), and drive 2.5 miles west. Turn right (north) onto County Road A18 (Lake Boulevard) and drive 4 miles, crossing Shasta Dam en route.

About the campground: Situated on the Sacramento River adjacent to the Chappie-Shasta Off Highway Vehicle Area, this campground is of primary interest to OHV enthusiasts. A boat ramp at Centimudi, 1.5 miles to the east, provides access to Shasta Lake. The 4.5-mile Dry Fork Creek Trail begins at the western end of Shasta Dam, providing shoreline fishing access, swimming opportunities, and great views of Mount Shasta. Stay limit 14 days. Open all year.

18 Shasta Unit: Upper and Lower Jones Valley

Location: 13 miles northeast of Redding.
Sites: In Lower Jones, 14 sites for tents and RVs up to 16 feet long; in Upper Jones, 13 sites for tents and RVs up to 10 feet long.
Facilities: Tables, fire rings, drinking water, vault toilets.
Fee per night: $12.
Management: Shasta-Trinity National Forest, 530-275-1587.
Activities: Fishing, boating.
Finding the campground: From the intersection of Interstate 5 and California Highway 299 in Redding, drive east 5 miles on CA 299, turn left (north) onto Dry Creek Road (County Road 4J02), and drive 6.5 miles. Bear right at the Y intersection and drive 1 mile.

About the campground: Two adjacent campgrounds near an attractive cove in the Pit River Arm of the lake. A boat ramp is located about a mile north. Stay limit 14 days. Open all year.

19 Shasta Unit: Jones Inlet

Location: 13 miles northeast of Redding.
Sites: Open camping for tents and RVs up to 30 feet long.
Facilities: Drinking water, vault toilets.
Fee per night: $6.
Management: Shasta-Trinity National Forest, 530-275-1587.
Activities: Swimming, fishing, boating, waterskiing, hiking.
Finding the campground: From the intersection of Interstate 5 and California Highway 299 in Redding, drive east 5 miles on CA 299, turn left (north) onto Dry Creek Road (County Road 4J02), and drive 6.5 miles. Bear right at the Y intersection and drive 1.5 miles.

About the campground: Situated on the shoreline of the Pit River Arm of the lake. The Clickapudi Trail, a pretty, 4-mile loop, samples the forest and shoreline coves in the area and is open to hikers, mountain bikers, and equestrians. Stay limit 14 days. Open from March through October.

20 Shasta Unit: Mariners Point

Location: 14 miles northeast of Redding.
Sites: Open camping for tents and RVs up to 16 feet long.
Facilities: Drinking water, vault toilets.
Fee per night: $8.
Management: Shasta-Trinity National Forest, 530-275-1587.
Activities: Swimming, fishing, boating, waterskiing.
Finding the campground: From the intersection of Interstate 5 and California Highway 299 in Redding, drive east 5 miles on CA 299, turn left (north) onto Dry Creek Road (County Road 4J02), and drive 9 miles (the last 4 miles are actually on County Road 5J050, which joins from the left).

About the campground: Situated on the shoreline of the Pit River Arm of the lake. Stay limit 14 days. Open from March through October.

21 Madrone

Location: 44 miles northeast of Redding.
Sites: 10 sites for tents and RVs up to 16 feet long.
Facilities: Tables, fire rings, vault toilets. No drinking water.
Fee per night: None.
Management: Shasta-Trinity National Forest, 530-275-1587.
Activities: Fishing, hiking.
Finding the campground: From the intersection of Interstate 5 and California Highway 299, drive 29 miles northeast on CA 299, turn left (north) onto Fenders Ferry Road (Forest Road 27), and drive 15 miles.

About the campground: An isolated campground pretty much in the middle of nowhere, on the bank of Squaw Creek. A trail leads north from the campground along Beartrap Creek. Elevation 1,500 feet. Stay limit 14 days. Open from May through September.

22 Whiskeytown Unit: Brandy Creek

Location: 14 miles west of Redding.
Sites: 46 sites for self-contained RVs up to 25 feet long.
Facilities: Drinking water, dump station. Boat ramp nearby.
Fee per night: $14, winter months $7.
Management: Whiskeytown-Shasta-Trinity National Recreation Area, 530-241-6584.
Activities: Swimming, fishing, boating, waterskiing, hiking.
Finding the campground: From Redding, drive west 10 miles on California Highway 299, turn left at the Whiskeytown Unit Visitor Center, and drive 4 miles.

Whiskeytown-Shasta-Trinity National Recreation Area: Whiskeytown Unit

Whiskeytown Lake, with a 3,200-acre surface area and 36 miles of shoreline, is the central attraction of this smallest of the the three units in the national recreation area. In addition to most water sports (including scuba diving), you can hike 45 miles of trails, explore historical gold rush sites, and pan for gold (there is a $1 permit fee; check at the visitor center for permit and best panning locations). Gathering dead wood for campfires is allowed, but a $10 permit is required. The lake is stocked annually with 50,000 rainbow trout and 2,000 brown trout. There is also a resident population of largemouth, smallmouth, and spotted bass, as well as kokanee salmon.

About the campground: Situated on Brandy Creek less than a quarter of a mile from the lakeshore. A marina and boat ramp are located within a quarter of a mile. Stay limit 14 days from May 15 through September 15, 30 days from October through April. Open all year.

23 Whiskeytown Unit: Dry Creek Group Camp

Location: 15 miles west of Redding.
Sites: 2 group sites for tents, accommodating up to 50 people each.
Facilities: Tables, fire rings, drinking water, vault toilets.
Fee per night: $60. Reservations required; call 800-365-CAMP.
Management: Whiskeytown-Shasta-Trinity National Recreation Area, 530-241-6584.
Activities: Swimming, fishing, boating, waterskiing, hiking.
Finding the campground: From Redding, drive west 10 miles on California Highway 299, turn left at the Whiskeytown Unit Visitor Center, and drive 5 miles.

About the campground: Situated on a small peninsula on the lakeshore at the end of the paved road. A marina and boat ramp are located within 2 miles. Stay limit 14 days from May 15 through September 15, 30 days from October through April. Open all year.

24 Whiskeytown Unit: Oak Bottom

Location: 14 miles west of Redding.
Sites: 100 sites for tents and 50 spaces for RVs in a large parking area.
Facilities: Tables, fire rings, drinking water, showers, flush toilets, dump station, store, boat ramp and rentals. The facilities are wheelchair accessible.
Fee per night: $18 for lakeside tent, $16 for nonlakeside tent, $14 for RV. In the winter, $8 tent, $7 RV. For reservations between May 13 and September 15, call 800-365-CAMP. Reservations not accepted the rest of the year.
Management: Whiskeytown-Shasta-Trinity National Recreation Area, 530-241-6584.
Activities: Swimming, fishing, boating, waterskiing, hiking, mountain biking.
Finding the campground: From Redding, drive west 14 miles on California Highway 299.

About the campground: The best sites go to the tents in this large campground on the northern shore of the lake, but the location is excellent for both lake access and hiking and mountain biking trails. Stay limit 14 days from May 15 to September 15, 30 days remainder of year. Open all year.

25 Clear Creek

Location: 44 miles northwest of Redding.
Sites: 22 sites for tents and RVs up to 22 feet long.
Facilities: Tables, fire rings, vault toilets. No drinking water.
Fee per night: None.

Management: Shasta-Trinity National Forest, 530-623-2121.
Activities: Hunting.
Finding the campground: From the intersection of Interstate 5 and California 299 at Redding, take CA 299 west for 17 miles, turn right (north) onto Trinity Lake Road and continue 14 miles. Turn right (north) onto East Side Road (County Road 106) and drive 11 miles, then turn right onto Dog Creek Road and drive 2 miles.

About the campground: There is little reason to stay at this isolated campground unless you are looking for solitude or a hunting base camp. Elevation 3,400 feet. Stay limit 14 days. Open all year.

26 East Weaver

Location: 4 miles north of Weaverville.
Sites: 15 sites for tents and RVs up to 16 feet long.
Facilities: Tables, fire rings, drinking water (April-November only), vault toilets.
Fee per night: $8.
Management: Shasta-Trinity National Forest, 530-623-2121.
Activities: Fishing, hiking.
Finding the campground: From Weaverville (about 40 miles west of Redding on California Highway 299), drive 2 miles north on California Highway 3, turn left onto County Road 228, and drive 2 miles.

About the campground: Situated on the East Branch of Weaver Creek. A trail leads northwest from the campground into the Monument Peak area of the Trinity Alps Wilderness. Elevation 2,700 feet. Stay limit 14 days. Open all year.

27 Rush Creek

Location: 9 miles northeast of Weaverville.
Sites: 10 sites for tents and RVs up to 16 feet long.
Facilities: Tables, fire rings, vault toilets. No drinking water.
Fee per night: $5.
Management: Shasta-Trinity National Forest, 530-623-2121.
Activities: None.
Finding the campground: From Weaverville (about 40 miles west of Redding on California Highway 299), drive 9 miles north on California Highway 3.

About the campground: Situated on Rush Creek, the campground serves mainly as an overflow if Trinity Lake campgrounds are full. Elevation 2,700 feet. Stay limit 14 days. Open from April through mid-September.

28 Bridge Camp

Location: 17 miles north of Weaverville.
Sites: 10 sites for tents and RVs up to 12 feet long.

Facilities: Tables, fire rings, drinking water (April-October only), vault toilets, corrals.
Fee per night: $8 from April through October, free rest of year.
Management: Shasta-Trinity National Forest, 530-623-2121.
Activities: Hiking, horseback riding.
Finding the campground: From Weaverville (about 40 miles west of Redding on California Highway 299), drive 14 miles north on California Highway 3, turn left onto Trinity Alps Road (County Road 112), and drive 3 miles.

About the campground: Bridge Camp is one of the major starting points for hikes into the Trinity Alps Wilderness. The Stuarts Fork Trail (for hikers and equestrians) begins half a mile northwest of the campground and leads to Alpine Lake (7 miles) and Emerald and Sapphire Lakes (11 and 13 miles). The campground is 3 miles from the shore of Trinity Lake. Elevation 2,700 feet. Stay limit 14 days. Open all year.

29 Preacher Meadow

Location: 29 miles northeast of Weaverville.
Sites: 45 sites for tents and RVs up to 32 feet long.
Facilities: Tables, fire rings, drinking water, vault toilets.
Fee per night: $8.
Management: Shasta-Trinity National Forest, 530-623-2121.
Activities: None.
Finding the campground: From Weaverville (about 40 miles west of Redding on California Highway 299), drive 29 miles northeast on California Highway 3.

About the campground: Best used as an overflow area if lakeside campgrounds are full, Preacher Meadow has no access to Trinity Lake. Elevation 2,900 feet. Stay limit 14 days. Open from mid-May through mid-October.

30 Goldfield

Location: 44 miles northeast of Weaverville.
Sites: 6 sites for tents and RVs up to 16 feet long.
Facilities: Tables, fire rings, vault toilets. No drinking water.
Fee per night: None.
Management: Shasta-Trinity National Forest, 530-623-2121.
Activities: Hiking.
Finding the campground: From Weaverville (about 40 miles west of Redding on California Highway 299), drive 38 miles northeast on California Highway 3, turn left (west) at the Coffee Creek Ranger Station onto County Road 104, and drive 6 miles.

About the campground: The Boulder Creek Trail begins a short distance west of the campground and leads to a series of small lakes in the Trinity Alps Wilderness. Elevation 3,000 feet. Stay limit 14 days. Open all year.

31 Big Flat

Location: 60 miles north of Weaverville.
Sites: 5 sites for tents and RVs up to 16 feet long.
Facilities: Tables, fire rings, vault toilets. No drinking water.
Fee per night: None.
Management: Shasta-Trinity National Forest, 530-623-2121.
Activities: Hiking.
Finding the campground: From Weaverville (about 40 miles west of Redding on California Highway 299), drive 38 miles northeast on California Highway 3, turn left (west) at the Coffee Creek Ranger Station onto County Road 104, and drive 22 miles.

About the campground: Deep within the Trinity Alps Wilderness, the campground offers an ideal base for day hikes and backpacking trips. Trails lead north, west, and south to lovely small lakes and abandoned gold mines. Elevation 5,000 feet. Stay limit 14 days. Open all year.

32 Trinity River

Location: 40 miles northeast of Weaverville.
Sites: 7 sites for tents and RVs up to 32 feet long.
Facilities: Tables, fire rings, drinking water (May through October only), vault toilets.
Fee per night: $8.
Management: Shasta-Trinity National Forest, 530-623-2121.
Activities: Fishing.
Finding the campground: From Weaverville (about 40 miles west of Redding on California Highway 299), drive 40 miles northeast on California Highway 3.

About the campground: Situated on the upper Trinity River, which offers fair fishing for small trout. Elevation 2,500 feet. Stay limit 14 days. Open all year.

33 Eagle Creek

Location: 45 miles northeast of Weaverville.
Sites: 17 sites for tents and RVs up to 27 feet long.
Facilities: Tables, fire rings, drinking water (except in winter), vault toilets.
Fee per night: $8.
Management: Shasta-Trinity National Forest, 530-623-2121.
Activities: Fishing.
Finding the campground: From Weaverville (about 40 miles west of Redding on California Highway 299), drive 45 miles northeast on California Highway 3.

About the campground: Situated at the confluence of Eagle Creek and the upper Trinity River, with fair fishing for small trout. Elevation 2,800 feet. Stay limit 14 days. Open all year.

34 Horse Flat

Location: 47 miles northeast of Weaverville.
Sites: 16 sites for tents and RVs up to 16 feet long.
Facilities: Tables, fire rings, vault toilets, hitching rails. No drinking water.
Fee per night: None.
Management: Shasta-Trinity National Forest, 530-623-2121.
Activities: Hiking, horseback riding.
Finding the campground: From Weaverville (about 40 miles west of Redding on California Highway 299), drive 45 miles northeast on California Highway 3, turn left onto Forest Road 36N27, and drive 2 miles.

About the campground: The Eagle Creek Trail begins at the campground, providing access to the northern part of the Trinity Alps Wilderness for day hikers, backpackers, and equestrians. Elevation 3,200 feet. Stay limit 14 days. Open from mid-May through October.

35 Trinity Unit: Mary Smith

Location: 2 miles north of Lewiston.
Sites: 18 sites for tents.
Facilities: Tables, fire rings, drinking water, flush and vault toilets.
Fee per night: $9.
Management: Shasta-Trinity National Forest, 530-623-2121.
Activities: Fishing, canoeing, kayaking, bird watching.
Finding the campground: From Lewiston (27 miles west of Redding via California Highway 299 and County Road 105), drive 2 miles north on CR 105.

About the campground: Situated on Lewiston Lake, this campground is small but in a beautiful setting south of Trinity Dam. Car top boats may be launched from the campground, and a boat ramp is located 3 miles north. There is a 10-mile-per-hour speed limit on the lake, which is stocked annually with more than 20,000 catchable-size rainbow, brown, and brook trout. Lewiston is a magnet for water birds and other birds and is a designated wildlife viewing area. Elevation 2,000 feet. Stay limit 14 days. Open from May through October.

36 Trinity Unit: Cooper Gulch

Location: 3 miles north of Lewiston.
Sites: 5 sites for tents and RVs up to 16 feet long.
Facilities: Tables, fire rings, drinking water, vault toilets. The facilities are wheelchair accessible. Boat ramp 2 miles north.
Fee per night: $10.
Management: Shasta-Trinity National Forest, 530-623-2121.
Activities: Fishing, canoeing, kayaking, bird watching.
Finding the campground: From Lewiston (27 miles west of Redding via California Highway 299 and County Road 105), drive 3 miles north on CR 105.

Whiskeytown-Shasta-Trinity National Recreation Area: Trinity Unit

Trinity Lake, also known as Clair Engle Lake, is the westernmost and second largest of the three major lakes that make up the Whiskeytown-Shasta-Trinity National Recreation Area. The Trinity Unit contains 24 public campgrounds, most of them either on the lake or a tributary stream. In addition, there are several private camping resorts and three full-service marinas. Boat rentals are available, including houseboats.

Trinity Lake occupies 17,000 acres of surface area at an elevation of 2,400 feet and is surrounded by scenic mountains. Fishing is varied, but the lake is noted particularly for smallmouth bass. Trout fishing is also good; each year the lake is stocked with 40,000 rainbows and 5,000 browns. Other catches include largemouth bass, bullhead, kokanee, and catfish. The Trinity Heritage National Scenic Byway begins at Weaverville and follows California Highway 3 along the western shore of the lake. Area campgrounds provide an excellent base from which to explore the beautiful Trinity Alps Wilderness, which lies to the west.

For car and RV campers who have boats and want to get away from the road-bound crowd for a day or so, Trinity Lake features four boat-in campgrounds. Three are on the southwestern arm of the lake, and one is farther northeast. They all have picnic tables, fire rings, and vault toilets. They have no drinking water, and no fee is charged. They are Ridgeville, 21 sites; Ridgeville Island, 3 sites; Mariners Roost, 7 sites; and Captains Point, 3 sites. From the first three, you have great views of the Trinity Alps.

About the campground: See Mary Smith Campground (number 35). Open from April through November.

37 Trinity Unit: Tunnel Rock

Location: 6 miles north of Lewiston.
Sites: 6 sites for tents and RVs up to 15 feet long.
Facilities: Tables, fire rings, vault toilets. No drinking water. Boat ramp 1 mile south.
Fee per night: $5.
Management: Shasta-Trinity National Forest, 530-623-2121.
Activities: Fishing, canoeing, kayaking, bird watching.
Finding the campground: From Lewiston (27 miles west of Redding via California Highway 299 and County Road 105), drive 6 miles north on CR 105.

About the campground: See Mary Smith Campground (number 35). Open all year.

38 Trinity Unit: Ackerman

Location: 7 miles north of Lewiston.
Sites: 66 sites for tents and RVs up to 40 feet long.
Facilities: Tables, fire rings, drinking water (April-November only), flush toilets, dump station. Boat ramp 2 miles south.
Fee per night: $10.
Management: Shasta-Trinity National Forest, 530-623-2121.
Activities: Fishing, canoeing, kayaking, bird watching.
Finding the campground: From Lewiston (27 miles west of Redding via California Highway 299 and County Road 105), drive 7 miles north on CR 105.

About the campground: See Mary Smith Campground (number 35). Open all year.

39 Trinity Unit: Jackass Springs

Location: 44 miles northwest of Redding.
Sites: 21 sites for tents and RVs up to 32 feet long.
Facilities: Tables, fire rings, vault toilets. No drinking water in the winter.
Fee per night: None.
Management: Shasta-Trinity National Forest, 530-623-2121.
Activities: Fishing, swimming.
Finding the campground: From the intersection of Interstate 5 and California Highway 299 at Redding, take CA 299 west for 17 miles, turn right (north) onto Trinity Mountain Road, and drive 14 miles. Turn right (north) onto East Side Road (County Road 106) and drive 11 miles, then turn right onto Delta Road and drive 2 miles.

About the campground: This is the only campground on the isolated eastern shore of the lake. It is situated in an attractive cove, and there is an island offshore. But the setting is affected by water drawdowns in the fall. Stay limit 14 days. Open all year.

40 Trinity Unit: Tannery Gulch

Location: 13 miles northeast of Weaverville.
Sites: 83 family sites, plus 4 double sites for tents and RVs up to 40 feet long.
Facilities: Tables, fire rings, drinking water, flush toilets, boat ramp.
Fee per night: $12, double sites $18. For reservations call 800-280-CAMP. There is a one-time reservation fee of $8.65.
Management: Shasta-Trinity National Forest, 530-623-2121.
Activities: Boating, fishing, swimming, waterskiing, hiking.
Finding the campground: From Weaverville (about 40 miles west of Redding on California Highway 299), drive 12 miles north on California Highway 3, turn right onto Tannery Gulch Road, and drive 1 mile.

About the campground: Situated on the southwest shore of Trinity Lake, with a good swimming beach nearby. A hiking trail follows the shoreline east from the campground. Elevation 2,400 feet. Stay limit 14 days. Open from May through September.

41 Trinity Unit: Stoney Point

Location: 15 miles northeast of Weaverville.
Sites: 22 sites for tents.
Facilities: Tables, fire rings, drinking water, flush toilets. Boat ramp half a mile northwest at Stuart Fork.
Fee per night: $10 from April through October, remaining months free.
Management: Shasta-Trinity National Forest, 530-623-2121.
Activities: Boating, fishing, swimming, waterskiing.
Finding the campground: From Weaverville (about 40 miles west of Redding on California Highway 299), drive 15 miles northeast on California Highway 3.

About the campground: Situated on the southwest shore of Trinity Lake, with a swimming beach nearby. Elevation 2,400 feet. Stay limit 14 days. Open all year.

42 Trinity Unit: Stoney Creek Group Camp

Location: 16 miles northeast of Weaverville.
Sites: 1 site for tents, accommodates up to 50 people.
Facilities: Tables, fire rings, drinking water, flush toilets. The facilities are wheelchair accessible. Boat ramp 1 mile west at Stuart Fork.
Fee per night: $50. Reservations are required; call 800-280-CAMP. There is a one-time reservation fee of $15.
Management: Shasta-Trinity National Forest, 530-623-2121.
Activities: Boating, fishing, swimming, waterskiing.
Finding the campground: From Weaverville (about 40 miles west of Redding on California Highway 299), drive 15.5 miles northeast on California Highway 3.

About the campground: Situated on the Stoney Creek Arm of Trinity Lake, with a swimming beach nearby. Elevation 2,400 feet. Stay limit 14 days. Open from May through September.

43 Trinity Unit: Fawn Group Camp

Location: 17 miles northeast of Weaverville.
Sites: 1 site for tents and RVs up to 37 feet long, accommodates up to 300 people.
Facilities: Tables, fire rings, drinking water, flush toilets. Boat ramp 2 miles west at Stuart Fork.
Fee per night: $60. Reservations required; call 800-280-CAMP. There is a one-time reservation fee of $15.
Management: Shasta-Trinity National Forest, 530-623-2121.
Activities: Boating, fishing, swimming, waterskiing.

Finding the campground: From Weaverville (about 40 miles west of Redding on California Highway 299), drive 16.5 miles northeast on California Highway 3.

About the campground: Situated near the shore of Trinity Lake, with a swimming beach nearby. Elevation 2,400 feet. Stay limit 14 days. Open from May through September.

44 Trinity Unit: Bushy Tail Group Camp

Location: 18 miles northeast of Weaverville.
Sites: 30 sites for tents and RVs up to 20 feet long.
Facilities: Tables, fire rings, drinking water, flush toilets. Boat ramp nearby.
Fee per night: $30. Reservations required; call 800-280-CAMP. There is a one-time reservation fee of $15.
Management: Shasta-Trinity National Forest, 530-623-2121.
Activities: Boating, fishing, swimming, waterskiing.
Finding the campground: From Weaverville (about 40 miles west of Redding on California Highway 299), drive 17.5 miles northeast on California Highway 3.

About the campground: Situated about half a mile from the shore of Trinity Lake, with a swimming beach nearby. Elevation 2,400 feet. Stay limit 14 days. Open from May through September.

45 Trinity Unit: Minersville

Location: 19 miles northeast of Weaverville.
Sites: 21 sites for tents and RVs up to 18 feet long.
Facilities: Tables, fire rings, drinking water (April-October only), flush toilets, boat ramp.
Fee per night: $10-$17 from April through October, remaining months free.
Management: Shasta-Trinity National Forest, 530-623-2121.
Activities: Boating, fishing, swimming, waterskiing.
Finding the campground: From Weaverville (about 40 miles west of Redding on California Highway 299), drive 18.5 miles northeast on California Highway 3.

About the campground: Situated close to the shore of Trinity Lake, with a swimming beach nearby. Elevation 2,400 feet. Stay limit 14 days. Open all year.

46 Trinity Unit: Clark Springs

Location: 19 miles northeast of Weaverville.
Sites: 21 sites for tents and RVs up to 20 feet long.
Facilities: Tables, fire rings, drinking water, flush toilets. Boat ramp nearby.
Fee per night: $8.
Management: Shasta-Trinity National Forest, 530-623-2121.

Activities: Boating, fishing, swimming, waterskiing.
Finding the campground: From Weaverville (about 40 miles west of Redding on California Highway 299), drive 19 miles northeast on California Highway 3.

About the campground: Situated on the shore of Trinity Lake, with a swimming beach nearby. Elevation 2,400 feet. Stay limit 14 days. Open from April through mid-September.

47 Trinity Unit: Hayward Flat

Location: 24 miles northeast of Weaverville.
Sites: 94 single, 4 double sites for tents and RVs up to 40 feet long.
Facilities: Tables, fire rings, drinking water, flush toilets, swimming beach.
Fee per night: $12, double sites $18. For reservations call 800-280-CAMP. There is a one-time reservation fee of $8.65.
Management: Shasta-Trinity National Forest, 530-623-2121.
Activities: Boating, fishing, swimming, waterskiing.
Finding the campground: From Weaverville (about 40 miles west of Redding on California Highway 299), drive 22 miles northeast on California Highway 3, turn right (east) onto Forest Road 35N26Y, and drive 2 miles.

About the campground: Situated in an attractive spot on the shore of Trinity Lake, with its own private swimming beach. Elevation 2,400 feet. Stay limit 14 days. Open from mid-May through mid-September.

48 Trinity Unit: Alpine View

Location: 27 miles northeast of Weaverville.
Sites: 66 sites, including 4 double sites, for tents and RVs up to 32 feet long.
Facilities: Tables, fire rings, drinking water, flush toilets. Boat ramp half a mile north.
Fee per night: $12 single, $18 double site.
Management: Shasta-Trinity National Forest, 530-623-2121.
Activities: Boating, fishing, swimming, waterskiing.
Finding the campground: From Weaverville (about 40 miles west of Redding on California Highway 299), drive 25 miles northeast on California Highway 3, turn right (east) onto County Road 160, and drive 2 miles.

About the campground: As the name implies, this shoreline campground has great views across the water toward the Trinity Alps. Elevation 2,400 feet. Stay limit 14 days. Open from mid-May through mid-September.

49 Steelbridge

Location: 9 miles south of Weaverville.
Sites: 9 sites for tents and RVs.
Facilities: Tables, fire rings, vault toilets. No drinking water.
Fee per night: None.

Management: Bureau of Land Management, 530-224-2100.
Activities: Fishing, swimming, paddling.
Finding the campground: From Weaverville, drive south on California Highway 299 for 7 miles, turn left onto Steel Bridge Road, and drive 2 miles.

About the campground: Situated on the Trinity River in a grove of ponderosa pine, oak, and willow. Fishing is good for salmon in summer and steelhead in late fall. The Trinity is a designated Wild and Scenic River, and experienced rafters and kayakers will enjoy this stretch. Elevation 1,700 feet. Stay limit 14 days. Open all year.

50 Douglas City

Location: 7 miles south of Weaverville.
Sites: 18 sites for tents and RVs.
Facilities: Tables, fire rings, drinking water, flush and vault toilets, beach.
Fee per night: $8.
Management: Bureau of Land Management, 530-224-2100.
Activities: Fishing, swimming, paddling.
Finding the campground: From Weaverville, drive south on California Highway 299 for 6 miles, turn right onto Steiner Flat Road, and drive half a mile.

About the campground: Situated on the bank of the Trinity amid ponderosa pine, Douglas fir, and oak trees, with good access to the river. Fishing is good for salmon in summer and steelhead in late fall. The Trinity is a designated Wild and Scenic River, and experienced rafters and kayakers will enjoy this stretch. Elevation 1,600 feet. Stay limit 14 days. Open from May through October.

51 Junction City

Location: 10 miles west of Weaverville.
Sites: 22 sites for tents and RVs.
Facilities: Tables, fire rings, drinking water, vault toilets.
Fee per night: $7.
Management: Bureau of Land Management, 530-224-2100.
Activities: Fishing, swimming, paddling.
Finding the campground: From Weaverville, drive west on California Highway 299 for 10 miles.

About the campground: Situated on the banks of the Trinity River amid ponderosa pine and madrone. Fishing is good for salmon in summer and steelhead in late fall. The Trinity is a designated Wild and Scenic River, and experienced rafters and kayakers will enjoy this stretch. Elevation 1,500 feet. Stay limit 14 days. Open from May through October.

52 Ripstein

Location: 21 miles northwest of Weaverville.
Sites: 10 sites for tents.

Facilities: Tables, fire rings, vault toilets. No drinking water.
Fee per night: None.
Management: Shasta-Trinity National Forest, 530-623-6106.
Activities: Hiking.
Finding the campground: From Weaverville, drive west on California Highway 299 for 8 miles; at Junction City turn right (north) onto County Road 401 (Canyon Creek Road) and drive 13 miles.

About the campground: Used primarily as a base for day hikes and backpack trips into the Trinity Alps Wilderness, this campground is half a mile south of the Canyon Creek trailhead. Trails lead to Little Granite Peak, Sawtooth Mountain, and the Canyon Creek Lakes. Elevation 2,600 feet. Stay limit 14 days. Open all year.

53 Pigeon Point

Location: 14 miles west of Weaverville.
Sites: 35 sites for tents and RVs up to 25 feet long.
Facilities: Tables, fire rings, vault toilets, beach. No drinking water. The facilities are wheelchair accessible.
Fee per night: $6.
Management: Shasta-Trinity National Forest, 530-623-6106.
Activities: Fishing, swimming, paddling.
Finding the campground: From Weaverville, drive west on California Highway 299 for 14 miles.

About the campground: Pigeon Point is on the Trinity River, a designated Wild and Scenic River, and experienced rafters and kayakers will enjoy this stretch. Fishing is good for salmon in summer and steelhead in late fall. Although there is a nice beach, the campground itself is across the highway from the river. Elevation 1,100 feet. Stay limit 14 days. Open from May through October.

54 Hobo Gulch

Location: 29 miles northwest of Weaverville.
Sites: 10 sites for tents and RVs.
Facilities: Tables, fire rings, vault toilets. No drinking water.
Fee per night: None.
Management: Shasta-Trinity National Forest, 530-623-6106.
Activities: Hiking.
Finding the campground: From Weaverville, drive west on California Highway 299 for 14 miles, turn right (north) at Helena onto County Road 421, and drive 15 miles.

About the campground: Surrounded on three sides by the Trinity Alps Wilderness, the campground serves primarily as a base for hiking and backpacking trips. Trails lead north from the campground toward the Salmon Mountains. Elevation 3,000 feet. Stay limit 14 days. Open all year.

55 Big Flat

Location: 19 miles west of Weaverville.
Sites: 10 sites for tents and RVs up to 25 feet long.
Facilities: Tables, fire rings, drinking water, vault toilets.
Fee per night: $8.
Management: Shasta-Trinity National Forest, 530-623-6106.
Activities: Fishing, swimming, paddling.
Finding the campground: From Weaverville, drive west on California Highway 299 for 19 miles.

About the campground: Big Flat is on the Trinity River, a designated Wild and Scenic River, and experienced rafters and kayakers will enjoy this stretch. Fishing is good for salmon in summer and steelhead in late fall. Elevation 1,300 feet. Stay limit 14 days. Open all year.

56 Skunk Point Group Camp

Location: 20 miles west of Weaverville.
Sites: 2 group sites for tents and RVs, accommodate up to 30 people each.
Facilities: Tables, fire rings, drinking water, vault toilets.
Fee per night: $20 for up to 10 people, $2 per person thereafter. Reservations required; call 800-280-CAMP. There is a one-time reservation fee of $15.
Management: Shasta-Trinity National Forest, 530-623-6106.
Activities: Fishing, swimming, paddling.
Finding the campground: From Weaverville, drive west on California Highway 299 for 20 miles.

About the campground: Skunk Point is on the Trinity River, a designated Wild and Scenic River, and experienced rafters and kayakers will enjoy this stretch. Fishing is good for salmon in summer and steelhead in late fall. Elevation 1,200 feet. Stay limit 14 days. Open all year.

57 Big Bar

Location: 22 miles west of Weaverville.
Sites: 3 sites for tents.
Facilities: Tables, fire rings, drinking water, vault toilets.
Fee per night: None.
Management: Shasta-Trinity National Forest, 530-623-6106.
Activities: Fishing, swimming, paddling.
Finding the campground: From Weaverville, drive west on California Highway 299 for 22 miles.

About the campground: Big Bar offers easy access to the Trinity River, a designated Wild and Scenic River. Experienced rafters and kayakers will enjoy this stretch, and fishing is good for salmon in summer and steelhead in late fall. Elevation 1,200 feet. Stay limit 14 days. Open all year.

58 Hayden Flat

Location: 29 miles west of Weaverville.
Sites: 35 sites for tents and RVs up to 25 feet long.
Facilities: Tables, fire rings, drinking water, vault toilets. The facilities are wheelchair accessible.
Fee per night: $10 river sites, $8 other.
Management: Shasta-Trinity National Forest, 530-623-6106.
Activities: Fishing, swimming, paddling.
Finding the campground: From Weaverville, drive west on California 299 for 29 miles.

About the campground: Hayden Flat is divided in two, with some sites along the Trinity River and some across CA 299 in a small grove of trees. The Trinity is a Wild and Scenic River, and experienced rafters and kayakers will enjoy this stretch. Fishing is good for salmon in summer and steelhead in late fall. Campers here have easy access to the river, including a swimming beach. Elevation 1,200 feet. Stay limit 14 days. Open all year.

59 Burnt Ranch

Location: 38 miles west of Weaverville.
Sites: 16 sites for tents and RVs up to 25 feet long.
Facilities: Tables, fire rings, drinking water, vault toilets. The facilities are wheelchair accessible.
Fee per night: $8.
Management: Shasta-Trinity National Forest, 530-623-6106.
Activities: Fishing, swimming, paddling.
Finding the campground: From Weaverville, drive west on California Highway 299 for 38 miles.

About the campground: Burnt Ranch is situated on a bluff above the Wild and Scenic Trinity River. Experienced rafters and kayakers will enjoy this stretch of the river, and fishing is good for salmon in summer and steelhead in late fall. Elevation 1,000 feet. Stay limit 14 days. Open all year.

60 Denny

Location: 52 miles northwest of Weaverville.
Sites: 16 sites for tents and RVs up to 25 feet long.
Facilities: Tables, fire rings, drinking water, vault toilets.
Fee per night: None.
Management: Shasta-Trinity National Forest, 530-623-6106.
Activities: Hiking, fishing.
Finding the campground: From Weaverville, drive west on California Highway 299 for 39 miles, turn right (north) onto County Road 402, and drive 13 miles.

About the campground: Denny is situated on the New River, a designated Wild and Scenic River like the Trinity, which it flows into. Fishing is fair for small trout. The New River Trail, which leads into the Trinity Alps Wilderness, begins 6 miles north of the campground. Elevation 1,400 feet. Stay limit 14 days. Open all year.

61 Big Slide

Location: 24 miles northwest of Hayfork.
Sites: 8 sites for tents and RVs.
Facilities: Tables, fire rings, vault toilets. No drinking water.
Fee per night: None.
Management: Shasta-Trinity National Forest, 530-628-5227.
Activities: Fishing.
Finding the campground: From the intersection of California Highway 3 and County Road 301 in Hayfork (70 miles west of Redding on CA 3), drive about 19 miles northwest on CR 301 to Hyampom, turn right onto Country Road 311, and drive 5 miles.

About the campground: Situated on the South Fork of the Trinity River, this campground has little to recommend it except isolation. Fishing for small trout is only fair. Elevation 1,250 feet. Stay limit 14 days. Open all year; not serviced in winter.

62 Slide Creek

Location: 25 miles northwest of Hayfork.
Sites: 5 sites for tents and RVs.
Facilities: Tables, fire rings, vault toilets. No drinking water.
Fee per night: None.
Management: Shasta-Trinity National Forest, 530-628-5227.
Activities: Fishing.
Finding the campground: From the intersection of California Highway 3 and County Road 301 in Hayfork (70 miles west of Redding on CA 3), drive about 19 miles northwest on CR 301 to Hyampom, turn right onto Country Road 311, and drive 5.5 miles.

About the campground: See Big Slide Campground (number 61).

63 Shiell Gulch

Location: 12 miles southeast of Hayfork.
Sites: 5 sites for tents and RVs.
Facilities: Tables, fire rings, vault toilets. No drinking water.
Fee per night: None.
Management: Shasta-Trinity National Forest, 530-628-5227.
Activities: None.
Finding the campground: From the intersection of California Highway 3 and County Road 301 in Hayfork (70 miles west of Redding on CA 3), drive 5

miles east on CA 3, turn right (south) onto Country Road 302, and drive about 7 miles.

About the campground: Situated on the banks of a small stream, the campground offers seclusion and not much else. Elevation 2,600 feet. Stay limit 14 days. Open all year; not serviced in winter.

64 Philpot

Location: 8 miles south of Hayfork.
Sites: 6 sites for tents and RVs.
Facilities: Tables, fire rings, vault toilets. No drinking water.
Fee per night: None.
Management: Shasta-Trinity National Forest, 530-628-5227.
Activities: None.
Finding the campground: From the intersection of California Highway 3 and County Road 301 in Hayfork (70 miles west of Redding on CA 3), drive 6 miles south on CA 3, turn right (west) onto the road to Plummer Peak Lookout (initially Country Road 353) and drive 1.5 miles.

About the campground: Situated near a small stream, the campground offers little except solitude. Elevation 2,600 feet. Stay limit 14 days. Open all year; not serviced in winter.

65 Hell Gate

Location: 19 miles southwest of Hayfork.
Sites: 17 sites for tents and RVs up to 15 feet long.
Facilities: Tables, fire rings, drinking water, vault toilets. The facilities are wheelchair accessible.
Fee per night: $6.
Management: Shasta-Trinity National Forest, 530-628-5227.
Activities: Fishing, swimming, hiking, paddling.
Finding the campground: From the intersection of California Highway 3 and County Road 301 in Hayfork (70 miles west of Redding on CA 3), drive south 11 miles on CA 3, turn right (west) onto California Highway 36, and drive 8 miles.

About the campground: Situated in an attractive location on the South Fork of the Trinity River, with a beach and easy river access. The South Fork National Recreation Trail begins at the campground. Elevation 2,300 feet. Stay limit 14 days. Open all year; not serviced in winter.

66 Scotts Flat

Location: 20 miles southwest of Hayfork.
Sites: 10 sites for tents and RVs up to 20 feet long.
Facilities: Tables, fire rings, vault toilets. No drinking water.
Fee per night: None.

Management: Shasta-Trinity National Forest, 530-628-5227.
Activities: Fishing, swimming, hiking, paddling.
Finding the campground: From the intersection of California Highway 3 and County Road 301 in Hayfork (70 miles west of Redding on CA 3), drive south 11 miles on CA 3, turn right (west) onto California Highway 36, and drive 8.5 miles.

About the campground: See Hell Gate Campground (number 65).

67 Forest Glen

Location: 20 miles southwest of Hayfork.
Sites: 15 sites for tents and RVs up to 15 feet long.
Facilities: Tables, fire rings, drinking water, vault toilets. The facilities are wheelchair accessible.
Fee per night: $6.
Management: Shasta-Trinity National Forest, 530-628-5227.
Activities: Fishing, hiking.
Finding the campground: From the intersection of California Highway 3 and County Road 301 in Hayfork (70 miles west of Redding on CA 3), drive south 11 miles on CA 3, turn right (west) onto California Highway 36, and drive 9 miles.

About the campground: Situated near the South Fork of the Trinity River. Elevation 2,300 feet. Stay limit 14 days. Open all year; not serviced in winter.

68 Mad River

Location: 39 miles southwest of Hayfork.
Sites: 40 sites for tents and RVs up to 30 feet long.
Facilities: Tables, fire rings, drinking water, vault toilets.
Fee per night: $10.
Management: Six Rivers National Forest, 707-574-6233.
Activities: Fishing.
Finding the campground: From the intersection of California Highway 3 and County Road 301 in Hayfork (70 miles west of Redding on CA 3), drive south 11 miles on CA 3, turn right (west) onto California Highway 36, and drive 23 miles. Turn left onto Lower Mad River Road and drive 5 miles.

About the campground: Situated on the banks of the Mad River. Although the river is famous for its steelhead fishing, the campground is too far upstream for good fishing. A better option is Ruth Lake (numbers 69, 70). Elevation 2,600 feet. Stay limit 14 days. Open all year.

69 Ruth Lake: Fir Cove

Location: 45 miles southwest of Hayfork.
Sites: 19 single sites and 3 group sites for tents and RVs.
Facilities: Tables, fire rings, drinking water, vault toilets.

Fee per night: $10, group sites $35-$45. Group sites must be reserved; call the number below.
Management: Six Rivers National Forest, 707-574-6233.
Activities: Fishing, swimming, boating, waterskiing.
Finding the campground: From the intersection of California Highway 3 and County Road 301 in Hayfork (70 miles west of Redding on CA 3), drive south 11 miles on CA 3, turn right (west) onto California Highway 36, and drive 23 miles. Turn left onto Lower Mad River Road and drive 11 miles.

About the campground: Fir Cove is on the eastern shore of Ruth Lake, which is noted for black bass. Catchable-size rainbow trout are stocked annually, and there is a resident crappie population. The campground is open on weekends (from 2 P.M. Friday to 2 P.M. Monday) for individual camping only. The rest of the week it operates as a group camp only. Elevation 2,800 feet. Stay limit 14 days. Open from May 22 through September 13.

70 Ruth Lake: Bailey Canyon

Location: 45 miles southwest of Hayfork.
Sites: 25 sites for tents and RVs up to 22 feet long.
Facilities: Tables, fire rings, drinking water, vault toilets.
Fee per night: $10.
Management: Six Rivers National Forest, 707-574-6233.
Activities: Fishing, swimming, boating, waterskiing.
Finding the campground: From the intersection of California Highway 3 and County Road 301 in Hayfork (70 miles west of Redding on CA 3), drive south 11 miles on CA 3, turn right (west) onto California Highway 36, and drive 23 miles. Turn left onto Lower Mad River Road and drive a little over 11 miles.

About the campground: See Fir Cove Campground (number 69). Stay limit 14 days. Open from May 22 through September 13.

71 Deer Lick Springs

Location: 37 miles southeast of Hayfork.
Sites: 13 sites for tents and RVs.
Facilities: Tables, fire rings, vault toilets. No drinking water.
Fee per night: None.
Management: Shasta-Trinity National Forest, 530-352-4211.
Activities: Hiking, fishing, hot springs.
Finding the campground: From the intersection of California Highway 3 and County Road 301 in Hayfork (70 miles west of Redding on CA 3), drive south 11 miles on CA 3, turn left (east) onto California Highway 36, and continue about 16 miles. Turn left (north) onto Harrison Gulch Road and drive about 10 miles.

About the campground: Situated on Browns Creek adjacent to Deerlick Springs Resort, which has hot springs pools open to campers for a fee. Trails lead in several directions from the campground, including to Sugarloaf Peak (3 miles). Elevation 3,100 feet. Stay limit 14 days. Open all year; not serviced in winter.

72 White Rock

Location: 33 miles south of Hayfork.
Sites: 3 sites for tents.
Facilities: Tables, fire rings, vault toilets. No drinking water.
Fee per night: None.
Management: Shasta-Trinity National Forest, 530-352-4211.
Activities: None.
Finding the campground: From the intersection of California Highway 3 and County Road 301 in Hayfork (70 miles west of Redding on CA 3), drive south 11 miles on CA 3, turn left (east) onto California Highway 36, and continue about 7 miles. Turn right (south) onto Forest Road 30 and drive 8 miles. Then turn left onto Forest Road 35 and drive 7 miles.

About the campground: There is nothing at this campground to make the long, winding drive worthwhile. Elevation 4,800 feet. Stay limit 14 days. Open all year; not serviced in winter.

73 Basin Gulch

Location: 29 miles southeast of Hayfork.
Sites: 13 sites for tents and RVs up to 20 feet long.
Facilities: Tables, fire rings, vault toilets. No drinking water.
Fee per night: None.
Management: Shasta-Trinity National Forest, 530-352-4211.
Activities: None.
Finding the campground: From the intersection of California Highway 3 and County Road 301 in Hayfork (70 miles west of Redding on CA 3), drive south 11 miles on CA 3, turn left (east) onto California Highway 36, and proceed about 17 miles to Yolla Bolla Ranger Station. Turn right onto Forest Road 28N10 and drive 1 mile.

About the campground: Situated near a small creek with sparse vegetation, this rarely used campground may appeal to those seeking solitude. Elevation 2,700 feet. Stay limit 14 days. Open all year; not serviced in winter.

74 Beegum Gorge

Location: 37 miles southeast of Hayfork.
Sites: 2 sites for tents and RVs.
Facilities: Tables, fire rings, vault toilets. No drinking water.
Fee per night: None.
Management: Shasta-Trinity National Forest, 530-352-4211.
Activities: Hiking.

Finding the campground: From the intersection of California Highway 3 and County Road 301 in Hayfork (70 miles west of Redding on CA 3), drive south 11 miles on CA 3, turn left (east) onto California Highway 36, and continue about 21 miles to Platina. Turn right onto Forest Road 29N06 and drive 5 miles. The road is not recommended for trailers.

About the campground: Situated in dry country with sparse vegetation, Beegum Gorge has little to make the long trip there worthwhile. A trail leads west from the campground along Beegum Creek. Elevation 2,200 feet. Stay limit 14 days. Open all year; not serviced in winter.

75 Tomhead Saddle

Location: 36 miles west of Red Bluff.
Sites: 5 sites for tents and RVs.
Facilities: Tables, fire rings, vault toilets, corral. No drinking water.
Fee per night: None.
Management: Shasta-Trinity National Forest, 530-352-4211.
Activities: Hiking, horseback riding.
Finding the campground: From the intersection of Interstate 5 and California Highway 36 in Red Bluff, drive west 13 miles on CA 36, turn left onto Cannon Road, and drive about 5 miles. Turn right (west) onto Pettijohn Road and drive about 15 miles. Then turn left onto Forest Road 27N06 and drive 3 miles.

About the campground: This campground will mainly interest equestrians and hikers. Trails extend west from the campground into the Yolla Bolly-Middle Eel Wilderness; several loop back to camp. The area is dry and sparsely vegetated and better suited to horses than hikers. Elevation 5,600 feet. Stay limit 14 days. Open all year; not serviced in winter.

76 Reading Island

Location: 21 miles south of Reading.
Sites: 9 sites for tents and RVs up to 30 feet long.
Facilities: Tables, fire rings, drinking water, vault toilets. Boat ramp nearby. The facilities are wheelchair accessible.
Fee per night: $5.
Management: Bureau of Land Management, 530-224-2100.
Activities: Fishing, swimming, boating, bird watching.
Finding the campground: From the intersection of California Highway 44 and Interstate 5 in Redding, drive south 16 miles on I-5, turn left (east) onto Balls Ferry Road, and drive 5 miles.

About the campground: Situated on the banks of the Sacramento River, with fishing for trout, salmon, steelhead, and bass. Swimmers should take care during periods of high water. Stay limit 14 days. Open all year.

77 Lake Red Bluff

Location: 3 miles southeast of Red Bluff.
Sites: 25 sites for tents and RVs.
Facilities: Tables, fire rings, drinking water (except in winter), showers, flush/vault toilets, boat ramps. The facilities are wheelchair accessible.
Fee per night: $10.
Management: Mendocino National Forest, 530-824-5196.
Activities: Fishing, swimming, boating, waterskiing, bird watching.
Finding the campground: From the intersection of Interstate 5 and California Highway 36 in Red Bluff, drive about 100 yards east on CA 36 to the first turnoff, which is Sale Lane. Turn south and travel about half a mile to the end of the road.

About the campground: This seasonal lake on the Sacramento River is a popular summer water sports location, heavily used due to its proximity to town. In early spring, a diversion dam opens to allow salmon to migrate upriver, and the lake disappears for the season. Stay limit 14 days. Open all year.

78 Woodson Bridge State Recreation Area

Location: 26 miles south of Red Bluff.
Sites: 41 individual sites, plus 5 group sites for tents and RVs up to 31 feet long.
Facilities: Tables, fire rings, drinking water, showers, flush toilets, dump station, playground. Boat ramp nearby. The facilities are wheelchair accessible.
Fee per night: $14, group sites $60. For reservations call 800-444-7275. There is a one-time reservation fee of $7.50.
Management: California Department of Parks and Recreation, 530-839-2112.
Activities: Fishing, boating, swimming, hiking.
Finding the campground: From the intersection of Interstate 5 and California Highway 99 in Red Bluff, take CA 99 south for 24 miles, turn right (west) onto South Avenue (County Road A9), and drive 2 miles.

About the campground: Situated in an attractive oak grove on the banks of the Sacramento River, this campground is just a short walk away from a gravel swimming beach. Shad, catfish, striped and largemouth bass, steelhead, and bluegill are all possible catches in the river. A short nature loop trail begins at the campground. Stay limit 15 days from June through September, 30 days from October through May. Open all year.

79 Black Butte Lake: Buckhorn

Location: 40 miles southwest of Red Bluff.
Sites: 65 improved sites, 20 unimproved sites, plus 1 group site for tents and RVs up to 35 feet long.
Facilities: Tables, fire rings, drinking water, flush toilets, showers, dump station, boat ramp, fish-cleaning station, playground, beach.

Fee per night: $12 improved, $10 unimproved. Group site $75. Reservations required for the group site; call the number below.
Management: U.S. Army Corps of Engineers, 530-865-4781.
Activities: Fishing, swimming, boating, hiking.
Finding the campground: From the intersection of California Highway 36 and Interstate 5 in Red Bluff, drive south on I-5 for 27 miles, take the Black Butte Lake exit, and drive northwest 12 miles on Newville Road. Turn left onto Buckhorn Road and drive 1 mile.

About the campground: Buckhorn is situated on the north shore of Black Butte Lake, which is 7 miles long, covers a surface area of almost 4,500 acres, and has 40 miles of shoreline. Fishing is best in the spring, and catches include crappie, bass, catfish, and bluegill. The lake is subject to heavy water drawdowns in summer and fall. Summers are usually hot. Three self-guided nature trails are located at different parts of the lake. Stay limit 14 days. Open all year.

80 Black Butte Lake: Orland Buttes

Location: 40 miles southwest of Red Bluff.
Sites: 35 sites, plus 1 group site, for tents and RVs up to 35 feet long.
Facilities: Tables, fire rings, drinking water, flush toilets, showers, dump station, boat ramp, fish-cleaning station.
Fee per night: $12. Group site $50. Reservation required for group site; call the number below.
Management: U.S. Army Corps of Engineers, 530-865-4781.
Activities: Fishing, swimming, boating, hiking.
Finding the campground: From the intersection of California Highway 36 and Interstate 5 in Red Bluff, drive south on I-5 for 27 miles, take the Black Butte Lake exit, and drive northwest 12 miles on Newville Road. Turn left onto Buckhorn Road and drive 1 mile. Orland Buttes is adjacent to Buckhorn Campground (above).

About the campground: See Buckhorn Campground (number 79). Open from April through September.

81 Whitlock

Location: 55 miles southwest of Red Bluff.
Sites: 3 sites for tents and RVs.
Facilities: Tables, fire rings, grill, drinking water, vault toilet.
Fee per night: None.
Management: Mendocino National Forest, 530-824-5196.
Activities: Hiking.
Finding the campground: From the intersection of California Highway 36 and Interstate 5 in Red Bluff, drive 18 miles south on I-5, take the Corning exit, and drive west on Corning Road for 21 miles to Paskenta. Drive west on Forest Road 23N01 (also signed Forest Road M2) for about 15 miles, turn right onto Forest Road 24N41, and drive about 1 mile.

About the campground: A small, quiet campground in a grove of large oaks and ponderosa pines. Elevation 4,300 feet. Stay limit 14 days. Open from June through October.

82 Rocky Cabin

Location: 27 miles northwest of Paskenta.
Sites: 3 sites for tents and RVs.
Facilities: Tables, fire rings, grills, vault toilet. No drinking water.
Fee per night: None.
Management: Mendocino National Forest, 530-824-5196.
Activities: Hiking.
Finding the campground: From Paskenta, drive west for 27 miles on Forest Road M2. A campground sign will be on the right.

About the campground: With a long, winding approach via dirt road, this camp has little to offer except solitude and is hardly worth the effort. Elevation 6,250 feet. Stay limit 14 days. Open from June through October.

83 Three Prong

Location: 25 miles west of Paskenta.
Sites: 6 sites for tents and RV.
Facilities: Tables, fire rings, drinking water, vault toilet.
Fee per night: None.
Management: Mendocino National Forest, 530-824-5196.
Activities: Hiking.
Finding the campground: From Paskenta, drive west on Forest Road 23N01 (also signed FR M2), turn left onto Forest Road 24N13, to the campground. The route is well marked.

About the campground: Situated in a grove of fir and pine trees along the edge of a large meadow. Elevation 5,800 feet. Stay limit 14 days. Open from June through October.

84 Kingsley Glade

Location: 22 miles west of Paskenta.
Sites: 6 sites for tents and RVs.
Facilities: Tables, fire rings, drinking water, vault toilets, corral, hitching posts.
Fee per night: None.
Management: Mendocino National Forest, 530-824-5196.
Activities: Hiking, horseback riding.
Finding the campground: From Paskenta, drive west on Forest Road 23N01 (also signed Forest Road M2), turn left onto Forest Road 24N01 to the campground. The route is well marked.

About the campground: Situated in forest at the edge of a meadow, with riding trails leading from camp. Thomes Creek, located about 5 road miles from the camp, is a popular fishing and swimming spot. Elevation 4,500 feet. Stay limit 14 days. Open from June through October.

85 Wells Cabin

Location: 33 miles west of Paskenta.
Sites: 25 sites for tents.
Facilities: Tables, fire rings, stoves, drinking water, vault toilets.
Fee per night: None.
Management: Mendocino National Forest, 530-824-5196.
Activities: Hiking.
Finding the campground: From Paskenta, drive west for about 30 miles on Forest Road 23N02, turn right (north) onto Forest Road 23N69, and drive about 3 miles.

About the campground: Situated in a red fir forest, with beautiful high-elevation scenery. Nearby Anthony Peak Lookout provides excellent views all the way to the Pacific Ocean on a clear day. Elevation 6,300 feet. Stay limit 14 days. Open from July through October.

MODOC AREA

Most of this area lies within the borders of the Modoc National Forest, 1.6 million acres of varied terrain that includes meadows, wetlands, forests, and lava fields. The national forest shelters more than 300 species of wildlife, including pronghorn antelope, wild horses and burros, and bald eagles.

The Medicine Lake Shield Volcano, about 10 miles south of Lava Beds National Monument, is one of North America's most unusual geological features. At about 20 miles in diameter, it is the largest volcano in California. Its gently sloping profile hides the fact that, in mass, it is larger than nearby Mount Shasta.

This sprawling area northeast of California Highway 89 contains extensive lava flows, cinder cones, pumice deposits, and lava tubes. Scenic attractions include Lava Beds National Monument, Giant Crater, Tilted Rocks, and Burnt Lava Flows.

1 Lava Beds National Monument: Indian Well

Location: 48 miles northwest of Canby.
Sites: 40 sites for tents and RVs, plus 1 group site for up to 40 people.
Facilities: Tables, fire rings, grills, drinking water (except in winter), flush toilets. The facilities are wheelchair accessible.
Fee per night: $10 summer, $6 winter. Group site $30-$40, must be reserved by calling the number below.

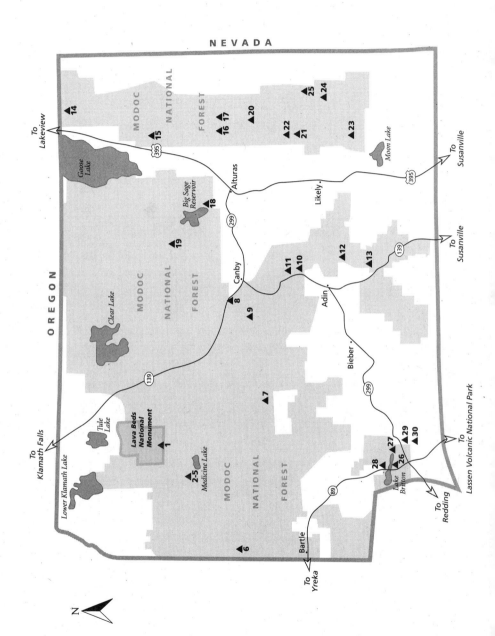

MODOC AREA CAMPGROUNDS

		Group sites	RV sites	Total sites	Max. RV length	Hookups	Toilets	Showers	Drinking water	Dump station	Pets	Wheelchair	Recreation	Fee ($)	Season	Can reserve	Length of stay
1	Lava Beds National Monument	•	•	41			F		•		•	•	H	6–40		•	14

Medicine Lake (2–5)

		Group sites	RV sites	Total sites	Max. RV length	Hookups	Toilets	Showers	Drinking water	Dump station	Pets	Wheelchair	Recreation	Fee ($)	Season	Can reserve	Length of stay
2	Hemlock		•	19	22		V		•		•		HS FB	7	July–October		14
3	A. H. Hogue		•	24	22		V		•		•		HS FB	7	July–October		14
4	Modoc		•	22	22		V		•		•		HS FB	7	July–October		14
5	Headquarters		•	8	22		V		•		•		HS FB	7	July–October		14
6	Harris Spring		•	15	32		V		•		•		H		June–October		14
7	Lava Camp		•	12	32		V				•		H		May–October		14
8	Howard's Gulch		•	11	22		V		•		•	•	H		May–October		14
9	Cottonwood Flat		•	10	22		V		•		•				June–October		14
10	Lower Rush Creek		•	10	22		V		•		•		F	5	May–October		14
11	Upper Rush Creek		•	13	22		V		•		•		F	4	May–October		14
12	Ash Creek		•	7	22		V				•		F		May–October		14
13	Willow Creek		•	8	32		V		•		•	•	F	5	May–October		14
14	Cave Lake		•	6	16		V		•		•		SFB		July–October		14
15	Plum Valley		•	7	16		V				•		F		June–October		14
16	Cedar Pass		•	17	16		V				•				May–October		14
17	Stowe Reservoir		•	8	20		V		•		•				May–October		14
18	Big Sage Reservoir		•	6	22		V				•		FBL		May–October		14
19	Reservoir C		•	6	22		V				•		F		May–October		14

		Group sites	RV sites	Total sites	Max. RV length	Hookups	Toilets	Showers	Drinking water	Dump station	Pets	Wheelchair	Recreation	Fee ($)	Season	Can reserve	Length of stay
20	Pepperdine		•	5	15		V		•		•		HR		July–October		14
21	Mill Creek Falls		•	19	22		V		•		•		H	5	June–October		14
22	Soup Spring		•	14	22		V		•		•		HR		June–October		14
23	Blue Lake		•	48	32		V		•		•	•	HSF BL	6	June–October		14
24	Patterson		•	5	16		V		•		•		HR		July–October		14
25	Emerson		•	4	16		V				•		HF		July–October		14
26	McArthur–Burney Falls Memorial State Park		•	128	32		F	•	•	•	•	•	HSF BL	12–17		•	15/30
27	Dusty	•	•	7	20		V				•		HS FB	6–12			14
28	Lake Britton		•	30	16		V		•		•		HSF BL	15			14
29	Pit River		•	10			V				•		F				14
30	Cassel		•	27	20		V		•		•		F	11			15

Hookups: W = Water E = Electric S = Sewer
Toilets: F = Flush V = Vault P = Pit C = Chemical
Recreation: H = Hiking S = Swimming F = Fishing B = Boating L = Boat Launch O = Off-highway Driving R = Horseback Riding
Maximum Trailer/RV Length given in feet. Stay Limit given in days. Fee given in dollars.
If no entry under Season, campground is open all year. If no entry under Fee, camping is free.

Management: Lava Beds National Monument, 530-667-2282.
Activities: Hiking, cave exploring.
Finding the campground: From Canby, drive northwest on California Highway 139 for 30 miles, turn left onto Forest Road 97, and drive about 18 miles, following signs to Lava Beds National Monument. Turn right at the visitor center and drive 0.2 mile.

About the campground: Selected by *Sunset Magazine* as one of the 100 best campgrounds in the western United States, Indian Well offers a unique opportunity to explore more than 30 caves and lava tubes and to hike over ancient lava beds and fields. While ranger-led tours of the caves are offered, visitors are encouraged to explore the tubes on their own, and you may check out a lantern free of charge at the visitor center, which also provides maps and information about the caves and hiking trails. Some of the more popular caves are Mushpot, the only illuminated cave, located at the visitor center; Skull Cave, a deep hole with a staircase leading down to a narrow tube; and Sentinel, more than two-thirds of a mile long, with entrances at each end. A trail leads to the top of Schonchin Butte, a 30,000-year-old cinder cone, with an excellent view of Mount Shasta. The area was also the stronghold for the last stand of the Modoc Indians against the U.S. Army in the 1870s, and several interesting historical sites are located throughout the monument. As of this writing, space in the campground is almost always available, even on summer weekends. Stay limit 14 days. Although the campground is open all year, there is no water in winter months, and only pit toilets are available at that time. However, water and flush toilets are available year-round at the visitor center.

2 Medicine Lake: Hemlock

Location: 60 miles northeast of the community of Mount Shasta.
Sites: 19 sites for tents and RVs up to 22 feet long.
Facilities: Tables, fire rings, drinking water, vault toilets. A boat ramp is located on the east shore of the lake.
Fee per night: $7.
Management: Modoc National Forest, 530-677-2246.
Activities: Hiking, swimming, fishing, boating, waterskiing.
Finding the campground: From the intersection of Interstate 5 and California Highway 89 in Mount Shasta, drive east on CA 89 for 29 miles to Bartle. Just past town, turn left onto Forest Road 49 (Medicine Lake Road) and drive north about 31 miles. Turn left (east) at the campground sign.

About the campground: Medicine Lake, 1.5 miles long by about 1 mile wide, is the crater of a former volcano. It is stocked with more than 120,000 brown trout annually, and it receives much attention from anglers. Fishing is best from a trolling boat, and in summer most success occurs in the morning and the evening. Waterskiing is restricted to the hours between 10 A.M. and 4 P.M. The campground is located on the attractive, pine-shaded shoreline, but the sites are more crowded together than at the average Forest Service camp. The lake is 15 miles south of Lava Beds National Monument via FR 49, a washboard dirt road that is steep, winding, and not recommended for large

RVs or trailers. Elevation 6,700 feet. Stay limit 14 days. Open from July through October.

3 Medicine Lake: A. H. Hogue

Location: 60 miles northeast of the community of Mount Shasta.
Sites: 24 sites for tents and RVs up to 22 feet long.
Facilities: Tables, fire rings, drinking water, vault toilets. A boat ramp is located on the east shore of the lake.
Fee per night: $7.
Management: Modoc National Forest, 530-677-2246.
Activities: Hiking, swimming, fishing, boating, waterskiing.
Finding the campground: From the intersection of Interstate 5 and California Highway 89 in Mount Shasta, drive east on CA 89 for 29 miles to Bartle. Just past town, turn left onto Forest Road 49 (Medicine Lake Road) and drive north about 31 miles. Turn left (east) at the campground sign and continue west a short distance past Hemlock Campground (number 2).

About the campground: See Hemlock Campground (number 2).

4 Medicine Lake: Modoc

Location: 60 miles northeast of the community of Mount Shasta.
Sites: 22 sites for tents and RVs up to 22 feet long.
Facilities: Tables, fire rings, drinking water, vault toilets. A boat ramp is located on the east shore of the lake.
Fee per night: $7.
Management: Modoc National Forest, 530-677-2246.
Activities: Hiking, swimming, fishing, boating, waterskiing.
Finding the campground: From the intersection of Interstate 5 and California Highway 89 in Mount Shasta, drive east on CA 89 for 29 miles to Bartle. Just past town, turn left onto Forest Road 49 (Medicine Lake Road) and drive north about 31 miles. Turn left (east) at the campground sign and continue west a short distance past A. H. Hogue Campground (number 3).

About the campground: See Hemlock Campground (number 3).

5 Medicine Lake: Headquarters

Location: 60 miles northeast of the community of Mount Shasta.
Sites: 8 sites for tents and RVs up to 22 feet long.
Facilities: Tables, fire rings, drinking water, vault toilets. A boat ramp is located on the east shore of the lake.
Fee per night: $7.
Management: Modoc National Forest, 530-677-2246.
Activities: Hiking, swimming, fishing, boating, waterskiing.
Finding the campground: From the intersection of Interstate 5 and California Highway 89 in Mount Shasta, drive east on CA 89 for 29 miles to Bartle. Just past town, turn left onto Forest Road 49 (Medicine Lake Road) and drive

north about 31 miles. Turn left (east) at the campground sign and continue west 1.5 miles beyond Modoc Campground (number 4).

About the campground: See Hemlock Campground (number 3).

6 Harris Spring

Location: 32 miles northeast of McCloud.
Sites: 15 sites for tents and RVs up to 32 feet long.
Facilities: Tables, fire rings, drinking water, vault toilets.
Fee per night: None.
Management: Shasta-Trinity National Forest, 530-964-2184.
Activities: Sightseeing, hiking.
Finding the campground: From McCloud, drive 16 miles east on California Highway 89, turn left (north) at Bartle onto Forest Road 15 (Volcanic National Scenic Byway), and drive 16 miles.

About the campground: Harris Spring is best used as an overnight stop or as a base camp for exploring the lava flows, cinder cones, and craters of the surrounding Medicine Lake Highlands Volcanic Area. Elevation 4,800 feet. Stay limit 14 days. Open from June through October.

7 Lava Camp

Location: 32 miles northwest of Bieber.
Sites: 12 sites for tents and RVs up to 32 feet long.
Facilities: Tables, fire rings, vault toilets. No drinking water.
Fee per night: None.
Management: Modoc National Forest, 530-233-2162.
Activities: Cross-country hiking.
Finding the campground: From Bieber, drive 1 mile northeast on California Highway 299, turn left (north) onto County Road 91, and drive about 20 miles. Turn left (west) onto Forest Road 42N03 and drive 9 miles. Then turn right (north) onto Forest Road 42N23 and drive 2 miles.

About the campground: Surrounded by stark lava country, the campground earns its name. It is a long drive for little gain except solitude or exploring the lava highlands. Elevation 4,400 feet. Stay limit 14 days. Open from May through October.

8 Howard's Gulch

Location: 6 miles northwest of Canby.
Sites: 11 sites for tents and RVs up to 22 feet long.
Facilities: Tables, fire rings, drinking water, vault toilets. The facilities are wheelchair accessible.
Fee per night: None.
Management: Modoc National Forest, 530-233-5811.
Activities: Hiking.

Finding the campground: From Canby, drive 6 miles northwest on California Highway 139.

About the campground: This campground sits in an attractive setting: a mixed forest of pines with some aspens along the fringe of a meadow. It is especially nice in the fall, when the aspen leaves turn golden. Elevation 4,700 feet. Stay limit 14 days. Open from May through October.

9 Cottonwood Flat

Location: 12 miles west of Canby.
Sites: 10 sites for tents and RVs up to 22 feet long.
Activities: None.
Facilities: Tables, fire rings, drinking water, vault toilets.
Fee per night: None.
Management: Modoc National Forest, 530-233-5811.
Finding the campground: From Canby, drive southwest 4 miles on California Highway 139/299, turn right onto Forest Road 84, and drive west 7.6 miles.

About the campground: A remote camp, situated on lava flats strewn with junipers. Elevation 4,700 feet. Stay limit 14 days. Open from June through October.

10 Lower Rush Creek

Location: 9 miles northeast of Adin.
Sites: 10 sites for tents and RVs up to 22 feet long.
Facilities: Tables, fire rings, drinking water, vault toilets.
Fee per night: $5.
Management: Modoc National Forest, 530-299-3215.
Activities: Fishing.
Finding the campground: From the intersection of California Highways 139 and 299 in Adin, drive 8 miles northeast on CA 299, turn right at the campground sign, and drive half a mile.

About the campground: Situated on the banks of a small stream, with fair fishing for small native trout. Elevation 4,400 feet. Stay limit 14 days. Open from May through October.

11 Upper Rush Creek

Location: 10 miles northeast of Adin.
Sites: 13 sites for tents and RVs up to 22 feet long.
Facilities: Tables, fire rings, drinking water, vault toilets.
Fee per night: $4.
Management: Modoc National Forest, 530-299-3215.
Activities: Fishing.
Finding the campground: From the intersection of California Highways 139 and 299 in Adin, drive 10 miles northeast on CA 299.

About the campground: Situated along the banks of Upper Rush Creek, the campground offers fair fishing for small trout. Elevation 5,200 feet. Stay limit 14 days. Open from May through October.

12 Ash Creek

Location: 9 miles southeast of Adin.
Sites: 7 sites for tents and RVs up to 22 feet long.
Facilities: Tables, fire rings, vault toilet. No drinking water.
Fee per night: None.
Management: Modoc National Forest, 530-299-3215.
Activities: Fishing.
Finding the campground: From Adin, drive southeast on Ash Valley Road (County Road 527) for 8 miles, turn left at a sign for the campground, and drive 1 mile.

About the campground: Elevation 4,800 feet. Stay limit 14 days. Open from May through October.

13 Willow Creek

Location: 14 miles southeast of Adin.
Sites: 8 sites for tents and RVs up to 32 feet long.
Facilities: Tables, fire rings, drinking water, vault toilets. The facilities are wheelchair accessible.
Fee per night: $5.
Management: Modoc National Forest, 530-299-3215.
Activities: Fishing.
Finding the campground: From the intersection of California Highways 299 and 139 in Adin, drive southeast 14 miles on CA 139.

About the campground: Fishing in Willow Creek is possible directly from the campground. The catch is small rainbow trout, which are lightly stocked annually. Elevation 5,200 feet. Stay limit 14 days. Open from May through October.

14 Cave Lake

Location: 44 miles northeast of Alturas.
Sites: 6 sites for tents and RVs up to 16 feet long.
Facilities: Tables, fire rings, drinking water, vault toilets.
Fee per night: None.
Management: Modoc National Forest, 530-279-6116.
Activities: Fishing, boating, swimming.
Finding the campground: From the intersection of California Highway 299 and U.S. Highway 395 in Alturas, drive north on US 395 for 38 miles, turn right onto Forest Road 2, and drive 6 miles.

About the campground: The campground provides access to two nearby lakes: Cave and Lily. Trout fishing in both lakes is fair to good but usually better in Lily Lake. Both lakes are stocked annually. No motors are permitted on the lakes. FR 2 is a steep, dirt road, not recommended for trailers or large RVs. Elevation 6,600 feet. Stay limit 14 days. Open from July through October.

15 Plum Valley

Location: 22 miles northeast of Alturas.
Sites: 7 sites for tents and RVs up to 16 feet long.
Facilities: Tables, fire rings, vault toilet. No drinking water.
Fee per night: None.
Management: Modoc National Forest, 530-279-6116.
Activities: Fishing.
Finding the campground: From the intersection of California Highway 299 and U.S. Highway 395 in Alturas, drive north on US 395 for 19 miles, turn right onto County Road 11, and drive 2 miles. Bear right onto Forest Road 45N35 and drive 1 mile.

About the campground: Elevation 5,600 feet. Stay limit 14 days. Open from June through October.

16 Cedar Pass

Location: 15 miles northeast of Alturas.
Sites: 17 sites for tents and RVs up to 16 feet long.
Facilities: Tables, fire rings, vault toilets. No drinking water.
Fee per night: None.
Activities: None.
Management: Modoc National Forest, 530-279-6116.
Finding the campground: From the intersection of California Highway 299 and U.S. Highway 395 in Alturas, drive north on combined 395/299 for 5.6 miles, turn right onto CA 299, and drive east 9.2 miles.

About the campground: Best used as an overnight stop. Nonpotable water is available from two small streams adjacent to the campground. Elevation 5,900 feet. Stay limit 14 days. Open from May through October.

17 Stowe Reservoir

Location: 17 miles northeast of Alturas.
Sites: 8 sites for tents and RVs up to 20 feet long.
Facilities: Tables, fire rings, drinking water, vault toilets.
Fee per night: None.
Activities: None.
Management: Modoc National Forest, 530-279-6116.
Finding the campground: From the intersection of California Highway 299 and U.S. Highway 395 in Alturas, drive north on combined 395/299 for 5.6 miles, turn right onto CA 299, and drive east 11.2 miles.

About the campground: Stowe is a former cattle ranch, and the "reservoir" is a pond that provided water for the herd. Elevation 6,300 feet. Stay limit 14 days. Open from May through October.

18 Big Sage Reservoir

Location: 13 miles northwest of Alturas.
Sites: 6 sites for tents and RVs up to 22 feet long.
Facilities: Tables, vault toilets, boat ramp. No drinking water.
Fee per night: None.
Management: Modoc National Forest, 530-233-5811.
Activities: Fishing, boating.
Finding the campground: From the intersection of California Highway 299 and U.S. Highway 395 in Alturas, drive west on CA 299 for 3.6 miles, turn right onto Forest Road 73 (Crowder Flat Road), and drive 5.6 miles. Turn right onto County Road 180 and drive 3.3 miles.

About the campground: You can catch largemouth bass and catfish at Big Sage Reservoir. Elevation 5,100 feet. Stay limit 14 days. Open from May through October.

19 Reservoir C

Location: 19 miles northwest of Alturas.
Sites: 6 sites for tents and RVs up to 22 feet long.
Facilities: Tables, vault toilets. No drinking water.
Fee per night: None.
Management: Modoc National Forest, 530-233-5811.
Activities: Fishing.
Finding the campground: From the intersection of California Highway 299 and U.S. Highway 395 in Alturas, drive west on CA 299 for 3.6 miles, turn right onto Forest Road 73 (Crowder Flat Road), and drive 9.2 miles. Turn left onto Forest Road 43N18 (Triangle Ranch Road) and drive 5.6 miles. Then turn right onto Forest Road 44N32 and drive 0.7 mile.

About the campground: This small lake is stocked annually with brown and Eagle Lake trout. Fishing is best in early summer, before water drawdowns take place. Elevation 4,900 feet. Stay limit 14 days. Open from May through October.

20 Pepperdine

Location: 19 miles east of Alturas.
Sites: 5 sites for tents and RVs up to 15 feet long.
Facilities: Tables, fire rings, drinking water, vault toilets, corrals and watering facilities for horses.
Fee per night: None.
Management: Modoc National Forest, 530-279-6116.

Activities: Hiking, horseback riding.
Finding the campground: From the intersection of California Highway 299 and U.S. Highway 395 in Alturas, drive south on US 395 for 1.2 miles, turn left onto County Road 56, and drive east for 13 miles to a fork in the road. Bear left onto Forest Road 31 (Parker Creek Road) and drive 5 miles to the campground access sign.

About the campground: A trail leads from the campground to the summit of Squaw Peak (8,646 feet, 4 miles round trip). The Summit Trail leads to Patterson Lake in the South Warner Wilderness (12 miles round trip). Elevation 7,200 feet. Stay limit 14 days. Open from July through October.

21 Mill Creek Falls

Location: 33 miles southeast of Alturas.
Sites: 19 sites for tents and RVs up to 22 feet long.
Facilities: Tables, fire rings, drinking water, vault toilets.
Fee per night: $5.
Management: Modoc National Forest, 530-279-6116.
Activities: Hiking.
Finding the campground: From the intersection of California Highway 299 and U.S. Highway 395 in Alturas, drive south on US 395 for 19 miles to the town of Likely, turn left (east) onto County Road 64 (Jess Valley Road), and drive for 12 miles, bearing left when Forest Road 5 joins CR 64 from the south. Turn left onto Forest Road 40N46 and drive 1.5 miles.

About the campground: Located on the banks of Mill Creek, near Clear Lake. A trail leads from the campground to Mill Creek Falls, and Poison Flat Trail connects the campground to Mill Creek, Summit, and East Creek Trails in the South Warner Wilderness. Elevation 5,700 feet. Stay limit 14 days. Open from June through October.

22 Soup Spring

Location: 39 miles southeast of Alturas.
Sites: 14 sites for tents and RVs up to 22 feet long.
Facilities: Tables, fire rings, drinking water, vault toilets, corrals.
Fee per night: None.
Management: Modoc National Forest, 530-279-6116.
Activities: Hiking, horseback riding.
Finding the campground: From the intersection of California Highway 299 and U.S. Highway 395 in Alturas, drive south on US 395 for 19 miles to the town of Likely, turn left onto County Road 64 (Jess Valley Road), and drive 9 miles. Turn left onto Forest Road 5 (also still CR 64) and drive 4.5 miles. Turn right onto Forest Road 40N24 and drive 6 miles.

About the campground: A spur trail leads from the campground to the Mill Creek Trail and the Summit Trail in the South Warner Wilderness. Elevation 6,800 feet. Stay limit 14 days. Open from June through October.

23 Blue Lake

Location: 36 miles southeast of Alturas.
Sites: 48 sites for tents and RVs up to 32 feet long.
Facilities: Tables, fire rings, drinking water, vault toilets, boat ramp, fishing pier. The facilities are wheelchair accessible.
Fee per night: $6.
Management: Modoc National Forest, 530-279-6116.
Activities: Swimming, boating, fishing, hiking.
Finding the campground: From the intersection of California Highway 299 and U.S. Highway 395 in Alturas, drive south on US 395 for 19 miles to the town of Likely, turn left onto County Road 64 (Jess Valley Road), and drive 9 miles. Turn right onto Forest Road 64 and drive 6 miles. Then turn right onto Forest Road 38N60 and drive 2 miles.

About the campground: Campsites are situated to provide views of Blue Lake and the surrounding mountains. White fir and ponderosa pine surround the lake, which is noted for large brown trout, some as large as 10 pounds. The lake is also stocked annually with rainbow and Eagle Lake trout. A 5-mile-per-hour speed limit is in effect on the lake. A trail circles the lake and takes about an hour to walk. Elevation 6,000 feet. Stay limit 14 days. Open from June through October.

24 Patterson

Location: 44 miles southeast of Alturas.
Sites: 5 sites for tents and RVs up to 16 feet long.
Facilities: Tables, fire rings, drinking water, vault toilets.
Fee per night: None.
Management: Modoc National Forest, 530-279-6116.
Activities: Hiking, horseback riding.
Finding the campground: From the intersection of California Highway 299 and U.S. Highway 395 in Alturas, drive south on US 395 for 19 miles to the town of Likely, turn left onto County Road 64 (Jess Valley Road), and drive 9 miles. Turn right onto Forest Road 64 and drive 16 miles.

About the campground: The Summit Trail and the East Creek Trail lead north from the campground into the South Warner Wilderness. Elevation 7,200 feet. Stay limit 14 days. Open from July through October.

25 Emerson

Location: 20 miles south of Cedarville.
Sites: 4 sites for tents and RVs up to 16 feet long.
Facilities: Tables, fire rings, vault toilets. No drinking water.
Fee per night: None.
Management: Modoc National Forest, 530-279-6116.
Activities: Hiking, fishing.
Finding the campground: From the intersection of California Highway 299

and County Road 1 in Cedarville, drive south 17 miles on CR 1, turn right onto Country Road 40, and drive 3 miles.

About the campground: The Emerson Trail leads from the campground into the South Warner Wilderness, connecting to the Summit Trail. Elevation 6,000 feet. Stay limit 14 days. Open from July through October.

26 McArthur–Burney Falls Memorial State Park

Location: 11 miles northeast of Burney.
Sites: 128 sites for tents or RVs up to 32 feet long.
Facilities: Tables, grills, drinking water, flush toilets, showers, dump station, store, snack bar, boat launch and rentals. The facilities are wheelchair accessible.
Fee per night: $12-$17, pets $1. For reservations call 800-444-7275. There is a one-time reservation fee of $7.50.
Management: California Department of Parks and Recreation, 916-335-2777.
Activities: Hiking, swimming, fishing, boating.
Finding the campground: From Burney, drive 5 miles northeast on California Highway 299, turn left onto California Highway 89, and drive 6 miles.

About the campground: On the shores of Lake Britton and encompassing a beautiful waterfall and several hiking trails, this 875-acre forested park provides a full range of outdoor recreation. The campground here has been designated one of the 100 best in the West by *Sunset Magazine*. Campsites are well spaced in an attractive forest of tall pines, with some scattered oaks. Most campsites are only a short walk from 129-foot Burney Falls, a lovely double waterfall. One hundred million gallons of water spill over the falls daily, year-round.

Access to Lake Britton is at the end of the campground access road, where there is a boat launch, marina, and swimming beach. The lake contains bass, bluegill, trout, and crappie, although catches of the last two are not particularly good. The Falls Trail leads from the store parking lot to the bottom of the falls, crosses the creek, and ascends on the other side of the falls. Two trails, Headwaters Trail and the Fall Creek Loop Trail, explore different aspects of the falls and Burney Creek. Elevation 3,000 feet. Stay limit 15 days from June through September, 30 days from October through May. Open all year.

27 Dusty

Location: 13 miles northeast of Burney, near Lake Britton.
Sites: 5 sites for tents or RVs up to 20 feet long, plus 2 group sites for up to 25 people each.
Facilities: Tables, fire rings, vault toilets. No drinking water.
Fee per night: $6, pets $1, group site $12.
Management: PG&E, 916-386-5164.
Activities: Hiking, swimming, fishing, boating.
Finding the campground: From Burney, drive 5 miles northeast on California Highway 299, turn left onto California Highway 89, and drive 8 miles.

At Lake Britton's Northshore Campground, author Richard McMahon finds a serene moment in which to record his thoughts. PHOTO BY BEN BREITUNG

About the campground: Located in a wooded setting on the north bank of the Pit River, just before its juncture with Lake Britton. See McArthur–Burney Falls Memorial State Park Campground (number 26) for area information. Stay limit 14 days. Open all year.

28 Lake Britton: Northshore

Location: 15 miles north of Burney.
Sites: 30 sites for tents or RVs up to 16 feet long.
Facilities: Tables, grills, drinking water, vault toilets, boat ramp.
Fee per night: $15, pets $1.
Management: PG&E, 916-386-5164.
Activities: Hiking, swimming, fishing, boating.
Finding the campground: From Burney, drive 5 miles northeast on California Highway 299, turn left onto California Highway 89, and drive 9 miles. Turn left onto Clark Creek Road and drive 1 mile.

About the campground: Northshore is attractively located on Lake Britton, and many campsites have direct access to the lake and views over the water. See McArthur–Burney Falls Memorial State Park Campground (number 26) for area information. Elevation 2,800 feet. Stay limit 14 days. Open all year.

29 Pit River

Location: 12 miles northeast of Burney.
Sites: 10 sites for tents or RVs.
Facilities: Tables, grills, vault toilets. No drinking water.
Fee per night: None.
Management: Bureau of Land Management, 916-257-5381.
Activities: Fishing.
Finding the campground: From Burney, drive about 12 miles northeast on California Highway 299.

About the campground: Trout fishing along the Pit River is good if you are willing to fight the brush along its banks and do a lot of wading. Stay limit 14 days. Open all year.

30 Cassel

Location: 11 miles northeast of Burney.
Sites: 27 sites for tents or RVs up to 20 feet long.
Facilities: Tables, grills, drinking water, vault toilets.
Fee per night: $11, pets $1.
Management: PG&E, 916-335-2781.
Activities: Fishing.
Finding the campground: From Burney, drive 7.5 miles northeast on California Highway 299, turn right onto Cassel Road, and drive 3.5 miles.

About the campground: Cassel is on the banks of Lower Hat Creek, a stream famous for fly fishing for large trout. Check for catch-and-release regulations. Stay limit 15 days. Open all year.

LASSEN AREA

Welcome to "The Crossroads," where the lava of the Modoc Plateau, the granite of the Sierra Nevada, and the sagebrush of the Great Basin meet and blend. This is one of the most fascinating and geologically diverse areas of California. The centerpiece is Lassen Volcanic National Park, but other attractions also lure outdoor enthusiasts. Lassen National Forest offers miles of wooded trails, streams, and the Thousand Lakes Wilderness. Eagle Lake is the second largest natural lake in the state, and Lake Almanor is one of the most beautiful of the manmade ones. Hat Creek offers challenging trout fishing, and Subway Cave features a self-guided tour through the largest lava tube in California. Lassen National Scenic Byway makes a 170-mile loop through four major geophysical regions, providing an excellent tour of "The Crossroads."

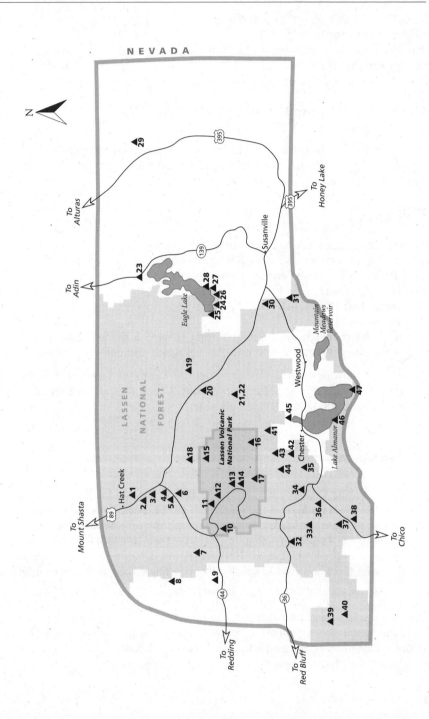

Lassen Area Campgrounds

		Group sites	RV sites	Total sites	Max. RV length	Hookups	Toilets	Showers	Drinking water	Dump station	Pets	Wheelchair	Recreation	Fee ($)	Season	Can reserve	Length of stay
1	Honn			6			V		•				F	6			14
2	Bridge		•	25	22		V	•	•				F	11	May–October		14
3	Rocky			8			V	/	•				F	6	May–October		14
4	Cave		•	46	22		V	•	•	•	•		F	11			14
5	Hat Creek	•	•	76	22		F	•	•	•	•		F	11–44	May–October	•	14
6	Big Pine		•	19	22		V	•	•				F	8	May–October		14
7	North Battle Creek Reservoir		•	15			V	•	•				SFBL	15			14
8	Latour Demonstration State Forest		•	7			P		•				H		June–October		15
9	McCumber Reservoir		•	7			V	•	•				SFBL	15			14
Lassen Volcanic National Park (10–17)																	
10	Manzanita Lake		•	179	35		F	•	•	•	•		•	HSF BL	14	May–October		15
11	Crags		•	45	35		V	•	•	•	•		H	8	May–October		15
12	Lost Creek Group Camp	•	•	7			V	•	•				H	45	June–September	•	14
13	Summit Lake North		•	46	35		F	•	•	•	•		HS FB	14	June–October		15
14	Summit Lake South		•	48	35		V	•	•				HS FB	12	June–October		15
15	Butte Lake		•	98	35		F	•	•	•	•		HSF BL	10	June–October		15
16	Juniper Lake	•		20			V		•				HS BL	10	June–October		14
17	Warner Valley		•	18			V	•	•	•	•		H	12	May–October		15
18	Butte Creek		•	10	22		P		•				HF		May–October		14
19	Crater Lake		•	17	22		P	•	•				HF SB	10.50	June–October		14
20	Bogard		•	21	27		V	•	•				HF	8.50	May–October		14

Silver Lake (21–22)

		Group sites	RV sites	Total sites	Max. RV length	Hookups	Toilets	Showers	Drinking water	Dump station	Pets	Wheelchair	Recreation	Fee ($)	Season	Can reserve	Length of stay
21	Rocky Knoll		•	18			V		•		•		HSF BL	10	May–October		14
22	Silver Bowl		•	18			V		•		•		HSF BL	10	May–October		14

Eagle Lake (23–28)

		Group sites	RV sites	Total sites	Max. RV length	Hookups	Toilets	Showers	Drinking water	Dump station	Pets	Wheelchair	Recreation	Fee ($)	Season	Can reserve	Length of stay
23	North Eagle Lake		•	20			V		•	•	•		HS FB	6	Mem. Day–December		14
24	Merrill		•	181	35		F	•	•	•	•	•	HS FB	13–15	May–October	•	14
25	Christie		•	69			F	•	•	•	•	•	HS FB	13–20	May–October		14
26	West Eagle Group Camp	•	•	2	35		F	•		•		•	HS FB	70–120	May–October	•	14
27	Eagle		•	45	32		F	•		•		•	HS FB	13–20	May–October	•	14
28	Aspen Grove			26			F	•		•		•	HSF BL	11	May–October		14
29	Ramhorn Springs		•	10	27		V	•		•			HR	5			14
30	Goumaz		•	10	30		V			•			HF	5	May–October		14
31	Roxie Peconom			10			V	•		•			HF		May–October		14
32	Battle Creek		•	50			F	•		•			HF	12	May–October		14
33	Hole in the Ground		•	11			V	•		•			HF	10	May–October		14
34	Gurnsey Creek	•	•	33			V	•		•			HF	10–75	May–October	•	14
35	Willow Springs			8			V			•			F	8	May–October		14
36	Elam		•	15			V	•		•			F	11	May–October		14
37	Alder Creek			5			V			•			HF	8	April–October		14
38	Potato Patch		•	32			V	•		•			HF	10	May–October		14
39	South Antelope			4			V			•			HF				14
40	Black Rock			4			V	•		•			HF	5			14

	Group sites	RV sites	Total sites	Max. RV length	Hookups	Toilets	Showers	Drinking water	Dump station	Pets	Wheelchair	Recreation	Fee ($)	Season	Can reserve	Length of stay
41 Benner Creek		•	9	20		V		•	•				8	May–October		14
42 High Bridge			12			V		•	•			HF	10	May–October		14
43 Warner Creek			13			V			•			F	8	May–October		14
44 Domingo Springs			18			V		•	•			HF	10	May–October		14
45 Last Chance Creek	•	•	25			V		•	•			F	15-20	May–October	•	14
Lake Almanor (46–47)																
46 Almanor	•	•	121			V		•	•	•		SFBL	12-55	May–October	•	14
47 Lake Almanor	•	•	132			V		•	•	•		SFBL	15	May–October	•	14

Hookups: W = Water E = Electric S = Sewer
Toilets: F = Flush V = Vault P = Pit C = Chemical
Recreation: H = Hiking S = Swimming F = Fishing B = Boating L = Boat Launch O = Off-highway Driving R = Horseback Riding
Maximum Trailer/RV Length given in feet. Stay Limit given in days. Fee given in dollars.
If no entry under **Season**, campground is open all year. If no entry under Fee, camping is free.

1 Honn

Location: 17 miles southeast of Burney.
Sites: 6 sites for tents.
Facilities: Tables, grills, vault toilets. No drinking water.
Fee per night: $6.
Management: Lassen National Forest, 530-336-5521.
Activities: Fishing.
Finding the campground: From Burney, drive 5.5 miles northeast on California Highway 299, turn right onto California Highway 89, and drive southeast for 12 miles.

About the campground: In the shadow of Lassen Peak, Honn is one of six campgrounds located along Hat Creek, providing opportunities for trout fishing, hiking, camping, and wildlife observation. Lava tubes, dormant and extinct volcanoes, lava flows, and fault lines all attest to a turbulent volcanic past. The campgrounds are used almost exclusively by anglers during the fishing season, and Upper Hat Creek is stocked annually with nearly 100,000 trout. Honn is not recommended for trailers, due to limited turnaround space. Elevation 3,500 feet. Stay limit 14 days. Open all year.

2 Bridge

Location: 23 miles southeast of Burney.
Sites: 25 sites for tents and RVs up to 22 feet long.
Facilities: Tables, grills, drinking water, vault toilets.
Fee per night: $11.
Management: Lassen National Forest, 530-336-5521.
Activities: Fishing.
Finding the campground: From Burney, drive 5.5 miles northeast on California Highway 299, turn right onto California Highway 89, and drive southeast for 17 miles.

About the campground: See Honn Campground (number 1). Elevation 4,000 feet. Stay limit 14 days. Open from May through October.

3 Rocky

Location: 24 miles southeast of Burney.
Sites: 8 sites for tents, no RVs.
Facilities: Tables, grills, vault toilets. No drinking water.
Fee per night: $6.
Management: Lassen National Forest, 530-336-5521.
Activities: Fishing.
Finding the campground: From Burney, drive 5.5 miles northeast on California Highway 299, turn right onto California Highway 89, and drive southeast for 18 miles.

About the campground: See Honn Campground (number 1). Elevation 4,000 feet. Stay limit 14 days. Open from May through October.

4 Cave

Location: 27 miles southeast of Burney.
Sites: 46 sites for tents and RVs up to 22 feet long.
Facilities: Tables, grills, drinking water, vault toilets. The facilities are wheelchair accessible.
Fee per night: $11.
Management: Lassen National Forest, 530-336-5521.
Activities: Fishing.
Finding the campground: From Burney, drive 5.5 miles northeast on California Highway 299, turn right onto CA 89, and drive southeast for 21 miles.

About the campground: Located on the banks of Hat Creek at a point where the stream is stocked with rainbow trout every two weeks during the fishing season. A trail runs along the creek; part of it is wheelchair-accessible. Directly across the highway from the campground is Subway Cave, a large lava tube 0.7 mile long, with interpretive displays along its length. The cave is not illuminated, so bring a flashlight. The campground is 15 miles northeast of the entrance to Lassen Volcanic National Park. Elevation 4,400 feet. For additional area description, see Honn Campground (number 1). Stay limit 14 days. Open all year.

5 Hat Creek

Location: 29 miles southeast of Burney.
Sites: 73 sites for tents and RVs up to 22 feet long, plus 3 group sites.
Facilities: Tables, grills, drinking water, flush and vault toilets, dump station.
Fee per night: $11, group sites $44. Reservations may be made for sites 1-9 by calling 800-280-CAMP. Group sites must be reserved. There is a one-time reservation fee of $8.65.
Management: Lassen National Forest, 530-336-5521.
Activities: Fishing.
Finding the campground: From Burney, drive 5.5 miles northeast on California Highway 299, turn right onto California Highway 89, and drive southeast for 23 miles.

About the campground: For an area description, see Honn Campground (number 1). Elevation 4,400 feet. The campground is about 12 miles northeast of the entrance to Lassen Volcanic National Park. Stay limit 14 days. Open from May through October.

6 Big Pine

Location: 32 miles southeast of Burney.
Sites: 19 sites for tents and RVs up to 22 feet long.

Facilities: Tables, grills, drinking water, vault toilets.
Fee per night: $8.
Management: Lassen National Forest, 530-336-5521.
Activities: Fishing.
Finding the campground: From Burney, drive 5.5 miles northeast on California Highway 299, turn right onto California Highway 89, and drive south for 26 miles.

About the campground: For an area description, see Honn Campground (number 1). Elevation 4,700 feet. Stay limit 14 days. Open from May through October.

---

7 North Battle Creek Reservoir

Location: 45 miles south of Burney.
Sites: 10 sites for tents and RVs, plus 5 walk-in sites.
Facilities: Tables, grills, drinking water, vault toilets, boat ramp.
Fee per night: $15, pets $1.
Management: PG&E, 530-386-5164.
Activities: Fishing, boating, swimming.
Finding the campground: From Burney, drive 5.5 miles northeast on California Highway 299, turn right onto California Highway 89, and drive south for 34 miles. Turn right onto Forest Road 32N31 and drive 5 miles.

About the campground: Fishing can be good at this little-known lake, which is stocked annually with brown trout. No gas engines are allowed on the lake. Lassen Volcanic National Park is 8 miles to the southeast. Elevation 5,600 feet. Stay limit 14 days. Open all year.

---

8 Latour Demonstration State Forest

Location: 47 miles south of Burney.
Sites: Total of 7 sites for tents and RVs in 4 primitive campgrounds within 2 miles of each other.
Facilities: Tables, grills. No drinking water. Old Cow Creek (2 sites) and South Cow Creek Meadows (2 sites) have pit toilets. Butcher's Gulch (1 site) and Old Headquarters (2 sites) have no toilet facilities.
Fee per night: None.
Management: Latour Demonstration State Forest, 530-225-2505.
Activities: Hiking.
Finding the campgrounds: From Burney, drive 5.5 miles northeast on California Highway 299, turn right onto California Highway 89, and drive southeast for 32 miles. Turn right onto Forest Road 16 (a gravel road) and drive 9.6 miles to its intersection with Forest Road 32N48 on the right. Turn left onto a dirt road and drive 0.3 mile to the state forest boundary. A series of criss-cross-

ing dirt roads are confusing here, and it is best to call for a brochure before visiting the forest.

About the campgrounds: The purpose of this remote state forest is to teach and demonstrate conservation logging practices. It also protects a unique stand of old-growth sugar pines, many of which are 40 to 60 inches in diameter. Elevation 5,500 to 5,900 feet. Stay limit 15 days. Open from June through October.

9 McCumber Reservoir

Location: 14 miles west of the Manzanita entrance to Lassen Volcanic National Park.
Sites: 7 sites for tents or RVs.
Facilities: Tables, grills, drinking water, vault toilets, boat ramp.
Fee per night: $15.
Management: PG&E, 530-386-5164.
Activities: Swimming, fishing, boating.
Finding the campground: From the point where California Highways 89 and 44 separate, 1 mile west of the northwestern (Manzanita) entrance to Lassen Volcano National Park, drive west 10.5 miles on CA 44, turn right onto Lake McCumber Road (dirt), and drive 2.5 miles.

About the campground: This small, often overlooked lake is stocked annually with 6,000 rainbow trout. No gas engines are allowed on the lake. Elevation 3,500 feet. Stay limit 14 days. Open all year.

Lassen Volcanic National Park

In May 1915, Mount Lassen exploded with a fury similar to that of Mount St. Helens in 1980. Today, ecologists are studying the Mount Lassen area to see what the future has in store for the devastated terrain of Mount St. Helens. Although Mount Lassen itself is dormant, volcanic activity is evident in the steam vents, mud pots, and boiling springs of Sulphur Works and Bumpass Hell, which you can visit via a combination of short trails and boardwalks. Several small, pretty lakes line the main road through the park. The most attractive is Manzanita, near the visitor center and the park's northwest entrance. A trail zigzags up Mount Lassen to its 10,457-foot summit. The hike is 5 miles round trip, and you gain 2,000 feet in altitude. On a clear day, you can easily see Mount Shasta 75 miles to the north. The park contains eight vehicle-accessible campgrounds.

Boardwalks allow visitors to get closeup views of the vents and fumaroles of Bumpass Hell, in Lassen Volcanic National Park.

10 Lassen Volcanic National Park: Manzanita Lake

Location: 46 miles east of Redding.
Sites: 179 sites for tents and RVs up to 35 feet long.
Facilities: Tables, grills, drinking water, showers, flush toilets, dump station, laundry, store, boat launch. The facilities are wheelchair accessible.
Fee per night: $14.
Management: Lassen Volcanic National Park, 530-595-4444.
Activities: Hiking, fishing, boating, swimming.
Finding the campground: From the intersection of Interstate 5 and California Highway 44 in Redding, drive about 45 miles east on CA 44. Turn right onto California Highway 89 and drive less than 1 mile to the park entrance station. Continue a short distance and make a right turn onto the campground entrance road.

About the campground: Small but beautiful Manzanita Lake is one of the main attractions of the park. It offers great reflections of Mount Lassen and Chaos Crags, and the campground gets heavy use. To accommodate the crowds, the sites are closer together than at other park campgrounds. The park visitor center is also here, on CA 89 just past the campground entrance road. The Nobles Emigrant Trail leads northeast to Chaos Crags and beyond. Trout fishing can be good, but catch-and-release rules are in effect. No motorized boats are permitted on the lake. Elevation 5,900 feet. Stay limit 15 days. Open May through October.

Mount Lassen dominates the view from campsites on Manzanita Lake, one of the main attractions of Lassen Volcanic National Park.

11 Lassen Volcanic National Park: Crags

Location: 5 miles northeast of the Manzanita Visitor Center.
Sites: 45 sites for tents and RVs up to 35 feet long.
Facilities: Tables, grills, drinking water, portable vault toilets. The facilities are wheelchair accessible.
Fee per night: $8.
Management: Lassen Volcanic National Park, 530-595-4444.
Activities: Hiking.
Finding the campground: From the Manzanita Visitor Center, drive northeast for 5 miles on California Highway 89.

About the campground: Directly across the highway from towering Chaos Crags, campsites here offer more room and privacy than Manzanita and Summit Lake North and South. The Emigrant Trail crosses the highway about a mile east of the campground, en route to Lost Creek, a little more than a mile away. Elevation 5,700 feet. Stay limit 15 days. Crags Campground is usually open only to accommodate overflow when other campgrounds are crowded.

12 Lassen Volcanic National Park: Lost Creek Group Camp

Location: 6 miles east of Manzanita Visitor Center.
Sites: 7 group sites for tents and RVs; each accommodates up to 35 people.
Facilities: Tables, grills, drinking water, vault toilets.

Fee per night: $45. Reservations required; call the number below.
Management: Lassen Volcanic National Park, 530-595-4444.
Activities: Hiking.
Finding the campground: From the Manzanita Visitor Center, drive north and then southeast for 5.5 miles on California Highway 89.

About the campground: Elevation 5,700 feet. Stay limit 14 days. Open from June through September.

13 Lassen Volcanic National Park: Summit Lake North

Location: 12 miles east of the Manzanita Visitor Center.
Sites: 46 sites for tents and RVs up to 35 feet long.
Facilities: Tables, grills, drinking water, flush toilets. The facilities are wheelchair accessible.
Fee per night: $14.
Management: Lassen Volcanic National Park, 530-595-4444.
Activities: Hiking, fishing, swimming, boating.
Finding the campground: From the Manzanita Visitor Center, drive 12 miles north and then southeast on California Highway 89.

About the campground: Summit is a small but beautiful lake. Deer often graze in a nearby meadow. Campsites are not on the shoreline but are close to it. They are also close together, as at Manzanita. The Summit Lake Trail (8 miles round trip) begins at the north end of the lake and leads to Echo Lake and Upper and Lower Twin Lakes. Fishing is poor in Summit Lake, because it is no longer stocked and has been overfished. Elevation 6,700 feet. Stay limit 15 days. Open from June through October.

14 Lassen Volcanic National Park: Summit Lake South

Location: 13 miles east of the Manzanita Visitor Center.
Sites: 48 sites for tents and RVs up to 35 feet long.
Facilities: Tables, grills, drinking water, vault toilets.
Fee per night: $12.
Management: Lassen Volcanic National Park, 530-595-4444.
Activities: Hiking, fishing, swimming, boating.
Finding the campground: From the Manzanita Visitor Center, drive 12.5 miles north and then southeast on California Highway 89.

About the campground: See Summit Lake North Campground (number 13).

15 Lassen Volcanic National Park: Butte Lake

Location: 89 miles east of Redding.
Sites: 98 sites for tents and RVs up to 35 feet long.
Facilities: Tables, grills, drinking water, flush toilets, boat ramp. The facilities are wheelchair accessible.

Climbers near the 10,457-foot summit of Mount Lassen, a dormant volcano that last erupted in 1915, creating the landscape encompassed by Lassen Volcanic National Park.

Fee per night: $10.
Management: Lassen Volcanic National Park, 530-595-4444.
Activities: Hiking, swimming, fishing, boating.
Finding the campground: From Redding, drive east 82 miles on California Highway 44, turn right onto Forest Road 32N21, and drive about 7 miles.

About the campground: Only nonmotorized boats are allowed on Butte Lake, which offers poor to mediocre fishing for trout. A 4-mile round-trip hike leads from the campground to the top of Cinder Cone (6,907 feet), from which there are excellent views of the surrounding wilderness. Elevation 6,100 feet. Stay limit 15 days. Open from June through October.

16 Lassen Volcanic National Park: Juniper Lake

Location: 12 miles north of Chester.
Sites: 18 sites for tents (RVs not recommended), plus 2 group sites for up to 15 people each.
Facilities: Fire rings, vault toilets, boat ramp. No drinking water.
Fee per night: $10.
Management: Lassen Volcanic National Park, 530-595-4444.
Activities: Hiking, swimming, boating.
Finding the campground: From Chester, on the north end of Lake Almanor, take Warner Valley Road north for 1 mile, bear left onto Juniper Lake Road, and drive 11 miles. The dirt road is rough and not suitable for RVs.

About the campground: The campground is on the east side of the lake. Fishing is only fair to poor, as the lake is not stocked. On the north end of the lake, a half-mile climb of Inspiration Point affords wide views of the park. Only nonmotorized boats are permitted on the lake. Elevation 6,800 feet. Stay limit 14 days. Open from June through October.

17 Lassen Volcanic National Park: Warner Valley

Location: 16 miles north of Chester.
Sites: 18 sites for tents and RVs.
Facilities: Tables, fire rings, drinking water, vault toilets. The facilities are wheelchair accessible.
Fee per night: $12.
Management: Lassen Volcanic National Park, 530-595-4444.
Activities: Hiking.
Finding the campground: From Chester, drive north on Warner Valley Road for 16 miles. The dirt road, often rutted, is not recommended for large RVs.

About the campground: The Drake Lake Trail begins half a mile north of the campground and ascends steeply in just over 2 miles to emerald green Drake Lake. Elevation 5,650 feet. Stay limit 15 days. Open from May through October.

18 Butte Creek

Location: 40 miles southeast of Burney.
Sites: 10 sites for tents and RVs up to 22 feet long.
Facilities: Tables, fire rings, pit toilets. No drinking water.
Fee per night: None.
Management: Lassen National Forest, 530-258-2141.
Activities: Fishing, hiking.
Finding the campground: From Burney, drive 5.5 miles northeast on California Highway 299, turn right onto California Highway 89, and drive southeast for 21 miles. Turn left onto California Highway 44 and drive 11 miles. Then turn right onto Forest Road 32N21 and drive 3 miles.

About the campground: Fishing is only fair in this stream, and then only in spring, after the meager annual stocking of trout. Butte Lake Campground in Lassen Volcanic National Park lies 4 miles to the south on the same road. Elevation 5,600 feet. Stay limit 14 days. Open from May through October.

19 Crater Lake

Location: 57 miles southeast of Burney.
Sites: 17 sites for tents and RVs up to 22 feet long.
Facilities: Tables, fire rings, drinking water, pit toilets.
Fee per night: $10.50.

Management: Lassen National Forest, 530-257-4188.
Activities: Fishing, boating, swimming, hiking.
Finding the campground: From Burney, drive 5.5 miles northeast on California Highway 299, turn right onto California Highway 89, and drive southeast for 21 miles. Turn left onto California Highway 44 and drive east 23 miles to Bogard Work Center. Turn left onto Forest Road 32N08 and drive 7 miles.

About the campground: Only nonmotorized boats are permitted on the lake, which is stocked annually with brook trout. Elevation 6,800 feet. Stay limit 14 days. Open from June through October.

20 Bogard

Location: 54 miles southeast of Burney.
Sites: 21 sites for tents and RVs up to 27 feet long.
Facilities: Tables, fire rings, drinking water, vault toilets.
Fee per night: $8.50.
Management: Lassen National Forest, 530-257-4188.
Activities: Hiking, fishing.
Finding the campground: From Burney, drive 5.5 miles northeast on California Highway 299, turn right onto California Highway 89, and drive southeast for 21 miles. Turn left onto California Highway 44 and drive east 23 miles to Bogard Work Center. Continue on CA 44 for 2 miles, turn right onto Forest Road 31N26, and drive 1.6 miles. Turn right onto Forest Road 31N21 and drive almost half a mile.

About the campground: Elevation 5,600 feet. Stay limit 14 days. Open from May through October.

21 Silver Lake: Rocky Knoll

Location: 20 miles northwest of Westwood.
Sites: 18 sites for tents and RVs.
Facilities: Tables, fire rings, drinking water, vault toilets, boat ramp.
Fee per night: $10.
Management: Lassen National Forest, 530-258-2141.
Activities: Hiking, swimming, fishing, boating.
Finding the campground: From Westwood (20 miles west of Susanville on California Highway 36), drive north on County Road A21 for 12 miles, turn left onto Country Road 110 (Silver Lake Road), and drive 8 miles to Silver Lake. Turn left at the lake.

About the campground: Silver Lake is a small but beautiful lake adjacent to the Caribou Wilderness. It is stocked annually with 10,000 trout. Only car top boats are allowed. There are two campgrounds on the lakeshore less than half a mile apart (see Silver Bowl Campground, number 22). Trails lead into the wilderness and to other nearby lakes. Elevation 6,400 feet. Stay limit 14 days. Open from May through October.

22 Silver Lake: Silver Bowl

Location: 20 miles northwest of Westwood.
Sites: 18 sites for tents and RVs.
Facilities: Tables, fire rings, drinking water, vault toilets, boat ramp.
Fee per night: $10.
Management: Lassen National Forest, 530-258-2141.
Activities: Hiking, swimming, fishing, boating.
Finding the campground: From Westwood (20 miles west of Susanville on California Highway 36), drive north on County Road A21 for 12 miles, turn left onto Country Road 110 (Silver Lake Road), and drive 8 miles to Silver Lake. Turn right at the lake.

About the campground: See Rocky Knoll Campground (number 21).

23 Eagle Lake: North Eagle Lake

Location: 41 miles north of Susanville.
Sites: 20 sites for tents and RVs.
Facilities: Tables, grills, drinking water, vault toilets. Dump station and boat ramp nearby (fee charged).
Fee per night: $6.
Management: Bureau of Land Management, 530-257-5381.
Activities: Fishing, swimming, boating, waterskiing, hiking.
Finding the campground: From Susanville, drive north on California Highway 139 for 40 miles, turn left (east) onto County Road A1 (Eagle Lake Road), and drive half a mile.

About the campground: Eagle Lake is the second largest natural lake in California. Six campgrounds are located on its pine-lined shores—this one at the north end of the lake and five on the south shore. All water activities can be enjoyed here, and the lake is known for its trophy-size trout, which average three to five pounds. Eagle Lake is stocked annually with 200,000 trout, 10 to 12 inches long. This campground offers direct access to the water. Elevation 5,100 feet. Stay limit 14 days. Open from Memorial Day to December 31.

24 Eagle Lake: Merrill

Location: 17 miles northwest of Susanville.
Sites: 181 sites for tents and RVs up to 35 feet long.
Facilities: Tables, grills, drinking water, flush toilets, dump station. The facilities are wheelchair accessible.
Fee per night: $13-$15. For reservations call 800-280-CAMP. There is a one-time reservation fee of $8.65.
Management: Lassen National Forest, 530-257-4188.
Activities: Fishing, swimming, boating, waterskiing, hiking, cycling.
Finding the campground: From the junction of California Highways 139

and 36 in Susanville, drive west on CA 36 for 3 miles, turn right (northeast) onto County Highway A1, and drive 14 miles.

About the campground: Situated on the south shore of the lake in a pine grove. A store, pay showers, and a full-service marina are close by. A boat ramp is located at Aspen Grove, 2 miles to the east. The 5-mile South Shore Trail is ideal for cycling or hiking. See North Eagle Lake Campground (number 23) for information about Eagle Lake. Elevation 5,100 feet. Stay limit 14 days. Open from May through October, but will remain open to the end of the fishing season, weather permitting.

25 Eagle Lake: Christie

Location: 19 miles northwest of Susanville.
Sites: 69 sites for tents and RVs, including some pull-thrus.
Facilities: Tables, grills, drinking water, flush toilets, dump station. The facilities are wheelchair accessible.
Fee per night: $13, double sites $20.
Management: Lassen National Forest, 530-257-4188.
Activities: Fishing, swimming, boating, waterskiing, hiking.
Finding the campground: From the junction of California Highways 139 and 36 in Susanville, drive west on CA 36 for 3 miles, turn right (northeast) onto County Highway A1, and drive 16 miles.

About the campground: See North Eagle Lake Campground (number 23) and Merrill Campground (number 24) for area information. Elevation 5,100 feet. Stay limit 14 days. Open from May through October.

26 Eagle Lake: West Eagle Group Camp

Location: 17 miles northwest of Susanville.
Sites: 2 group sites for tents and RVs up to 35 feet long; camp 1 accommodates 100 people, camp 2 holds 75 people.
Facilities: Tables, grills, drinking water, flush toilets. The facilities are wheelchair accessible.
Fee per night: Camp 1 $70-$120, camp 2 $60-$80. Reservations are required; call 800-280-CAMP. There is a one-time reservation fee of $8.65.
Management: Lassen National Forest, 530-257-4188.
Activities: Fishing, swimming, boating, waterskiing, hiking.
Finding the campground: From the junction of California Highways 139 and 36 in Susanville, drive west on CA 36 for 3 miles, turn right (northeast) onto County Highway A1, and drive 13 miles. Turn right (east) onto County Road 231 and drive 0.7 mile.

About the campground: See North Eagle Lake Campground (number 23) and Merrill Campground (number 24) for area information. Elevation 5,100 feet. Stay limit 14 days. Open from May through October.

27 Eagle Lake: Eagle

Location: 17 miles northwest of Susanville.
Sites: 45 sites for tents and RVs up to 32 feet long.
Facilities: Tables, grills, drinking water, flush toilets. The facilities are wheelchair accessible.
Fee per night: $13, double sites $20. For reservations call 800-280-CAMP. There is a one-time reservation fee of $8.65.
Management: Lassen National Forest, 530-257-4188.
Activities: Fishing, swimming, boating, waterskiing, hiking.
Finding the campground: From the junction of California Highways 139 and 36 in Susanville, drive west on CA 36 for 3 miles, turn right (northeast) onto County Highway A1, and drive 13 miles. Turn right (east) onto County Road 231 and drive a little over a mile.

About the campground: See North Eagle Lake Campground (number 23) and Merrill Campground (number 24) for area information. Elevation 5,100 feet. Stay limit 14 days. Open from May through October.

28 Eagle Lake: Aspen Grove

Location: 18 miles northwest of Susanville.
Sites: 26 sites for tents.
Facilities: Tables, grills, drinking water, flush toilets, boat ramp. The facilities are wheelchair accessible.
Fee per night: $11.
Management: Lassen National Forest, 530-257-4188.
Activities: Fishing, swimming, boating, waterskiing, hiking.
Finding the campground: From the junction of California Highways 139 and 36 in Susanville, drive west on CA 36 for 3 miles, turn right (northeast) onto County Highway A1, and drive 13 miles. Turn right (east) onto County Road 231 and drive 2.2 miles.

About the campground: See North Eagle Lake Campground (number 23) and Merrill Campground (number 24) for area information. Elevation 5,100 feet. Stay limit 14 days. Open from May through October.

29 Ramhorn Springs

Location: 52 miles northeast of Susanville.
Sites: 10 sites for tents and RVs up to 27 feet long.
Facilities: Tables, grills, drinking water, vault toilets, corrals.
Fee per night: $5.
Management: Bureau of Land Management, 530-257-5381.
Activities: Hiking, horseback riding, hunting.
Finding the campground: From Susanville, drive east and then north 50 miles on U.S. Highway 395, turn right (east) onto Post Camp Road, and drive 2 miles.

About the campground: Hiking and horseback riding on undeveloped trails, not far from Shinn Peak (7,562 feet). Elevation 5,100 feet. Stay limit 14 days. Open all year.

30 Goumaz

Location: 16 miles west of Susanville.
Sites: 10 sites for tents and RVs up to 30 feet long.
Facilities: Tables, fire rings, vault toilets. No drinking water.
Fee per night: $5.
Management: Lassen National Forest, 530-257-4118.
Activities: Hiking, fishing, mountain biking.
Finding the campground: From the intersection of California Highways 139 and 36 in Susanville, drive 6 miles west on CA 36, turn right onto California Highway 44, and drive 6 miles. Turn left onto Goumaz Road (Forest Road 30N08) and drive 4 miles.

About the campground: Located on the banks of the Susan River, the camp is not far from the Bizz Johnson Trail, a 26-mile former railway right-of-way that offers fine views of the river as it passes through rugged, primitive Susan River Canyon. It is used by hikers, mountain bikers, and equestrians, as well as snowmobilers and cross-country skiers in winter. Elevation 5,200 feet. Stay limit 14 days. Open from May through October.

31 Roxie Peconom

Location: 11 miles southwest of Susanville.
Sites: 10 sites for tents.
Facilities: Tables, fire rings, drinking water, vault toilets.
Fee per night: None.
Management: Lassen National Forest, 530-257-4188.
Activities: Hiking, fishing.
Finding the campground: From the intersection of California Highways 139 and 36 in Susanville, drive west 9 miles on California Highway 36, turn left (south) onto Forest Road 29N03, and drive 2 miles.

About the campground: Elevation 4,800 feet. Stay limit 14 days. Open from May through October.

32 Battle Creek

Location: 41 miles east of Red Bluff.
Sites: 50 sites for tents and RVs.
Facilities: Tables, fire rings, drinking water, flush toilets.
Fee per night: $12.
Management: Lassen National Forest, 530-258-2141.
Activities: Fishing, hiking.

Finding the campground: From Red Bluff, drive east 41 miles on California Highway 36.

About the campground: Located on the banks of Battle Creek, the campground provides access to good trout fishing. The stream is well stocked annually with trout, mostly rainbows. The campground is 10 miles southwest of the southwest entrance to Lassen Volcanic National Park. Elevation 4,800 feet. Stay limit 14 days. Open from May through October.

33 Hole in the Ground

Location: 50 miles east of Red Bluff.
Sites: 11 sites for tents and RVs.
Facilities: Tables, fire rings, drinking water, vault toilets.
Fee per night: $10.
Management: Lassen National Forest, 530-258-2141.
Activities: Fishing, hiking.
Finding the campground: From Red Bluff, drive east 43 miles on California Highway 36 to Mineral, turn right onto County Road 172, and drive 5 miles. Turn right almost 180 degrees onto Forest Road 28N05 and drive 2 miles.

About the campground: Located on the banks of Mill Creek, which is stocked annually with rainbow trout. An 18-mile trail, following the creek most of the way, leads to Black Rock, where a campground is also located. Elevation 4,300 feet. Stay limit 14 days. Open from May through October.

34 Gurnsey Creek

Location: 54 miles east of Red Bluff.
Sites: 32 sites for tents and RVs, plus a group camp for up to 100 people.
Facilities: Tables, grills, drinking water, vault toilets.
Fee per night: $10 for family sites, $75 for group site. Reservations are required for the group camp; call 800-280-CAMP. There is a one-time reservation fee of $8.65.
Management: Lassen National Forest, 530-258-2141.
Activities: Fishing, hiking.
Finding the campground: From Red Bluff, drive east 54 miles on California Highway 36 to the campground sign.

About the campground: Fishing is fair in the spring, when the water level of the creek is highest. The stream is stocked annually with a small number of rainbow trout. Elevation 5,000 feet. Stay limit 14 days. Open from May through October.

35 Willow Springs

Location: 57 miles east of Red Bluff.
Sites: 8 sites for tents, RVs and trailers not recommended.
Facilities: Tables, fire rings, vault toilet. No drinking water.

Fee per night: $8.
Management: Lassen National Forest, 530-258-2141.
Activities: Fishing.
Finding the campground: From Red Bluff, drive east 51 miles on California Highway 36, turn left onto County Road 769, and drive 1.3 miles. Turn right onto Forest Road 29N19 and drive 5 miles.

About the campground: On the banks of Lost Creek, where a stray trout may occasionally nibble. Elevation 5,200 feet. Stay limit 14 days. Open from May through October.

36 Elam

Location: 59 miles east of Red Bluff.
Sites: 15 sites for tents and RVs.
Facilities: Tables, fire rings, drinking water, vault toilets.
Fee per night: $11.
Management: Lassen National Forest, 530-258-2141.
Activities: Fishing.
Finding the campground: From Red Bluff, drive east 56 miles on California Highway 36, turn right onto California Highway 32, and drive 3 miles.

About the campground: Located on the banks of Deer Creek, which is one of the better trout streams in the area. It is stocked annually with more than 65,000 rainbow and brook trout. Fishing season is in May and June. Elevation 4,600 feet. Stay limit 14 days. Open from May through October.

37 Alder Creek

Location: 63 miles east of Red Bluff.
Sites: 5 sites for tents only, RVs with trailers not recommended.
Facilities: Tables, fire rings, vault toilet. No drinking water.
Fee per night: $8.
Management: Lassen National Forest, 530-258-2141.
Activities: Hiking, fishing.
Finding the campground: From Red Bluff, drive east 56 miles on California Highway 36, turn right onto California Highway 32, and drive 7 miles.

About the campground: On Deer Creek; see Elam Campground (number 36) for fishing information. Elevation 3,900 feet. Stay limit 14 days. Open from April through October.

38 Potato Patch

Location: 66 miles east of Red Bluff.
Sites: 32 sites for tents and RVs.
Facilities: Tables, fire rings, drinking water, vault toilets.
Fee per night: $10.
Management: Lassen National Forest, 530-258-2141.

Activities: Fishing, hiking.
Finding the campground: From Red Bluff, drive east 56 miles on California Highway 36, turn right onto California Highway 32, and drive 9.6 miles.

About the campground: See Elam Campground (number 36) for fishing information. Elevation 3,400 feet. Stay limit 14 days. Open from May through October.

39 South Antelope

Location: 41 miles east of Red Bluff.
Sites: 4 sites for tents.
Facilities: Tables, fire rings, vault toilet. No drinking water.
Fee per night: None.
Management: Lassen National Forest, 530-258-3844.
Activities: Hiking, fishing.
Finding the campground: From Red Bluff, drive east on California Highway 36 for about 24 miles, turn right (south) onto Plum Creek Road, and drive 8 miles. Turn right (south) onto Ponderosa Way and drive 9 miles.

About the campground: Catches of small native trout are possible in the South Fork of Antelope Creek, and hikers can use its course for off-trail hiking. Better hiking options are available at Black Rock Campground (number 40), which is a gateway to the Ishi Wilderness. Elevation 2,700 feet. Stay limit 14 days. Open all year.

40 Black Rock

Location: 50 miles east of Red Bluff.
Sites: 4 sites for tents.
Facilities: Tables, fire rings, drinking water, vault toilet.
Fee per night: $5.
Management: Lassen National Forest, 530-258-3844.
Activities: Hiking, fishing.
Finding the campground: From Red Bluff, drive east on California Highway 36 for about 24 miles, turn right (south) onto Plum Creek Road, and drive 8 miles. Turn right (south) onto Ponderosa Way and drive 18 miles.

About the campground: Located on the banks of Mill Creek and at the base of Black Rock, one of the oldest geological features of the area. A trail leads west from the campground into the Ishi Wilderness. Elevation 2,100 feet. Stay limit 14 days. Open all year.

41 Benner Creek

Location: 7 miles north of Chester.
Sites: 9 sites for tents and RVs up to 20 feet long.
Facilities: Tables, fire rings, drinking water, vault toilets.
Fee per night: $8.

Management: Lassen National Forest, 530-258-2141.
Activities: None.
Finding the campground: From Chester, drive north 6.5 miles on County Road 318 (Juniper Lake Road).

About the campground: The campground is 5 miles south of Juniper Lake, which is in Lassen Volcanic National Park. Stay limit 14 days. Open from May through October.

42 High Bridge

Location: 5 miles northwest of Chester.
Sites: 12 sites for tents, RVs/trailers not recommended.
Facilities: Tables, fire rings, drinking water, vault toilets.
Fee per night: $10.
Management: Lassen National Forest, 530-258-2141.
Activities: Hiking, fishing.
Finding the campground: From the intersection of California Highway 36 and County Road 312 (Warner Valley Road) in Chester, drive northwest on Country Road 312 for 5 miles.

About the campground: Trout fishing can be good in the usually overlooked stream that flows beside the campground. The Warner Valley entrance to Lassen Volcanic National Park is 9 miles to the north. CR 312 is a dirt road, often rough, and is not suited for large vehicles. Elevation 5,200 feet. Stay limit 14 days. Open from May through October.

43 Warner Creek

Location: 7 miles northwest of Chester.
Sites: 13 sites for tents, RVs/trailers not recommended.
Facilities: Tables, fire rings, vault toilets. No drinking water.
Fee per night: $8.
Management: Lassen National Forest, 530-258-2141.
Activities: Fishing.
Finding the campground: From the intersection of California Highway 36 and County Road 312 (Warner Valley Road) in Chester, drive northwest on CR 312 for 7 miles.

About the campground: See High Bridge Campground (number 42).

44 Domingo Springs

Location: 8 miles northwest of Chester.
Sites: 18 sites for tents, RVs/trailers not recommended.
Facilities: Tables, fire rings, drinking water, vault toilets.
Fee per night: $10.
Management: Lassen National Forest, 530-258-2141.
Activities: Hiking, fishing.

Finding the campground: From the intersection of California Highway 36 and County Road 312 (Warner Valley Road) in Chester, drive northwest on CR 312 for 6 miles, bear left onto Country Road 311, and drive 2.2 miles.

About the campground: The Pacific Crest Trail passes half a mile west of the campground on its way north to Lassen Volcanic National Park (4 miles). The dirt road to the campground is not suitable for large vehicles. Elevation 5,200 feet. Stay limit 14 days. Open from May through October.

45 Last Chance Creek

Location: 6 miles north of Chester.
Sites: 12 sites for tents and RVs, plus 13 group sites.
Facilities: Tables, fire grills, drinking water, vault toilets.
Fee per night: $15 for individual, $20 for group sites. Reservations required for group sites.
Management: PG&E, 530-894-4687.
Activities: Fishing.
Finding the campground: From the Chester fire station, drive east 2.3 miles on California Highway 36 (crossing the causeway), turn left (north), and drive 3.2 miles.

About the campground: Situated where Last Chance Creek flows into the north end of Lake Almanor. Elevation 4,500 feet. Stay limit 14 days. Open from May through October.

46 Lake Almanor: Almanor

Location: 9 miles southeast of Chester.
Sites: 101 sites for tents and RVs, plus 20 group sites.
Facilities: Tables, fire rings, drinking water, vault toilets, boat ramp. The facilities are wheelchair accessible.
Fee per night: $12, group sites $55. For reservations call 800-280-CAMP; a reservation is required for group sites. There is a one-time reservation fee of $8.65.
Management: Lassen National Forest, 530-258-2141.
Activities: Swimming, fishing, boating, waterskiing.
Finding the campground: From Chester, drive 2 miles south on California Highway 36, turn left onto California Highway 89, and drive 5.5 miles southeast to the group camp. Turn left here and drive an additional 1.5 miles to the family camp.

About the campground: Lake Almanor, 27 miles west of Susanville, is one of the largest manmade lakes in California. Its sapphire blue waters reflect Mount Lassen from almost any angle, providing great photos for camera buffs. Virtually all water sports may be enjoyed on the lake, and Almanor offers good fishing for trout, salmon, and smallmouth bass. The lake is stocked annually with nearly a quarter of a million fish, including Chinook salmon and brown and Eagle Lake trout. Fishing is best in early spring and fall. Boat ramps, docks, and marinas are located along the shores of the lake.

Lake Almanor Campground sprawls along almost 2 miles of shoreline, and many of its campsites are directly on the water.

Sunset Magazine has listed Lake Almanor as one of the 100 best campgrounds in the western United States. The family campground is on the lake side of the highway, several hundred feet from the water. The group camp is 1.5 miles from the water on the opposite side of the highway. Elevation 4,500 feet. Stay limit 14 days. Open from May through October.

47 Lake Almanor: Lake Almanor

Location: 14 miles southeast of Chester.
Sites: 131 sites for tents and RVs, plus 1 group camp for up to 40 people.
Facilities: Tables, grills, drinking water, vault toilets, dump station, boat ramp.
Fee per night: $15, pets $1. Reservations required for group camp; call number below for fees.
Management: PG&E, 530-894-4687.
Activities: Swimming, fishing, boating, waterskiing.
Finding the campground: From Chester, drive 2 miles south on California Highway 36, turn left onto California Highway 89, and drive 12 miles.

About the campground: Lake Almanor Campground enjoys an inviting location. It spreads almost 2 miles along the lakeshore. Many of its sites are attractively located directly on the water. For more information about the area, see Almanor Campground (number 46). Elevation 4,500 feet. Stay limit 14 days. Open from May through October.

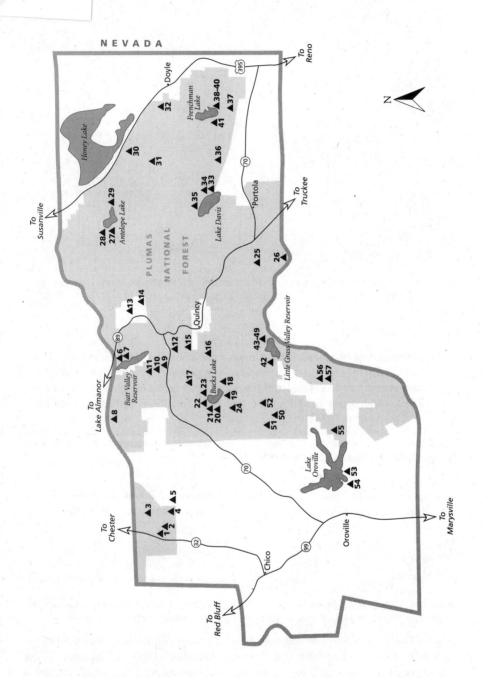

PLUMAS AREA

Plumas National Forest covers most of this region, providing more than 1.1 million acres of opportunity for nature lovers. The forest contains more than 1,000 miles of rivers and streams and over 100 lakes. Lake Oroville, which lies outside the national forest, is one of California's larger lakes. It offers good fishing for trout and salmon on more than 15,000 surface acres.

The Feather River National Scenic Byway, which begins about 10 miles north of Oroville on California Highway 70, travels along the rugged canyon of the North Fork of the Feather River, climbing over the Sierra crest at Beckwourth Pass and passing huge rock formations, waterfalls, and forested slopes en route. Feather Falls, the sixth highest waterfall in the United States with a spectacular 640-foot drop, can be reached either by boat from Lake Oroville or via the Feather Falls National Recreation Trail, a strenuous 8-mile round trip with a 2,500-foot elevation gain. Frazier Falls (100-foot drop), near Gold Lake, can be reached by an easy half-mile hike.

1 Soda Springs

Location: 52 miles northeast of Chico.
Sites: 10 sites for tents.
Facilities: Tables, fire rings, vault toilets. No drinking water.
Fee per night: None.
Management: Lassen National Forest, 530-258-2141.
Activities: Fishing.
Finding the campground: From the intersection of California Highways 99 and 32 in Chico, drive 52 miles northeast on CA 32.

About the campground: Elevation 3,900 feet. Stay limit 14 days. Open from May through October.

2 Butte Meadows

Location: 32 miles northeast of Chico.
Sites: 12 sites for tents and RVs.
Facilities: Tables, fire rings, drinking water, vault toilets.
Fee per night: $8.
Management: Lassen National Forest, 530-258-2141.
Activities: Fishing.
Finding the campground: From the intersection of California Highways 99 and 32 in Chico, drive northeast about 27 miles on CA 32, turn right (northeast) onto Humboldt Road, and drive 5 miles.

About the campground: Located on the banks of Butte Creek, which is stocked annually with rainbow trout. Elevation 4,600 feet. Stay limit 14 days. Open from May through October.

Plumas Area Campgrounds

		Group sites	RV sites	Total sites	Max. RV length	Hookups	Toilets	Showers	Drinking water	Dump station	Pets	Wheelchair	Recreation	Fee ($)	Season	Can reserve	Length of stay
1	Soda Springs			10			V				•		F		May–October		14
2	Butte Meadows		•	12			V		•		•		F	8	May–October		14
3	Cherry Hill		•	25			V		•		•		F	9	May–October	•	14
4	West Branch		•	15			V		•		•		F	8	May–October		14
5	Philbrook Lake		•	20			V		•		•		SFB	15	May–October		14
Butt Valley Reservoir (6–7)																	
6	Ponderosa Flat		•	63			V		•		•		SFB	15	May–October		14
7	Cool Springs		•	30			V		•		•		SFB	15	May–October		14
8	Yellow Creek		•	10			V		•		•		F	15	May–October		14
9	Gansner Bar		•	14	31	F		•		•		•	HSF	11	April–October		14
10	North Fork		•	20	32	F		•	•	•		•	HSF	11	May–October		14
11	Queen Lily		•	12	17	F		•		•			HSF	11	May–October		14
12	Hallsted		•	20	23	F		•		•			SF	9	May–October	•	14
13	Greenville		•	14			V		•	•	•		H	8			14
14	Taylorsville County Park		•	47			F	•	•	•	•		R	10			14
15	Snake Lake			7			V				•		FB		May–October		14
16	Deanes Valley			7			V				•		F		May–October		14
17	Silver Lake			8			V				•		FB		May–October		14
Bucks Lake (18–24)																	
18	Whitehorse		•	20			V		•		•		F	12	June–October		14
19	Haskins Valley		•	65			V		•	•	•		SFBL	15	June–October		14
20	Lower Bucks		•	6							•		SFB	6	June–October		14

		Group sites	RV sites	Total sites	Max. RV length	Hookups	Toilets	Showers	Drinking water	Dump station	Pets	Wheelchair	Recreation	Fee ($)	Season	Can reserve	Length of stay
21	Sundew		•	19	22		V		•		•		SFB	12	June–October		14
22	Hutchins Group Camp	•	•	3			V		•	•	•	•	HS FB	45	June–October		14
23	Mill Creek		•	10			V		•		•		HS FB	12	June–October		14
24	Grizzly Creek		•	8			V				•		F	9	June–October		14
25	Plumas-Eureka State Park		•	67			F	•	•	•	•	•	HF	15–17	May–Oct. 15		15
26	Lakes Basin	•	•	25			V		•		•		HSF	10	June–October	•	14

Antelope Lake (27–29)

		Group sites	RV sites	Total sites	Max. RV length	Hookups	Toilets	Showers	Drinking water	Dump station	Pets	Wheelchair	Recreation	Fee ($)	Season	Can reserve	Length of stay
27	Boulder Creek		•	70			V		•	•	•		SFB	12	May–October	•	14
28	Lone Rock		•	86			V		•	•	•		SFBL	12–14	May–October	•	14
29	Long Point	•	•	42			V		•		•	•	SFB	12–35	May–October	•	14
30	Laufman		•	6			V				•						14
31	Conklin Park		•	9			V				•		F				14
32	Meadow View		•	6			V				•						14

Lake Davis (33–35)

		Group sites	RV sites	Total sites	Max. RV length	Hookups	Toilets	Showers	Drinking water	Dump station	Pets	Wheelchair	Recreation	Fee ($)	Season	Can reserve	Length of stay
33	Grizzly		•	55			F		•	•	•		SFBL	12	May–October		14
34	Grasshopper Flat		•	70			F		•	•	•		SFBL	12	May–October		14
35	Lightning Tree		•	38							•		SFBL		May–October		14
36	Crocker		•	10			V				•		F		May–November		14
37	Chilcoot		•	40			F		•		•		HF	12	May–October		14

Frenchman Lake Recreation Area (38–41)

		Group sites	RV sites	Total sites	Max. RV length	Hookups	Toilets	Showers	Drinking water	Dump station	Pets	Wheelchair	Recreation	Fee ($)	Season	Can reserve	Length of stay
38	Frenchman		•	38			V		•		•		SFBL	12	May–October	•	14
39	Spring Creek		•	39			V		•		•		SFB	12	May–October	•	14
40	Big Cove		•	38			V		•		•		SFB	12–24	May–October	•	14

	Group sites	RV sites	Total sites	Max. RV length	Hookups	Toilets	Showers	Drinking water	Dump station	Pets	Wheelchair	Recreation	Fee ($)	Season	Can reserve	Length of stay
41 Cottonwood Springs	•	•	22			V		•	•	•		SFB	12–87	May–October	•	14

Little Grass Valley Reservoir (42–49)

	Group sites	RV sites	Total sites	Max. RV length	Hookups	Toilets	Showers	Drinking water	Dump station	Pets	Wheelchair	Recreation	Fee ($)	Season	Can reserve	Length of stay
42 Black Rock		•	30			V		•		•		HSF BL	10	May–October		14
43 Peninsula			25			F		•		•		HSF BL	12	May–October		14
44 Tooms		•	20			V		•		•		HSF BL	9	May–October		14
45 Wyandotte		•	28			F		•	•	•		HSF BL	11–15	May–October		14
46 Little Beaver		•	120			F		•	•	•		HSF BL	11–12	May–October		14
47 Red Feather		•	60			F	•	•	•	•	•	HSF BL	12	May–October	•	14
48 Running Deer		•	40			F		•	•	•		HSF BL	12	May–October		14
49 Horse Camp		•	10			V		•		•		HSF BLR	15	May–October		14
50 Milsap Bar		•	20	19		V				•		HSF		May–October		14
51 Rogers Cow Camp		•	5			V				•				May–October		14
52 Little North Fork		•	8			V				•		HSF		May–October		14

Lake Oroville State Recreation Area (53–54)

	Group sites	RV sites	Total sites	Max. RV length	Hookups	Toilets	Showers	Drinking water	Dump station	Pets	Wheelchair	Recreation	Fee ($)	Season	Can reserve	Length of stay
53 Bidwell Canyon		•	75		WES	F	•	•	•	•	•	FBL	16–20		•	30
54 Loafer Creek	•	•	144			F	•	•	•	•		SFB LR	10–40		•	30
55 Feather Falls Trailhead			5			V		•		•		H		April–October		14

Sly Creek Reservoir (56–57)

	Group sites	RV sites	Total sites	Max. RV length	Hookups	Toilets	Showers	Drinking water	Dump station	Pets	Wheelchair	Recreation	Fee ($)	Season	Can reserve	Length of stay
56 Sly Creek		•	26			V		•		•	•	FSBL	10	May–October		14
57 Strawberry		•	17			V		•		•		FSBL	8	May–October		14

Hookups: W = Water E = Electric S = Sewer
Toilets: F = Flush V = Vault P = Pit C = Chemical
Recreation: H = Hiking S = Swimming F = Fishing B = Boating L = Boat Launch O = Off-highway Driving R = Horseback Riding
Maximum Trailer/RV Length given in feet. Stay Limit given in days. Fee given in dollars.
If no entry under **Season,** campground is open all year. If no entry under **Fee,** camping is free.

3 Cherry Hill

Location: 36 miles northeast of Chico.
Sites: 13 walk-in tent sites, 12 sites for tents and RVs.
Facilities: Tables, fire rings, drinking water, vault toilets.
Fee per night: $9. For reservations call 800-280-CAMP. There is a one-time reservation fee of $8.65.
Management: Lassen National Forest, 530-258-2141.
Activities: Fishing.
Finding the campground: From the intersection of California Highways 99 and 32 in Chico, drive northeast about 27 miles on CA 32, turn right (northeast) onto Humboldt Road, and drive 8.6 miles.

About the campground: Situated on the banks of Butte Creek, which is stocked annually with rainbow trout. Elevation 4,700 feet. Stay limit 14 days. Open from May through October.

4 West Branch

Location: 39 miles northeast of Chico.
Sites: 15 sites for tents and RVs.
Facilities: Tables, fire rings, drinking water, vault toilets.
Fee per night: $8.
Management: Lassen National Forest, 530-258-2141.
Activities: Fishing.
Finding the campground: From the intersection of California Highways 99 and 32 in Chico, drive northeast about 27 miles on CA 32, turn right (northeast) onto Humboldt Road, and drive 5 miles. Drive southeast 4.5 miles on Skyway Road, turn left onto Humbug Summit Road and drive 1.5 miles. Turn right onto West Branch Road and drive 0.5 mile.

About the campground: Located on the West Branch of the Feather River. Elevation 4,800 feet. Stay limit 14 days. Open from May through October.

5 Philbrook Lake

Location: 42 miles northeast of Chico.
Sites: 20 sites for tents and RVs.
Facilities: Tables, grills, drinking water, vault toilets. The facilities are wheelchair accessible.
Fee per night: $15, pets $1.
Management: PG&E, 530-386-5164.
Activities: Swimming, fishing, boating.
Finding the campground: From the intersection of California Highways 99 and 32 in Chico, drive northeast about 27 miles on CA 32, turn right (northeast) onto Humboldt Road, and drive 5 miles. Drive southeast 4.5 miles on Skyway Road, turn left onto Humbug Summit Road and drive 1.5 miles. Turn right onto West Branch Road (which becomes Philbrook Road) and drive 3.5 miles.

About the campground: The campground is near the shoreline of Philbrook Reservoir, a pretty lake stocked annually with small trout, which never seem to grow. Elevation 5,600 feet. Stay limit 14 days. Open from May through October.

6 Butt Valley Reservoir: Ponderosa Flat

Location: 12 miles south of Chester.
Sites: 63 sites for tents and RVs.
Facilities: Tables, grills, drinking water, vault toilets, boat ramp.
Fee per night: $15, pets $1.
Management: PG&E, 530-894-4687.
Activities: Swimming, fishing, boating.
Finding the campground: From Chester, drive 2 miles south on California Highway 36, turn left onto California Highway 89, and drive 7 miles. Turn right onto Butt Valley Road (County Road 305) and drive 3 miles.

About the campground: Located on the north end of Butt Valley Reservoir, which is subject to heavy drawdowns of water but contains some large rainbow trout. Elevation 4,150 feet. Stay limit 14 days. Open from May through October.

7 Butt Valley Reservoir: Cool Springs

Location: 14 miles south of Chester.
Sites: 30 sites for tents and RVs.
Facilities: Tables, grills, drinking water, vault toilets.
Fee per night: $15, pets $1.
Management: PG&E, 530-894-4687.
Activities: Swimming, fishing, boating.
Finding the campground: From Chester, drive 2 miles south on California Highway 36, turn left onto California Highway 89, and drive 7 miles. Turn right onto Butt Valley Road (County Road 305) and drive 5 miles.

About the campground: See Ponderosa Flat Campground (number 6).

8 Yellow Creek

Location: 15 miles south of Chester.
Sites: 10 sites for tents and RVs.
Facilities: Tables, grills, drinking water, vault toilets.
Fee per night: $15, pets $1.
Management: PG&E, 530-894-4687.
Activities: Fishing.
Finding the campground: From Chester, drive 2 miles south on California Highway 36, turn left onto California Highway 89, and drive 5 miles. Turn right onto Humbug Road (County Road 308/309) and drive 0.7 mile. Bear left onto CR 309 and drive 1.3 miles, turn right onto Country Road 307 and drive 4.5 miles, and then turn left at a Y intersection and drive 1.2 miles.

About the campground: Elevation 4,400 feet. Stay limit 14 days. Open from May through October.

9 Gansner Bar

Location: 51 miles northeast of Oroville.
Sites: 14 sites for tents and RVs up to 31 feet long.
Facilities: Tables, fire rings, drinking water, flush toilets. The facilities are wheelchair accessible.
Fee per night: $11.
Management: Plumas National Forest, 530-283-0555.
Activities: Hiking, swimming, fishing.
Finding the campground: From Oroville, drive northeast 50 miles on California Highway 70 to Gansner Ranch Ranger Station, at the intersection with Caribou Road. Turn left (north) onto Caribou and drive 0.5 mile.

About the campground: Located on the banks of the North Fork of the Feather River, which is stocked annually with rainbow trout. Elevation 2,300 feet. Stay limit 14 days. Open from April through October.

10 North Fork

Location: 52 miles northeast of Oroville.
Sites: 20 sites for tents and RVs up to 32 feet long.
Facilities: Tables, grills, drinking water, flush toilets, dump station. The facilities are wheelchair accessible.
Fee per night: $11.
Management: Plumas National Forest, 530-283-0555.
Activities: Hiking, swimming, fishing.
Finding the campground: From Oroville, drive northeast 50 miles on California Highway 70 to Gansner Ranch Ranger Station, at the intersection with Caribou Road. Turn left (north) onto Caribou and drive 2 miles.

About the campground: Located on the banks of the North Fork of the Feather River, which is stocked annually with rainbow trout. Elevation 2,600 feet. Stay limit 14 days. Open from May through October.

11 Queen Lily

Location: 53 miles northeast of Oroville.
Sites: 12 sites for tents and RVs up to 17 feet long.
Facilities: Tables, fire rings, drinking water, flush toilets.
Fee per night: $11.
Management: Plumas National Forest, 530-283-0555.
Activities: Hiking, swimming, fishing.
Finding the campground: From Oroville, drive northeast 50 miles on California Highway 70 to Gansner Ranch Ranger Station, at the intersection with Caribou Road. Turn left (north) onto Caribou and drive 3 miles.

About the campground: See North Fork Campground (number 10).

12 Hallsted

Location: 60 miles northeast of Oroville.
Sites: 20 sites for tents and RVs up to 23 feet long.
Facilities: Tables, fire rings, drinking water, flush toilets.
Fee per night: $9. For reservations call 800-280-CAMP. There is a one-time reservation fee of $8.65.
Management: Plumas National Forest, 530-283-0555.
Activities: Swimming, fishing.
Finding the campground: From Oroville, drive northeast on California Highway 70 for 60 miles.

About the campground: Located on the banks of the East Branch of the North Fork of the Feather River, which is a stocked trout stream. Elevation 2,800 feet. Stay limit 14 days. Open from May through October.

13 Greenville

Location: 2 miles north of Greenville.
Sites: 14 sites for tents and RVs.
Facilities: Tables, fire rings, grills, drinking water, vault toilets, dump station.
Fee per night: $8.
Management: Indian Valley Community Services District, 530-284-7224.
Activities: Hiking, biking.
Finding the campground: From Greenville, drive north on California Highway 89 for 1.5 miles.

About the campground: A partially wooded location close to town, with a stream nearby. Nine miles from Lake Almanor and 3.5 miles from Round Valley Reservoir. Stay limit 14 days. Open all year.

14 Taylorsville County Park

Location: At the east end of Taylorsville.
Sites: 47 sites for tents and RVs, divided into a lower and an upper level.
Facilities: Tables, drinking water, showers, flush and vault toilets, dump station.
Fee per night: $10.
Management: Plumas County Recreation Department, 530-284-6646.
Activities: Biking, horseback riding.
Finding the campground: From Taylorsville, drive east on County Road 207 to the park at the end of town.

About the campground: A wooded site close to town with a stream nearby. Most campsites have makeshift fire rings, and campfires are permitted. Horses may be tethered at the campsite at no additional charge. Stay limit 14 days. Open all year.

15 Snake Lake

Location: 7 miles northwest of Quincy.
Sites: 7 sites for tents.
Facilities: Tables, fire rings, vault toilets. No drinking water.
Fee per night: None.
Management: Plumas National Forest, 530-283-0555.
Activities: Fishing, boating.
Finding the campground: From Quincy, drive 5 miles west on Bucks Lake Road (Forest Road 119), turn right onto County Road 422, and drive 1.6 miles. Turn right onto Snake Lake Access Road and drive 0.5 mile.

About the campground: Snake Lake is relatively shallow, allowing catfish, bass, and bluegill to thrive. In addition, the lake is stocked annually with rainbow trout fingerlings. Elevation 4,200 feet. Stay limit 14 days. Open from May through October.

16 Deanes Valley

Location: 9 miles southwest of Quincy.
Sites: 7 sites for tents and RVs.
Facilities: Tables, fire rings, vault toilets. No drinking water.
Fee per night: None.
Management: Plumas National Forest, 530-283-0555.
Activities: Fishing.
Finding the campground: From Quincy, drive west 3.5 miles on Bucks Lake Road (Forest Road 119), turn left onto Forest Road 24N28, and drive 5 miles.

About the campground: Located on the South Fork of Rock Creek. Fishing is limited to small trout. Elevation 4,400 feet. Stay limit 14 days. Open from May through October.

17 Silver Lake

Location: 13 miles west of Quincy.
Sites: 8 sites for tents.
Facilities: Tables, fire rings, vault toilets. No drinking water.
Fee per night: None.
Management: Plumas National Forest, 530-283-0555.
Activities: Fishing, boating.
Finding the campground: From Quincy, drive 8 miles west on Bucks Lake Road (Forest Road 119), turn right (north) onto Silver Lake Road (Forest Road 24N29X), and drive 5 miles.

About the campground: No powerboats are allowed on this beautiful, secluded lake. Fishing is limited to small trout. Elevation 5,800 feet. Stay limit 14 days. Open from May through October.

18 Bucks Lake: Whitehorse

Location: 15 miles west of Quincy.
Sites: 20 sites for tents and RVs.
Facilities: Tables, fire rings, drinking water, vault toilets.
Fee per night: $12.
Management: Plumas National Forest, 530-283-0555.
Activities: Fishing.
Finding the campground: From Quincy, drive west 15 miles on Bucks Lake Road.

About the campground: Whitehorse is on the banks of Bucks Creek, about half a mile east of Bucks Lake, where you can engage in most water sports. The lake is stocked annually with more than 20,000 rainbow, brook, and Eagle Lake trout, and it is noted for good trout fishing. Two boat ramps are located on the south shore of the lake and one on the north shore. Elevation 5,200 feet. Stay limit 14 days. Open from June through October.

19 Bucks Lake: Haskins Valley

Location: 17 miles west of Quincy.
Sites: 65 sites for tents and RVs.
Facilities: Tables, grills, drinking water, vault toilets, dump station, boat ramp.
Fee per night: $15, pets $1.
Management: PG&E, 530-386-5164.
Activities: Swimming, fishing, boating, waterskiing.
Finding the campground: From Quincy, drive west 17 miles on Bucks Lake Road.

About the campground: See Whitehorse Campground (number 18) for a description of Bucks Lake.

20 Bucks Lake: Lower Bucks

Location: 19 miles west of Quincy.
Sites: 6 sites for self-contained RVs only.
Facilities: Tables, fire rings. No water or toilet facilities.
Fee per night: $6.
Management: Plumas National Forest, 530-283-0555.
Activities: Swimming, fishing, boating, waterskiing.
Finding the campground: From Quincy, drive west 16 miles on Bucks Lake Road, turn right onto Bucks Lake Dam Road (Forest Road 33), and drive 3 miles.

About the campground: See Whitehorse Campground (number 18) for a description of Bucks Lake.

21 Bucks Lake: Sundew

Location: 19 miles west of Quincy.
Sites: 19 sites for tents and RVs up to 22 feet long.
Facilities: Tables, fire rings, drinking water, vault toilets.
Fee per night: $12.
Management: Plumas National Forest, 530-283-0555.
Activities: Swimming, fishing, boating, waterskiing.
Finding the campground: From Quincy, drive west 16 miles on Bucks Lake Road, turn right onto Bucks Lake Dam Road (Forest Road 33), and drive 3.3 miles.

About the campground: See Whitehorse Campground (number 18) for a description of Bucks Lake.

22 Bucks Lake: Hutchins Group Camp

Location: 20 miles west of Quincy.
Sites: 3 group sites for tents and RVs, each for 10 to 25 people.
Facilities: Tables, fire rings, drinking water, vault toilets, dump station. The facilities are wheelchair accessible.
Fee per night: $45.
Management: Plumas National Forest, 530-283-0555.
Activities: Hiking, swimming, fishing, boating, waterskiing.
Finding the campground: From Quincy, drive west 16 miles on Bucks Lake Road, turn right onto Bucks Lake Dam Road (Forest Road 33), and drive 3.6 miles.

About the campground: See Whitehorse Campground (number 18) for a description of Bucks Lake.

23 Bucks Lake: Mill Creek

Location: 21 miles west of Quincy.
Sites: 10 sites for tents and RVs.
Facilities: Tables, fire rings, drinking water, vault toilets.
Fee per night: $12.
Management: Plumas National Forest, 530-283-0555.
Activities: Hiking, swimming, fishing, boating, waterskiing.
Finding the campground: From Quincy, drive west 16 miles on Bucks Lake Road, turn right onto Bucks Lake Dam Road (Forest Road 33), and drive 5 miles.

About the campground: See Whitehorse Campground (number 18) for a description of Bucks Lake.

24 Bucks Lake: Grizzly Creek

Location: 19 miles west of Quincy.
Sites: 8 sites for tents and RVs.
Facilities: Tables, fire rings, vault toilets. No drinking water.
Fee per night: $9.
Management: Plumas National Forest, 530-283-0555.
Activities: Fishing.
Finding the campground: From Quincy, drive west about 18 miles on Bucks Lake Road to its intersection with Bucks Lake Dam Road (Forest Road 33). Bear left at the fork onto Forest Road 36 (County Road 414), and drive 0.7 mile.

About the campground: See Whitehorse Campground (number 18) for a description of Bucks Lake. Grizzly Creek Campground is about 1.5 miles west of the lake at an elevation of 5,400 feet.

25 Plumas-Eureka State Park: Upper Jamison

Location: 15 miles west of Portola.
Sites: 67 sites for tents and RVs.
Facilities: Tables, grills, drinking water, showers, flush toilets, dump station. The facilities are wheelchair accessible.
Fee per night: $15-$17, pets $1.
Management: California Department of Parks and Recreation, 916-836-2380.
Activities: Hiking, fishing.
Finding the campground: From Portola, drive west on California Highway 70 for 9 miles, turn left onto California Highway 89, and drive south 1 mile. Turn right onto County Road A14 and drive 5 miles.

About the campground: The park blends the history of California's hard-rock gold-mining period with the beauty of the northern Sierra Nevada peaks, lakes, and meadows. A mining museum and a restored stamp mill are located at the park headquarters, and the historic mining town of Johnsville is nearby. Two small lakes, Eureka and Madora, lie within the park. A 1.5-mile loop trail circles Madora. Another loop trail, 3 miles long, climbs 1,300 feet to the summit of Eureka Peak (7,447 feet).

The campground, selected by *Sunset Magazine* as one of the 100 best in the western United States, is attractively laid out in a tall pine forest, with trails leading to the museum/mining complex, Jamison Mine, and Grass and Smith Lakes (outside the park boundary). Elevation 4,700 feet. Stay limit 15 days. Open from May 1 through October 15.

26 Lakes Basin

Location: 17 miles southwest of Portola.
Sites: 24 individual sites for tents and RVs, plus 1 group site for up to 25 people.

Facilities: Tables, fire rings, drinking water, vault toilets.
Fee per night: $10; call for group fees. Reservations a~~r~~
group camp; call 800-280-CAMP. There is a one-time reser~~~~
Management: Plumas National Forest, 530-836-2575.
Activities: Hiking, mountain biking, swimming, fishing.
Finding the campground: From Portola, drive 7.5 miles ~~southwest on Coun~~
ty Road 114, turn right onto California Highway 89, and drive almost 2 miles.
Turn left onto Gold Lake Highway (County Road 519), and drive 7 miles.

About the campground: A scenic alpine landscape, 25 lakes and ponds connected by a well-maintained trail system, and unusual geological features make this campground an ideal base for exploration. A half-mile long trail leads from the campground to 175-foot-high Frazier Falls, best visited in spring when the water level is highest and wildflowers are in bloom. Elevation 6,400 feet. Stay limit 14 days. Open from June through October.

27 | Antelope Lake: Boulder Creek

Location: 31 miles southeast of Susanville.
Sites: 70 sites for tents and RVs.
Facilities: Tables, fire rings, grills, drinking water, vault toilets, dump station. Boat ramp 2 miles east.
Fee per night: $12. For reservations call 800-280-CAMP. There is a one-time reservation fee of $8.65.
Management: Plumas National Forest, 530-283-0555.
Activities: Swimming, fishing, boating, waterskiing.
Finding the campground: From Susanville, drive southeast for 10 miles on U.S. Highway 395, turn right just past Janesville onto County Road 208 (which becomes Forest Road 28N01), and drive 15 miles. Turn right onto Forest Road 28N03 and drive 6 miles.

About the campground: One of the more remote lakes in the Plumas National Forest, Antelope Lake is a good wildlife viewing area. The lake is heavily stocked annually with rainbow and brook trout, as well as Eagle Lake trout fingerlings. The campground is on the shoreline in an attractive pine forest. The dump station is located at Boulder Creek Work Center, about half a mile northeast of the campground. The boat ramp is at Lost Cove on the north shore of the lake, about 2 miles east of the campground. Elevation 5,000 feet. Stay limit 14 days. Open from May through October.

28 | Antelope Lake: Lone Rock

Location: 33 miles southeast of Susanville.
Sites: 86 sites for tents and RVs.
Facilities: Tables, fire rings, grills, drinking water, vault toilets, dump station, boat ramp.
Fee per night: $12-$14. For reservations call 800-280-CAMP. There is a one-time reservation fee of $8.65.

gement: Plumas National Forest, 530-283-0555.
vities: Swimming, fishing, boating, waterskiing.
nding the campground: From Susanville, drive southeast for 10 miles on U.S. Highway 395, turn right onto County Road 208, and drive 15 miles. Turn right onto Forest Road 28N03 and drive 2 miles. Then turn right onto Forest Road 27N41 and drive 6 miles.

About the campground: See Boulder Creek Campground (number 27).

---

29 | Antelope Lake: Long Point

Location: 29 miles southeast of Susanville.
Sites: 38 individual sites, plus 4 group sites for tents and RVs.
Facilities: Tables, fire rings, grills, drinking water, vault toilets.
Fee per night: $12-$14 individual sites, $23-$35 group sites. For reservations call 800-280-CAMP. There is a one-time reservation fee of $8.65.
Management: Plumas National Forest, 530-283-0555.
Activities: Swimming, fishing, boating, waterskiing.
Finding the campground: From Susanville, drive southeast for 10 miles on U.S. Highway 395, turn right onto County Road 208, and drive 15 miles. Turn right onto Forest Road 28N03 and drive 2 miles. Then turn right onto Forest Road 27N41 and drive 1.5 miles.

About the campground: See Boulder Creek Campground (number 27). This campground has a wheelchair-accessible nature trail and fishing dock.

---

30 | Laufman

Location: 23 miles southeast of Susanville.
Sites: 6 sites for tents and RVs.
Facilities: Tables, fire rings, vault toilet. No drinking water.
Fee per night: None.
Management: Plumas National Forest, 530-836-2575.
Finding the campground: From Susanville, drive southeast 20 miles on U.S. Highway 395, turn right onto County Road 336, and drive 3 miles.

About the campground: Laufman has little to recommend it except that it is a free place to stop for a night. Elevation 5,100 feet. Stay limit 14 days. Open all year.

---

31 | Conklin Park

Location: 31 miles southeast of Susanville.
Sites: 9 sites for tents and RVs.
Facilities: Tables, fire rings, vault toilets. No drinking water.
Fee per night: None.
Management: Plumas National Forest, 530-836-2575.
Activities: Fishing.

Finding the campground: From Susanville, drive southeast 20 miles on U.S. Highway 395, turn right onto County Road 336, and drive 11 miles. CR 336 becomes Forest Road 70 when the pavement begins.

About the campground: Situated in a quiet location on the banks of Willow Creek, which has a population of small, native trout. Elevation 5,900 feet. Stay limit 14 days. Open all year.

32 Meadow View

Location: 6 miles west of Doyle.
Sites: 6 sites for tents and RVs.
Facilities: Tables, fire rings, vault toilets. No drinking water.
Fee per night: None.
Management: Plumas National Forest, 530-836-2575.
Finding the campground: From the intersection of U.S. Highway 395 and County Road 331 in Doyle, drive west 6 miles on CR 331.

About the campground: Meadow View appeared rundown and has little to recommend it except as a free place to stop for a night. Elevation 6,100 feet. Stay limit 14 days. Open all year.

33 Lake Davis: Grizzly

Location: 9 miles north of Portola.
Sites: 55 sites for tents and RVs.
Facilities: Tables, fire rings, grills, drinking water, flush toilets, dump station, boat ramp.
Fee per night: $12.
Management: Plumas National Forest, 530-836-2575.
Activities: Swimming, fishing, boating, waterskiing.
Finding the campground: From Portola, drive east 3 miles on California Highway 70, turn left onto County Road 112 (Grizzly Road), and drive 6 miles.

About the campground: Davis is a beautiful mountain lake destination for those seeking a water sports vacation. It provides good trout fishing in the late spring and fall and bass fishing in summer. Almost 30,000 Eagle Lake and rainbow trout are stocked annually. The campground is on the southeast shore of the lake. Elevation 5,900 feet. Stay limit 14 days. Open from May through October.

34 Lake Davis: Grasshopper Flat

Location: 9 miles north of Portola.
Sites: 70 sites for tents and RVs.
Facilities: Tables, fire rings, grills, drinking water, flush toilets, dump station, boat ramp.
Fee per night: $12.

Management: Plumas National Forest, 530-836-2575.
Activities: Swimming, fishing, boating, waterskiing.
Finding the campground: From Portola, drive east 3 miles on California Highway 70, turn left onto County Road 112 (Grizzly Road), and drive 6 miles. The campground is on the shoreline of the lake, a short distance beyond Grizzly Campground (number 33).

About the campground: See Grizzly Campground (number 33).

35 Lake Davis: Lightning Tree

Location: 12 miles north of Portola.
Sites: 38 sites for self-contained RVs only; no tents.
Facilities: Tables, fire rings. No drinking water, no toilets. Dump station and boat ramp, 1 mile.
Fee per night: None.
Management: Plumas National Forest, 530-836-2575.
Activities: Swimming, fishing, boating, waterskiing.
Finding the campground: From Portola, drive east 3 miles on California Highway 70, turn left onto County Road 112 (Grizzly Road), and drive 9 miles.

About the campground: See Grizzly Campground (number 33).

36 Crocker

Location: 11 miles northeast of Portola.
Sites: 10 sites for tents and RVs.
Facilities: Tables, fire rings, vault toilets. No drinking water.
Fee per night: None.
Management: Plumas National Forest, 530-836-2575.
Activities: Fishing.
Finding the campground: From Portola, drive 5 miles east on California Highway 70, turn left onto County Road 111 at Beckwourth, and drive north 6 miles.

About the campground: Situated on the banks of intermittent Crocker Creek, where a few wild trout may be available. Elevation 5,800 feet. Stay limit 14 days. Open from May through November.

37 Chilcoot

Location: 23 miles northeast of Portola.
Sites: 35 sites for tents and RVs, 5 sites for tents only.
Facilities: Tables, fire rings, drinking water, flush toilets.
Fee per night: $12.
Management: Plumas National Forest, 530-836-2575.
Activities: Hiking, fishing.
Finding the campground: From Portola, drive 18 miles east on California Highway 70, turn left in Chilcoot onto Forest Road 176, and drive 5 miles.

About the campground: Situated on Little Last Chance Creek about 4 miles south of Frenchman Lake. See Frenchman Campground (number 38) for lake activities. Elevation 5,400 feet. Stay limit 14 days. Open from May through October.

38 Frenchman Lake Recreation Area: Frenchman

Location: 29 miles northeast of Portola.
Sites: 38 sites for tents and RVs.
Facilities: Tables, grills, drinking water, vault toilets, boat ramp. Dump station at Cottonwood Springs Campground (number 41).
Fee per night: $12. For reservations call 800-280-CAMP. There is a one-time reservation fee of $8.65.
Management: Plumas National Forest, 530-836-2575.
Activities: Swimming, fishing, boating, waterskiing.
Finding the campground: From Portola, drive 18 miles east on California Highway 70, turn left in Chilcoot onto Forest Road 176, and drive 9 miles. At the lake, take the right fork and drive 1.5 miles.

About the campground: Frenchman Lake Recreation Area contains four campgrounds, three along the lakeshore (Frenchman, Spring Creek, and Big Cove) and one on a stream 1.5 miles west of the lake (Cottonwood Springs). The lake provides a good place for a complete water sport vacation. The gambling halls of Reno, Nevada, are only 35 miles away. The lake is heavily stocked with trout annually to make up for a decision to kill pike by poisoning the lake in 1991; everything else died, too. Elevation 5,500 feet. Stay limit 14 days. Open from May through October.

39 Frenchman Lake Recreation Area: Spring Creek

Location: 28 miles northeast of Portola.
Sites: 39 sites for tents and RVs.
Facilities: Tables, grills, drinking water, vault toilets. Dump station at Cottonwood Springs Campground (number 41).
Fee per night: $12. For reservations call 800-280-CAMP. There is a one-time reservation fee of $8.65.
Management: Plumas National Forest, 530-836-2575.
Activities: Swimming, fishing, boating, waterskiing.
Finding the campground: From Portola, drive 18 miles east on California Highway 70, turn left in Chilcoot onto Forest Road 176, and drive 9 miles. At the lake, take the right fork and drive 1.7 miles.

About the campground: For a description of Frenchman Lake Recreation Area, see Frenchman Campground (number 38). Spring Creek is the only campground on the lake that has some sites directly on the water, making swimming and small boat inputs possible right from the campsite. Larger boats may launch at the ramp at Frenchman or the beach at Spring Creek. Elevation 5,500 feet. Stay limit 14 days. Open from May through October.

40 Frenchman Lake Recreation Area: Big Cove

Location: 29 miles northeast of Portola.
Sites: 19 single sites and 19 multifamily sites for tents and RVs.
Facilities: Tables, grills, drinking water, vault toilets. Dump station at Cottonwood Springs Campground (number 41).
Fee per night: $12 for individual/family sites, $24 for multiple sites. For reservations call 800-280-CAMP. There is a one-time reservation fee of $8.65.
Management: Plumas National Forest, 530-836-2575.
Activities: Swimming, fishing, boating, waterskiing.
Finding the campground: From Portola, drive 18 miles east on California Highway 70, turn left in Chilcoot onto Forest Road 176, and drive 9 miles. At the lake, take the right fork and drive 2.5 miles.

About the campground: For a description of Frenchman Lake Recreation Area, see Frenchman Campground (number 38). Big Cove has an overflow area across the road from the main campground.

41 Frenchman Lake Recreation Area: Cottonwood Springs

Location: 29 miles northeast of Portola.
Sites: 20 sites for tents and RVs, plus 2 group sites for tents and RVs, one for up to 25 people, the other for up to 50.
Facilities: Tables, grills, drinking water, vault toilets. Dump station across the road.
Fee per night: $12 for individual/family sites, $45 and $87 for group sites. For reservations call 800-280-CAMP. There is a one-time reservation fee of $8.65.
Management: Plumas National Forest, 530-836-2575.
Activities: Swimming, fishing, boating, waterskiing.
Finding the campground: From Portola, drive 18 miles east on California Highway 70, turn left in Chilcoot onto Forest Road 176, and drive 9 miles. At the lake, take the left fork and drive 1.5 miles.

About the campground: For a description of Frenchman Lake Recreation Area, see Frenchman Campground (number 38). The dump station across the road charges $3.

42 Little Grass Valley Reservoir: Black Rock

Location: 53 miles northeast of Oroville.
Sites: 10 walk-in sites for tents, plus 20 RV sites in the parking lot.
Facilities: Tables, fire rings, drinking water, vault toilets, boat ramp.
Fee per night: $10.
Management: Plumas National Forest, 530-534-6500.
Activities: Hiking, fishing, swimming, boating, waterskiing.
Finding the campground: From the intersection of California Highways 70 and 162 in Oroville, drive east 8 miles on CA 162. Turn right onto Forbestown Road (signed TO CHALLENGE/LA PORTE) and drive about 40 miles, passing

through Forbestown, Challenge, Strawberry Valley, and La Porte. Turn left onto Little Grass Valley Road (County Road 514) and drive about 5 miles.

About the campground: The reservoir is a popular water sports location, and eight campgrounds line its shores. Black Rock is the only one on the western shore. The lake is heavily stocked annually with rainbow trout and kokanee. Elevation 5,060 feet. Stay limit 14 days. Open from May through October.

43 Little Grass Valley Reservoir: Peninsula

Location: 50 miles northeast of Oroville.
Sites: 25 sites for tents.
Facilities: Tables, fire rings, drinking water, flush toilets, boat ramp.
Fee per night: $12.
Management: Plumas National Forest, 530-534-6500.
Activities: Hiking, fishing, swimming, boating, waterskiing.
Finding the campground: From the intersection of California Highways 70 and 162 in Oroville, drive east 8 miles on CA 162. Turn right onto Forbestown Road (signed TO CHALLENGE/LA PORTE) and drive about 40 miles, passing through Forbestown, Challenge, Strawberry Valley, and La Porte. Turn left onto Little Grass Valley Road (County Road 514) and drive about 2 miles to the campground road on the right.

About the campground: See Black Rock Campground (number 42).

44 Little Grass Valley Reservoir: Tooms

Location: 50 miles northeast of Oroville.
Sites: 20 sites for RVs only; no tents.
Facilities: Drinking water, vault toilets, boat ramp.
Fee per night: $9.
Management: Plumas National Forest, 530-534-6500.
Activities: Hiking, fishing, swimming, boating, waterskiing.
Finding the campground: From the intersection of California Highways 70 and 162 in Oroville, drive east 8 miles on CA 162. Turn right onto Forbestown Road (signed TO CHALLENGE/LA PORTE) and drive about 40 miles, passing through Forbestown, Challenge, Strawberry Valley, and La Porte. Turn left onto Little Grass Valley Road (County Road 514) and drive about 2 miles to the campground road on the right. Tooms is adjacent to Peninsula Campground (number 43).

About the campground: The "campground" is actually the upper parking lot of the Tooms boat ramp. See Black Rock Campground (number 42).

45 Little Grass Valley Reservoir: Wyandotte

Location: 50 miles northeast of Oroville.
Sites: 26 individual sites and 2 double sites for tents and RVs.

Facilities: Tables, fire rings, drinking water, flush toilets, dump station, boat ramp.
Fee per night: $11 individual site, $15 double site.
Management: Plumas National Forest, 530-534-6500.
Activities: Hiking, fishing, swimming, boating, waterskiing.
Finding the campground: From the intersection of California Highways 70 and 162 in Oroville, drive east 8 miles on CA 162. Turn right onto Forbestown Road (signed TO CHALLENGE/LA PORTE) and drive about 40 miles, passing through Forbestown, Challenge, Strawberry Valley, and La Porte. Turn left onto Little Grass Valley Road (County Road 514) and drive about 2 miles to the campground road on the right. Drive about a quarter-mile beyond Peninsula Campground (number 43).

About the campground: See Black Rock Campground (number 42).

46 Little Grass Valley Reservoir: Little Beaver

Location: 51 miles northeast of Oroville.
Sites: 120 sites for tents and RVs.
Facilities: Tables, fire rings, drinking water, flush toilets, dump station, boat ramp.
Fee per night: $11-$12.
Management: Plumas National Forest, 530-534-6500.
Activities: Hiking, fishing, swimming, boating, waterskiing.
Finding the campground: From the intersection of California Highways 70 and 162 in Oroville, drive east 8 miles on CA 162. Turn right onto Forbestown Road (signed TO CHALLENGE/LA PORTE) and drive about 40 miles, passing through Forbestown, Challenge, Strawberry Valley, and La Porte. Turn left onto Little Grass Valley Road (County Road 514) and drive 1 mile. Make a sharp right turn onto Forest Road 22N68 and drive 2 miles.

About the campground: See Black Rock Campground (number 42).

47 Little Grass Valley Reservoir: Red Feather

Location: 52 miles northeast of Oroville.
Sites: 60 sites for tents and RVs.
Facilities: Tables, fire rings, drinking water, flush toilets, dump station, boat ramp. The facilities are wheelchair accessible.
Fee per night: $12. For reservations call 800-280-CAMP. There is a one-time reservation fee of $8.65.
Management: Plumas National Forest, 530-534-6500.
Activities: Hiking, fishing, swimming, boating, waterskiing.
Finding the campground: From the intersection of California Highways 70 and 162 in Oroville, drive east 8 miles on CA 162. Turn right onto Forbestown Road (signed TO CHALLENGE/LA PORTE) and drive about 40 miles, passing through Forbestown, Challenge, Strawberry Valley, and La Porte. Turn left onto Little Grass Valley Road (County Road 514) and drive 1 mile. Make a sharp right turn onto Forest Road 22N68 and drive almost 2.5 miles.

About the campground: See Black Rock Campground (number 42).

---

48 Little Grass Valley Reservoir: Running Deer

Location: 52 miles northeast of Oroville.
Sites: 40 sites for tents and RVs.
Facilities: Tables, fire rings, drinking water, flush toilets, dump station, boat ramp.
Fee per night: $12.
Management: Plumas National Forest, 530-534-6500.
Activities: Hiking, fishing, swimming, boating, waterskiing.
Finding the campground: From the intersection of California Highways 70 and 162 in Oroville, drive east 8 miles on CA 162. Turn right onto Forbestown Road (signed TO CHALLENGE/LA PORTE) and drive about 40 miles, passing through Forbestown, Challenge, Strawberry Valley, and La Porte. Turn left onto Little Grass Valley Road (County Road 514) and drive 1 mile. Make a sharp right turn onto Forest Road 22N68 and drive about 3 miles.

About the campground: See Black Rock Campground (number 42).

---

49 Little Grass Valley Reservoir: Horse Camp

Location: 53 miles northeast of Oroville.
Sites: 10 sites for tents and RVs.
Facilities: Tables, fire rings, drinking water, vault toilets, 10 hitching posts, boat launch.
Fee per night: $15.
Management: Plumas National Forest, 530-534-6500.
Activities: Hiking, fishing, swimming, boating, waterskiing, horseback riding.
Finding the campground: From the intersection of California Highways 70 and 162 in Oroville, drive east 8 miles on CA 162. Turn right onto Forbestown Road (signed TO CHALLENGE/LA PORTE) and drive about 40 miles, passing through Forbestown, Challenge, Strawberry Valley, and La Porte. Turn left onto Little Grass Valley Road (County Road 514) and drive 1 mile. Make a sharp right turn onto Forest Road 22N68 and drive about 3.5 miles. The camp is near the point at which the South Fork Feather River enters the lake.

About the campground: See Black Rock Campground (number 42) for information about the area. Elevation 5,000 feet. Stay limit 14 days. Open from May through October.

---

50 Milsap Bar

Location: 33 miles northeast of Oroville.
Sites: 20 sites for tents and RVs up to 19 feet long.
Facilities: Tables, fire rings, vault toilets. No drinking water.
Fee per night: None.
Management: Plumas National Forest, 530-534-6500.
Activities: Hiking, swimming, fishing, kayaking, rafting.

Finding the campground: From the intersection of California Highways 70 and 162 in Oroville, drive east and then north on CA 162 for 24 miles to Brush Creek Work Center. Turn right (south) onto Forest Road 62 (Milsap Bar Road) and drive about 9 miles. FR 62 is a narrow, winding, dirt road not suitable for trailers or large RVs.

About the campground: Milsap Bar provides access to Middle Fork Feather River, a designated National Wild and Scenic River. The portion of the river fronting the campground is called the Milsap Bar Scenic River Zone. It is 3.6 miles long and suitable for experienced kayakers. However, since it is bordered on both the north and south by wild-river zones (precipitous cliffs, waterfalls, and huge boulders), local knowledge of the area is essential. Elevation 1,600 feet. Stay limit 14 days. Open from May through October.

51 Rogers Cow Camp

Location: 32 miles northeast of Oroville.
Sites: 5 sites for tents and RVs.
Facilities: Tables, fire rings, vault toilets. No drinking water.
Fee per night: None.
Management: Plumas National Forest, 530-534-6500.
Activities: None.
Finding the campground: From the intersection of California Highways 70 and 162 in Oroville, drive east and then north on CA 162 for 32 miles, passing the Brush Creek Work Center. Watch for the campground sign on the left side of the road.

About the campground: There is little to recommend a stay at this campground. The access road is dirt and poorly maintained, and there is nothing to do when you get there. Elevation 4,100 feet. Stay limit 14 days. Open from May through October.

52 Little North Fork

Location: 37 miles northeast of Oroville.
Sites: 8 sites for tents and small RVs.
Facilities: Tables, fire rings, vault toilets. No drinking water.
Fee per night: None.
Management: Plumas National Forest, 530-534-6500.
Activities: Hiking, fishing, swimming.
Finding the campground: From the intersection of California Highways 70 and 162 in Oroville, drive east and then north on CA 162 for about 30 miles, passing the Brush Creek Work Center. Turn right (west) onto Forest Road 60 and drive about 7 miles on a narrow, winding, dirt road not suitable for trailers or large RVs.

About the campground: Little North Fork is a hard place to reach for activities that can be enjoyed elsewhere. Elevation 3,700 feet. Stay limit 14 days. Open from May through October.

Lake Oroville State Recreation Area

Created by the tallest earth-filled dam in the United States, Lake Oroville is one of California's larger lakes, with more than 15,800 acres of surface area and 167 miles of mostly undeveloped shoreline. It is primarily a boater's lake in that much of the shoreline is accessible only by boat. Recreation areas, including boat-in campgrounds, are located at various places around the lake. Boaters may land at any point to explore the shoreline and surrounding country, which is state-owned from 300 feet to as much as a mile from the high-water line.

More than a million fish have been stocked in Lake Oroville in the past few years, and annual stocking includes 50,000 brown trout and more than 150,000 chinook salmon. The lake also has a sizable population of other fish, including bass, rainbow trout, bluegill, crappie, and catfish. Feather Falls, with its spectacular 640-foot drop, is the sixth highest waterfall in the United States and a highlight of the recreation area. You can reach it by boat or trail. When the lake is at high water, boats can get to within a quarter-mile of the falls. Hikers must drive about 16 miles to reach the Feather Falls National Recreation Trail, an 8-mile round trip to the falls, with a 2,500-foot elevation gain.

The recreation area is divided into two parts, Lake Oroville itself and the much smaller North and South Forebays, about 5 miles to the north.

53 Lake Oroville State Recreation Area: Bidwell Canyon

Location: 9 miles east of Oroville.
Sites: 75 sites with full hookups, primarily for RVs but tents are allowed.
Facilities: Tables, grills, drinking water, showers, flush toilets, dump station, seven-lane boat ramp, boat rentals, marina, store. The facilities are wheelchair accessible.
Fee per night: $16-$20. For reservations call 800-444-7275. There is a one-time reservation fee of $7.50.
Management: California Department of Parks and Recreation, 530-538-2200.
Activities: Fishing, boating, waterskiing.
Finding the campground: From the intersection of California Highways 70 and 162 in Oroville, drive east on CA 162 for 6.5 miles, turn left (north) onto Kelly Ridge Road, and drive 2.5 miles.

About the campground: The campground is not on the shore of the lake but on a small hill just above the marina. The nearby visitor center features an open-air lookout tower with views over the lake. Stay limit 30 days. Open all year.

54 Lake Oroville State Recreation Area: Loafer Creek

Location: 8 miles east of Oroville.
Sites: 137 sites for tents and RVs (Coyote Campground), plus 6 group sites (Grasshopper Campground) for up to 25 people each, and a horse camp.

Facilities: Tables, grills, drinking water, showers, flush toilets, dump station, seven-lane boat ramp, swimming beach.

Fee per night: $10-$14, group sites $40. For reservations call 800-444-7275. There is a one-time reservation fee of $7.50 ($15 for groups).

Management: California Department of Parks and Recreation, 530-538-2200.

Activities: Fishing, swimming, boating, waterskiing, hiking, horseback riding.

Finding the campground: From the intersection of California Highways 70 and 162 in Oroville, drive east on CA 162 for 8 miles to the campground entrance on the left.

About the campground: More rustic and spacious than Bidwell Canyon (number 53), Loafer Creek is located in a mixed deciduous forest. It has a swimming beach and a 4.6-mile forested loop trail. Stay limit 30 days. Open all year.

55 Feather Falls Trailhead

Location: 27 miles northeast of Oroville.

Sites: 5 sites for tents.

Facilities: Tables, fire rings, drinking water, vault toilet.

Fee per night: None.

Management: Plumas National Forest, 530-534-6500.

Activities: Hiking.

Finding the campground: From the intersection of California Highways 70 and 162 in Oroville, drive east 8 miles on CA 162 (Olive Highway), turn right onto Forbestown Road, and drive 7 miles. Turn left onto Lumpkin Road and drive 10 miles to the trailhead turnoff. Turn left and drive 1.5 miles.

About the campground: Feather Falls, with its spectacular 640-foot drop, is the sixth highest waterfall in the United States. Feather Falls National Recreation Trail, which leads to the falls, is actually now two trails. The original trail involves an 8-mile round trip with a 2,500-foot elevation gain. A new trail, 9.5 miles round trip, provides an easier climb. Elevation 2,500 feet. Stay limit 14 days. Open from April through October.

56 Sly Creek Reservoir: Sly Creek

Location: 40 miles northeast of Oroville.

Sites: 26 sites for tents and RVs.

Facilities: Tables, fire rings, drinking water, vault toilets, boat ramp. The facilities are wheelchair accessible.

Fee per night: $10.

Management: Plumas National Forest, 530-675-2462.

Activities: Fishing, swimming, boating.

Finding the campground: From the intersection of California Highways 70 and 162 in Oroville, drive east 8 miles on CA 162. Turn right onto Forbestown Road (signed TO CHALLENGE/LA PORTE) and drive about 15 miles to Challenge.

From there, drive 12 miles northeast on La Porte Road, turn left at the campground turnoff, and drive 4.5 miles.

About the campground: The campground is on the southwest shore of the lake, which offers reasonably good trout fishing. Elevation 3,530 feet. Stay limit 14 days. Open from May through October.

57 Sly Creek Reservoir: Strawberry

Location: 41 miles northeast of Oroville.
Sites: 17 sites for tents and RVs.
Facilities: Tables, fire rings, drinking water, vault toilets, boat ramp.
Fee per night: $8.
Management: Plumas National Forest, 530-675-2462.
Activities: Fishing, swimming, boating.
Finding the campground: From the intersection of California Highways 70 and 162 in Oroville, drive east 8 miles on CA 162. Turn right onto Forbestown Road (signed TO CHALLENGE/LA PORTE) and drive about 15 miles to Challenge. From there, drive 16 miles northeast on La Porte Road, turn left at the campground turnoff, and drive 2 miles.

About the campground: Situated on the eastern shore of the lake. See Sly Creek Campground (number 56).

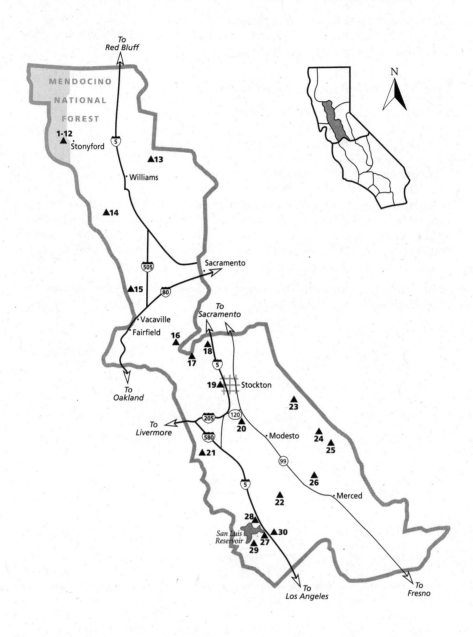

Central Valley

California's Central Valley is one of the most productive farming areas in the world. A drive along Interstate 5 through the Sacramento Valley reveals an astoundingly diverse agricultural bounty rarely seen anywhere. Miles and miles of orchards, vineyards, rice, and vegetable crops seem to stretch to an endless horizon. To a traveler accustomed to the smaller farms of the eastern United States, California agriculture boggles the mind.

But not all of the Central Valley is farmland. The eastern foothills of the Sierra Nevada offer a variety of outdoor adventures. Large lakes provide opportunities for a full range of water sports, and the foothills offer miles of hiking, equestrian, and mountain biking trails, as well as picnicking and wildlife-watching opportunities.

Cool winters and warm summers produce a long growing season, which contributes significantly to the Central Valley's agricultural bounty. In the summer, the average low temperature is 65 degrees Fahrenheit, while the average high is 96 degrees. In the winter, the low averages 39 degrees and the high 56. Spring sees readings of between 73 and 49, and in the fall temperatures are somewhat warmer, with an average high of 78 and low of 52. The percentage of average days of sunshine is 91 percent in summer, 71 in fall, 44 in winter, and 61 in the spring.

Although the Central Valley Tour Region (as defined by the California Division of Tourism) extends into Southern California, this book features only the campgrounds in its northern half. For the southern campgrounds, please see the companion FalconGuide *Camping Southern California,* also by Richard McMahon.

1 Mill Creek

Location: 8 miles west of Stonyford.
Sites: 6 sites for tents.
Facilities: Tables, fire rings, grills, vault toilet. No drinking water.
Fee per night: None.
Management: Mendocino National Forest, 530-963-3128.
Activities: Fishing, OHV driving.
Finding the campground: From Stonyford, drive west 8 miles on Fouts Spring Road (Forest Road M10), turn right (north) onto Forest Road 18N03, and drive a short distance.

About the campground: Situated on Mill Creek, in an area where vegetation is pretty much limited to brush and digger pine trees. The campground receives high OHV use from October through June. Elevation 1,700 feet. Stay limit 14 days. Open all year.

CENTRAL VALLEY CAMPGROUNDS

		Group sites	RV sites	Total sites	Max. RV length	Hookups	Toilets	Showers	Drinking water	Dump station	Pets	Wheelchair	Recreation	Fee ($)	Season	Can reserve	Length of stay
1	Mill Creek			6			V				•		FO				14
2	Fouts		•	11	16		V	•		•	•		FO				14
3	Davis Flat		•	70			V	•	•				O				14
4	Gray Pine Group Camp	•	•	1			V	•	•				O			•	14
5	South Fork		•	5			V		•				O				14
6	North Fork		•	6			V		•				O				14
7	Old Mill		•	10	16		V		•				H		May–October		14
8	Cedar Camp		•	5			V		•				H		mid-June–mid-Oct.		14
9	Digger Pine Flat		•	7			V		•				O				14
10	Dixie Glade		•	5			V	•	•		•		H		April–October		14
11	Mill Valley		•	15			V	•	•					3	April–October		14
12	Letts Lake Complex		•	40	20		V	•	•				SFB	5	mid-April–October		14
13	Colusa-Sacramento River State Recreation Area		•	14	30		F	•	•	•	•		FBL	12–14		•	15/30
14	Cache Creek Canyon Regional Park	•	•	48			F	•	•	•	•	•	HF	10–15			14
15	Lake Solano County Park		•	67	40	WES	F	•	•	•	•		FBL	15–18			14
16	Sandy Beach County Park		•	42		E	F	•	•	•	•	•	FBL	10–15			14
17	Brannan Island State Recreation Area	•	•	104	31		F	•	•	•	•	•	SFBL	15–17		•	15
18	Westgate Landing County Park		•	14			F	•		•	•	•	SFBL	9		•	14
19	Dos Reis County Park		•	26		WES	F	•	•		•	•	FBL	13		•	14
20	Caswell Memorial State Park		•	65	24		F	•	•		•		HF	15–17		•	15
21	Frank Raines–Deer Creek, OHV Park		•	34		ES	F	•	•		•		O	12–16			14
22	George J. Hatfield State Recreation Area	•	•	22	32		F	•		•			F	12–14		•	15
23	Woodward Reservoir County Park		•	155			F	•	•	•	•		SFBL	12–16			14

	Group sites	RV sites	Total sites	Max. RV length	Hookups	Toilets	Showers	Drinking water	Dump station	Pets	Wheelchair	Recreation	Fee ($)	Season	Can reserve	Length of stay
24 Modesto Reservoir Regional Park	•		170		WES	F	•	•	•		•	SFBL	12–16			14
25 Turlock Lake State Recreation Area	•		67	27		F	•	•		•	•	SFBL	12–16		•	15
26 McConnell State Recreation Area	•		21	27		F	•	•		•		SF	12–16	March–September		15

San Luis Reservoir State Recreation Area (27–30)

	Group sites	RV sites	Total sites	Max. RV length	Hookups	Toilets	Showers	Drinking water	Dump station	Pets	Wheelchair	Recreation	Fee ($)	Season	Can reserve	Length of stay
27 Medeiros	•		350			C	•		•			SFBL	9–11			15/30
28 San Luis Creek	•		53		WES	V		•	•			SFBL	14–16		•	15/30
29 Basalt	•		79			F	•	•	•	•	•	HSF BL	14–16		•	15/30
30 Los Banos Creek Reservoir	•		25	30		V			•			HSF BL	7–9			15/30

Hookups: W = Water E = Electric S = Sewer
Toilets: F = Flush V = Vault P = Pit C = Chemical
Recreation: H = Hiking S = Swimming F = Fishing B = Boating L = Boat Launch O = Off-highway Driving R = Horseback Riding
Maximum Trailer/RV Length given in feet. Stay Limit given in days. Fee given in dollars.
If no entry under **Season,** campground is open all year. If no entry under Fee, camping is free.

2 Fouts

Location: 9 miles west of Stonyford.
Sites: 11 sites for tents and RVs up to 16 feet long.
Facilities: Tables, fire rings, grills, drinking water, vault toilets. The facilities are wheelchair accessible.
Fee per night: None.
Management: Mendocino National Forest, 530-963-3128.
Activities: Fishing, OHV driving.
Finding the campground: From Stonyford, drive west 8 miles on Fouts Spring Road (Forest Road M10), turn right (north) onto Forest Road 18N03, and drive about 1 mile.

About the campground: Situated on a small creek, in an area where vegetation is pretty much limited to brush and digger pine trees. The campground receives high OHV use October through June. Elevation 1,700 feet. Stay limit 14 days. Open all year.

3 Davis Flat

Location: 9 miles west of Stonyford.
Sites: 70 dispersed sites for tents and RVs.
Facilities: Tables, fire rings, drinking water, vault toilets.
Fee per night: None.
Management: Mendocino National Forest, 530-963-3128.
Activities: OHV driving.
Finding the campground: From Stonyford, drive west 8 miles on Fouts Spring Road (Forest Road M10), turn right (north) onto Forest Road 18N03, and drive about 1 mile.

About the campground: Situated in the Davis Flat OHV Driving Area, the campground is used mainly for this purpose, especially from October through June. There are only 12 tables and fire rings for the 70 campsites. Elevation 1,700 feet. Stay limit 14 days. Open all year.

4 Gray Pine Group Camp

Location: 10 miles west of Stonyford.
Sites: 1 group site for tents and RVs, accommodates up to 70 people.
Facilities: Tables, fire rings, drinking water, vault toilets.
Fee per night: None, but reservations are required; call the number below.
Management: Mendocino National Forest, 530-963-3128.
Activities: OHV driving.
Finding the campground: From Stonyford, drive west 8 miles on Fouts Spring Road (Forest Road M10), turn right (north) onto Forest Road 18N03, and drive about 1.5 miles.

About the campground: Located in the Davis Flat OHV Driving Area, with vegetation consisting of manzanita, brush, and gray pine trees. The campground receives high OHV use from October through June. Elevation 1,700 feet. Stay limit 14 days. Open all year.

5 South Fork

Location: 10 miles west of Stonyford.
Sites: 5 sites for tents and RVs.
Facilities: Tables, fire rings, vault toilet. No drinking water.
Fee per night: None.
Management: Mendocino National Forest, 530-963-3128.
Activities: OHV driving.
Finding the campground: From Stonyford, drive west 8 miles on Fouts Spring Road (Forest Road M10), turn right (north), onto Forest Road 18N03 and drive 1.5 miles.

About the campground: Situated on the South Fork of Stony Creek in an area of high OHV use, especially from October through June. Elevation 1,900 feet. Stay limit 14 days. Open all year.

6 North Fork

Location: 10 miles west of Stonyford.
Sites: 6 sites for tents and RVs.
Facilities: Tables, stoves, vault toilet. No drinking water.
Fee per night: None.
Management: Mendocino National Forest, 530-963-3128.
Activities: OHV driving.
Finding the campground: From Stonyford, drive west 8 miles on Fouts Spring Road (Forest Road M10), turn right (north) onto Forest Road 18N03, and drive 1.5 miles.

About the campground: Situated adjacent to a stream in an open grove of oak trees. The area receives high OHV use, especially from October through June. Elevation 1,700 feet. Stay limit 14 days. Open all year.

7 Old Mill

Location: 11 miles southwest of Stonyford.
Sites: 10 sites for tents and RVs up to 16 feet long.
Facilities: Tables, fire rings, vault toilets. No drinking water.
Fee per night: None.
Management: Mendocino National Forest, 530-963-3128.
Activities: Hiking.
Finding the campground: From Stonyford, drive west 6 miles on Fouts Spring Road (Forest Road M10), turn left (south) onto Trough Springs Road (Forest Road M5), and drive about 5 miles. FR M5 is a narrow dirt road, not recommended for large vehicles.

About the campground: Elevation 3,700 feet. Stay limit 14 days. Open from May through October.

8 Cedar Camp

Location: 17 miles southwest of Stonyford.
Sites: 5 sites for tents and small RVs.
Facilities: Tables, fire rings, vault toilets. No drinking water.
Fee per night: None.
Management: Mendocino National Forest, 530-963-3128.
Activities: Hiking.
Finding the campground: From Stonyford, drive west 6 miles on Fouts Spring Road (Forest Road M10), turn left (south) onto Trough Springs Road (Forest Road M5), and drive about 11 miles. FR M5 is a narrow dirt road, not recommended for large vehicles or trailers.

About the campground: Situated in an area of mature fir and pine near the base of Goat Mountain (6,121 feet), this campground has little to recommend it or make it worth the long, slow drive to get here. Elevation 4,300 feet. Stay limit 14 days. Open from mid-June through mid-October.

9 Digger Pine Flat

Location: 10 miles southwest of Stonyford.
Sites: 7 sites for tents and small RVs.
Facilities: Tables, fire rings, vault toilets. No drinking water.
Fee per night: None.
Management: Mendocino National Forest, 530-963-3128.
Activities: OHV driving.
Finding the campground: From Stonyford, drive south 5 miles on Lodoga-Stonyford Road, turn right (southwest), onto Goat Mountain Road, and drive about 5 miles. The access road is not suited to trailers.

About the campground: The area receives high OHV use from October 1 to June 1. Elevation 1,500 feet. Stay limit 14 days. Open all year.

10 Dixie Glade

Location: 11 miles west of Stonyford.
Sites: 5 sites for tents and RVs.
Facilities: Tables, fire rings, drinking water, vault toilets. The facilities are wheelchair accessible.
Fee per night: None.
Management: Mendocino National Forest, 530-963-3128.
Activities: Hiking.
Finding the campground: From Stonyford, drive west 11 miles on Fouts Spring Road (Forest Road M10).

About the campground: Situated in a small, quiet location amid ponderosa pine, Douglas fir, and oak. The Bathhouse Trail leads northeast from the campground, connecting to other trails in the Snow Mountain Wilderness. Elevation 3,700 feet. Stay limit 14 days. Open from April through October.

11 Mill Valley

Location: 15 miles west of Stonyford.
Sites: 15 sites for tents and RVs.
Facilities: Tables, fire rings, drinking water, vault toilets.
Fee per night: $3.
Management: Mendocino National Forest, 530-963-3128.
Activities: None.
Finding the campground: From Stonyford, drive west about 13.5 miles on Fouts Spring Road (Forest Road M10), turn left onto Forest Road 17N02, and drive 1.5 miles.

About the campground: Situated beside pretty Lily Pond. Trout fishing 1 mile south at Letts Lake. Elevation 4,200 feet. Stay limit 14 days. Open from mid-April through October.

12 Letts Lake Complex

Location: 16 miles west of Stonyford.
Sites: 40 sites for tents and RVs up to 20 feet long.
Facilities: Tables, fire rings, drinking water, vault toilets.
Fee per night: $5.
Management: Mendocino National Forest, 530-963-3128.
Activities: Fishing, swimming, boating.
Finding the campground: From Stonyford, drive west about 13.5 miles on Fouts Spring Road (Forest Road M10), turn left onto Forest Road 17N02, and drive 2.5 miles.

About the campground: Campsites are distributed throughout a mixed pine forest in four separate campgrounds: Main Letts, Saddle, Stirrup, and Spillway. They are all close together and all have access to 30-acre Letts Lake. The lake is stocked annually with brook trout. No motorized boats are permitted. Elevation 4,500 feet. Stay limit 14 days. Open from mid-April through October.

13 Colusa-Sacramento River State Recreation Area

Location: In Colusa.
Sites: 14 sites for tents and RVs up to 30 feet long.
Facilities: Tables, fire rings, drinking water, flush toilets, showers, dump station, boat ramp.
Fee per night: $12-$14. For reservations call 800-444-7275. There is a one-time reservation fee of $7.50.
Management: California Department of Parks and Recreation, 530-458-4927.
Activities: Fishing, boating, bird watching.
Finding the campground: From the junction of Interstate 5 and California Highway 20 near Williams, drive east on CA 20 for 9 miles, turn left (north) onto 10th Street in Colusa, and drive 1 mile.

About the campground: Situated on the Sacramento River, with a variety of fishing options: striped bass in spring, shad in summer, salmon in late summer-early fall, and sturgeon in winter. Other catches include catfish, bluegill, and carp. Stay limit 15 days from June through September, 30 days from October through May. Open all year.

14 Cache Creek Canyon Regional Park

Location: 44 miles northwest of Woodland.
Sites: 48 sites for tents and RVs, including 3 group sites for 20 to 50 people each.
Facilities: Tables, fire rings, drinking water, flush toilets, dump station. The facilities are wheelchair accessible.
Fee per night: $10-$15. Call for group rates.
Management: Yolo County Parks and Recreation, 530-666-8115.
Activities: Fishing, hiking, kayaking, rafting.

Finding the campground: From the intersection of Interstate 505 and California Highway 16 (10 miles west of Woodland), drive about 34 miles northwest on CA 16.

About the campground: Cache Creek is the closest whitewater rafting to the San Francisco Bay area. The stretch near the campground can be good fishing grounds for catfish and sometimes for bass. Stay limit 14 days. Open all year.

15 Lake Solano County Park

Location: 18 miles north of Vacaville.
Sites: 67 sites for tents and RVs up to 40 feet long, 17 with full hookups.
Facilities: Tables, fire rings, drinking water, flush toilets, showers, dump station, boat ramp and rentals.
Fee per night: $15-$18, pets $1.
Management: Solano County Parks Department, 530-795-2990.
Activities: Fishing, boating.
Finding the campground: From the intersection of Interstates 80 and 505 at Vacaville, drive north 11 miles on I-505, turn left (west) onto California Highway 128, and drive 7 miles. Turn left (south) onto Pleasants Valley Road and drive about 300 yards.

About the campground: This small lake is actually a dammed section of Putah Creek, and its size varies. It is stocked with rainbow trout, and you can also catch catfish and sunfish. No motorized boats are permitted on the lake. Stay limit 14 days. Open all year.

16 Sandy Beach County Park

Location: 25 miles west of Stockton.
Sites: 42 sites for tents and RVs, with electric hookups.
Facilities: Tables, fire rings, drinking water, flush toilets, showers, dump station, playground, boat ramp. The facilities are wheelchair accessible.
Fee per night: $10-$15, pets $1.
Management: Sacramento County Parks Department, 707-374-2097.
Activities: Fishing, boating.
Finding the campground: From Stockton, drive north 7 miles on Interstate 5, turn left (west) onto California Highway 12, and drive 17 miles. After crossing the Sacramento River and entering Rio Vista, turn left onto Main Street and then right onto Second and proceed to Beach Avenue. Follow Beach to the campground.

About the campground: Situated on the Sacramento River at a popular fishing location. For fishing information, see Colusa-Sacramento River Campground (number 13). Stay limit 14 days. Open all year.

17 Brannan Island State Recreation Area

Location: 26 miles west of Stockton.
Sites: 102 sites for tents and RVs up to 31 feet long, 32 boat-berth sites with walk-in campsites, plus 2 group sites for tents and RVs up to 31 feet long.
Facilities: Tables, fire rings, drinking water, flush toilets, dump station, boat ramp, swimming area. The facilities are wheelchair accessible.
Fee per night: $15-$17, pets $1. For reservations call 800-444-7275 (required for group sites). There is a one-time reservation fee of $7.50 ($15 for a group).
Management: California Department of Parks and Recreation, 530-777-6671.
Activities: Swimming, fishing, boating, waterskiing, bird watching.
Finding the campground: From Stockton, drive north 7 miles on Interstate 5, turn left (west) onto California Highway 12, and drive 16 miles. Turn left (south) onto California Highway 160 and drive 3 miles.

About the campground: Situated on the Sacramento River, the campground provides an excellent base for fishing and exploring the many miles of waterway in the Sacramento-San Joaquin Delta. For fishing information, see Colusa-Sacramento River Campground (number 13). Nearby Frank's Tract is ideal for waterskiing. Stay limit 15 days. Open all year.

18 Westgate Landing County Park

Location: 13 miles northwest of Stockton.
Sites: 14 sites for tents and RVs.
Facilities: Tables, grills, drinking water, flush toilets, boat slips. The facilities are wheelchair accessible.
Fee per night: $9, pets $1, boat slips $10. Reservations accepted; call the number below.
Management: San Joaquin County Parks Department, 209-953-8800.
Activities: Swimming, fishing, boating, waterskiing,
Finding the campground: From Stockton, drive north 7 miles on Interstate 5, turn left (west) onto California Highway 12, and drive 5 miles. Turn right (north) onto Glasscock Road and drive 1 mile.

About the campground: Situated on the South Mokelumne River, the campground provides access to the waterways of the Sacramento-San Joaquin Delta. For fishing information, see Colusa-Sacramento River Campground (number 13). Stay limit 14 days. Open all year.

19 Dos Reis County Park

Location: In Stockton.
Sites: 26 sites for RVs with full hookups, tents accepted.
Facilities: Tables, grills, drinking water, flush toilets, showers, boat ramp. The facilities are wheelchair accessible.
Fee per night: $13, pets $1. Reservations accepted; call the number below.
Management: San Joaquin County Parks Department, 209-953-8800.

Activities: Fishing, boating.

Finding the campground: From Interstate 5 in Stockton, take the Lathrop exit west to an immediate right onto Manthey Road. Drive about 1 mile, turn left onto Dos Reis Road, and drive a short distance.

About the campground: Situated on the San Joaquin River, where fishing for striped bass is sometimes good. Stay limit 14 days. Open all year.

20 Caswell Memorial State Park

Location: 6 miles south of Manteca.

Sites: 65 sites for tents and RVs up to 24 feet long.

Facilities: Tables, fire rings, drinking water, flush toilets, showers.

Fee per night: $15-$17. For reservations call 800-444-7275. There is a one-time reservation fee of $7.50.

Management: California Department of Parks and Recreation, 209-826-1196.

Activities: Fishing, hiking.

Finding the campground: From the intersection of California Highways 120 and 99 at Manteca, drive southeast 1 mile on CA 99, turn right onto Austin Road, and drive 4.5 miles.

About the campground: Situated on the Stanislaus River. Although parts of the river are fairly heavily stocked with rainbow trout, this section of sluggish, green water more often yields catfish. A nature trail and a visitor center are also located here. Stay limit 15 days. Open all year.

21 Frank Raines–Deer Creek OHV Park

Location: 23 miles west of Patterson.

Sites: 34 sites with electric and sewer hookups, for tents and RVs.

Facilities: Tables, grills, drinking water, flush toilets, showers, playground.

Fee per night: $12-$16, pets $2, ATVs $2.

Management: Stanislaus County Department of Parks and Recreation, 408-897-3127.

Activities: OHV driving.

Finding the campground: From Interstate 5 at Patterson, take the Patterson exit, turn west onto Del Puerto Canyon Road, and drive 23 miles.

About the campground: This park encompasses 860 acres of steep terrain for OHV use (all-terrain vehicles, dune buggies, motorcycles, four-wheel-drive vehicles). Stay limit 14 days. Open all year.

22 George J. Hatfield State Recreation Area

Location: 42 miles west of Merced.

Sites: 21 sites, plus 1 group site for tents and RVs up to 32 feet long.

Facilities: Tables, grills, drinking water, flush toilets.

Fee per night: $12-$14, pets $1. Reservations required for group site; call 800-444-7275. There is a one-time reservation fee of $7.50.

Management: California Department of Parks and Recreation, 209-826-1196.
Activities: Fishing.
Finding the campground: From the intersection of California Highways 99 and 140 in Merced, drive west on CA 140 for 33 miles, turn right (north) onto California Highway 33, and drive 3.7 miles. Turn right onto Merced Street in Newman (which becomes Hills Ferry Road, then Kelley Road) and drive about 5 miles.

About the campground: Situated on the Merced River near its confluence with the San Joaquin. Catfish are the main catch. Stay limit 15 days. Open all year.

23 Woodward Reservoir County Park

Location: 5 miles north of Oakdale.
Sites: 155 sites for tents and RVs.
Facilities: Tables, grills, drinking water, flush toilets, showers, dump station, store, boat ramp and rentals.
Fee per night: $12-$16, pets $2.
Management: Stanislaus County Department of Parks and Recreation, 408-897-3127.
Activities: Swimming, fishing, boating, waterskiing.
Finding the campground: From the intersection of California Highway 120 and County Road J14 in Oakdale, drive north on CR J14 (26 Mile Road) for 5 miles.

About the campground: Woodward Reservoir covers almost 3,000 acres and has more than 20 miles of shoreline. Boating rules separate the lake into fishing and waterskiing areas. The lake is stocked annually with rainbow trout, and catfish and small bass can also be taken. Stay limit 14 days. Open all year.

24 Modesto Reservoir Regional Park

Location: 21 miles east of Modesto.
Sites: 170 sites for tents and RVs, including 130 with full hookups.
Facilities: Tables, fire rings, drinking water, showers, flush toilets, dump station, boat ramp. The facilities are wheelchair accessible.
Fee per night: $12-$16. Boat fee $5 per day.
Management: Stanislaus County Parks Department, 209-874-9540.
Activities: Swimming, fishing, boating, waterskiing.
Finding the campground: From the intersection of California Highways 99 and 132 in Modesto, drive east on CA 132 about 19 miles, turn left (north) onto Reservoir Road, and drive 2 miles.

About the campground: Modesto is a medium-sized lake covering about 2,700 acres. It has 30 miles of shoreline. Small to medium bass and trout are the main catches. A portion of the southern part of the lake has a speed limit of 5 miles per hour, which prevents waterskiing and benefits anglers. Stay limit 14 days. Open all year. No pets allowed.

25 | Turlock Lake State Recreation Area

Location: 26 miles east of Modesto.
Sites: 67 sites for tents and RVs up to 27 feet long.
Facilities: Tables, fire rings, drinking water, showers, flush toilets, boat ramp, fishing pier. The facilities are wheelchair accessible.
Fee per night: $12-$16. For reservations call 800-444-7275. There is a one-time reservation fee of $7.50.
Management: California Department of Parks and Recreation, 209-874-2008.
Activities: Fishing, swimming, boating, waterskiing.
Finding the campground: From the intersection of California Highways 99 and 132 in Modesto, drive east on CA 132 for about 23 miles, turn right (south) onto Roberts Ferry Road, and drive 1 mile. Turn left (east) onto Lakeside Road and drive 2 miles.

About the campground: Turlock Lake has 26 miles of shoreline and covers 3,500 acres. However, this surface area can be cut in half during the summer due to heavy drawdowns. The lake can provide good trout fishing in the spring and fair bass fishing in summer. It is stocked annually with rainbow trout. Other catches include bluegill, crappie, and catfish. Stay limit 15 days. Open all year.

26 | McConnell State Recreation Area

Location: 13 miles southeast of Turlock.
Sites: 21 sites for tents and RVs up to 27 feet long (trailers to 24 feet).
Facilities: Tables, grills, drinking water, showers, flush toilets, swimming beach.
Fee per night: $12-$16, pets $1.
Management: California Department of Parks and Recreation, 209-826-1196.
Activities: Fishing, swimming.
Finding the campground: From the intersection of County Road J17 and California Highway 99 in Turlock, drive southeast on CA 99 for 5.7 miles. Take the El Capitan Way exit and drive east 4.5 miles, turn right (south) onto Pepper Street, and drive 2.7 miles.

About the campground: This 74-acre park enjoys an attractive location on the banks of the Merced River. Large sycamores and evergreens shade spacious lawns in the campsite area. Fishing is primarily for catfish and bass. Stay limit 15 days. Open from March through September.

27 | San Luis Reservoir State Recreation Area: Medeiros

Location: 11 miles west of Los Banos.
Sites: 350 primitive sites for tents and motor homes.
Facilities: Tables, fire rings, ramadas, drinking water, chemical toilets, boat ramp.
Fee per night: $9-$11, pets $1.

Management: California Department of Parks and Recreation, 209-826-1196.
Activities: Fishing, swimming, boating, waterskiing, sailboarding.
Finding the campground: From the intersection of California Highways 165 and 152 in Los Banos, drive 10 miles west on CA 152, turn right (north) onto California Highway 33, and drive about 1 mile.

About the campground: Situated on the southeast shore of O'Neill Forebay, with fishing for striped bass, crappie, bluegill, and catfish. Stay limit 15 days from June through September, 30 days from October through May. Open all year.

28 San Luis Reservoir State Recreation Area: San Luis Creek

Location: 15 miles west of Los Banos.
Sites: 53 sites with full hookups for tents and RVs.
Facilities: Tables, fire rings, drinking water, vault toilets, boat ramp.
Fee per night: $14-$16, pets $1. For reservations call 800-444-7275. There is a one-time reservation fee of $7.50.
Management: California Department of Parks and Recreation, 209-826-1196.
Activities: Fishing, swimming, boating, waterskiing, sailboarding, cycling.
Finding the campground: From the intersection of California Highways 165 and 152 in Los Banos, drive 13 miles west on CA 152, turn right at the campground entry sign, and drive about 2 miles.

About the campground: Situated on the northwest shore of O'Neill Forebay, with fishing for striped bass, crappie, bluegill, and catfish. Access to the California Aqueduct Bikeway is 0.2 mile north of the campground. Stay limit 15 days from June through September, 30 days from October through May. Open all year.

San Luis Reservoir State Recreation Area

This recreation area encompasses more than 26,000 acres of low, grassy hills in the eastern Diablo Mountains. It features three manmade lakes: San Luis Reservoir, O'Neill Forebay, and Los Banos Creek Reservoir. San Luis Reservoir is the largest, covering 14,000 acres. It has 65 miles of virtually treeless shoreline. Its water can be drawn down significantly during the summer and fall. O'Neill Forebay, below the San Luis Dam, covers about 2,000 acres and has 14 miles of mostly treeless shoreline. Its water level is more constant than that of San Luis Reservoir. Los Banos Creek Reservoir, the most scenic of the three, has a 12-mile shoreline and occupies 400 acres in a narrow, steep-sided canyon. High winds can blow up quickly on San Luis and O'Neill Forebay in spring and early summer. The recreation area contains four campgrounds—two on O'Neill Forebay and one on each of the other lakes.

29 San Luis Reservoir State Recreation Area: Basalt

Location: 14 miles west of Los Banos.
Sites: 79 sites for tents and RVs.
Facilities: Tables, fire rings, drinking water, flush toilets, showers, dump station, boat ramp. The facilities are wheelchair accessible.
Fee per night: $14-$16, pets $1. For reservations call 800-444-7275. There is a one-time reservation fee of $7.50.
Management: California Department of Parks and Recreation, 209-826-1196.
Activities: Fishing, swimming, boating, waterskiing, sailboarding, cycling, hiking.
Finding the campground: From the intersection of California Highways 165 and 152 in Los Banos, drive 12 miles west on CA 152, turn left at the campground entry sign, and drive about 2 miles.

About the campground: Situated on the eastern shore of San Luis Reservoir. Striped bass, crappie, bluegill, and catfish are the main catches. A 1.5-mile loop trail leads from the campground to a hilltop viewpoint. Access to the California Aqueduct Bikeway is 0.2 mile north of San Luis Creek Campground (number 28). Stay limit 15 days from June through September, 30 days from October through May. Open all year.

30 San Luis Reservoir State Recreation Area: Los Banos Creek Reservoir

Location: 11 miles south of Los Banos.
Sites: 25 sites for tents and RVs up to 30 feet long.
Facilities: Tables, fire rings, vault toilets, boat ramp. No drinking water.
Fee per night: $7-$9, pets $1.
Management: California Department of Parks and Recreation, 209-826-1196.
Activities: Fishing, swimming, boating, sailboarding, hiking.
Finding the campground: From the intersection of California Highways 165 and 152 in Los Banos, drive 5 miles west on CA 152, turn left (south) onto Volta Road, and drive 1 mile. Turn left (east) onto Pioneer Road and drive 1 mile. Then turn right (south) onto Canyon Road and drive about 4 miles.

About the campground: Situated on the eastern shore of Los Banos Creek Reservoir, which is stocked annually in the fall and winter with rainbow trout. You can also catch bluegill, black bass, crappie, and catfish. An excellent guided hike is offered on weekends during March and April, beginning with a boat trip to the western end of the canyon and then followed by a hike upstream along Los Banos Creek. A fee is charged. Stay limit 15 days from June through September, 30 days from October through May. Open all year.

Gold Country

The glitter of gold once lured more than 300,000 fortune hunters to this region from all over the world. Boomtowns were created almost overnight and then, when the gold panned out, disappeared almost as quickly. Fortunes were indeed made, but mostly by wily merchants and saloon owners, who knew where the real gold was. Today, the promise of wealth is gone, but the Gold Country still attracts visitors, this time seeking a different kind of riches: history, natural beauty, and outdoor recreation.

California Highway 49, which runs from Mariposa in the south part of the region to Downieville in the north, forges a pathway through the center of Gold Country. It passes through towns and districts whose very names evoke the days of the gold rush: Coulterville, Sonora, Angel's Camp, Placerville, and Nevada City. Lining the route are old mines and mining towns—some preserved, some restored, and some slowly fading away.

Sacramento, the capital of the Golden State, is a sophisticated city with a gold rush past. Its Old Sacramento district, on the riverfront, encompasses 26 acres of restaurants and shops in buildings dating from 1849 to 1870. It also includes the California State Railroad Museum. To the northeast, a large portion of Tahoe National Forest provides forested lakes, streams, and rivers in the high country.

Temperatures in Gold Country vary considerably from summer to winter and from the high forest in the northeast to the lowlands of the Sacramento River valley. Precipitation is moderate; the heaviest rains fall in the winter months. Average temperatures range from 53 to 39 degrees F in the winter, 72 to 46 in the spring, 91 to 57 in the summer, and 72 to 49 in the fall. The average percentage of sunny days rises from a low of 52 percent in the winter to 81 in the spring, 95 in the summer, and 81 in the fall.

This guidebook divides Gold Country into two areas: the High Forest and Motherlode Territory.

THE HIGH FOREST

A large portion of Tahoe National Forest covers most of the High Forest, providing woodlands, lakes, rivers, and streams for outdoor enjoyment. Five large manmade lakes offer a variety of water sports. The era of the gold rush is brought to life along the Yuba Donner National Scenic Byway, which travels to both slopes of the Sierra Nevada as it follows the North Yuba River from Truckee to Nevada City. Of particular interest is the portion of the byway between Bassetts and Oregon Creek, known as "49 Miles on Highway 49," with its quaint gold rush towns along the river.

GOLD COUNTRY

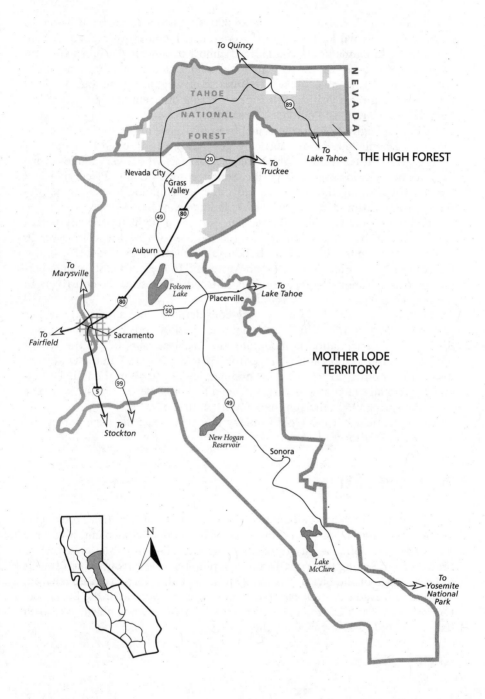

To Quincy

TAHOE

NEVADA

NATIONAL

89

FOREST

To
Lake Tahoe

THE HIGH FOREST

20

Nevada City

To
Truckee

Grass
Valley

49   80

Auburn

To
Marysville

Folsom
Lake

Placerville

To
Lake Tahoe

80

50

To
Fairfield

Sacramento

MOTHER LODE
TERRITORY

99

49

5

To
Stockton

New Hogan
Reservoir

Sonora

N

Lake
McClure

To
Yosemite
National
Park

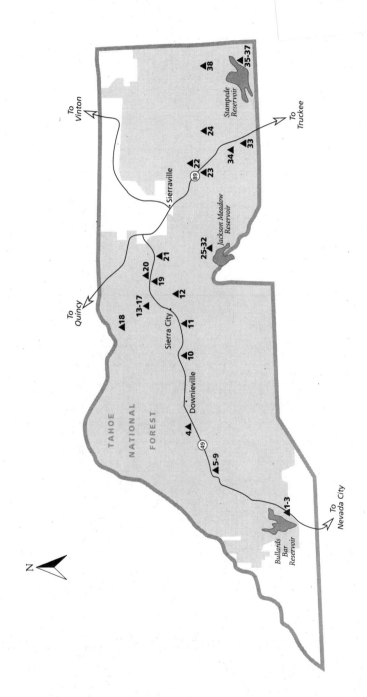

H Forest Campgrounds

	Group sites	RV sites	Total sites	Max. RV length	Hookups	Toilets	Showers	Drinking water	Dump station	Pets	Wheelchair	Recreation	Fee ($)	Season	Can reserve	Length of stay
Bullards Bar Reservoir (1–3)																
1 Dark Day			16			V		•		•		HSF BL	14	May–October	•	14
2 Hornswoggle Group Camp	•	•	5			F		•		•		HS FB	35–65	May–October	•	14
3 Schoolhouse		•	56			F		•		•		HS FB	14	May–October	•	14
4 Ramshorn		•	16	25		V		•		•		SF	10	May–October		14
5 Rocky Rest		•	10			V		•		•		HSF	10	May–October		14
6 Indian Valley		•	17	25		V		•		•		HSF	14	May–October		14
7 Fiddle Creek			15			V		•		•	•	HSF	10	May–October		14
8 Cal-Ida		•	20			V		•		•		HSF	10	May–October		14
9 Carlton Flat		•	20			V		•		•		HSF	10	May–October		14
10 Union Flat		•	11	23		V		•		•	•	HSF	10	May–October		14
11 Loganville		•	19	25		V		•		•		HSF	10	May–October		14
12 Wild Plum		•	44	25		V		•		•		HF	10	May–October		14
13 Salmon Creek		•	31	25		V		•		•		HF	10	May–October		14
14 Sardine Lake		•	27	25		V		•		•		HS FB	10	May–October		14
15 Diablo		•	20			V				•		F		May–October		14
16 Berger		•	9	17		V				•				May–October		14
17 Packsaddle		•	15			V				•		HFR	10	May–October		14
18 Snag Lake		•	12	19		V				•		SF		June–October		14
19 Sierra		•	16	23		V				•		SF	10	June–October		14
20 Chapman Creek		•	29	23		V		•		•		HSF	10	June–October		14
21 Yuba Pass		•	20	25		V		•		•		H	10	June–November	•	14

	Group sites	RV sites	Total sites	Max. RV length	Hookups	Toilets	Showers	Drinking water	Dump station	Pets	Wheelchair	Recreation	Fee ($)	Season	Can reserve	Length of stay
22 Cottonwood		•	24	27		V		•		•		H	10	May–October	•	14
23 Cold Creek		•	10	25		V		•		•		H	10	May–October	•	14
24 Bear Valley		•	10			V		•		•		O		June–October		14

Jackson Meadow Reservoir (25–32)

	Group sites	RV sites	Total sites	Max. RV length	Hookups	Toilets	Showers	Drinking water	Dump station	Pets	Wheelchair	Recreation	Fee ($)	Season	Can reserve	Length of stay
25 Pass Creek		•	30	23		F		•	•	•		HSF BL	13	June–October	•	14
26 East Meadow		•	46	25		F		•		•	•	HS FB	13	June–October	•	14
27 Little Laiser Meadow Horse Camp		•	6			V		•		•		R	13	June–October	•	14
28 Aspen Group Camp	•	•	3	25		V		•		•		HS FB	55–110	June–October	•	14
29 Firtop		•	12	23		F		•		•		HS FB	12	June–October	•	14
30 Findley		•	14	25		F		•		•	•	HS FB	12	June–October	•	14
31 Woodcamp		•	20	23		F		•		•		HS FB	12	June–October	•	14
32 Silver Tip Group Camp	•	•	2			V		•		•		HS FB	60	June–October	•	14
33 Lower Little Truckee		•	15	23		V		•		•		HF	10	May–October	•	14
34 Upper Little Truckee		•	26	23		V		•		•		HF	10	May–October	•	14

Stampede Reservoir (35–37)

	Group sites	RV sites	Total sites	Max. RV length	Hookups	Toilets	Showers	Drinking water	Dump station	Pets	Wheelchair	Recreation	Fee ($)	Season	Can reserve	Length of stay
35 Emigrant Group Camp	•	•	4			V		•	•	•	•	SFB	55–110	May–October	•	14
36 Logger		•	252	32		V		•	•	•	•	HS FB	12	May–October	•	14
37 Davies Creek		•	10			V				•		R		May–October		14
38 Lookout	•	•	23			V		•		•		HF	8–30	June–September		14

Hookups: W = Water E = Electric S = Sewer
Toilets: F = Flush V = Vault P = Pit C = Chemical
Recreation: H = Hiking S = Swimming F = Fishing B = Boating L = Boat Launch O = Off-highway Driving R = Horseback Riding
Maximum Trailer/RV Length given in feet. Stay Limit given in days. Fee given in dollars.
If no entry under **Season,** campground is open all year. If no entry under Fee, camping is free.

1 Bullards Bar Reservoir: Dark Day

Location: 22 miles northwest of Nevada City.
Sites: 16 sites for tents.
Facilities: Tables, fire rings, drinking water, vault toilets, boat ramp.
Fee per night: $14. Reservations required; call 530-692-3200.
Management: Yuba County Water Agency, 530-741-6278.
Activities: Hiking, swimming, fishing, boating.
Finding the campground: From the intersection of California Highways 20 and 49 in Nevada City, drive 18 miles northwest on CA 49 to North Yuba Ranger Station in Log Cabin. Turn left (west) onto Forest Road 8 (Marysville Road) and drive 3.5 miles.

About the campground: Although listed as a walk-in campground, Dark Day is only a short distance from the parking lot. The campsites are almost close enough to the lakeshore to be considered on the water. Bullards Bar is an attractive lake with 55 miles of shoreline. Fishing can be excellent, as the lake is heavily stocked with rainbow trout fingerlings and kokanee, but a boat is almost a must. Two boat-in campgrounds are located on the north shore of the lake. Elevation 2,200 feet. Stay limit 14 days. Open from May through October.

2 Bullards Bar Reservoir: Hornswoggle Group Camp

Location: 22 miles northwest of Nevada City.
Sites: 5 group sites for tents and RVs, 4 for 25 people each and 1 for 50 people.
Facilities: Tables, fire rings, drinking water, flush toilets. Boat ramp half a mile away, at Dark Day Campground (number 1).
Fee per night: $35-$65. Reservations required; call 530-692-3200.
Management: Tahoe National Forest, 530-288-3232.
Activities: Hiking, swimming, fishing, boating.
Finding the campground: From the intersection of California Highways 20 and 49 in Nevada City, drive 18 miles northwest on CA 49 to North Yuba Ranger Station in Log Cabin. Turn left (west) onto Forest Road 8 (Marysville Road) and drive about 4 miles.

About the campground: See Dark Day Campground (number 1).

3 Bullards Bar Reservoir: Schoolhouse

Location: 22 miles northwest of Nevada City.
Sites: 56 sites for tents and RVs.
Facilities: Tables, fire rings, drinking water, flush toilets. Boat ramp half a mile away, at Dark Day Campground (number 1).
Fee per night: $14. Reservations required; call 530-692-3200.
Management: Tahoe National Forest, 530-288-3232.
Activities: Hiking, swimming, fishing, boating.
Finding the campground: From the intersection of California Highways 20 and 49 in Nevada City, drive 18 miles northwest on CA 49 to North Yuba

Ranger Station in Log Cabin. Turn left (west) onto Forest Road 8 (Marysville Road) and drive about 4 miles. Schoolhouse is across the road from Hornswoggle Campground (number 2).

About the campground: See Dark Day Campground (number 1).

4 Ramshorn

Location: 5 miles west of Downieville.
Sites: 16 sites for tents and RVs up to 25 feet long.
Facilities: Tables, fire rings, drinking water, vault toilets.
Fee per night: $10.
Management: Tahoe National Forest, 530-288-3232.
Activities: Fishing, swimming, gold panning.
Finding the campground: From Downieville, drive west 5 miles on California Highway 49.

About the campground: Situated on the banks of the North Yuba River, one of the prettiest rivers in the region. Although this is a stocked trout stream, it is impacted by gold-mining operations. Recreational gold panning is featured at the campground, but be careful not to infringe on commercial claims in the vicinity. Elevation 2,600 feet. Stay limit 14 days. Open from May through October.

5 Rocky Rest

Location: 9 miles west of Downieville.
Sites: 10 sites for tents and RVs.
Facilities: Tables, fire rings, drinking water, vault toilets.
Fee per night: $10.
Management: Tahoe National Forest, 530-288-3232.
Activities: Hiking, fishing, swimming, gold panning.
Finding the campground: From Downieville, drive 9 miles west on California Highway 49.

About the campground: See Ramshorn Campground (number 4). Elevation 2,200 feet.

6 Indian Valley

Location: 10 miles west of Downieville.
Sites: 17 sites for tents and RVs up to 25 feet long.
Facilities: Tables, fire rings, drinking water, vault toilets.
Fee per night: $14.
Management: Tahoe National Forest, 530-288-3232.
Activities: Hiking, fishing, swimming, mountain biking, gold panning.
Finding the campground: From Downieville, drive 9.5 miles west on California Highway 49.

About the campground: See Ramshorn Campground (number 4). Elevation 2,200 feet.

7 Fiddle Creek

Location: 11 miles west of Downieville.
Sites: 15 sites for tents.
Facilities: Tables, fire rings, drinking water, vault toilets. The facilities are wheelchair accessible.
Fee per night: $10.
Management: Tahoe National Forest, 530-288-3232.
Activities: Hiking, fishing, swimming, gold panning.
Finding the campground: From Downieville, drive 11 miles west on California Highway 49.

About the campground: See Ramshorn Campground (number 4). Elevation 2,200 feet.

8 Cal-Ida

Location: 11 miles west of Downieville.
Sites: 20 sites for tents and RVs.
Facilities: Tables, fire rings, drinking water, vault toilets.
Fee per night: $10.
Management: Tahoe National Forest, 530-288-3232.
Activities: Hiking, fishing, swimming, gold panning.
Finding the campground: From Downieville, drive 11.3 miles west on California Highway 49.

About the campground: See Ramshorn Campground (number 4). Elevation 2,200 feet.

9 Carlton Flat

Location: 11 miles west of Downieville.
Sites: 20 sites for tents and RVs.
Facilities: Tables, fire rings, drinking water, vault toilets.
Fee per night: $10.
Management: Tahoe National Forest, 530-288-3232.
Activities: Hiking, fishing, swimming, gold panning.
Finding the campground: From Downieville, drive 11.3 miles west on California Highway 49.

About the campground: See Ramshorn Campground (number 4). Elevation 2,200 feet.

10 Union Flat

Location: 5 miles east of Downieville.
Sites: 11 sites for tents and RVs up to 23 feet long.
Facilities: Tables, fire rings, drinking water, vault toilets. The facilities are wheelchair accessible.
Fee per night: $10.

Management: Tahoe National Forest, 530-288-3232.
Activities: Hiking, fishing, swimming, gold panning.
Finding the campground: From Downieville, drive 5 miles east on California Highway 49.

About the campground: See Ramshorn Campground (number 4). Elevation 3,400 feet.

11 Loganville

Location: 2 miles west of Sierra City.
Sites: 19 sites for tents and RVs up to 25 feet long.
Facilities: Tables, fire rings, drinking water, vault toilets.
Fee per night: $10.
Management: Tahoe National Forest, 530-288-3232.
Activities: Hiking, fishing, swimming.
Finding the campground: From Sierra City, drive 2 miles west on California Highway 49.

About the campground: Situated on the North Yuba River, a stocked trout stream impacted by area gold-mining operations. Gold panning is prohibited here. Elevation 3,800 feet. Stay limit 14 days. Open from May through October.

12 Wild Plum

Location: 2 miles east of Sierra City.
Sites: 44 sites for tents and RVs up to 25 feet long.
Facilities: Tables, fire rings, drinking water, vault toilets.
Fee per night: $10.
Management: Tahoe National Forest, 530-288-3232.
Activities: Hiking, fishing.
Finding the campground: From Sierra City, drive 2 miles east on Wild Plum Road.

About the campground: Located on the banks of a small creek, with several attractive waterfalls in the vicinity. The Haypress Creek Trail (6 miles round trip) passes by the campground, rises steeply along the creek, and goes through a canyon into an old-growth forest and past a scenic waterfall. Elevation 4,400 feet. Stay limit 14 days. Open from May through October.

13 Salmon Creek

Location: 5 miles north of Sierra City.
Sites: 31 sites for tents and RVs up to 25 feet long.
Facilities: Tables, fire rings, drinking water, vault toilets.
Fee per night: $10.
Management: Tahoe National Forest, 530-288-3232.
Activities: Hiking, fishing.

Finding the campground: From Sierra City, drive 3 miles northeast on California Highway 49, turn left (west) at Bassetts onto Gold Lake Road, and drive 2 miles.

About the campground: Situated at the junction of Salmon and Packer Creeks, at an elevation of 5,800 feet. Stay limit 14 days. Open from May through October.

14 Sardine Lake

Location: 5 miles north of Sierra City.
Sites: 27 sites for tents and RVs up to 25 feet long.
Facilities: Tables, fire rings, drinking water, vault toilets.
Fee per night: $10.
Management: Tahoe National Forest, 530-288-3232.
Activities: Hiking, fishing, swimming, boating.
Finding the campground: From Sierra City, drive 3 miles northeast on California Highway 49, turn left (west) at Bassetts onto Gold Lake Road, and drive 1.5 miles. Turn left onto Packer Lake Road and drive less than a quarter-mile, bearing left at the fork.

About the campground: Situated 1 mile east of Lower Sardine Lake, which, along with Upper Sardine Lake, makes the prettiest pair of lakes seen anywhere. The lower lake is well stocked annually with brook and rainbow trout; the upper lake is not stocked. Elevation 5,800 feet. Stay limit 14 days. Open from May through October.

15 Diablo

Location: 6 miles north of Sierra City.
Sites: 20 sites for tents and RVs.
Facilities: Tables, fire rings, vault toilets. No drinking water.
Fee per night: None.
Management: Tahoe National Forest, 530-288-3232.
Activities: Fishing.
Finding the campground: From Sierra City, drive 3 miles northeast on California Highway 49, turn left (west) at Bassetts onto Gold Lake Road, and drive 1.5 miles. Turn left onto Packer Lake Road and drive about 1 mile, bearing right at the fork.

About the campground: Located on the banks of Packer Creek. Elevation 5,800 feet. Stay limit 14 days. Open from May through October.

16 Berger

Location: 7 miles north of Sierra City.
Sites: 9 sites for tents and RVs up to 17 feet long.
Facilities: Tables, fire rings, vault toilets. No drinking water.

Fee per night: None.
Management: Tahoe National Forest, 530-288-3232.
Activities: None.
Finding the campground: From Sierra City, drive 3 miles northeast on California Highway 49, turn left (west) at Bassetts onto Gold Lake Road, and drive 1.5 miles. Turn left onto Packer Lake Road and drive about 2 miles, bearing right at the fork.

About the campground: Berger is mainly used as an overflow campground if others in the Lakes Basin area are full. Elevation 5,900 feet. Stay limit 14 days. Open from May through October.

17 Packsaddle

Location: 7 miles north of Sierra City.
Sites: 15 sites for tents and RVs.
Facilities: Tables, fire rings, vault toilets, hitching posts. No drinking water.
Fee per night: $10.
Management: Tahoe National Forest, 530-288-3232.
Activities: Hiking, fishing, horseback riding, mountain biking.
Finding the campground: From Sierra City, drive 3 miles northeast on California Highway 49, turn left (west) at Bassetts onto Gold Lake Road, and drive 1.5 miles. Turn left onto Packer Lake Road and drive about 2.5 miles, bearing right at the fork.

About the campground: The Sierra Buttes Trail (5 miles round trip) begins a few hundred yards south of the campground. The trail climbs 2,500 feet to one of the finest lookouts in the state, located at 8,587 feet. There is no extra charge for horses at the campground, and equestrians may hitch their horses at the campsite. Elevation 6,000 feet. Stay limit 14 days. Open from May through October.

18 Snag Lake

Location: 8 miles north of Sierra City.
Sites: 12 sites for tents and RVs up to 19 feet long.
Facilities: Tables, fire rings, vault toilets. No drinking water.
Fee per night: None.
Management: Tahoe National Forest, 530-288-3232.
Activities: Fishing, swimming, canoeing, kayaking.
Finding the campground: From Sierra City, drive 3 miles northeast on California Highway 49, turn left (west) at Bassetts onto Gold Lake Road, and drive 5 miles.

About the campground: Only hand-launched boats are permitted on this small, peaceful lake, which is stocked annually with a modest number of rainbow trout. The campground is only 2 miles from Gold Lake and scenic Lakes Basin (see Plumas Area, page 183). Here, an alpine landscape, 25 lakes

TRY 233

connected by a well-maintained trail system, unusual geological
nd 175-foot-high Frazier Falls provide a memorable outdoor expe-
evation 6,600 feet. Stay limit 14 days. Open from June through Oc-
to.

19 Sierra

Location: 7 miles northeast of Sierra City.
Sites: 16 sites for tents and RVs up to 23 feet long.
Facilities: Tables, fire rings, vault toilets. No drinking water.
Fee per night: $10.
Management: Tahoe National Forest, 530-288-3232.
Activities: Fishing, swimming.
Finding the campground: From Sierra City drive northeast 7 miles on California Highway 49.

About the campground: Situated on the banks of the North Fork Yuba River, which is stocked with rainbow trout annually. Elevation 5,600 feet. Stay limit 14 days. Open from June through October.

20 Chapman Creek

Location: 8 miles northeast of Sierra City.
Sites: 29 sites for tents and RVs up to 23 feet long.
Facilities: Tables, fire rings, drinking water, vault toilets.
Fee per night: $10.
Management: Tahoe National Forest, 530-288-3232.
Activities: Fishing, swimming, hiking.
Finding the campground: From Sierra City drive northeast 8 miles on California Highway 49.

About the campground: Situated on the banks of Chapman Creek at its junction with the North Fork Yuba River. For fishing information, see Sierra Campground (number 19). The Chapman Creek Trail begins at the campground and follows the creek through a thick forest, gaining a modest 500 feet in elevation in 1.5 miles. Elevation 6,000 feet. Stay limit 14 days. Open from June through October.

21 Yuba Pass

Location: 11 miles northeast of Sierra City.
Sites: 20 sites for tents and RVs up to 25 feet long.
Facilities: Tables, fire rings, drinking water, vault toilets.
Fee per night: $10. For reservations call 800-280-CAMP. There is a one-time reservation fee of $8.65.
Management: Tahoe National Forest, 530-994-3401.
Activities: Hiking, mountain biking.

Finding the campground: From Sierra City, drive northeast 11 miles on California Highway 49.

About the campground: Situated at the top of the pass at an elevation of 6,700 feet. Stay limit 14 days. Open from June through November.

22 Cottonwood

Location: 5 miles southeast of Sierraville.
Sites: 24 sites for tents and RVs up to 27 feet long.
Facilities: Tables, fire rings, drinking water, vault toilets.
Fee per night: $10. For reservations call 800-280-CAMP. There is a one-time reservation fee of $8.65.
Management: Tahoe National Forest, 530-994-3401.
Activities: Hiking.
Finding the campground: From Sierraville, drive southeast on California Highway 89 for 4.5 miles.

About the campground: A short interpretive trail makes a loop from the campground. Elevation 5,600 feet. Stay limit 14 days. Open from May through October.

23 Cold Creek

Location: 5 miles southeast of Sierraville.
Sites: 10 sites for tents and RVs up to 25 feet long.
Facilities: Tables, fire rings, drinking water, vault toilets.
Fee per night: $10. For reservations call 800-280-CAMP. There is a one-time reservation fee of $8.65.
Management: Tahoe National Forest, 530-994-3401.
Activities: Hiking.
Finding the campground: From Sierraville, drive southeast on California Highway 89 for 5 miles.

About the campground: Elevation 5,800 feet. Stay limit 14 days. Open from May through October.

24 Bear Valley

Location: 12 miles southeast of Sierraville.
Sites: 10 sites for tents and RVs.
Facilities: Tables, fire rings, drinking water, vault toilets.
Fee per night: None.
Management: Tahoe National Forest, 530-994-3401.
Activities: OHV driving, mountain biking.
Finding the campground: From Sierraville, drive southeast on California Highway 89 for 8 miles, turn left (north) onto Forest Road 451, and drive 4 miles.

About the campground: The region surrounding the camp was burned extensively by a forest fire in 1994 and has not yet recovered. Routes suitable for OHV driving radiate in almost every direction from the campground, and mountain bikers can use many of them. One leads to Sardine Peak (8,134 feet), which overlooks the burn area. Elevation 6,600 feet. Stay limit 14 days. Open from June through October.

25 Jackson Meadow Reservoir: Pass Creek

Location: 30 miles northwest of Truckee.
Sites: 30 sites for tents and RVs up to 23 feet long.
Facilities: Tables, fire rings, drinking water, flush toilets, dump station, boat ramp.
Fee per night: $13. For reservations call 800-280-CAMP. There is a one-time reservation fee of $8.65.
Management: Tahoe National Forest, 530-994-3401.
Activities: Hiking, fishing, boating, swimming.
Finding the campground: From the intersection of Interstate 80 and California Highway 89 in Truckee, drive north 14 miles on CA 89, turn left (west) onto Forest Road 07, and drive 16 miles.

About the campground: Jackson Meadow is a high mountain reservoir with beautiful views of the surrounding mountains. It offers cool weather in the summer and provides good fishing. Nearly 35,000 rainbow and brown trout, 10 to 12 inches long, are stocked annually, as are 50,000 fingerlings, mostly rainbows. Pass Creek Campground is on the northeastern shoreline of the lake. A swimming beach is nearby at Aspen Creek Picnic Area. The Pacific Crest Trail passes half a mile east of the campground. Elevation 6,100 feet. Stay limit 14 days. Open from June through October.

26 Jackson Meadow Reservoir: East Meadow

Location: 30 miles northwest of Truckee.
Sites: 46 sites for tents and RVs up to 25 feet long.
Facilities: Tables, fire rings, drinking water, flush toilets. The facilities are wheelchair accessible. Dump station and boat ramp at Pass Creek Campground (number 25), 2 miles north.
Fee per night: $13. For reservations call 800-280-CAMP. There is a one-time reservation fee of $8.65.
Management: Tahoe National Forest, 530-994-3401.
Activities: Hiking, fishing, boating, swimming.
Finding the campground: From the intersection of Interstate 80 and California Highway 89 in Truckee, drive north 14 miles on CA 89, turn left (west) onto Forest Road 07, and drive 15 miles. Turn left (south) onto the campground entrance road and drive 1 mile.

About the campground: Situated near the shoreline in a wooded cove on the eastern shore of the lake. See Pass Creek Campground (number 25) for lake and area description. Elevation 6,100 feet. Stay limit 14 days. Open from June through October.

27 Jackson Meadow Reservoir: Little Laiser Meadow Horse Camp

Location: 31 miles northwest of Truckee.
Sites: 6 sites for tents and RVs.
Facilities: Tables, fire rings, drinking water, vault toilets, corrals, hitching posts.
Fee per night: $13. For reservations call 800-280-CAMP. There is a one-time reservation fee of $8.65.
Management: Tahoe National Forest, 530-994-3401.
Activities: Horseback riding. Swimming, fishing, and boating at the lake, 3 miles north.
Finding the campground: From the intersection of Interstate 80 and California Highway 89 in Truckee, drive north 14 miles on CA 89, turn left (west) onto Forest Road 07, and drive 15 miles. Turn left (south) onto the campground entrance road and drive 2 miles.

About the campground: See Pass Creek Campground (number 25) for lake and area description. Elevation 6,100 feet. Stay limit 14 days. Open from June through October.

28 Jackson Meadow Reservoir: Aspen Group Camp

Location: 31 miles northwest of Truckee.
Sites: 3 group sites for tents and RVs up to 25 feet long; 1 for up to 50 people, 2 for up to 25.
Facilities: Tables, fire rings, drinking water, vault toilets. Dump station, boat ramp, and swimming beach available at Pass Creek Campground (number 25), 1 mile east.
Fee per night: $55-$110. Reservations required; call 800-280-CAMP. There is a one-time reservation fee of $8.65.
Management: Tahoe National Forest, 530-994-3401.
Activities: Hiking, fishing, boating, swimming.
Finding the campground: From the intersection of Interstate 80 and California Highway 89 in Truckee, drive north 14 miles on CA 89, turn left (west) onto Forest Road 07, and drive 17 miles.

About the campground: See Pass Creek Campground (number 25) for lake and area description. Elevation 6,200 feet. Stay limit 14 days. Open from June through October.

29 Jackson Meadow Reservoir: Firtop

Location: 34 miles northwest of Truckee.
Sites: 12 sites for tents and RVs up to 23 feet long.

Facilities: Tables, fire rings, drinking water, flush toilets. Boat ramp nearby. Dump station and swimming beach available at Pass Creek Campground (number 25), 3 miles to the north.
Fee per night: $12. For reservations call 800-280-CAMP. There is a one-time reservation fee of $8.65.
Management: Tahoe National Forest, 530-994-3401.
Activities: Hiking, fishing, boating, swimming.
Finding the campground: From the intersection of Interstate 80 and California Highway 89 in Truckee, drive north 14 miles on CA 89, turn left (west) onto Forest Road 07, and drive 19.5 miles. FR 07 becomes Forest Road 956 en route.

About the campground: See Pass Creek Campground (number 25) for lake and area description. Elevation 6,200 feet. Stay limit 14 days. Open from June through October.

30 Jackson Meadow Reservoir: Findley

Location: 34 miles northwest of Truckee.
Sites: 14 sites for tents and RVs up to 25 feet long.
Facilities: Tables, fire rings, drinking water, flush toilets. Boat ramp nearby. The facilities are wheelchair accessible. Dump station and swimming beach available at Pass Creek Campground (number 25), 3.5 miles to the north.
Fee per night: $12. For reservations call 800-280-CAMP. There is a one-time reservation fee of $8.65.
Management: Tahoe National Forest, 530-994-3401.
Activities: Hiking, fishing, boating, swimming.
Finding the campground: From the intersection of Interstate 80 and California Highway 89 in Truckee, drive north 14 miles on CA 89, turn left (west) onto Forest Road 07, and drive 19.5 miles. FR 07 becomes Forest Road 956 en route.

About the campground: See Pass Creek Campground (number 25) for lake and area description. Elevation 6,200 feet. Stay limit 14 days. Open from June through October.

31 Jackson Meadow Reservoir: Woodcamp

Location: 34 miles northwest of Truckee.
Sites: 20 sites for tents and RVs up to 23 feet long.
Facilities: Tables, fire rings, drinking water, flush toilets. Boat ramp nearby. Dump station and swimming beach available at Pass Creek Campground (number 25), 4 miles to the north.
Fee per night: $12. For reservations call 800-280-CAMP. There is a one-time reservation fee of $8.65.
Management: Tahoe National Forest, 530-994-3401.
Activities: Hiking, fishing, boating, swimming.

Finding the campground: From the intersection of Interstate 80 and California Highway 89 in Truckee, drive north 14 miles on CA 89, turn left (west) onto Forest Road 07, and drive 19.5 miles. FR 07 becomes Forest Road 956 en route. Watch for the campground access road.

About the campground: See Pass Creek Campground (number 25) for lake and area description. Elevation 6,100 feet. Stay limit 14 days. Open from June through October.

32 Jackson Meadow Reservoir: Silver Tip Group Camp

Location: 34 miles northwest of Truckee.
Sites: 2 group sites for tents and RVs, each for up to 25 people.
Facilities: Tables, fire rings, drinking water, vault toilets. Boat ramp nearby. Dump station and swimming beach available at Pass Creek Campground (number 25), 4.5 miles to the north.
Fee per night: $60. Reservations required; call 800-280-CAMP. There is a one-time reservation fee of $8.65.
Management: Tahoe National Forest, 530-994-3401.
Activities: Hiking, fishing, boating, swimming.
Finding the campground: From the intersection of Interstate 80 and California Highway 89 in Truckee, drive north 14 miles on CA 89, turn left (west) onto Forest Road 07, and drive 20 miles. FR 07 becomes Forest Road 956 en route. Watch for the campground access road.

About the campground: See Pass Creek Campground (number 25) for lake and area description. Elevation 6,200 feet. Stay limit 14 days. Open from June through October.

33 Lower Little Truckee

Location: 11 miles north of Truckee.
Sites: 15 sites for tents and RVs up to 23 feet long.
Facilities: Tables, fire rings, drinking water, vault toilets.
Fee per night: $10. For reservations call 800-280-CAMP. There is a one-time reservation fee of $8.65.
Management: Tahoe National Forest, 530-994-3401.
Activities: Hiking, fishing.
Finding the campground: From the intersection of Interstate 80 and California Highway 89 in Truckee, drive north 11 miles on CA 89.

About the campground: Situated on the banks of the Little Truckee River, an attractive and fairly productive trout stream. Elevation 6,000 feet. Stay limit 14 days. Open from May through October.

34 Upper Little Truckee

Location: 11 miles north of Truckee.
Sites: 26 sites for tents and RVs up to 23 feet long.

Facilities: Tables, fire rings, drinking water, vault toilets.
Fee per night: $10. For reservations call 800-280-CAMP. There is a one-time reservation fee of $8.65.
Management: Tahoe National Forest, 530-994-3401.
Activities: Hiking, fishing.
Finding the campground: From the intersection of Interstate 80 and California Highway 89 in Truckee, drive north 11.3 miles on CA 89.

About the campground: Situated on the banks of the Little Truckee River, an attractive and fairly productive trout stream. Elevation 6,100 feet. Stay limit 14 days. Open from May through October.

35 Stampede Reservoir: Emigrant Group Camp

Location: 16 miles northeast of Truckee.
Sites: 4 group sites for tents and RVs; 2 for up to 25 people each, 2 for up to 50 people each.
Facilities: Tables, fire rings, drinking water, vault toilets, dump station. Boat ramp 2 miles east. The facilities are wheelchair accessible.
Fee per night: $55-$110. Reservations required; call 800-280-CAMP. There is a one-time reservation fee of $8.65.
Management: Tahoe National Forest, 530-587-3558.
Activities: Fishing, swimming, boating, mountain biking.
Finding the campground: From the intersection of Interstate 80 and California Highway 89 in Truckee, drive northeast on I-80 for 6 miles. Take the Boca-Hirschdale exit and drive north on County Road 894/270 for about 8 miles. Turn left (west) onto Country Road 261 and drive 1.5 miles. Then turn right at the campground sign and drive about half a mile.

About the campground: Beautiful Stampede Reservoir encompasses almost 3,500 acres of surface area. Annual fish stockage includes 20,000 rainbow trout and a quarter-million kokanee fingerlings. Because the reservoir is heavily drawn down in summer and fall, fishing is best in the spring. Elevation 6,000 feet. Stay limit 14 days. Open from May through October.

36 Stampede Reservoir: Logger

Location: 16 miles northeast of Truckee.
Sites: 252 sites for tents and RVs up to 32 feet long.
Facilities: Tables, fire rings, drinking water, vault toilets, dump station. Boat ramp 1 mile north. The facilities are wheelchair accessible.
Fee per night: $12. Reservations accepted; call 800-280-CAMP. There is a one-time reservation fee of $8.65.
Management: Tahoe National Forest, 530-587-3558.
Activities: Hiking, Fishing, swimming, boating, mountain biking.
Finding the campground: From the intersection of Interstate 80 and California Highway 89 in Truckee, drive northeast on I-80 for 6 miles, take the Boca-Hirschdale exit, and drive north on County Road 894/270 for about 8 miles. Turn left (west) onto Country Road 261 and drive 2 miles.

About the campground: See Emigrant Campground (number 35) for details about the lake. The Commemorative Overland Emigrant Trail passes the campground, running east to Dutch Flat and west to Nevada City. Elevation 6,000 feet. Stay limit 14 days. Open from May through October.

37 Stampede Reservoir: Davies Creek

Location: 16 miles northeast of Truckee.
Sites: 10 sites for tents and RVs.
Facilities: Tables, fire rings, vault toilets. No drinking water.
Fee per night: None.
Management: Tahoe National Forest, 530-587-3558.
Activities: Horseback riding.
Finding the campground: From the intersection of Interstate 80 and California Highway 89 in Truckee, drive northeast on I-80 for 6 miles, take the Boca-Hirschdale exit, and drive north on County Road 894/270 for about 10 miles.

About the campground: Horses are permitted at the campground. Elevation 6,000 feet. Stay limit 14 days. Open from May through October.

38 Lookout

Location: 30 miles northeast of Truckee.
Sites: 22 sites for tents and RVs up to 23 feet long, plus 1 group site for up to 16 people.
Facilities: Tables, fire rings, drinking water, vault toilets.
Fee per night: $8. Group fee $30.
Management: Toiyabe National Forest, 702-884-8123.
Activities: Hiking, fishing.
Finding the campground: From the intersection of Interstate 80 and California Highway 89 in Truckee, drive northeast on I-80 for 20 miles (into Nevada), take the Verdi exit, and drive north on Dog Valley Road for 10 miles.

About the campground: A former quartz crystal mine is located a short distance from the campground. Elevation 6,700 feet. Stay limit 14 days. Open from June through September.

MOTHER LODE TERRITORY

Tourists traveling to Mother Lode Territory from the north via the Golden Chain Highway (California Highway 49) are welcomed to the region by the gold rush towns of Nevada City and Grass Valley. Once rivaling San Francisco and Sacramento in population, Nevada City has reinvented itself, turning from gold fields to grape fields as it hosts a flourishing wine industry. North of the town lies Malakoff Diggins, the world's largest hydraulic mining site,

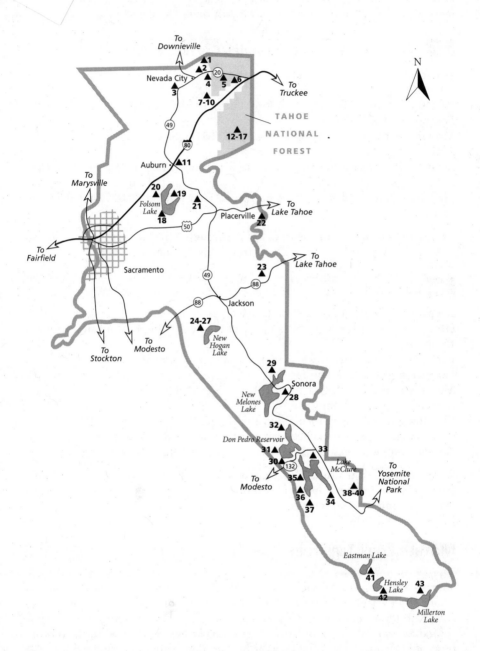

N

MOTHER LODE TERRITORY CAMPGROUNDS

	Group sites	RV sites	Total sites	Max. RV length	Hookups	Toilets	Showers	Drinking water	Dump station	Pets	Wheelchair	Recreation	Fee ($)	Season	Can reserve	Length of stay
1 Malakoff Diggins State Historic Park		•	30	24		F		•	•		•	HSF	12		•	30
2 South Yuba		•	16	27		P		•	•			HSF	5	March–October		15
3 Nevada County Fairgrounds		•	145		WE	F		•	•	•			15			14
4 Scotts Flat Lake Recreation Area		•	187			F	•	•	•	•	•	SFB	16–19		•	15
5 White Cloud		•	46	27		F		•	•			H	11	May–October		14
6 Skillman Group Camp	•	•	2			V			•			HR	18–60	May–November	•	14
Rollins Reservoir (7–10)																
7 Greenhorn		•	36			F		•	•			SFBL	15			14
8 Orchard Springs		•	55		WES	F	•	•	•			SFBL	16–19			14
9 Peninsula		•	58			F		•	•			SFBL	15			14
10 Long Ravine		•	58			F		•	•			SFBL	15			14
11 Auburn State Recreation Area			63			P			•			HSF BR	7–13			15
12 Parker Flat OHV Staging Area		•	7			V		•	•			O		May–October		14
13 Sugar Pine OHV Staging Area		•	open			V		•	•			O		May–October		14
Sugar Pine Reservoir (14–16)																
14 Forbes Creek Group Camp	•	•	2	30		V		•	•		•	HSF	55 BLO	May–October	•	14
15 Giant Gap		•	30	30		V		•	•			HSF	10 BO	May–October	•	14
16 Shirttail Creek		•	30	30		V		•	•			HSF	10 BO	May–October	•	14
17 Big Reservoir		•	100	27		V		•	•			SF	15 BO	May–October	•	14

Folsom Lake State Recreation Area (18–20)

	Group sites	RV sites	Total sites	Max. RV length	Hookups	Toilets	Showers	Drinking water	Dump station	Pets	Wheelchair	Recreation	Fee ($)	Season	Can reserve	Length of stay
18 Beal's Point		•	49	31		F	•	•	•	•	•	HSF BLR	12–16		•	7/30
19 Peninsula		•	100	31		F	•	•	•	•	•	HSF BLR	12–16		•	7/30
20 Negro Bar			20			F	•		•	•	•	HSF BLR	12–16		•	7/30
21 Marshall Gold Discovery State Historic Park	•		80		WES	F	•	•	•	•	•	H	27–29		•	
22 Sly Park Recreation Area	•	•	192			V	•			•	•	SFB LR	13–110+		•	14
23 Chaw'se Indian Grinding Rock State Historic Park	•	•	24	27		F	•	•		•	•		15–17		•	15

New Hogan Lake (24–27)

	Group sites	RV sites	Total sites	Max. RV length	Hookups	Toilets	Showers	Drinking water	Dump station	Pets	Wheelchair	Recreation	Fee ($)	Season	Can reserve	Length of stay
24 Acorn East		•	71			F	•	•	•	•		SFBL	8–14			14
25 Acorn West		•	61			F	•	•	•	•		SFB	8–14	April–October		14
26 Oak Knoll		•	50			V		•		•		SFB	8	April–October		14
27 Coyote Point Group Camp	•	•	1			V		•		•		SFB	90	April–September	•	14

New Melones Lake (28–29)

	Group sites	RV sites	Total sites	Max. RV length	Hookups	Toilets	Showers	Drinking water	Dump station	Pets	Wheelchair	Recreation	Fee ($)	Season	Can reserve	Length of stay
28 Tuttletown Recreation Area		•	95			F	•	•	•	•		SFBL	10			14
29 Glory Hole		•	144			F	•	•	•	•		SFB	10			14

Don Pedro Reservoir (30–32)

	Group sites	RV sites	Total sites	Max. RV length	Hookups	Toilets	Showers	Drinking water	Dump station	Pets	Wheelchair	Recreation	Fee ($)	Season	Can reserve	Length of stay
30 Blue Oaks		•	195		WE	F	•	•	•		•	SFB	10–22		•	14
31 Fleming Meadows		•	238		WES	F	•	•	•			SFB	10–22		•	14
32 Moccasin Point		•	85		WES	F	•	•	•			SFBL	10–22		•	14

Lake McClure (33–36)

	Group sites	RV sites	Total sites	Max. RV length	Hookups	Toilets	Showers	Drinking water	Dump station	Pets	Wheelchair	Recreation	Fee ($)	Season	Can reserve	Length of stay
33 Horseshoe Bend Recreation Area		•	110		WE	F	•	•	•	•		SFBL	14–18		•	14
34 Bagby Recreation Area		•	30		WE	F	•	•		•		SFBL	14–18		•	14
35 Barrett Cove Recreation Area		•	275		WE	F	•	•	•	•	•	SFBL	14–18		•	14
36 McClure Point Recreation Area		•	100		WE	F	•	•				SFBL	14–18		•	14
37 Lake McSwain Recreation Area		•	99		WE	F	•	•	•	•		SFBL	14–18		•	14

Merced River Recreation Area (38–40)

	Group sites	RV sites	Total sites	Max. RV length	Hookups	Toilets	Showers	Drinking water	Dump station	Pets	Wheelchair	Recreation	Fee ($)	Season	Can reserve	Length of stay
38 McCabe Flat		•	14			V		•		•		HS FR	10			14
39 Willow Placer		•	8			V		•				HS FR	10			14
40 Railroad Flat		•	9			V		•				HS FR	10			14
41 Eastman Lake	•	•	70		WES	F	•	•	•	•	•	SFB LR	8–18		•	14
42 Hensley Lake	•	•	53			F	•	•	•	•	•	SF BL	12–50		•	14
43 Millerton Lake State Recreation Area	•	•	142	36		F	•	•	•	•	•	HSF BLR	12–112		•	15/30

Hookups: W = Water E = Electric S = Sewer
Toilets: F = Flush V = Vault P = Pit C = Chemical
Recreation: H = Hiking S = Swimming F = Fishing B = Boating L = Boat Launch O = Off-highway Driving R = Horseback Riding
Maximum Trailer/RV Length given in feet. Stay Limit given in days. Fee given in dollars.
If no entry under **Season,** campground is open all year. If no entry under Fee, camping is free.

while to the south Empire Mine State Historic Park preserves what was once California's largest and richest hardrock mine.

Farther south, at Coloma, a replica of Sutter's Mill stands on the original site of the 1848 gold discovery that started the worldwide rush to California. Placerville, once called "Hangtown" because of its speedy law enforcement, has the distinction of owning its own gold mine, which is open for tours. Columbia State Historic Park, near Sonora, provides the opportunity to tour an actual gold rush era town, with its original buildings, covered boardwalks, and storefronts. Fortunately, the tourist wares for sale in most of the shops fail to dent the authentic feel of the town, which even has two operating Victorian-style hotels. Coulterville, listed on the National Register of Historic Places, once had 50 saloons.

But all that glitters in Mother Lode Territory is not gold. Twelve large lakes offer their shining surfaces to water sports enthusiasts. This represents a very favorable lake to population ratio, enhanced by the fact that the lakes are spread out almost evenly from north to south through the region. The Chaw'se Indian Grinding Rock Historic Park, about 9 miles east of Jackson, features a museum and a large, flat rock outcropping pitted by more than 1,000 mortar holes used by early peoples for grinding acorns into flour.

1 Malakoff Diggins State Historic Park

Location: 25 miles northeast of Nevada City.
Sites: 30 sites for tents and RVs up to 24 feet long (trailers 18 feet), plus 3 rustic cabins.
Facilities: Tables, grills, drinking water, flush toilets. The facilities are wheelchair accessible.
Fee per night: $12, pets $1. For reservations call 800-444-7275. There is a one-time reservation fee of $7.50. Call the number below for cabin reservations.
Management: California Department of Parks and Recreation, 530-265-2740.
Activities: Hiking, swimming, fishing, gold panning.
Finding the campground: From the intersection of California Highways 20 and 49 in Nevada City, drive west and then north on CA 49 for 10.5 miles. Turn right (east) onto Tyler Foote Crossing Road (which becomes Backbone Road) and drive about 14 miles. The last 2 miles of the road are unpaved and steep.

About the campground: Malakoff Diggins was once the world's largest hydraulic mining site, and North Bloomfield was a thriving community. Today, visitors can explore the "diggings" and walk the town's now-deserted streets, which are lined with the original, restored buildings. The park also features a museum, picnic sites, gold panning, and a small lake for swimming and shoreline fishing (bass, bluegill, and catfish). Diggins Trail, a 3-mile loop, tours the mining pit, its rim, and the surrounding facilities, including a tunnel used to bring water to the site (flashlight required). Elevation 3,400 feet. Stay limit 30 days. Open all year.

2 South Yuba

Location: 23 miles northeast of Nevada City.
Sites: 16 sites for tents and RVs up to 27 feet long.
Facilities: Tables, fire rings, drinking water, pit toilets.
Fee per night: $5.
Management: Bureau of Land Management, 530-985-4474.
Activities: Hiking. Swimming, fishing, kayaking, gold panning, 1 mile north.
Finding the campground: From the intersection of California Highways 20 and 49 in Nevada City, drive west and then north on CA 49 for 10.5 miles. Turn right (east) onto Tyler Foote Crossing Road and drive about 9 miles. Turn right (south) onto Grizzly Hills Road and drive 3 miles. Turn left (east) onto North Bloomfield Road and drive about a quarter-mile.

About the campground: Situated about a mile south of the South Yuba River in a thick pine forest, the campground is a good base from which to explore the Mother Lode Territory. Malakoff Diggins and the Empire Mine are close by (see above). The South Yuba provides trout fishing and whitewater kayaking and rafting. The campground is also one of the trailheads for the South Yuba River Trail, a wheelchair-accessible trail running east and west through the scenic Yuba River Canyon. This historic trail features flumes, waterworks, and the remains of equipment used in hydraulic mining. Another access to the trail is on CA 49, 8 miles northwest of Nevada City. Elevation 2,600 feet. Stay limit 15 days. Open from March through October.

3 Nevada County Fairgrounds

Location: 4 miles southwest of Nevada City.
Sites: 145 sites with water and electric hookups for RVs only; no tents. .
Facilities: Drinking water, flush toilets, dump station.
Fee per night: $15.
Management: Nevada County Fairgrounds, 530-273-6217.
Activities: None, unless a fair is in progress.
Finding the campground: From the junction of California Highways 20 and 49 in Nevada City, drive southwest on CA 20/49 for about 4 miles, take the McCourtney Street exit (large "Fairgrounds" sign), and follow signs to the fairgrounds.

About the campground: This campground is best used as an overnight stop or as a base from which to explore the surrounding Mother Lode Territory. The North Star Mining Museum and Empire Mine State Historic Park are nearby, and Malakoff Diggins State Historic Park (number 1) is about 30 miles to the north. The Empire Mine was formerly one of the largest and richest hard-rock gold mines in the state. Elevation 2,300 feet. Stay limit 14 days. Open all year.

4 Scotts Flat Lake Recreation Area

Location: 8 miles east of Nevada City.
Sites: 187 sites for tents and RVs.
Facilities: Tables, fire rings, grills, drinking water, flush toilets, showers, laundry, dump station. Boat ramp less than half a mile away. The facilities are wheelchair accessible.
Fee per night: $16-$19, pets $2. Reservations accepted; call the number below.
Management: Nevada Irrigation District, 530-265-5302.
Activities: Swimming, fishing, boating, waterskiing, horseshoes, volleyball.
Finding the campground: From the intersection of California Highways 20 and 49 in Nevada City, drive northeast 4 miles on CA 20, turn right (south) onto Scotts Flat Road, and drive 4 miles.

About the campground: This very attractive lake is stocked annually with rainbow and brown trout. The best fishing is in the spring and early summer. Elevation 3,000 feet. Stay limit 15 days. Open all year.

5 White Cloud

Location: 10 miles northeast of Nevada City.
Sites: 46 sites for tents and RVs up to 27 feet long.
Facilities: Tables, fire rings, drinking water, flush toilets.
Fee per night: $11.
Management: Tahoe National Forest, 530-265-4531.
Activities: Hiking, mountain biking.
Finding the campground: From the intersection of California Highways 20 and 49 in Nevada City, drive northeast on CA 20 for 10 miles.

About the campground: The Pioneer Trail, the first wagon route used by gold seekers in 1850, runs by the campground. It has become a popular mountain biking route, especially in the downhill direction (east to west). Elevation 5,300 feet. Stay limit 14 days. Open from May through October.

6 Skillman Group Camp

Location: 14 miles east of Nevada City.
Sites: 2 group sites for tents and RVs, each for up to 50 people.
Facilities: Tables, fire rings, vault toilets, corrals, nonpotable water.
Fee per night: $18-$60. Reservations required; call 800-280-CAMP. There is a one-time reservation fee of $8.65.
Management: Tahoe National Forest, 530-265-4531.
Activities: Hiking, mountain biking, horseback riding.
Finding the campground: From the intersection of California Highways 20 and 49 in Nevada City, drive northeast on CA 20 for 14 miles.

About the campground: See White Cloud Campground (number 5) for area information. The Pioneer Trail runs through the campground. Elevation 5,800 feet. Stay limit 14 days. Open from May through November.

7 Rollins Reservoir: Greenhorn

Location: 10 miles southeast of Nevada City.
Sites: 36 sites for tents and RVs.
Facilities: Tables, grill, drinking water, flush toilets, boat ramp.
Fee per night: $15, pets $2.
Management: Nevada Irrigation District, 530-272-6100.
Activities: Swimming, fishing, boating, waterskiing.
Finding the campground: From the intersection of California Highways 20 and 49 in Nevada City, drive 2 miles south on CA 49, turn left (southeast) onto California Highway 174, and drive 7 miles to Bear River Pines. Turn left (east) and drive 1 mile.

About the campground: Rollins Reservoir provides good trout fishing in the spring and bass fishing in the summer. The lake is well stocked annually with rainbow trout. Elevation 2,200 feet. Stay limit 14 days. Open all year.

8 Rollins Reservoir: Orchard Springs

Location: 12 miles southeast of Nevada City.
Sites: 18 sites for RVs (12 with full hookups, 6 with water and electric), 37 sites for tents.
Facilities: Tables, grill, drinking water, flush toilets, showers, boat ramp.
Fee per night: $16-19, pets $2.
Management: Nevada Irrigation District, 530-272-6100.
Activities: Swimming, fishing, boating, waterskiing.
Finding the campground: From the intersection of California Highways 20 and 49 in Nevada City, drive 2 miles south on CA 49, turn left (southeast) onto California Highway 174, and drive 9 miles. Turn left (east) onto Orchard Springs Road and drive 1 mile.

About the campground: See Greenhorn Campground (number 7).

9 Rollins Reservoir: Peninsula

Location: 14 miles southeast of Nevada City.
Sites: 58 sites for tents and RVs.
Facilities: Tables, grill, drinking water, flush toilets, boat ramp.
Fee per night: $15, pets $2.
Management: Nevada Irrigation District, 530-272-6100.
Activities: Swimming, fishing, boating, waterskiing.
Finding the campground: From the intersection of California Highways 20 and 49 in Nevada City, drive 2 miles south on CA 49, turn left (southeast) onto

California Highway 174, and drive 5 miles. Turn left (east) onto You Bet Road and drive 7 miles.

About the campground: See Greenhorn Campground (number 7).

10 Rollins Reservoir: Long Ravine

Location: 15 miles southeast of Nevada City.
Sites: 18 sites for RVs, 40 sites for tents.
Facilities: Tables, grills, drinking water, flush toilets, boat ramp.
Fee per night: $15, pets $2.
Management: Nevada Irrigation District, 530-272-6100.
Activities: Swimming, fishing, boating, waterskiing.
Finding the campground: From the intersection of California Highways 20 and 49 in Nevada City, drive 2 miles south on CA 49, turn left (southeast) onto California Highway 174, and drive about 11 miles to Shady Glen. Make a hard left and drive about 2 miles northeast to the access road on the left.

About the campground: See Greenhorn Campground (number 7).

11 Auburn State Recreation Area

Location: 1 mile east of Auburn.
Sites: 41 primitive, dispersed riverside and lakeside sites, plus 22 boat-in sites, for tents.
Facilities: Tables, fire rings, pit toilets. No drinking water.
Fee per night: $7-$13.
Management: California Department of Parks and Recreation, 530-885-4527.
Activities: Hiking, swimming, fishing, boating, waterskiing, kayaking, rafting, horseback riding, mountain biking, gold panning.
Finding the campground: From Auburn, drive east on California Highway 49 for 1 mile to the park headquarters. Obtain maps and information here about campsite location and availability. The two most popular camping areas are Ruck-A-Chucky, accessed from Forest Hill Road, and Cherokee Bar, reached via California Highway 193 and Sliger Mine Road.

About the campground: The 42,000 acres of this historic placer-mining area encompass 30 miles of the North and Middle Forks of the American River. Over 50 miles of hiking, biking, and equestrian trails (including an 11-mile segment of the Western States Pioneer Express Trail, which runs from Sacramento to Carson City, Nevada) run through the park along the Middle Fork of the American River, past inviting pools for swimming. A 3-mile round trip to Ruck-A-Chucky Falls begins at the campground and leads to an attractive waterfall and deep pool. Both the North and the Middle Forks of the river provide challenging runs for rafters and kayakers, and Lake Clementine offers water sports. The main access is from the boat ramp at its southwest end. Stay limit 15 days. Open all year.

12 Parker Flat OHV Staging Area

Location: 27 miles northeast of Auburn.
Sites: 7 sites for tents or RVs.
Facilities: Tables, fire rings, drinking water, vault toilets.
Fee per night: None.
Management: Tahoe National Forest, 530-367-2224.
Activities: OHV driving.
Finding the campground: From Interstate 80 at the north end of Auburn, take the Foresthill Road exit and drive about 24 miles northeast on Foresthill Road. Turn left (west) onto Sugar Pine Road (Forest Road 10) and drive 3 miles.

About the campground: The campground is a staging area for off-highway drivers and their vehicles. There is no other reason to camp here. A series of trails for motorcycles and ATVs extends in several directions from the campground. Elevation 3,700 feet. Stay limit 14 days. Open from May through October.

13 Sugar Pine OHV Staging Area

Location: 27 miles northeast of Auburn.
Sites: Undesignated sites for RVs only.
Facilities: Fire rings, drinking water, vault toilets.
Fee per night: None.
Management: Tahoe National Forest, 530-367-2224.
Activities: OHV driving.
Finding the campground: From Interstate 80 at the north end of Auburn, take the Foresthill Road exit and drive about 24 miles northeast on Foresthill Road. Turn left (west) onto Sugar Pine Road (Forest Road 10) and drive 3 miles. Sugar Pine is just north of Parker Flat Staging Area (number 12).

About the campground: See Parker Flat Campground, (number 12).

14 Sugar Pine Reservoir: Forbes Creek Group Camp

Location: 29 miles northeast of Auburn.
Sites: 2 group sites for tents and RVs up to 30 feet long; each accommodates up to 50 people.
Facilities: Tables, fire rings, drinking water, vault toilets. Dump station 1 mile southwest, boat ramp half-mile west. The facilities are wheelchair accessible.
Fee per night: $55. Reservations required; call 800-280-CAMP. There is a one-time reservation fee of $8.65.
Management: Tahoe National Forest, 530-367-2224.
Activities: Hiking, swimming, fishing, boating, OHV driving.
Finding the campground: From Interstate 80 at the north end of Auburn, take the Foresthill Road exit and drive about 24 miles northeast. Turn left (west) onto Sugar Pine Road (Forest Road 10) and drive just under 3 miles to a fork. Bear left and continue 1.5 miles.

About the campground: Sugar Pine Reservoir is 2 miles long and 1 mile wide at its widest point. It is stocked with 10,000 rainbow and brown trout annually. There is a 10-mile-per-hour speed limit for boats on the lake. A paved trail circles the lakeshore, and a series of OHV trails run north and east of the campground. Elevation 3,600 feet. Stay limit 14 days. Open from May through October.

15 Sugar Pine Reservoir: Giant Gap

Location: 32 miles northeast of Auburn.
Sites: 30 sites for tents and RVs up to 30 feet long.
Facilities: Tables, fire rings, drinking water, vault toilets, swimming beach. Dump station 2 miles southeast, boat ramp 2.5 miles southeast.
Fee per night: $10. For reservations call 800-280-CAMP. There is a one-time reservation fee of $8.65.
Management: Tahoe National Forest, 530-367-2224.
Activities: Hiking, swimming, fishing, boating, OHV driving.
Finding the campground: From Interstate 80 at the north end of Auburn, take the Foresthill Road exit and drive about 24 miles northeast. Turn left (west) onto Sugar Pine Road (Forest Road 10) and drive just under 3 miles to a fork. Bear left and continue 4.5 miles around the lake.

About the campground: See Forbes Creek Group Camp (number 14). Giant Gap has a swimming beach near the Manzanita Picnic Area.

16 Sugar Pine Reservoir: Shirttail Creek

Location: 32 miles northeast of Auburn.
Sites: 30 sites for tents and RVs up to 30 feet long.
Facilities: Tables, fire rings, drinking water, vault toilets. Dump station 2.5 mile southeast, boat ramp 3 miles southeast.
Fee per night: $10. For reservations call 800-280-CAMP. There is a one-time reservation fee of $8.65.
Management: Tahoe National Forest, 530-367-2224.
Activities: Hiking, swimming, fishing, boating, OHV driving.
Finding the campground: From Interstate 80 at the north end of Auburn, take the Foresthill Road exit and drive about 24 miles northeast. Turn left (west) onto Sugar Pine Road (Forest Road 10) and drive just under 3 miles to a fork. Bear left and continue 4.5 miles around the lake, past Giant Gap Campground (number 15).

About the campground: See Forbes Creek Group Camp (number 14).

17 Big Reservoir

Location: 29 miles northeast of Auburn.
Sites: 100 sites for tents and RVs up to 27 feet long.
Facilities: Tables, fire rings, drinking water, vault toilets.

Fee per night: $15. For reservations call 800-280-CAMP. There is a one-time reservation fee of $8.65.
Management: Tahoe National Forest, 530-367-2224.
Activities: Swimming, fishing, boating, OHV driving.
Finding the campground: From Interstate 80 at the north end of Auburn, take the Foresthill Road exit and drive about 24 miles northeast. Turn left (west) onto Sugar Pine Road (Forest Road 10) and drive just under 3 miles. Turn right onto Forest Road 24 and drive about 2 miles.

About the campground: This attractive 70-acre lake does not permit boats with motors, making it a good place for canoeing and kayaking. Fishing is poor but may improve, since private stocking of the lake with trout began a few years ago. Elevation 4,000 feet. Stay limit 14 days. Open from May through October.

18 Folsom Lake State Recreation Area: Beal's Point

Location: 13 miles southwest of Auburn.
Sites: 49 sites for tents and RVs up to 31 feet long.
Facilities: Tables, grills, drinking water, showers, flush toilets, dump station, boat launch and rentals, swimming beach. The facilities are wheelchair accessible.
Fee per night: $12-$16, pets $1. For reservations call 800-444-7275. There is a one-time reservation fee of $7.50.
Management: California Department of Parks and Recreation, 530-988-0205.
Activities: Hiking, swimming, fishing, boating, waterskiing, sailboarding, cycling, mountain biking, horseback riding.
Finding the campground: From the intersection of Interstate 80 and Auburn-Folsom Road in Auburn, drive southwest 13 miles on Auburn-Folsom Road.

About the campground: This 18,000-acre lake with 75 miles of shoreline is a complete water sports destination serving the heavily populated area between Auburn and Sacramento. Campground reservations are a good idea, especially in summer. Folsom is stocked annually with more than 30,000 rainbow trout, 100,000 kokanee fingerlings, and 30,000 bass fingerlings. In addition, the lake has a decent catfish population, and even sturgeon have been caught in the deeper waters.

Landlubbers, too, will find lots to do. The American River Bikeway runs from Beal's Point to Discovery Park in Old Town Sacramento, providing 32 paved miles of excellent cycling along the shores of Folsom and Natoma Lakes and the American River. Equestrians and hikers will enjoy the section of the Western States Pioneer Express Trail that passes near the campground. Stay limit 7 days from June through September, 30 days from October through April. Open all year.

19 Folsom Lake State Recreation Area: Peninsula

Location: 20 miles south of Auburn.
Sites: 100 sites for tents and RVs up to 31 feet long.

Facilities: Tables, grills, drinking water, flush toilets, dump station, boat launch. The facilities are wheelchair accessible.
Fee per night: $12-$16, pets $1. For reservations call 800-444-7275. There is a one-time reservation fee of $7.50.
Management: California Department of Parks and Recreation, 530-988-0205.
Activities: Hiking, swimming, fishing, boating, waterskiing, sailboarding, cycling, mountain biking, horseback riding.
Finding the campground: From the intersection of Interstate 80 and California Highway 49 in Auburn, drive south about 10 miles on CA 49, turn right (west) onto Rattlesnake Bar Road, and drive another 10 miles.

About the campground: See Beal's Point Campground (number 18) for area information. The Darrington Trail, open to hikers and mountain bikers, follows the South Fork American River for almost 8 miles. Stay limit 7 days from June through September, 30 days from October through April. Open all year.

20 Folsom Lake State Recreation Area: Negro Bar

Location: 16 miles southwest of Auburn.
Sites: 20 sites for tents only.
Facilities: Tables, grills, drinking water, flush toilets, boat launch. The facilities are wheelchair accessible.
Fee per night: $12-$16, pets $1. For reservations call 800-444-7275. There is a one-time reservation fee of $7.50.
Management: California Department of Parks and Recreation, 530-988-0205.
Activities: Hiking, swimming, fishing, boating, cycling, horseback riding.
Finding the campground: From the intersection of Interstate 80 and Auburn-Folsom Road in Auburn, drive southwest 16 miles on Auburn-Folsom Road.

About the campground: See Beal's Point Campground (number 18) for area information. The American River Bikeway and the Western States Pioneer Express Trail (for hikers and equestrians) pass by the campground. Stay limit 7 days from June through September, 30 days from October through April. Open all year.

21 Marshall Gold Discovery State Historic Park

Location: 18 miles southeast of Auburn, in Coloma.
Sites: 80 sites for tents and RVs, with full hookups available, plus tent cabins.
Facilities: Tables, grills, drinking water, showers, flush toilets, dump station, kayak/raft put-in and take-out, store. The facilities are wheelchair accessible.
Fee per night: $27-$29, pets $1. Tent cabins $37-$39. Reservations accepted; call 800-238-2298.
Management: Coloma Resort, 530-621-2267.
Activities: Hiking, rafting, gold panning, sightseeing.
Finding the campground: From the intersection of Interstate 80 and California Highway 49 in Auburn, drive south about 18 miles on CA 49 to Coloma. Turn left onto Bridge Street and cross the single-lane bridge over the

American River. The campground entrance is on the right immediately after clearing the bridge.

About the campground: The park is the site of Sutter's Mill, where gold was first discovered in California in 1848, and the town that grew up around it. The mill has been reconstructed, and some of its original timbers are housed at the site. The town contains a visitor center and museum and some of the original buildings, survivors of the gold rush days. The campground is along the American River, and most of its campsites are directly on the riverbank. No stay limit. Open all year.

22 Jenkinson Lake: Sly Park Recreation Area

Location: 17 miles east of Placerville.
Sites: 186 sites for tents and RVs, plus 5 group sites and an equestrian camp.
Facilities: Tables, fire rings, drinking water, vault toilets, boat ramp. The facilities are wheelchair accessible. In addition, equestrian and group sites have one electric outlet. The equestrian camp has hitching posts and corrals.
Fee per night: $13, pets $1.50. Group fee $110 for up to 50 people, $1.50 per person thereafter. Equestrian site $110. Reservations accepted (required for group sites); call 530-644-2792.
Management: El Dorado Irrigation District, 530-644-2545.
Activities: Swimming, fishing, boating, waterskiing, horseback riding.
Finding the campground: From Placerville, drive east on U.S. Highway 50 for 12 miles, take the Sly Park Road exit, and drive south 4 miles. Turn left onto the campground access road and drive half a mile.

About the campground: The campground is on the north shore of Jenkinson Lake, a good fishing location for trout in the spring and bass in the summer. A mix of more than 100,000 trout, from fingerlings to 12-inchers, are stocked annually. There is a 5-mile-per-hour speed limit on the upper end of the lake. Elevation 3,500 feet. Nine miles of horse trails circle the lake, and there are several hiking trails in the area. Stay limit 14 days. Open all year.

23 Chaw'se Indian Grinding Rock State Historic Park

Location: 11 miles northeast of Jackson.
Sites: 23 sites for tents and RVs up to 27 feet long, plus 1 environmental group site for up to 44 people.
Facilities: Tables, fire rings, drinking water, showers, flush toilets, food lockers. The facilities are wheelchair accessible.
Fee per night: $15-$17. Pets $1. Reservations for group site only; call number below for information and fees.
Management: California Department of Parks and Recreation, 209-296-7488.
Activities: Sightseeing.
Finding the campground: From the intersection of California Highways 49 and 88 in Jackson, drive 8.5 miles northeast on CA 88, turn right (east) onto California Highway 104, and drive 2.5 miles.

A ceremonial roundhouse, a replica of those once used by the Miwok Indians, is a popular attraction of Chaw'se Indian Grinding Rock State Historic Park.

About the campground: Chaw'se is the Miwok Indian word for a grinding rock used to grind acorns and other seeds into meal. The main rock in the park contains over 1,100 circular depressions created by this grinding, the largest grouping of such bedrock mortars in North America. The site also includes a museum, a reconstructed Miwok village and ceremonial roundhouse, and a half-mile-long nature trail. The family campground sits on a wooded hill above the field of grinding rocks. The environmental group camp consists of seven bark houses, each suitable for up to six people. It is in a secluded part of the park where all supplies, including water, must be hauled in on foot. Stay limit 15 days. Open all year.

24 New Hogan Lake: Acorn East

Location: 10 miles west of San Andreas.
Sites: 71 sites for tents and RVs.
Facilities: Tables, fire rings, drinking water, showers, flush toilets, dump station, fish-cleaning station, boat ramp.
Fee per night: $8-$14
Management: U.S. Army Corps of Engineers, 209-772-1343.
Activities: Swimming, fishing, boating, waterskiing.
Finding the campground: From San Andreas, drive northwest on CA 49 for 1 mile. Turn left (west) onto California Highway 12 and drive 6 miles. Turn left onto Lime Creek Road and drive 0.5 mile, then turn left onto South Petersburg Road and drive 2.5 miles.

About the campground: New Hogan Lake has a surface area of 4,400 acres and 50 miles of shoreline. You can catch bass, bluegill, crappie, and catfish here. A good portion of the campsites are on the lakeshore, and boats can be anchored or beached at the sites. Stay limit 14 days. Open all year.

25 New Hogan Lake: Acorn West

Location: 10 miles west of San Andreas.
Sites: 61 sites for tents and RVs.
Facilities: Tables, fire rings, drinking water, showers, flush toilets, dump station.
Fee per night: $8-$14.
Management: U.S. Army Corps of Engineers, 209-772-1343.
Activities: Swimming, fishing, boating, waterskiing.
Finding the campground: From San Andreas, drive northwest on CA 49 for 1 mile. Turn left (west) onto California Highway 12 and drive 6 miles. Turn left onto Lime Creek Road and drive 0.5 mile, then turn left onto South Petersburg Road and drive 2.5 miles.

About the campground: See Acorn East Campground (number 24) for lake information. A boat ramp is available at Acorn East. Stay limit 14 days. Open from April through October.

26 New Hogan Lake: Oak Knoll

Location: 10 miles west of San Andreas.
Sites: 50 sites for tents and RVs.
Facilities: Tables, fire rings, drinking water, vault toilets.
Fee per night: $8.
Management: U.S. Army Corps of Engineers, 209-772-1343.
Activities: Swimming, fishing, boating, waterskiing.
Finding the campground: From San Andreas, drive northwest on CA 49 for 1 mile. Turn left (west) onto California Highway 12 and drive 6 miles. Turn left onto Lime Creek Road and drive 0.5 mile, then turn left onto South Petersburg Road and drive 2.5 miles.

About the campground: See Acorn East Campground (number 24) for lake information. A boat ramp and dump station are available at Acorn East. Stay limit 14 days. Open from April through October as needed for overflow.

27 New Hogan Lake: Coyote Point Group Camp

Location: 10 miles west of San Andreas.
Sites: Undesignated number of sites for tents and RVs, camp holds up to 80 people.
Facilities: Tables, fire rings, drinking water, vault toilets, group barbecue.
Fee per night: $90. Reservations required; call the number below.
Management: U.S. Army Corps of Engineers, 209-772-1343.

Activities: Swimming, fishing, boating, waterskiing.
Finding the campground: From San Andreas, drive northwest on CA 49 for 1 mile. Turn left (west) onto California Highway 12 and drive 6 miles. Turn left onto Lime Creek Road and drive 0.5 mile, then turn left onto South Petersburg Road and drive 2.5 miles.

About the campground: See Acorn East Campground (number 24) for lake information. A boat ramp and dump station are available at Acorn East. Stay limit 14 days. Open from April through September.

28 New Melones Lake: Tuttletown Recreation Area

Location: 10 miles west of Sonora.
Sites: 95 sites for tents and RVs.
Facilities: Tables, grills, drinking water, showers, flush toilets, dump station, playground, boat ramp.
Fee per night: $10.
Management: U.S. Bureau of Reclamation, 209-536-9094.
Activities: Swimming, fishing, boating, waterskiing.
Finding the campground: From Sonora, drive about 8 miles northwest on California Highway 49 to Tuttletown, turn left (west) onto Reynolds Ferry Road, and drive 2 miles.

About the campground: This large reservoir has a surface area of more than 12,000 acres and almost 100 miles of shoreline. Rainbow trout, bass, bluegill, and catfish are the catches here, and the lake is heavily stocked annually with rainbow trout. Stay limit 14 days. Open all year.

29 New Melones Lake: Glory Hole

Location: 19 miles northwest of Sonora.
Sites: 144 sites for tents and RVs.
Facilities: Tables, grills, drinking water, showers, flush toilets, dump station, playground, marina. Boat ramp 0.7 mile south.
Fee per night: $10.
Management: U.S. Bureau of Reclamation, 209-536-9094.
Activities: Swimming, fishing, boating, waterskiing.
Finding the campground: From Sonora, drive about 15 miles northwest on California Highway 49, turn left (west) onto Glory Hole Road, and drive 4 miles.

About the campground: See Tuttletown Recreation Area (number 28).

30 Don Pedro Reservoir: Blue Oaks

Location: 39 miles east of Modesto.
Sites: 195 sites for tents and RVs, including 35 with water and electric hookups.

Facilities: Tables, grills, fire rings, drinking water, showers, flush toilets, dump station. Boat ramp nearby. The facilities are wheelchair accessible.
Fee per night: $10-$22. Reservations accepted.
Management: Don Pedro Recreation Agency, Turlock Irrigation District, 209-852-2396.
Activities: Swimming, fishing, boating, waterskiing.
Finding the campground: From the intersection of California Highways 99 and 132 in Modesto, drive east on CA 132 about 33 miles, turn left (north) onto County Road J59 (La Grange Road), and drive 5 miles. Turn right (east) onto Bonds Flat Road and drive about 1 mile.

About the campground: A large lake with 160 miles of shoreline and covering more than 12,000 acres, Don Pedro provides good trout and bass fishing, with the added possibility of catching kokanee and bluegill. The lake is heavily stocked annually with mature rainbow trout and bass fingerlings. Stay limit 14 days. Open all year. No pets allowed.

31 Don Pedro Reservoir: Fleming Meadows

Location: 40 miles east of Modesto.
Sites: 238 sites for tents and RVs, including 89 with full hookups.
Facilities: Tables, grills, fire rings, drinking water, showers, flush toilets, dump station. Boat ramp nearby.
Fee per night: $10-$22. Reservations accepted.
Management: Don Pedro Recreation Agency, Turlock Irrigation District, 209-852-2396.
Activities: Swimming, fishing, boating, waterskiing.
Finding the campground: From the intersection of California Highways 99 and 132 in Modesto, drive east on CA 132 about 33 miles, turn left (north) onto County Road J59 (La Grange Road), and drive 5 miles. Turn right (east) onto Bonds Flat Road and drive about 2 miles.

About the campground: See Blue Oaks Campground (number 30). No pets allowed.

32 Don Pedro Reservoir: Moccasin Point

Location: 15 miles south of Sonora.
Sites: 85 sites for tents and RVs, including 15 with full hookups.
Facilities: Tables, grills, fire rings, drinking water, showers, flush toilets, dump station, boat ramp and rentals, store, snack bar.
Fee per night: $10-$22. Reservations accepted.
Management: Don Pedro Recreation Agency, Turlock Irrigation District, 209-852-2396.
Activities: Swimming, fishing, boating, waterskiing.
Finding the campground: From the intersection of California Highways 108 and 49 just south of Sonora, drive south 14 miles on CA 49.

About the campground: See Blue Oaks Campground (number 30), except no wheelchair-accessible facilities. No pets allowed.

33 Lake McClure: Horseshoe Bend Recreation Area

Location: 3 miles west of Coulterville.
Sites: 110 sites for tents and RVs, including 35 with water and electric hookups.
Facilities: Tables, drinking water, showers, flush toilets, dump station, two-lane boat ramp, swimming lagoon, fish-cleaning station, store, laundry.
Fee per night: $14-$18, pets $2. Reservations accepted; call 800-468-8889 Tuesdays through Fridays between 8 A.M. and 2 P.M.
Management: Merced Irrigation District, 209-378-2521.
Activities: Swimming, fishing, boating, waterskiing.
Finding the campground: From the intersection of California Highways 49 and 132 in Coulterville, drive west on CA 132 about 3 miles.

About the campground: Shaped like a huge letter "H," Lake McClure has more than 80 miles of shoreline and is noted for its waterskiing and houseboats. The lake has populations of salmon, bluegill, crappie, shad, and catfish spread generally throughout the lake, while trout can best be caught in the eastern leg of the "H," and bass seem to favor the western leg. The lake is heavily stocked annually with rainbow trout. Stay limit 14 days. Open all year.

34 Lake McClure: Bagby Recreation Area

Location: 10 miles south of Coulterville.
Sites: 30 sites for tents and RVs, including 10 with water and electric hookups.
Facilities: Tables, drinking water, flush toilets, showers, fish-cleaning station, boat ramp.
Fee per night: $14-$18, pets $2. Reservations accepted; call 800-468-8889 Tuesdays through Fridays between 8 A.M. and 2 P.M.
Management: Merced Irrigation District, 209-378-2521.
Activities: Swimming, fishing, boating, waterskiing.
Finding the campground: From the intersection of California Highways 49 and 132 in Coulterville, drive south about 10 miles on CA 49.

About the campground: See Horseshoe Bend Recreation Area (number 33).

35 Lake McClure: Barrett Cove Recreation Area

Location: 44 miles east of Modesto.
Sites: 275 sites for tents and RVs, including 89 with water and electric hookups.
Facilities: Tables, drinking water, showers, flush toilets, dump station, playground, swimming area, five-lane boat ramp, marina and boat rentals (including houseboats), store, fish-cleaning station, laundry, gas station. The facilities are wheelchair accessible.
Fee per night: $14-$18, pets $2. Reservations accepted; call 800-468-8889 Tuesdays through Fridays between 8 A.M. and 2 P.M.

Management: Merced Irrigation District, 209-378-2521.

Activities: Swimming, fishing, boating, waterskiing.

Finding the campground: From the intersection of California Highways 99 and 132 in Modesto, drive east about 38 miles on CA 132, turn right (south) onto Merced Falls Road, and drive 3.5 miles. Turn left (east) onto Barrett Cove Road and drive 2 miles.

About the campground: See Horseshoe Bend Recreation Area (number 33).

36 Lake McClure: McClure Point Recreation Area

Location: 41 miles east of Modesto.

Sites: 100 sites for tents and RVs, including 52 with water and electric hookups.

Facilities: Tables, drinking water, showers, flush toilets, three-lane boat ramp, marina and boat rentals, swimming lagoon, fish-cleaning station, store, laundry, gas station.

Fee per night: $14-$18, pets $2. Reservations accepted; call 800-468-8889 Tuesdays through Fridays between 8 A.M. and 2 P.M.

Management: Merced Irrigation District, 209-378-2521.

Activities: Swimming, fishing, boating, waterskiing.

Finding the campground: From the intersection of California Highway 99 and County Road J16 just southeast of Modesto, drive east on CR J16 about 33 miles to Merced Falls, turn right onto Lake McClure Road, and drive about 8 miles.

About the campground: See Horseshoe Bend Recreation Area (number 33).

37 Lake McSwain Recreation Area

Location: 34 miles east of Modesto.

Sites: 99 sites for tents and RVs, including 65 with water and electric hookups.

Facilities: Tables, drinking water, showers, flush toilets, dump station, playground, two-lane boat ramp, marina and boat rentals, swimming lagoon, store, laundry, gas station.

Fee per night: $14-$18, pets $2. Reservations accepted; call 800-468-8889 Tuesdays through Fridays between 8 A.M. and 2 P.M.

Management: Merced Irrigation District, 209-378-2521.

Activities: Swimming, fishing, boating, kayaking.

Finding the campground: From the intersection of California 99 and County Road J16 just southeast of Modesto, drive east on CR J16 about 33 miles to Merced Falls, turn right onto Lake McClure Road, and drive about 1 mile.

About the campground: Lake McSwain is small compared to its neighboring reservoirs—roughly 2 miles long by half a mile wide. It is stocked annually with more than 35,000 catchable-size trout, which makes for good fishing until summer's hot weather. Stay limit 14 days. Open all year.

Originating in the high country of Yosemite National Park, the Merced River rushes headlong through glacially carved valleys and rugged mountains before spilling into the San Joaquin River.

38 Merced River Recreation Area: McCabe Flat

Location: 18 miles north of Mariposa.
Sites: 11 walk-in sites for tents, plus 3 sites for RVs.
Facilities: Tables, fire rings, vault toilets. No drinking water. The facilities are wheelchair accessible.
Fee per night: $10.
Management: Bureau of Land Management, 916-985-4475.
Activities: Hiking, fishing, swimming, rafting, horseback riding, gold panning, mountain biking.
Finding the campground: From Mariposa, drive 15 miles north on California Highway 140, turn left at Briceburg BLM Visitor Center, and cross the Merced River Bridge (not recommended for trailers over 18 feet long and large RVs). Turn left and drive downriver 2.5 miles.

About the campground: Situated in a great setting on the scenic Merced River, the campground is also adjacent to the old Yosemite Railroad Grade, which is now a trail for hikers, mountain bikers, and equestrians. Rafting access is also available to the Class III to Class V rapids of the Merced. Swimming is usually excellent, if cold. The river is stocked in summer with rainbow trout. Recreational gold panning is permitted along this section of the Merced. As if all this is not enough, the main entrance to Yosemite National Park (Arch Rock) is only 18 miles to the east. Stay limit 14 days. Open all year.

39 Merced River Recreation Area: Willow Placer

Location: 19 miles north of Mariposa.
Sites: 7 walk-in sites for tents, plus 1 RV site.
Facilities: Tables, fire rings, vault toilets. No drinking water.
Fee per night: $10.
Management: Bureau of Land Management, 916-985-4475.
Activities: Hiking, fishing, swimming, rafting, horseback riding, gold panning, mountain biking.
Finding the campground: From Mariposa, drive 15 miles north on California Highway 140, turn left at Briceburg BLM Visitor Center, and cross the Merced River Bridge (not recommended for trailers over 18 feet long and large RVs). Turn left and drive downriver 3.8 miles.

About the campground: See McCabe Flat Campground (number 38).

40 Merced River Recreation Area: Railroad Flat

Location: 21 miles north of Mariposa.
Sites: 3 walk-in sites for tents, plus 6 RV sites.
Facilities: Tables, fire rings, vault toilets. No drinking water.
Fee per night: $10.
Management: Bureau of Land Management, 916-985-4475.
Activities: Hiking, fishing, swimming, rafting, horseback riding, gold panning.
Finding the campground: From Mariposa, drive 15 miles north on California Highway 140, turn left at Briceburg BLM Visitor Center, and cross the Merced River Bridge (not recommended for trailers over 18 feet long and large RVs). Turn left and drive downriver 5.8 miles.

About the campground: See McCabe Flat Campground (number 38).

41 Eastman Lake: Codorniz

Location: 24 miles northeast of Chowchilla.
Sites: 66 sites for tents and RVs, including 6 with full hookups and 4 with water and electric, plus 3 group sites and an equestrian site with corrals.
Facilities: Tables, fire rings/grills, lantern holders, drinking water, flush toilets, showers, dump station, boat ramp, fish-cleaning stations, playground. The facilities are wheelchair accessible.
Fee per night: $8-$18. Call for group and equestrian rates. Reservations accepted.
Agency: U.S. Army Corps of Engineers, 209-689-3255.
Activities: Fishing, boating, swimming, waterskiing, horseback riding.
Finding the campground: From California Highway 99 in Chowchilla, take the Avenue 26 exit and drive east 16 miles. Turn left onto Road 29 and drive about 8 miles.

About the campground: A first-class campground with facilities as good as those at Hidden View Campground on nearby Hensley Lake (see below). Campsites are not on the lakeshore but are just above it; ten of them have views over the water. Campsites 9 and 10 are especially attractive, with trails leading down to small coves for swimming or shore fishing. Largemouth bass, rainbow trout, crappie, bluegill, sunfish, and catfish can be taken here, but the fishing is not as good as at Hensley Lake. Wildcat, a primitive campground nearby, has been closed and will probably not reopen. Stay limit 14 days. Open all year.

42 Hensley Lake: Hidden View

Location: 16 miles northeast of Madera.
Sites: 52 sites for tents and RVs, plus 1 group site.
Facilities: Tables, barbecue grills, fire rings, lantern holders, drinking water, flush toilets, showers, dump station, boat ramp, swimming beach, fish-cleaning stations.
Fee per night: $12-$18, $3 boat launch fee. Group site $50, includes launch fee. Reservations recommended for the group site.
Agency: U.S. Army Corps of Engineers, 209-673-5151.
Activities: Fishing, boating, swimming, waterskiing.
Finding the campground: From the intersection of California Highways 99 and 145 in Madera, go east on CA 145 for 6 miles, bear left on Road 400, and drive about 10 miles. Turn left onto Road 603 and follow signs to the campground.

About the campground: Located in dry, rolling hill country, where the grass only greens up in the spring, Hensley and nearby Eastman Lakes (see above) provide the only standing water for miles. Everything about this campground is first class. The sites are especially well situated to take advantage of waterfront locations and views over the lake. Tables at most sites are under trees or have ramada shelters over them—a blessing on hot summer days. The restrooms are modern and tiled, and they have hot water at sinks and showers. There is no extra charge for the showers. Fish-cleaning stations are state of the art, and the boat ramp is more than large enough to handle anything that can be towed by vehicle. After launching at the ramp, boats can pull right up to many of the campsites (depending on the water level). The lake is a good place to fish for largemouth bass, and it is also stocked with rainbow trout annually. Bluegill, crappie, and catfish are also caught. Shore fishing is good from the lake's many coves, including those at the campground. Stay limit 14 days. Open all year.

43 Millerton Lake State Recreation Area

Location: 26 miles east of Madera.
Sites: 138 sites for tents and RVs up to 36 feet long, plus 2 equestrian sites and 2 group sites, one for up to 40 people and the other up to 75 people.
Facilities: Tables, fire rings, grills, drinking water, showers, flush toilets, dump station, boat ramp. The facilities are wheelchair accessible.

Sailboats fill the "back yard" of a campsite at Millerton Lake State Recreation Area, near Madera.

Fee per night: $12-$17, pets $1. Group sites $60 and $112. For reservations call 800-444-7275. There is a one-time reservation fee of $7.50.

Management: California Department of Parks and Recreation, 209-822-2332.

Activities: Hiking, swimming, fishing, boating, sailboarding, waterskiing, horseback riding.

Finding the campground: From the intersection of California Highways 99 and 145 in Madera, drive east about 20 miles on CA145, turn right (north) onto Oneal Road, and drive 1.7 miles. Turn left (east) onto Millerton Road and drive about 4 miles.

About the campground: This 15-mile-long lake provides excellent sailing and sailboarding, as well as access to the scenic San Joaquin River Gorge. Its main fish catch is small- to medium-sized bass. A multipurpose trail circles the landward side of the campground, and a 1.2-mile round-trip hiking trail climbs to Buzzard's Roost, a fine overlook of the lake and the surrounding area. Campsites are spread out along several attractive coves on the north shore of the lake. Scattered trees supply some shade. One campsite, Number 59, sits alone on a small peninsula at least 300 yards from its nearest neighbor. It is completely private, with its own small cove and beach. Stay limit 15 days from June through September, 30 days from October through May. Open all year.

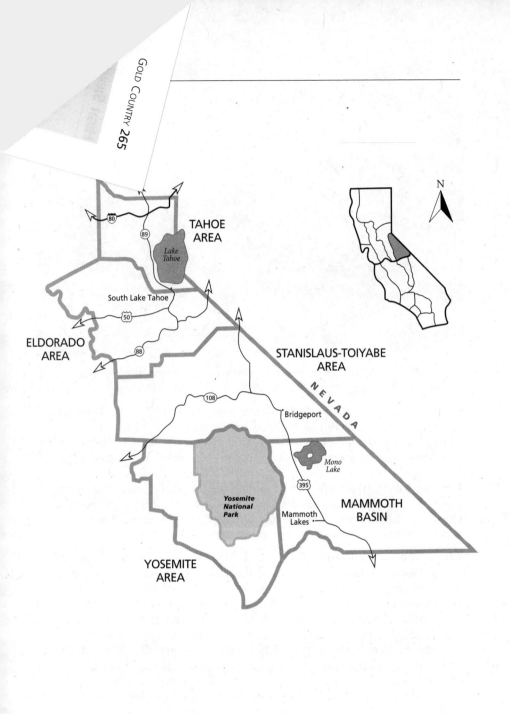

TAHOE
AREA

Lake
Tahoe

South Lake Tahoe

ELDORADO
AREA

STANISLAUS-TOIYABE
AREA

N E V A D A

108

Bridgeport

Mono
Lake

395

Yosemite
National
Park

Mammoth
Lakes

MAMMOTH
BASIN

YOSEMITE
AREA

N

80

89

50

88

High Sierra

Some of the most majestic scenery in all of California is found in the high country that separates the fertile Sacramento Valley in the west from the arid Nevada desert to the east. The Sierra Nevada, the highest mountain range on the North American continent, is the centerpiece of this tour region. Extending like a giant spine from north to south, its rugged peaks and granite-walled valleys deny access to its interior to all but hikers and backpackers. The region is a year-round paradise for outdoor enthusiasts, and virtually every type of outdoor activity takes place within its borders.

Yosemite, the crown jewel of the National Park Service, lies within this region, as do six national forests encompassing more than 5 million acres and containing hundreds of miles of roads, trails, and breathtaking scenery. Hundreds of lakes, large and small, dot the landscape. Many of them are in wild, remote places—havens of solitude where nothing but an angler's line disturbs their placid surfaces. Others, such as Lake Tahoe, North America's largest alpine lake, are more easily accessible by car and RV and welcome powerboats and waterskiers. Stands of giant sequoia, the largest trees on earth, are found along the western slopes of the Sierra Nevada. Wild and Scenic Rivers beckon kayakers and whitewater rafters, while special trails attract equestrians, mountain bikers, and off-highway drivers. Ski areas cater to both downhill and cross-country skiers.

Although most campgrounds in the High Sierra are closed in the winter, national forests permit camping anywhere within their borders as long as certain rules are followed (see How to Use This Guide, page 6). This allows the self-contained RVer and the hardy all-seasons camper the opportunity to enjoy these special places in their wonderful winter settings.

The climate of the High Sierra is typical of mountainous areas: warm summers, cool springs and falls, and cold winters—although the winters here are relatively moderate for a mountain environment. Average maximum/minimum temperatures range in summer from 79 to 45 degrees Fahrenheit and in winter from 44 to 16 degrees. Spring brings temperatures from 60 to 32 and fall 51 to 35. Of course, altitude affects the climate; the higher elevations have colder averages, while the lowest elevations tend to be warmer. The percentage of average days of sunshine is fairly consistent year-round: 80 percent in the summer, 79 in the fall, 74 in the winter, and 77 in the spring.

Although the High Sierra region, as defined by the California Division of Tourism, extends into Southern California, this book features campgrounds only in its northern half. For the southern campgrounds, please see the FalconGuide *Camping Southern California*, also by Richard McMahon.

This book divides the High Sierra into five areas: Tahoe, El Dorado, Stanislaus-Toiyabe, Yosemite, and Mammoth Basin. Each contains a variety of campgrounds that will satisfy virtually all lovers of the outdoors, whatever their preferred activities may be.

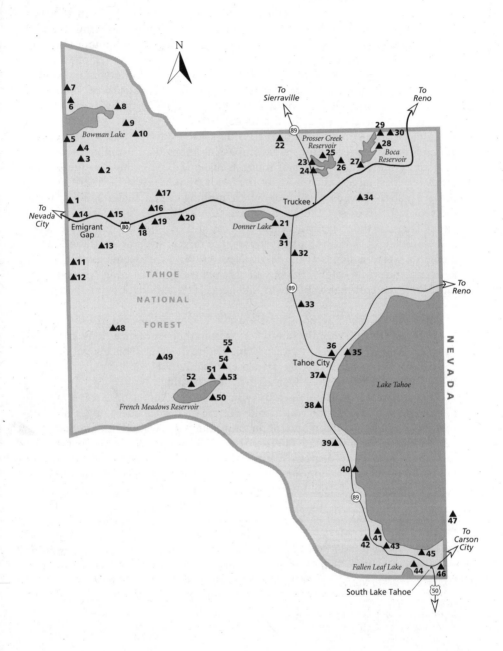

TAHOE AREA

The centerpiece of this area is magnificent Lake Tahoe. Ringed by snowcapped mountains and lying at an elevation of 6,225 feet, it is the largest and deepest alpine lake in North America. Smaller, less crowded lakes are located in the surrounding Tahoe National Forest, which also features half a million acres of woodland, rivers, and streams, and hundreds of miles of hiking, equestrian, OHV, and mountain biking trails. Also located within the forest is Big Trees Grove, the northernmost stand of giant sequoia in the Sierra Nevada.

1 Fuller Lake

Location: 26 miles northeast of Nevada City.
Sites: 9 sites for tents.
Facilities: Tables, fire rings, vault toilets, boat ramp. No drinking water.
Fee per night: None.
Management: Tahoe National Forest, 530-265-4538.
Activities: Swimming, fishing, boating.
Finding the campground: From the intersection of California Highways 49 and 20 in Nevada City, drive east 22 miles on CA 20, turn left (north) onto Bowman Road (Forest Road 18), and drive 4 miles.

About the campground: Fuller Lake is the first and easiest to reach of six lakes accessible from Bowman Road. It is stocked annually with rainbow and brown trout. The campground is on the west shore of the lake. Elevation 5,600 feet. Stay limit 14 days. Open from May through October.

2 Sanford Lake: Grouse Ridge

Location: 33 miles northeast of Nevada City.
Sites: 9 sites for tents and RVs up to 17 feet long.
Facilities: Tables, fire rings, drinking water, vault toilets.
Fee per night: None.
Management: Tahoe National Forest, 530-265-4531.
Activities: Swimming, fishing, boating, hiking, mountain biking.
Finding the campground: From the intersection of California Highways 49 and 20 in Nevada City, drive east 22 miles on CA 20, turn left (north) onto Bowman Road (Forest Road 18), and drive 6 miles. Turn right (east) onto Grouse Ridge Road and drive 5 miles.

About the campground: Situated near the shore of tiny Sanford Lake, the campground serves as the trailhead for hikes to a dozen small lakes within a 3-mile radius north and west of the camp, as well as to Five Lakes Basin, 3 miles to the east. A half-mile hike up to Grouse Ridge Lookout (7,707 feet) provides a fine view of the many small lakes in the area. Grouse Ridge Road is rough gravel, and its condition sometimes makes driving difficult for large vehicles. Elevation 7,400 feet. Stay limit 14 days. Open from June through October.

Tahoe Area Campgrounds

		Group sites	RV sites	Total sites	Max. RV length	Hookups	Toilets	Showers	Drinking water	Dump station	Pets	Wheelchair	Recreation	Fee ($)	Season	Can reserve	Length of stay
1	Fuller Lake			9			V				•		SFBL		May–October		14
2	Sanford Lake: Grouse Ridge		•	9	17		V	•			•		HS FB		June–October		14
3	Carr Lake			20			V				•		HS FB		June–October		14
4	Lindsey Lake			10			V				•		HS FB		June–October		14
5	Bowman Lake			7			V				•		HS FB		June–October		14
6	McMurray Lake			4			V				•		SB		June–October		14
7	Weaver Lake			4			V				•		SB		June–October		14
8	Jackson Creek			14			V				•		HF		June–October		14
9	Canyon Creek		•	20	23		V				•		HF		June–October		14
10	Faucherie Lake Group Camp	•	•	1	23		V				•		HF	30	June–October	•	14
11	North Fork		•	17	17		V	•			•		HF	11	May–October	•	14
12	Tunnel Mills Group Camp	•	•	1			V	•			•		F	40	May–October		14
13	Lake Valley Reservoir		•	18	23		F	•			•		SFB	15	May–October		14
14	Lake Spaulding		•	25	23		F	•			•		SFBL	15	May–October		14
15	Indian Springs		•	35	27		V	•			•		SFO	11	May–October	•	14
16	Woodchuck		•	8	17		V				•		FO		May–October		14
17	Sterling Lake			6			V				•		HFO		May–October		14
18	Big Bend		•	15	19		V	•			•		HF	10	May–October	•	14
19	Hampshire Rocks		•	31	23		V	•			•		HF	11	May–October	•	14
20	Kidd Lake Group Camp	•	•	1			F	•			•		SFB	call	May–October	•	14
21	Donner Memorial State Park		•	154	28		F	•	•		•	•	HS FB	12–17	Mem.Day– mid-Sept.	•	15
22	Sagehen Creek		•	10	17		V				•		HFO	8	June–October		14

	Group sites	RV sites	Total sites	Max. RV length	Hookups	Toilets	Showers	Drinking water	Dump station	Pets	Wheelchair	Recreation	Fee ($)	Season	Can reserve	Length of stay
Prosser Reservoir (23–26)																
23 Lakeside		•	30			V		•		•		SFB	8	June–October		14
24 Prosser		•	29			V		•		•		SFB	10	June–October		14
25 Prosser Ranch Group Camp	•	•	1			V		•		•		SFBL	75	June–October	•	14
26 Annie McCloud		•	10			C				•		SF BO		June–October		14
Boca Reservoir (27–29)																
27 Boca		•	20	27		V				•		SF	10 BO	May–October		14
28 Boca Rest		•	25	19		V		•		•		SFB	10	May–October		14
29 Boca Spring		•	17	19		V		•		•		RO	10	May–October		14
30 Boyington Mill		•	12	32		V				•		OF	10	May–October		14
31 Granite Flat		•	75			V		•		•	•	HF	12	May–October	•	14
32 Goose Meadow		•	25	31		V		•		•		HF	10	May–October	•	14
33 Silver Creek		•	19			V		•				HF	10	May–October	•	14
34 Martis Creek Lake		•	25	30		V		•		•	•	FB	10	May–October		14
Lake Tahoe (35–47)																
35 Lake Forest		•	21	20		F		•		•	•	SFB	12	April–October		14
36 Tahoe State Recreation Area	• 30 Area	30	30		F	•	•		•			HSF	14–17	May–September	•	15
37 William Kent		•	95	24		F		•		•		SF	12–14	June–September	•	14
38 Kaspian		•	10			F		•		•		HSF	10–12	May–September		14
39 Sugar Pine Point State Park		•	175	32		F	•	•	•	•	•	HSF	12–17		•	15/30
40 Meeks Bay		•	40	20		F		•		•		SFB	14–16	May–October	•	14
41 D. L. Bliss State Park		•	168	18		F	•	•		•		HSF	12–20	June–October	•	14

		Group sites	RV sites	Total sites	Max. RV length	Hookups	Toilets	Showers	Drinking water	Dump station	Pets	Wheelchair	Recreation	Fee ($)	Season	Can reserve	Length of stay
42	Bayview			10			V				•		H	5	June–October		2
43	Emerald Bay State Park		•	100	21		F	•	•		•		HSF	12–17	June–September	•	15
44	Fallen Leaf		•	205	40		F		•		•		SF BR	15	May–October	•	14
45	Camp Richardson	•	•	332		WES	F	•	•	•		•	HSF BL	19–25	April 15–Oct. 15	•	14
46	Campground by the Lake		•	170			F	•	•	•	•	•	SF	18	April–October	•	14
47	Nevada Beach		•	54			F		•		•		SF	16–18	May–October		14
48	Secret House			2			V				•		H		May–October		14
49	Robinson Flat			5			V		•		•		H		May–October		14

French Meadows Reservoir (50–54)

		Group sites	RV sites	Total sites	Max. RV length	Hookups	Toilets	Showers	Drinking water	Dump station	Pets	Wheelchair	Recreation	Fee ($)	Season	Can reserve	Length of stay
50	French Meadows		•	75	23		F		•		•		HS FB	10	June–October	•	14
51	Coyote Group Camp	•	•	4	23		V		•		•		HS FB	40–55	June–October	•	14
52	Lewis		•	40	23		V		•		•		HS FB	10	June–October	•	14
53	Gates Group Camp	•	•	3	23		V		•		•		HSF	40–55	June–October	•	14
54	Ahart		•	12	23		V		•		•		HSF	7	June–October		14
55	Talbot			5			V				•		HFR		June–October		14

Hookups: W = Water E = Electric S = Sewer
Toilets: F = Flush V = Vault P = Pit C = Chemical
Recreation: H = Hiking S = Swimming F = Fishing B = Boating L = Boat Launch O = Off-highway Driving R = Horseback Riding
Maximum Trailer/RV Length given in feet. Stay Limit given in days. Fee given in dollars.
If no entry under **Season,** campground is open all year. If no entry under Fee, camping is free.

3 Carr Lake

Location: 33 miles northeast of Nevada City.
Sites: 20 sites for tents.
Facilities: Tables, fire rings, vault toilets. No drinking water.
Fee per night: None.
Management: Tahoe National Forest, 530-265-4531.
Activities: Swimming, fishing, boating, hiking, mountain biking.
Finding the campground: From the intersection of California Highways 49 and 20 in Nevada City, drive east 22 miles on CA 20, turn left (north) onto Bowman Road (Forest Road 18), and drive 8.5 miles. Turn right (east) onto Forest Road 17 and drive 2.5 miles.

About the campground: Situated on the shore of a small lake, the campground provides hiking access to many small lakes in the area. See Grouse Ridge Campground (number 2). Elevation 6,700 feet. Stay limit 14 days. Open from June through October.

4 Lindsey Lake

Location: 33 miles northeast of Nevada City.
Sites: 10 sites for tents.
Facilities: Tables, fire rings, vault toilets. No drinking water.
Fee per night: None.
Management: Tahoe National Forest, 530-265-4531.
Activities: Swimming, fishing, boating, hiking, mountain biking.
Finding the campground: From the intersection of California Highways 49 and 20 in Nevada City, drive east 22 miles on CA 20, turn left (north) onto Bowman Road (Forest Road 18), and drive about 10 miles. Turn right (east) onto a gravel road signed "Lindsey Lake" and drive 1 mile.

About the campground: An 8-mile loop trail leads northeast from the campground, passing half a dozen small, pretty lakes. Elevation 5,900 feet. Stay limit 14 days. Open from June through October.

5 Bowman Lake

Location: 35 miles northeast of Nevada City.
Sites: 7 sites for tents.
Facilities: Tables, fire rings, vault toilets. No drinking water.
Fee per night: None.
Management: Tahoe National Forest, 530-265-4531.
Activities: Swimming, fishing, boating, hiking, mountain biking.
Finding the campground: From the intersection of California Highways 49 and 20 in Nevada City, drive east 22 miles on CA 20, turn left (north) onto Bowman Road (Forest Road 18), and drive about 13 miles. The last 3-mile stretch of the gravel road is rough and may not be suitable for large RVs.

About the campground: Bowman, a scenic 3-mile-long lake, is heavily stocked annually with rainbow trout fingerlings. It is also a good place to fish for brown trout. Stay limit 14 days. Open from June through October.

6 McMurray Lake

Location: 37 miles northeast of Nevada City.
Sites: 4 sites for tents.
Facilities: Tables, fire rings, vault toilets. No drinking water.
Fee per night: None.
Management: Tahoe National Forest, 530-265-4531.
Activities: Swimming, boating.
Finding the campground: From the intersection of California Highways 49 and 20 in Nevada City, drive east 22 miles on CA 20, turn left (north) onto Bowman Road (Forest Road 18), and drive about 13 miles. Turn east onto Meadow Lake Road (County Road 843) and drive 1 mile, then turn left (north) onto an unmarked road and drive half a mile. The last 4 miles are rough gravel and may not be suitable for large RVs.

About the campground: A tiny, attractive lake, which is stocked annually with rainbow trout. Elevation 6,200 feet. Stay limit 14 days. Open from June through October.

7 Weaver Lake

Location: 38 miles northeast of Nevada City.
Sites: 4 sites for tents.
Facilities: Tables, fire rings, vault toilets. No drinking water.
Fee per night: None.
Management: Tahoe National Forest, 530-265-4531.
Activities: Swimming, boating.
Finding the campground: From the intersection of California Highways 49 and 20 in Nevada City, drive east 22 miles on CA 20, turn left (north) onto Bowman Road (Forest Road 18), and drive about 13 miles. Turn east onto Meadow Lake Road (County Road 843) and continue 1 mile. Turn left (north) onto an unmarked road and drive 1.5 miles. The last 5 miles are rough gravel and may not be suitable for large RVs.

About the campground: A small, attractive lake, stocked with a mix of rainbow and brown trout, plus Eagle Lake trout fingerlings. Elevation 5,900 feet. Stay limit 14 days. Open from June through October.

8 Jackson Creek

Location: 39 miles northeast of Nevada City.
Sites: 14 sites for tents.
Facilities: Tables, fire rings, vault toilets. No drinking water.
Fee per night: None.

Management: Tahoe National Forest, 530-265-4531.
Activities: Fishing, hiking, mountain biking.
Finding the campground: From the intersection of California Highways 49 and 20 in Nevada City, drive east 22 miles on CA 20, turn left (north) onto Bowman Road (Forest Road 18), and drive about 17 miles to the campground. When FR 18 reaches Bowman Lake, it intersects with Meadow Lake Road (County Road 843). This section of the road may be difficult for conventional vehicles in wet weather.

About the campground: Situated on the banks of Jackson Creek, about half a mile east of its confluence with Bowman Lake. A trailhead 1 mile south of the campground leads to an area of small, pretty lakes. See Grouse Ridge Campground (number 2). Elevation 5,600 feet. Stay limit 14 days. Open from June through October.

9 Canyon Creek

Location: 41 miles northeast of Nevada City.
Sites: 20 sites for tents and RVs up to 23 feet long.
Facilities: Tables, fire rings, vault toilets. No drinking water.
Fee per night: None.
Management: Tahoe National Forest, 530-265-4531.
Activities: Fishing, hiking, mountain biking.
Finding the campground: From the intersection of California Highways 49 and 20 in Nevada City, drive east 22 miles on CA 20, turn left (north) onto Bowman Road (Forest Road 18), and drive about 17 miles to Jackson Creek Campground (number 8). [When FR 18 reaches Bowman Lake, it intersects with Meadow Lake Road (County Road 843).] From Jackson Creek Campground, take the road that intersects with Meadow Lake Road near the entrance to the campground and drive south about 2 miles. The last 7 miles to the campground is rough gravel road that may not be suitable for large RVs or trailers.

About the campground: Sawmill Lake is 1 mile north of the campground and Faucherie Lake 1 mile south. Faucherie receives a good annual stock of rainbow and brown trout fingerlings. The trailhead at the north end of Sawmill Lake leads to a series of small, attractive lakes. See Grouse Ridge Campground (number 2). Elevation 6,000 feet. Stay limit 14 days. Open from June through October.

10 Faucherie Lake Group Camp

Location: 42 miles northeast of Nevada City.
Sites: 1 group site for tents and RVs up to 23 feet long; accommodates up to 25 people.
Facilities: Tables, fire rings, vault toilets. No drinking water.
Fee per night: $30. Reservations required; call 800-280-CAMP. There is a one-time reservation fee of $8.65.

Management: Tahoe National Forest, 530-265-4531.
Activities: Fishing, hiking, mountain biking.
Finding the campground: From the intersection of California Highways 49 and 20 in Nevada City, drive east 22 miles on CA 20, turn left (north) onto Bowman Road (Forest Road 18), and drive about 17 miles to Jackson Creek Campground (number 8). [When FR 18 reaches Bowman Lake, it intersects with Meadow Lake Road (County Road 843).] From Jackson Creek Campground, take the road that intersects Meadow Lake Road near the entrance to the campground and drive south about 3 miles. The last 8 miles to the campground are on rough gravel road that may not be suitable for large RVs or trailers.

About the campground: Faucherie is a classically beautiful alpine lake in a secluded setting. It is stocked annually with brown and rainbow trout fingerlings. The campground is on the north shore of the lake. Elevation 6,100 feet. Stay limit 14 days. Open from June through October.

11 North Fork

Location: 6 miles south of Emigrant Gap.
Sites: 17 sites for tents and RVs up to 17 feet long.
Facilities: Tables, fire rings, drinking water, vault toilets.
Fee per night: $11. For reservations call 800-280-CAMP. There is a one-time reservation fee of $8.65.
Management: Tahoe National Forest, 530-265-4531.
Activities: Hiking, fishing, mountain biking.
Finding the campground: From Interstate 80, take the exit at Emigrant Gap and drive south about a quarter-mile. Turn right (west) onto Texas Hill Road (Forest Road 19), and drive 5.5 miles.

About the campground: An attractive location on the banks of one of the forks of the American River. Elevation 4,400 feet. Stay limit 14 days. Open from May through October.

12 Tunnel Mills Group Camp

Location: 7 miles south of Emigrant Gap.
Sites: 1 group site for tents and RVs; accommodates up to 50 people.
Facilities: Tables, fire rings, drinking water, vault toilets.
Fee per night: $40. Reservations required; call 800-280-CAMP. There is a one-time reservation fee of $8.65.
Management: Tahoe National Forest, 530-265-4531.
Activities: Fishing.
Finding the campground: From Interstate 80, take the exit at Emigrant Gap and drive south about a quarter-mile. Turn right (west) onto Texas Hill Road (Forest Road 19), and drive 6.5 miles.

About the campground: Situated on the banks of one of the forks of the American River. Elevation 4,000 feet. Stay limit 14 days. Open from May through October.

13 Lake Valley Reservoir: Lodgepole

Location: 6 miles east of Emigrant Gap.
Sites: 18 sites for tents and RVs up to 23 feet long.
Facilities: Tables, grills, drinking water, flush toilets. Boat ramp nearby.
Fee per night: $15, pets $1.
Management: PG&E, 530-386-5164.
Activities: Swimming, fishing, boating.
Finding the campground: From Emigrant Gap, drive east almost 4 miles on Interstate 80, take the Yuba Gap exit, and drive south a quarter-mile. Turn right onto Lake Valley Road and drive about 2 miles, bearing right at the fork.

About the campground: Situated on the southwestern shore of Lake Valley Reservoir, a scenic high-country lake. Trout fishing for rainbows is fair to good. A mix of catchable-size trout and fingerlings is stocked annually. Elevation 5,800 feet. Stay limit 14 days. Open from May through October.

14 Lake Spaulding

Location: 7 miles east of Emigrant Gap.
Sites: 25 sites for tents and RVs up to 23 feet long.
Facilities: Tables, grills, drinking water, flush toilets, boat ramp.
Fee per night: $15, pets $1.
Management: PG&E, 530-386-5164.
Activities: Swimming, fishing, boating, waterskiing.
Finding the campground: From Emigrant Gap, drive east 4.5 miles on Interstate 80, exit at California Highway 20, and drive west 1.5 miles. Turn right (north) onto Lake Spaulding Road and drive half a mile.

About the campground: Situated in a granite bowl, Lake Spaulding's cold water provides good trout fishing for rainbows and browns, as well as kokanee. A mix of trout fingerlings is stocked annually. Elevation 5,000 feet. Stay limit 14 days. Open from May through October.

15 Indian Springs

Location: 8 miles east of Emigrant Gap.
Sites: 35 sites for tents and RVs up to 27 feet long.
Facilities: Tables, fire rings, drinking water, vault toilets.
Fee per night: $11. For reservations call 800-280-CAMP. There is a one-time reservation fee of $8.65.
Management: Tahoe National Forest, 530-265-4531.
Activities: Swimming, fishing, OHV driving.
Finding the campground: From Emigrant Gap, drive east on Interstate 80 for 7 miles, take the Eagle Lakes exit, and drive north 1 mile on Eagle Lakes Road.

About the campground: Situated on the banks of the South Fork of the Yuba River at one of its most scenic points, this campground offers sparkling water tumbling over large boulders and deep pools for swimming, but only fair trout fishing. An OHV trail begins about 1 mile northwest of the campground. Elevation 5,600 feet. Stay limit 14 days. Open from May through October.

16 Woodchuck

Location: 11 miles northeast of Emigrant Gap.
Sites: 8 sites for tents and RVs up to 17 feet long.
Facilities: Tables, fire rings, vault toilets. No drinking water.
Fee per night: None.
Management: Tahoe National Forest, 530-265-4531.
Activities: Fishing, OHV driving.
Finding the campground: From Emigrant Gap, drive east on Interstate 80 for about 8 miles, take the Cisco Grove exit north, and turn left onto the frontage road. Drive less than half a mile to Fordyce Lake Road (Forest Road 85), turn right (northeast) onto Fordyce, and drive 3 miles. The road is steep and winding and not suitable for trailers or large RVs.

About the campground: Situated on the banks of Rattlesnake Creek. Elevation 6,300 feet. Stay limit 14 days. Open from May through October.

17 Sterling Lake

Location: 15 miles northeast of Emigrant Gap.
Sites: 6 sites for tents.
Facilities: Tables, fire rings, vault toilets. No drinking water.
Fee per night: None.
Management: Tahoe National Forest, 530-265-4531.
Activities: Hiking, fishing, OHV driving.
Finding the campground: From Emigrant Gap, drive east on Interstate 80 for about 8 miles, take the Cisco Grove exit north, and turn left onto the frontage road. Drive less than half a mile to Fordyce Lake Road (Forest Road 85), turn right (northeast) onto Fordyce, and drive 5 miles. Then turn left onto Sterling Lake Road and drive 2 miles. The road is steep and winding and not suitable for trailers or large RVs.

About the campground: Situated on the western shore of a secluded, scenic lake, with fair trout fishing. A 5-mile loop trail circles a series of attractive mountain ponds north of the camp. An OHV trail just west of the campground leads from Fordyce Lake to Meadow Lake and beyond. Elevation 6,500 feet. Stay limit 14 days. Open from May through October.

18 Big Bend

Location: 9 miles east of Emigrant Gap.
Sites: 15 sites for tents and RVs up to 19 feet long.
Facilities: Tables, fire rings, drinking water, vault toilets.
Fee per night: $10. For reservations call 800-280-CAMP. There is a one-time reservation fee of $8.65.

Management: Tahoe National Forest, 530-265-4531.
Activities: Hiking, fishing.
Finding the campground: From Emigrant Gap, drive east on Interstate 80 for about 9 miles, take the Big Bend exit south, turn left onto the frontage road, and drive east less than half a mile.

About the campground: Situated on the banks of the South Fork Yuba River. A trail begins south of the campground and leads to the Loch Leven Lakes (2 miles) and beyond. Elevation 5,800 feet. Stay limit 14 days. Open from May through October.

19 Hampshire Rocks

Location: 11 miles east of Emigrant Gap.
Sites: 31 sites for tents and RVs up to 23 feet long.
Facilities: Tables, fire rings, drinking water, vault toilets.
Fee per night: $11. For reservations call 800-280-CAMP. There is a one-time reservation fee of $8.65.
Management: Tahoe National Forest, 530-265-4531.
Activities: Hiking, fishing.
Finding the campground: From Emigrant Gap, drive east on Interstate 80 for about 9 miles, take the Big Bend exit south, turn left onto the frontage road, and drive east 1.5 miles.

About the campground: Situated on the South Fork Yuba River, which offers fair trout fishing and several swimming holes. Elevation 5,900 feet. Stay limit 14 days. Open from May through October.

20 Kidd Lake Group Camp

Location: 15 miles west of Truckee.
Sites: 1 group site for tents and RVs; accommodates up to 100 people.
Facilities: Tables, grills, drinking water, flush toilets.
Fee per night: Call number below for reservations and fee schedule.
Management: PG&E, 530-894-4687.
Activities: Swimming, fishing, boating.
Finding the campground: From the intersection of California Highway 89 North and Interstate 80 in Truckee, drive west on I-80 for 12 miles. Take the Soda Springs exit, drive a short distance, and then turn south onto Soda Springs Road. Drive 0.8 mile, turn west (right) onto Pahatsi Road, and drive 2 miles, bearing right at the fork. Turn left into the campground.

About the campground: Only hand-launched boats are allowed on Kidd Lake. Fishing is poor, the catch being mainly undersized trout. Elevation 6,500 feet. Stay limit 14 days. Open from May through October.

21 Donner Memorial State Park

Location: 3 miles west of Truckee.
Sites: 154 sites for tents and RVs up to 28 feet long.

Facilities: Tables, grills, drinking water, showers, flush toilets. The facilities are wheelchair accessible.

Fee per night: $12-$17, pets $1. For reservations call 800-444-7275. There is a one-time reservation fee of $7.50.

Management: California Department of Parks and Recreation, 530-587-3841.

Activities: Hiking, fishing, swimming, boating.

Finding the campground: From Interstate 80 at Truckee, take the California 89 South exit (1.5 miles west of town) and drive a short distance north. Turn left (west) onto Donner Pass Road and drive 1.5 miles.

About the campground: Donner is a beautiful lake in a mountain setting, but its proximity to the highway detracts somewhat from its ambiance. Although the lake receives an annual stock of 75,000 rainbow trout and 100,000 kokanee fingerlings, fishing is only fair. The park commemorates the Donner party, pioneers marooned near this spot by a snowstorm in 1846 and forced to resort to cannibalism before the survivors were finally rescued. The park includes a museum, two interpretive trails, and a swimming beach. A public boat ramp is located at the northwestern end of the lake. The campground is on the southeastern shore. Elevation 5,900 feet. Stay limit 15 days. Open from Memorial Day through mid-September.

22 Sagehen Creek

Location: 10 miles north of Truckee.

Sites: 10 sites for tents and RVs up to 17 feet long.

Facilities: Tables, fire rings, vault toilets. No drinking water.

Fee per night: $8.

Management: Tahoe National Forest, 530-587-3558.

Activities: Hiking, fishing, OHV driving.

Finding the campground: From the intersection of Interstate 80 and California Highway 89 in Truckee, drive north 8 miles on CA 89, turn left (west) onto Sagehen Summit Road, and drive 2 miles.

About the campground: Elevation 6,500 feet. Stay limit 14 days. Open from June through October.

23 Prosser Reservoir: Lakeside

Location: 5 miles north of Truckee.

Sites: 30 sites for tents and RVs.

Facilities: Tables, fire rings, drinking water, vault toilets. A boat ramp is about a mile east at Prosser Ranch Group Camp (number 25).

Fee per night: $8.

Management: Tahoe National Forest, 530-587-3558.

Activities: Fishing, boating, swimming.

Finding the campground: From the intersection of Interstate 80 and California Highway 89 in Truckee, drive north 4 miles on CA 89, turn right (east) onto the campground entrance road, and drive about 1 mile.

About the campground: Prosser is the most attractive of three large lakes just north of Truckee, and the campground is situated in a pretty cove on its northwestern shore. The lake is heavily stocked annually with more than 100,000 rainbow trout. There is a 5-mile-per-hour speed limit for all boats operating on the lake. Elevation 5,700 feet. Stay limit 14 days. Open from June through October.

24 Prosser Reservoir: Prosser

Location: 5 miles north of Truckee.
Sites: 29 sites for tents and RVs.
Facilities: Tables, fire rings, drinking water, vault toilets.
Fee per night: $10.
Management: Tahoe National Forest, 530-587-3558.
Activities: Fishing, boating, swimming.
Finding the campground: From the intersection of Interstate 80 and California Highway 89 in Truckee, drive north 4 miles on CA 89, turn right (east) onto the campground entrance road, and drive about 1.2 miles.

About the campground: Situated on a wooded rise overlooking the lake. See Lakeside Campground (number 23) for a description of the lake. A boat ramp is located less than half a mile east at Prosser Ranch Group Camp (number 25). Elevation 5,800 feet. Stay limit 14 days. Open from June through October.

25 Prosser Reservoir: Prosser Ranch Group Camp

Location: 6 miles north of Truckee.
Sites: 1 group sites for tents and RVs; accommodates up to 50 people.
Facilities: Tables, fire rings, drinking water, vault toilets, boat ramp.
Fee per night: $75. Reservations required; call 800-280-CAMP. There is a one-time reservation fee of $8.65.
Management: Tahoe National Forest, 530-587-3558.
Activities: Fishing, boating, swimming.
Finding the campground: From the intersection of Interstate 80 and California Highway 89 in Truckee, drive north 4 miles on CA 89, turn right (east) onto the campground entrance road, and drive about 1.5 miles.

About the campground: See Lakeside Campground (number 23) for a description of the lake. Elevation 5,700 feet. Stay limit 14 days. Open from June through October.

26 Prosser Reservoir: Annie McCloud

Location: 5 miles northeast of Truckee.
Sites: 10 sites for tents and RVs up to 17 feet long.
Facilities: Tables, fire rings, chemical toilets. No drinking water.
Fee per night: None.
Management: Tahoe National Forest, 530-587-3558.

Activities: Fishing, boating, swimming, OHV driving.
Finding the campground: From the intersection of Interstate 80 and California Highway 89 in Truckee, drive north half a mile on CA 89, turn right (east) onto Prosser Dam Road (Forest Road 787), and drive 4 miles.

About the campground: See Lakeside Campground (number 23) for a description of the lake. Elevation 6,600 feet. Stay limit 14 days. Open from June through October.

27 Boca Reservoir: Boca

Location: 7 miles northeast of Truckee.
Sites: 20 sites for tents and RVs up to 27 feet long.
Facilities: Tables, fire rings, vault toilets. Boat ramp half a mile east. No drinking water.
Fee per night: $10.
Management: Tahoe National Forest, 530-587-3558.
Activities: Fishing, boating, swimming, OHV driving.
Finding the campground: From the intersection of Interstate 80 and California Highway 89 in Truckee, drive northeast on I-80 for 6 miles, turn north at the Boca-Hirschdale exit, and drive a short distance. Turn left (west) onto Forest Road 73 and drive less than a mile.

About the campground: On the south shore of attractive Boca Reservoir, which is stocked annually with 13,000 rainbow trout and about 100,000 kokanee fingerlings. Elevation 5,600 feet. Stay limit 14 days. Open from May through October.

28 Boca Reservoir: Boca Rest

Location: 9 miles northeast of Truckee.
Sites: 25 sites for tents and RVs up to 19 feet long.
Facilities: Tables, fire rings, drinking water, vault toilets.
Fee per night: $10.
Management: Tahoe National Forest, 530-587-3558.
Activities: Fishing, boating, swimming.
Finding the campground: From the intersection of Interstate 80 and California Highway 89 in Truckee, drive northeast on I-80 for 6 miles, turn north at the Boca-Hirschdale exit, and drive north on County Road 894/270 for 2.5 miles.

About the campground: See Boca Campground (number 27).

29 Boca Reservoir: Boca Spring

Location: 10 miles northeast of Truckee.
Sites: 17 sites for tents and RVs up to 19 feet long.
Facilities: Tables, fire rings, drinking water, vault toilets.
Fee per night: $10.

Management: Tahoe National Forest, 530-587-3558.
Activities: Horseback riding, OHV driving.
Finding the campground: From the intersection of Interstate 80 and California Highway 89 in Truckee, drive northeast on I-80 for 6 miles, turn north at the Boca-Hirschdale exit, and drive north on County Road 894/270 for 3.5 miles.

About the campground: Located about a mile north of the water activities at Boca Reservoir. See Boca Campground (number 27) for a lake description. The campground permits horses at no additional charge. Elevation 5,650 feet. Stay limit 14 days. Open from May through October.

30 Boyington Mill

Location: 11 miles northeast of Truckee.
Sites: 12 sites for tents and RVs up to 32 feet long.
Facilities: Tables, fire rings, vault toilets. No drinking water.
Fee per night: $10.
Management: Tahoe National Forest, 530-587-3558.
Activities: Fishing, OHV driving.
Finding the campground: From the intersection of Interstate 80 and California Highway 89 in Truckee, drive northeast on I-80 for 6 miles, turn north at the Boca-Hirschdale exit, and drive north on County Road 894/270 for 4.5 miles.

About the campground: Located 2 miles north of the water activities of Boca Reservoir. See Boca Campground (number 27) for a lake description. Elevation 5,700 feet. Stay limit 14 days. Open from May through October.

31 Granite Flat

Location: 3 miles southwest of Truckee.
Sites: 75 sites for tents and RVs, including 10 walk-in sites.
Facilities: Tables, fire rings, drinking water, vault toilets. The facilities are wheelchair accessible.
Fee per night: $12. For reservations call 800-280-CAMP. There is a one-time reservation fee of $8.65.
Management: Tahoe National Forest, 530-587-3558.
Activities: Hiking, fishing, rafting.
Finding the campground: From Interstate 80 at Truckee, take the California Highway 89 South exit (1.5 miles west of town) and drive south on CA 89 for 1.5 miles.

About the campground: Situated on the bank of the Truckee River, which is a good trout stream. Elevation 5,900 feet. Stay limit 14 days. Open from May through October.

32 Goose Meadow

Location: 6 miles southwest of Truckee.
Sites: 25 sites for tents and RVs up to 31 feet long.
Facilities: Tables, fire rings, drinking water, vault toilets.
Fee per night: $10. For reservations call 800-280-CAMP. There is a one-time reservation fee of $8.65.
Management: Tahoe National Forest, 530-587-3558.
Activities: Hiking, fishing, rafting.
Finding the campground: From Interstate 80 at Truckee, take the California Highway 89 South exit (1.5 miles west of town) and drive south on CA 89 for 4.5 miles.

About the campground: Situated on the bank of the Truckee River, a good trout stream. Elevation 6,000 feet. Stay limit 14 days. Open from May through October.

33 Silver Creek

Location: 9 miles southwest of Truckee.
Sites: 19 sites for tents and RVs.
Facilities: Tables, fire rings, drinking water, vault toilets.
Fee per night: $10. For reservations call 800-280-CAMP. There is a one-time reservation fee of $8.65.
Management: Tahoe National Forest, 530-587-3558.
Activities: Hiking, fishing, rafting.
Finding the campground: From Interstate 80 at Truckee, take the California Highway 89 South exit (1.5 miles west of town) and drive south on CA 89 for 7.5 miles.

About the campground: Situated on the bank of the Truckee River, which is a good trout stream. The Deer Creek Trail runs from the campground northeast toward Mount Pluto (8,617 feet). Elevation 6,000 feet. Stay limit 14 days. Open from May through October.

34 Martis Creek Lake

Location: 5 miles east of Truckee.
Sites: 25 sites for tents and RVs up to 30 feet long.
Facilities: Tables, grills, drinking water, vault toilets. The facilities are wheelchair accessible.
Fee per night: $10.
Management: U.S. Army Corps of Engineers, 530-639-2342.
Activities: Fishing, boating.
Finding the campground: From Truckee, drive southeast 2.6 miles on California Highway 267, turn left onto a dirt road, and drive east and then north for 2.2 miles.

About the campground: The lake and campground are rather stark, especially when the water level is low. There are few big trees, and other vegetation is sparse. Fishing is catch-and-release, with only artificial lures and single barbless hooks permitted. No motorized boats are allowed on the lake. Elevation 5,800 feet. Stay limit 14 days. Open from May through October.

Lake Tahoe

The largest and deepest alpine lake in North America, Tahoe lies like a blue jewel in a green basin surrounded by a necklace of mountains. Although it is partly in Nevada, Tahoe is California's second largest lake. It is 21 miles long and 12 miles wide, and its shoreline is 71 miles long; 42 miles of shoreline are in California. Tahoe covers 193 square miles, and with a maximum depth of 1,645 feet and an average depth of 989 feet, it contains enough water to cover the entire state to a depth of 14 inches. Although 63 streams feed into the lake, only one, the Truckee River, flows out. Unlike most North American lakes, Tahoe's waters never reach the sea.

The lake is host to all water sports, and the surrounding hills and forests provide hiking, biking, and equestrian trails from spring through fall and ski runs and snowmobile trails in winter. Although fishing for kokanee and Mackinaw and rainbow trout can be good, local knowledge is pretty essential. When a body of water is as large and as pure as Tahoe, most of it is as barren of fish as a desert. But the fish are there; you just have to know where to find them.

The Tahoe Rim Trail, currently under construction, will make a 150-mile circuit of the lake, following the peaks that enclose the Tahoe Basin. Many segments of the trail are already open. The Tahoe portion of the Pacific Crest Trail runs along the Sierra crest on the west side of the lake, from Echo Summit to Carson Pass. The Tahoe Vista Trail starts at the top of the Heavenly Valley Tram, near the community of Stateline on the south shore of the lake. Other hiking, mountain biking, and equestrian trails can be found in the state parks bordering the lake: Burton Creek, Sugar Pine Point, D. L. Bliss, and Emerald Bay. A bicycle path extends along a good portion of the west shore of the lake, generally following the route of California Highway 89. Another along the south shore connects South Lake Tahoe with the Forest Service visitor center at Taylor Creek.

There are 12 public campgrounds along the shore of the lake in California, most of them providing direct access to the water. They are generally open from May through October (see individual listings). Only one, Sugar Pine Point State Recreation Area, is open all year. Reservations are advisable at all of them on weekends and during the summer months. One lakefront campground in Nevada, just across the stateline, is included in this guide in case California campgrounds in the vicinity are full.

35 Lake Tahoe: Lake Forest

Location: 1 mile northeast of Tahoe City.
Sites: 21 spaces for tents and RVs up to 20 feet long.
Facilities: Tables, grills, drinking water, flush toilets. Boat ramp half a mile west. The facilities are wheelchair accessible.
Fee per night: $12.
Agency: Tahoe City Parks Department, 916-583-5544, ext. 2.
Activities: Swimming, fishing, boating.
Finding the campground: From Tahoe City, drive 1.3 miles northeast on California Highway 28 and turn right at the sign for Lake Forest Park.

About the campground: Elevation 6,200 feet. Stay limit 14 days. Open from April through October.

36 Lake Tahoe: Tahoe State Recreation Area

Location: North side of Tahoe City.
Sites: 30 spaces for tents and RVs up to 30 feet long.
Facilities: Tables, grills, fire rings, drinking water, showers, flush toilets, pier.
Fee per night: $14-$17, pets $1. For reservations call 800-444-7275. There is a one-time reservation fee of $7.50.
Agency: California Department of Parks and Recreation, 916-525-7232.
Activities: Swimming, fishing, hiking.
Finding the campground: Off California Highway 28 on the north side of town.

About the campground: Lodgepole pine, alder, and willows partially shade this campground directly on the shore of Lake Tahoe. A pier and a 100-foot-long rocky beach provide access to the lake. A 5-mile loop trail runs through adjacent Burton Creek State Park. The Tahoe Gal makes daily lake cruises from a pier next to the campground, and a shopping center is within walking distance. Stay limit 15 days. Open from May through September.

37 Lake Tahoe: William Kent

Location: 2 miles south of Tahoe City.
Sites: 95 sites for tents and RVs up to 24 feet long.
Facilities: Tables, grills, drinking water, flush toilets.
Fee per night: $12-$14. For reservations call 800-280-CAMP. There is a one-time reservation fee of $8.65.
Agency: Tahoe National Forest, 916-573-2600.
Activities: Swimming, fishing.
Finding the campground: From the intersection of California Highways 28 and 89 in Tahoe City, drive south 2 miles on CA 89.

About the campground: Set in a stand of lodgepole pines, the campground is across the highway from the lakeshore, but a pebbly beach/picnic area belonging to the campground is on the lake side of the road. Stay limit 14 days. Open from June through September.

38 Lake Tahoe: Kaspian

Location: 4 miles south of Tahoe City.
Sites: 6 sites for tents, at least 4 sites for RVs.
Facilities: Tables, grills, drinking water, flush toilets.
Fee per night: $10-$12.
Agency: Tahoe National Forest, 916-573-2600.
Activities: Swimming, hiking, fishing.
Finding the campground: From the intersection of California Highways 28 and 89 in Tahoe City, drive south 4 miles on CA 89.

About the campground: Directly across the highway from the lake, the campground has a small picnic area and lake access on the lake side of the highway. All campers must park in the parking lot. Tenters climb a staircase to wooded campsites, while RVs use the parking lot. Kaspian also has access to the trailhead to Barker Peak (8,166 feet), where you can get a magnificent view of Lake Tahoe. Stay limit 14 days. Open from May through September.

39 Lake Tahoe: Sugar Pine Point State Park (General Creek)

Location: 9 miles south of Tahoe City.
Sites: 175 sites for tents and RVs up to 32 feet long.
Facilities: Tables, grills, drinking water, showers, flush toilets, dump station. The facilities are wheelchair accessible.
Fee per night: $12-$17, pets $1. For reservations call 800-280-CAMP. There is a one-time reservation fee of $8.65.
Agency: California Department of Parks and Recreation, 916-525-7982.
Activities: Swimming, fishing, hiking.
Finding the campground: From the intersection of California Highways 28 and 89 in Tahoe City, drive south 9 miles on CA 89.

About the campground: This 2,000-acre park contains nearly 2 miles of shoreline. However, the campground is on the opposite side of the highway from the lake, in a tall pine forest. Its sites are well spaced, affording relative privacy. The Dolder Nature Trail makes a 2-mile loop through the lakeside forest, and the General Creek Loop (for hikers and mountain bikers) makes a 5-mile circuit from the campground to Lily Pond through meadows and stands of lodgepole pine. Also of interest is the Hellman-Ehrman Mansion, a Queen Anne-style residence that was once the summer home of a frontier banker. Stay limit 15 days June through September, 30 days October through May. Open all year.

40 | Lake Tahoe: Meeks Bay

Location: 11 miles south of Tahoe City.
Sites: 40 sites for tents and RVs up to 20 feet long.
Facilities: Tables, grills, drinking water, flush toilets.
Fee per night: $14-$16. For reservations call 800-280-CAMP. There is a one-time reservation fee of $8.65.
Agency: Tahoe National Forest, 916-573-2600.
Activities: Swimming, boating, fishing, cycling.
Finding the campground: From the intersection of California Highways 28 and 89 in Tahoe City, drive south 11 miles on CA 89.

About the campground: The campground is in a stand of pine trees immediately behind a fine, sandy beach. The sites are fairly close together, but access to a beach makes a stay here worthwhile. Stay limit 14 days. Open from May through October.

41 | Lake Tahoe: D. L. Bliss State Park

Location: 11 miles northwest of South Lake Tahoe.
Sites: 168 sites for tents and RVs up to 18 feet long (trailers up to 15 feet).
Facilities: Tables, grills, drinking water, showers, flush toilets.
Fee per night: $12-$20, pets $1. For reservations call 800-280-CAMP. There is a one-time reservation fee of $8.65.
Agency: Tahoe National Forest, 916-573-2600.
Activities: Hiking, swimming, fishing, kayaking.
Finding the campground: From the intersection of U.S. Highway 50 and California Highway 89 in South Lake Tahoe, take CA 89 northwest for 11 miles.

About the campground: This state park preserves one of the most beautiful locations on the Lake Tahoe shoreline. Its campground has been selected by *Sunset Magazine* as one of the 100 best in the western United States. The camp is laid out in three separate loops. The northernmost lies just behind Lester Beach, the finest beach on the Tahoe shore, and Catawee Cove beach, a close second. A mile-long loop trail leads to Balancing Rock, a favorite geological feature of the Tahoe area since the 1800s. The premier hike along the lakeshore is the 4.5-mile Rubicon Trail, which connects D. L. Bliss and Emerald Bay State Parks and ends at Vikingsholm, a replica of an ancient Norse fortress. Stay limit 14 days. Open from June through October.

42 | Lake Tahoe: Bayview

Location: 7 miles northwest of South Lake Tahoe
Sites: 10 sites for tents.
Facilities: Vault toilet. No drinking water.
Fee per night: $5.
Management: Tahoe National Forest, 530-587-3558.

Activities: Hiking.

Finding the campground: From the intersection of U.S. Highway 50 and California Highway 89 in South Lake Tahoe, take CA 89 west for 6.5 miles to the campground entrance on the left, near the Inspiration Point parking lot.

About the campground: A trail leading southwest from the campground connects with the Pacific Crest Trail. Stay limit 2 days. Open June through October.

43 Lake Tahoe: Emerald Bay State Park (Eagle Point)

Location: 6 miles west of South Lake Tahoe.
Sites: 100 sites for tents and RVs up to 21 feet long (trailers up to 18 feet).
Facilities: Tables, grills, drinking water, showers, flush toilets.
Fee per night: $12-$17, pets $1. For reservations call 800-280-CAMP. There is a one-time reservation fee of $8.65.
Agency: Tahoe National Forest, 916-573-2600.
Activities: Swimming, fishing, hiking, kayaking.
Finding the campground: From the intersection of U.S. Highway 50 and California Highway 89 in South Lake Tahoe, take CA 89 west for 6 miles.

About the campground: The campground is laid out in two sections (Upper and Lower Eagle Point) overlooking beautiful Emerald Bay. The lower campground (sites 35-100) has some sites with great views overlooking the bay, but most are small and not level. The lower campground also has access to a trail leading to a beach on the bay and a 1.5-mile trail to Vikingsholm. Stay limit 15 days. Open from June through September.

44 Lake Tahoe: Fallen Leaf

Location: 4 miles west of South Lake Tahoe.
Sites: 205 sites for tents and RVs up to 40 feet long.
Facilities: Tables, fire rings, drinking water, flush toilets, horse rentals.
Fee per night: $15. For reservations call 800-280-CAMP. There is a one-time reservation fee of $8.65.
Agency: Tahoe National Forest, 530-544-5994.
Activities: Swimming, fishing, boating, horseback riding.
Finding the campground: From the intersection of U.S. Highway 50 and California Highway 89 in South Lake Tahoe, drive west 3 miles on CA 89, turn left (south) onto Fallen Leaf Road, and drive 1 mile.

About the campground: A little more than a mile from the south shore of Lake Tahoe, the campground is situated on the north shore of Fallen Leaf Lake, which is 3 miles long, 1 mile wide, and 430 feet deep. Fishing is for rainbow trout and kokanee. Fifty thousand kokanee fingerlings are stocked annually, but fishing is still only fair. A boat ramp is located at the south end of the lake, about 3 miles from camp. There is another ramp at Pope Beach (Lake Tahoe), about 2 miles to the northeast. Elevation 6,300 feet. Stay limit 14 days. Open from May through October.

A dozen public campgrounds rim the shore of Lake Tahoe, the largest and deepest alpine lake in North America.

45 Lake Tahoe: Camp Richardson

Location: 2.5 miles west of South Lake Tahoe.

Sites: 332 sites for tents and RVs, many with full or partial hookups, plus group sites and cabins.

Facilities: Tables, fire rings, drinking water, showers, flush toilets, dump station, playground, boat ramp and rental, horse rental, recreation hall, restaurant, store. The facilities are wheelchair accessible.

Fee per night: $19-$25. Call for cabin and group fee schedule. Reservations accepted; call 800-544-1801.

Agency: Tahoe National Forest, 530-541-1801.

Activities: Swimming, hiking, fishing, boating, waterskiing, cycling, horseback riding.

Finding the campground: From the intersection of U.S. Highway 50 and California Highway 89 in South Lake Tahoe, take CA 89 west for 2.5 miles.

About the campground: Situated on both sides of the highway in a pine forest, with sites close to but not on the shoreline, Camp Richardson has all the facilities of an upscale commercial campground, with the advantages of a woodland and lakeshore setting. The Forest Service Lake Tahoe Visitor Center is 1 mile west of the campground on CA 89. Hiking and equestrian trails lead from the campground, and a 3.2-mile bicycle path connects the camp with the visitor center and Baldwin Beach to the west and South Lake Tahoe and Poe Beach to the east. Parasailing, swimming beaches, and cruise boats are available in nearby South Lake Tahoe, and gambling casinos are located a few miles past the state line in Nevada. Elevation 6,300 feet. Stay limit 14 days. Open from April 15 through October 15. No pets allowed.

46 Lake Tahoe: Campground by the Lake

Location: In South Lake Tahoe.
Sites: 170 sites for tents and RVs.
Facilities: Tables, grills, drinking water, showers, flush toilets, dump station, playground, swimming pool, tennis and volleyball courts. The facilities are wheelchair accessible.
Fee per night: $18, pets $1. Reservations accepted.
Agency: City of South Lake Tahoe, 530-542-6096.
Activities: Swimming, fishing, cycling.
Finding the campground: From the intersection of U.S. Highway 50 and California Highway 89 in South Lake Tahoe, take US 50 northeast for 2.8 miles and turn right onto Rufus Allen Boulevard.

About the campground: Although not directly on the lakeshore, the campground is just across the highway from El Dorado Beach and a boat launch. Parasailing, swimming beaches, and cruise boats are available in nearby South Lake Tahoe, and gambling casinos are located a few miles past the state line in Nevada. Free shuttles to the casinos stop at the campground entrance. The Tahoe Vista Trail begins at the top of the Heavenly Valley Tram. (From the campground, drive east on US 50 for about 2 miles, turn right onto Ski Run Boulevard, and follow the signs to Heavenly Valley Ski Resort.) Traversing a ridge more than 2,000 feet above the lakeshore, this self-guided trail combines natural beauty with panoramic views over the entire Tahoe Basin. Elevation 6,200 feet. Stay limit 14 days. Open from April through October. This campground was formerly called South Lake Tahoe El Dorado Recreation Area.

47 Lake Tahoe: Nevada Beach

Location: 6 miles northeast of South Lake Tahoe, in Nevada.
Sites: 54 sites for tent and RVs.
Facilities: Tables, fire rings, drinking water, flush toilets.
Fee per night: $16-$18.
Management: Tahoe National Forest, 702-588-5562.
Activities: Swimming, fishing, canoeing, kayaking.
Finding the campground: From the intersection of U.S. Highway 50 and California Highway 89 in South Lake Tahoe, take US 50 northeast for 5 miles, turn left onto the road to Elk Point, and drive 1 mile.

About the campground: Although in Nevada, this campground is only a short distance across the state line and is a good place to enjoy the attractions of the south shore of the lake if the California campgrounds are full. Elevation 6,200 feet. Stay limit 14 days. Open from May through October.

48 Secret House

Location: 33 miles northeast of Auburn.
Sites: 2 sites for tents.
Facilities: Tables, fire rings, vault toilet. No drinking water.
Fee per night: None.
Management: Tahoe National Forest, 530-367-2224.
Activities: Hiking.
Finding the campground: From Interstate 80 at the north end of Auburn, take the Foresthill Road exit and drive about 33 miles northeast. The latter part of the road is gravel, narrow, and winding.

About the campground: The Beacroft Trail (4.5 miles round trip), 1 mile northeast of the campground, leads steeply down to the American River Trail, a scenic, historic route along the North Fork of the American River, which can be enjoyed in either direction. The disadvantage is the 3,000-foot climb back up. Elevation 5,400 feet. Stay limit 14 days. Open from May through October.

49 Robinson Flat

Location: 40 miles northeast of Auburn.
Sites: 5 sites for tents.
Facilities: Tables, fire rings, well water, vault toilets.
Fee per night: None.
Management: Tahoe National Forest, 530-367-2224.
Activities: Hiking.
Finding the campground: From Interstate 80 at the north end of Auburn, take the Foresthill Road exit and drive about 40 miles northeast. The latter part of the road is gravel, narrow, and winding.

About the campground: The Western States Trail passes the campground, leading down to French Meadows Reservoir (6 miles). Elevation 6,800 feet. Stay limit 14 days. Open May through October.

50 French Meadows Reservoir: French Meadows

Location: 52 miles northeast of Auburn.
Sites: 75 sites for tents and RVs up to 23 feet long.
Facilities: Tables, fire rings, drinking water, flush toilets. Boat ramp half-mile west.
Fee per night: $10. For reservations call 800-280-CAMP. There is a one-time reservation fee of $8.65.
Management: Tahoe National Forest, 530-367-2224.
Activities: Hiking, fishing, swimming, boating.
Finding the campground: From Interstate 80 at the north end of Auburn, take the Foresthill Road exit and drive 15 miles to the Foresthill Work Center. Turn right onto Mosquito Ridge Road (Forest Road 96) and drive about 33

miles to Anderson Dam. Continue around the south side of the lake for 4 miles.

About the campground: Situated on the southeast shore of the reservoir, which is 4 miles long and 1 mile wide and which covers about 2,000 acres when full. French Meadows is one of the better trout fishing lakes in the region and is well stocked annually with rainbows. Elevation 5,300 feet. Stay limit 14 days. Open from June through October.

51 French Meadows Reservoir: Coyote Group Camp

Location: 54 miles northeast of Auburn.
Sites: 4 group sites for tents and RVs up to 23 feet long: 3 for up to 25 people each, 1 for up to 50.
Facilities: Tables, fire rings, drinking water, vault toilets. Boat ramp 2 miles southwest.
Fee per night: $40-$55. Reservations required; call 800-280-CAMP. There is a one-time reservation fee of $8.65.
Management: Tahoe National Forest, 530-367-2224.
Activities: Hiking, fishing, swimming, boating.
Finding the campground: From Interstate 80 at the north end of Auburn, take the Foresthill Road exit and drive 15 miles to the Foresthill Work Center. Turn right onto Mosquito Ridge Road (Forest Road 96) and drive about 33 miles to Anderson Dam. Continue around the south side of the lake for 5.5 miles. Bear left at the fork at the east end of the lake.

About the campground: See French Meadows Campground (number 50).

52 French Meadows Reservoir: Lewis

Location: 55 miles northeast of Auburn.
Sites: 40 sites for tents and RVs up to 23 feet long.
Facilities: Tables, fire rings, drinking water, vault toilets. Boat ramp 1 mile southwest.
Fee per night: $10. For reservations call 800-280-CAMP. There is a one-time reservation fee of $8.65.
Management: Tahoe National Forest, 530-367-2224.
Activities: Hiking, fishing, swimming, boating.
Finding the campground: From Interstate 80 at the north end of Auburn, take the Foresthill Road exit and drive 15 miles to the Foresthill Work Center. Turn right onto Mosquito Ridge Road (Forest Road 96) and drive about 33 miles to Anderson Dam. Continue around the south side of the lake for 6.5 miles, bearing left at the fork at the east end of the lake.

About the campground: See French Meadows Campground (number 50). The Western States Trail passes Lewis Campground.

53 | French Meadows Reservoir: Gates Group Camp

Location: 54 miles northeast of Auburn.
Sites: 3 group sites for tents and RVs up to 23 feet long: 2 for up to 25 people each, 1 for up to 50.
Facilities: Tables, fire rings, drinking water, vault toilets. Boat ramp 2.5 miles southwest.
Fee per night: $40-$55. Reservations required; call 800-280-CAMP. There is a one-time reservation fee of $8.65.
Management: Tahoe National Forest, 530-367-2224.
Activities: Hiking, fishing, swimming.
Finding the campground: From Interstate 80 at the north end of Auburn, take the Foresthill Road exit and drive 15 miles to the Foresthill Work Center. Turn right onto Mosquito Ridge Road (Forest Road 96) and drive about 33 miles to Anderson Dam. Continue around the south side of the lake for 6 miles, bearing right at the fork at the east end of the lake.

About the campground: See French Meadows Campground (number 50). The Western States Trail passes near Gates Group Camp.

54 | French Meadows Reservoir: Ahart

Location: 55 miles northeast of Auburn.
Sites: 12 sites for tents and RVs up to 23 feet long.
Facilities: Tables, fire rings, drinking water, vault toilets. Boat ramp 3 miles southwest.
Fee per night: $7.
Management: Tahoe National Forest, 530-367-2224.
Activities: Hiking, fishing, swimming.
Finding the campground: From Interstate 80 at the north end of Auburn, take the Foresthill Road exit and drive 15 miles to the Foresthill Work Center. Turn right onto Mosquito Ridge Road (Forest Road 96) and drive about 33 miles to Anderson Dam. Continue around the south side of the lake for 6.5 miles, bearing right at the fork at the east end of the lake.

About the campground: Situated on the bank of the Middle Fork of the American River about 1 mile north of the lake. See French Meadows Campground (number 50). The Western States Trail passes near Ahart Campground.

55 | Talbot

Location: 58 miles northeast of Auburn.
Sites: 5 sites for tents.
Facilities: Tables, fire rings, vault toilets. No drinking water.
Fee per night: None.
Management: Tahoe National Forest, 530-367-2224.
Activities: Hiking, fishing, horseback riding.
Finding the campground: From Interstate 80 at the north end of Auburn, take the Foresthill Road exit and drive 15 miles to the Foresthill Work Center.

Turn right onto Mosquito Ridge Road (Forest Road 96) and drive about miles to Anderson Dam. Continue around the south side of the lake for 5 miles to a fork in the road at the east end of the lake. Bear right at the fork on FR 96 and drive 5 more miles.

About the campground: Situated on the banks of the Middle Fork of the American River, about 4 miles north of French Meadows Reservoir. The Western States Trail passes near the campground. The camp serves as a trailhead for hikers and equestrians and has 10 stalls for horses. Elevation 5,600 feet. Stay limit 14 days. Open from June through October.

ELDORADO AREA

The Eldorado National Forest is the main feature of this area, with its 4 rivers, 170 lakes, and 400 miles of trails for hikers, equestrians, and mountain bikers. The Carson National Scenic Byway (California Highway 88) winds for 58 miles across the forest, offering fine views of mountains and glacier-carved valleys. Camping, fishing, hiking, and mountain biking locations are available along or not far off the route.

1 Big Meadows

Location: 57 miles northeast of Auburn.
Sites: 54 sites for tents and RVs up to 27 feet long.
Facilities: Tables, fire rings, drinking water, flush and vault toilets. Boat ramp 1.5 miles south. The facilities are wheelchair accessible.
Fee per night: $8.
Management: Eldorado National Forest, 530-333-4312.
Activities: Hiking, fishing, boating.
Finding the campground: From Interstate 80 at the north end of Auburn, take the Foresthill Road exit and drive 15 miles to the Foresthill Work Center. Turn right onto Mosquito Ridge Road (Forest Road 96) and drive about 33 miles to Anderson Dam. Cross the dam, turn left (east) onto Forest Road 22, and drive 4.5 miles. Turn right onto Forest Road 2 and drive about 4 miles. The access road is long, winding, narrow, and not suitable for larger trailers and RVs.

About the campground: This is the only vehicle-accessible campground near Hell Hole Reservoir, 1.5 miles to the southeast. Hell Hole is situated in a huge rock-walled gorge and has virtually no shoreline. It is a beautiful setting. Fishing can be good for brown trout, which are stocked annually, along with fingerling kokanee and rainbow trout. Elevation 5,300 feet. Stay limit 14 days. Open from May 15 through November 15.

Hell Hole Reservoir

23,24

Loon Lake

20-22

▲18,19

ELDORADO

17

NATIONAL

Union Valley Reservoir

▲11-16

▲7-9

▲10

Ice House Reservoir

6

FOREST

▲1

▲2

▲5
▲4

▲3

26

27

28

25

29

50

To
Placerville

89

South Lake Tahoe

To
Carson City, NV

88

50

49

51 52

53

55 54

89

45-48

30

31

32

33

34

Silver Lake

40

41

Bear River Reservoir

44

43

42

36

37-39

35

88

To
Jackson

To
Topaz

N

Eldorado Area Campgrounds

	Group sites	RV sites	Total sites	Max. RV length	Hookups	Toilets	Showers	Drinking water	Dump station	Pets	Wheelchair	Recreation	Fee ($)	Season	Can reserve	Length of stay
1 Big Meadows		•	54	27		F		•		•	•	HFB	8	May 15–Nov. 15		14
2 Middle Meadows Group Camp	•		2			V		•		•		HF	25–50	May 15–Sept. 15	•	14
3 Dru Barner Equestrian Camp		•	16	23						•		HR				14
Stumpy Meadows Reservoir (4–5)																
4 Stumpy Meadows		•	40			V		•	•	•	•	HFB	10–20	April–Nov. 15	•	14
5 Black Oak Group Camp	•	•	4			V		•	•	•		HFB	50	April 15–October	•	14
6 Silver Creek			11			V				•		FS	6	June–Oct. 15		14
Ice House Reservoir (7–10)																
7 Ice House		•	83	25		V		•		•	•	SFB	13–20	June–Oct. 15	•	14
8 Northwind		•	10			V				•	•	SFB	5	May 15–October		14
9 Strawberry Point		•	10			V				•	•	SFB	5	May 15–October		14
10 Wrights Lake		•	70			V		•		•		SF BR	12–24	June 15–Oct. 15	•	14
Union Valley Reservoir (11–16)																
11 Jones Fork		•	10	27		V				•		SFB	5	May 15–October		14
12 Fashoda			30			V		•		•	•	SFB	13	May 15–October		14
13 Sunset		•	131			V		•		•	•	SFB	13–20	May 15–October	•	14
14 Wench Creek	•	•	102			F		•		•		SFB	13–60	May 15–October		14
15 Yellowjacket		•	40	23		F		•		•		SFBL	13	May 15–October		14
16 Wolf Creek		•	42			V		•		•	•	SFB	13–20	May 15–October	•	14
17 South Fork		•	17			V				•		F		June–Oct. 15		14

	Group sites	RV sites	Total sites	Max. RV length	Hookups	Toilets	Showers	Drinking water	Dump station	Pets	Wheelchair	Recreation	Fee ($)	Season	Can reserve	Length of stay
18 Gerle Creek Reservoir		•	50	23		V		•		•	•	HS FB	13	June–Oct. 15	•	14
19 Airport Flat		•	16	23		V				•	•	HF		June–Oct. 15		14

Loon Lake (20–24)

	Group sites	RV sites	Total sites	Max. RV length	Hookups	Toilets	Showers	Drinking water	Dump station	Pets	Wheelchair	Recreation	Fee ($)	Season	Can reserve	Length of stay
20 Loon Lake		•	68			V		•		•	•	HSF BL	13	June 15–Sept. 15	•	14
21 Loon Lake Equestrian Camp	•	•	10			V		•		•		HSF BR	13–50	June 15–Sept.15	•	14
22 Loon Lake Group Camp 2	•	•	6			V		•		•		HS FB	13	June 15–Sept. 15	•	14
23 Northshore		•	10			V				•	•	HS FB	5	June 15–Sept. 15		14
24 Red Fir Group Camp	•	•	1			V		•		•		HS FB	35	June 15–Sept. 15	•	14
25 Capps Crossing		•	11			V		•		•	•	HF	11	June 15–October		14
26 Sand Flat		•	29			V		•		•	•	SF	11–22	April 15–Nov. 15		14
27 China Flat		•	18			V		•		•	•	HSF	11–22	April 25–October		14
28 Silver Fork		•	35			V		•		•	•	HS FO	11–22	May 15–October		14
29 Lovers Leap			21			V		•		•		HFO		May 15–October		14
30 Woods Lake			25			V		•		•	•	HS FB	10–18	July–Oct. 15		14
31 Caples Lake		•	35			V		•		•		HSF BO	11	June–Oct. 15		14
32 Kirkwood Lake			12			V		•		•		HFB	10	June 16–Oct. 15		14
33 Silver Lake East		•	62			V		•		•		HSF BO	11	June–Oct. 15	•	14
34 Silver Lake West		•	35			V		•		•		HSF BO	10	June–Oct. 15		14
35 PiPi		•	51			V		•		•	•	HSF	10–18	April 15–Nov. 15		14
36 Lumberyard		•	5			V				•				June–Oct. 15		14
37 Mokelumne River			8			V				•		SF				14
38 Moore Creek			8			V				•		SF				14

	Group sites	RV sites	Total sites	Max. RV length	Hookups	Toilets	Showers	Drinking water	Dump station	Pets	Wheelchair	Recreation	Fee ($)	Season	Can reserve	Length of stay
39 White Azalea			6			V						HSF				14
40 Middle Fork Cosumnes River			5			V				•		HSF		June 15–Oct. 15		14

Bear River Reservoir (41–44)

	Group sites	RV sites	Total sites	Max. RV length	Hookups	Toilets	Showers	Drinking water	Dump station	Pets	Wheelchair	Recreation	Fee ($)	Season	Can reserve	Length of stay
41 Sugar Pine Point		•	10	25		V				•		SFB	8	June–Nov. 15		14
42 South Shore		•	22	25		V		•		•		SFB	11–22	June–Nov. 15		14
43 Pardoes Point			10			V				•		SFB	8	June–Nov. 15		14
44 Bear River Group Camp	•		3			V		•		•		SFB	50–100	June–Nov. 15	•	14

Blue Lake (45–48)

	Group sites	RV sites	Total sites	Max. RV length	Hookups	Toilets	Showers	Drinking water	Dump station	Pets	Wheelchair	Recreation	Fee ($)	Season	Can reserve	Length of stay
45 Lower Blue Lake		•	16			V		•		•		HSF	15 BL	July–Oct. 15		14
46 Middle Creek		•	5			V		•		•		HSFB	15	July–Oct. 15		14
47 Blue Lake Dam		•	25			V		•		•		HSFB	15	July–Oct. 15		14
48 Upper Blue Lake		•	32			V		•		•		HSFB	15	July–Oct. 15		14
49 Hope Valley	•	•	21			V		•		•		F	8–16	June–September	•	14
50 Kit Carson		•	12	23		V		•		•		F	8	June–September		14
51 Snowshoe Springs			13			V		•		•		F	8	May–September		14
52 Crystal Springs		•	22	23		V		•		•		F	8	May–September		14
53 Turtle Rock		•	28			V		•		•			10	May–October		none
54 Markleeville		•	10	23		V		•		•		F	8	May–September		14
55 Grover Hot Springs State Park		•	76			F	•	•		•	•	HSF	16	May–September	•	15

Hookups: W = Water. E = Electric S = Sewer
Toilets: F = Flush V = Vault P = Pit C = Chemical
Recreation: H = Hiking S = Swimming F = Fishing B = Boating L = Boat Launch O = Off-highway Driving R = Horseback Riding
Maximum Trailer/RV Length given in feet. Stay Limit given in days. Fee given in dollars.
If no entry Aunder **Season**, campground is open all year. If no entry under Fee, camping is free.

2 Middle Meadows Group Camp

Location: 61 miles northeast of Auburn.
Sites: 2 group sites for tents: one for up to 25 people, one for up to 50.
Facilities: Tables, fire rings, drinking water, vault toilets.
Fee per night: $25-$50. Reservations required; call 800-280-CAMP. There is a one-time reservation fee of $8.65.
Management: Eldorado National Forest, 530-333-4312.
Activities: Hiking, fishing.
Finding the campground: From Big Meadows Campground (number 1), continue southwest on Forest Road 24 for about 4 miles.

About the campground: Adjacent Long Canyon Creek offers wading and trout fishing. Elevation 5,000 feet. Stay limit 14 days. Open from May 15 through September 15.

3 Dru Barner Equestrian Camp

Location: 21 miles north of Placerville.
Sites: 16 sites for tents and RVs up to 23 feet long.
Facilities: None.
Fee per night: None.
Management: Eldorado National Forest, 209-333-4312.
Activities: Hiking, horseback riding.
Finding the campground: From Placerville, drive north on California Highway 193 for 13 miles to Georgetown, turn right (east) onto Wentworth Springs Road, and drive 6 miles to Balderson Station. Turn left onto Bypass Road (Forest Road 13N58) and drive 1.5 miles.

About the campground: Primarily for use of equestrians, but family camping is also permitted. A riding trail is near the campground. Elevation 3,000 feet. Stay limit 14 days. Open all year.

4 Stumpy Meadows Reservoir: Stumpy Meadows

Location: 30 miles northeast of Placerville.
Sites: 40 sites for tents and RVs, including 2 double sites.
Facilities: Tables, fire rings, drinking water, vault toilets. Boat ramp nearby. The facilities are wheelchair accessible.
Fee per night: $10, double units $20. For reservations call 800-280-CAMP. There is a one-time reservation fee of $8.65.
Management: Eldorado National Forest, 209-333-4312.
Activities: Hiking, fishing, boating.
Finding the campground: From Placerville, drive north on California Highway 193 for 13 miles to Georgetown, turn right (east) onto Wentworth Springs Road, and drive 17 miles.

About the campground: Situated on the shore of Stumpy Meadows Reservoir, which covers 320 acres and offers good spring trout fishing. The lake is stocked annually with rainbow and brown trout. There is a 5-mile-per-hour speed limit for boats. Elevation 4,400 feet. Stay limit 14 days. Open from April 1 through November 15.

5 | Stumpy Meadows Reservoir: Black Oak Group Camp

Location: 30 miles north of Placerville.
Sites: 3 group sites for tents (2 for up to 50 people, 1 for up to 25); 1 group site for self-contained RVs (for up to 75 people).
Facilities: Tables, fire rings, drinking water, vault toilets at tent sites. Boat ramp nearby. No toilets at RV site.
Fee per night: $50. Reservations required; call 800-280-CAMP. There is a one-time reservation fee of $8.65.
Management: Eldorado National Forest, 209-333-4312.
Activities: Hiking, fishing, boating.
Finding the campground: From Placerville, drive north on California Highway 193 for 13 miles to Georgetown, turn right (east) onto Wentworth Springs Road, and drive 17 miles.

About the campground: See Stumpy Meadows Reservoir (number 4). Stay limit 14 days. Open from April 15 through October 31.

6 | Silver Creek

Location: 30 miles east of Placerville.
Sites: 11 sites for tents.
Facilities: Tables, fire rings, vault toilet. No drinking water.
Fee per night: $6.
Management: Eldorado National Forest, 530-644-6048.
Activities: Fishing, swimming.
Finding the campground: From the intersection of California Highway 49 and U.S. Highway 50 in Placerville, drive east on US 50 for 21 miles, turn left (north) onto Ice House Road, and drive 9 miles.

About the campground: Adjacent to Silver Creek. Fishing and swimming are possible when the water level permits. Elevation 5,200 feet. Stay limit 14 days. Open from June 1 through October 15.

7 | Ice House Reservoir: Ice House

Location: 32 miles northeast of Placerville.
Sites: 83 sites for tents and RVs up to 25 feet long, including 6 double units.
Facilities: Tables, fire rings, drinking water, vault toilets. Dump station and boat ramp nearby. The facilities are wheelchair accessible.
Fee per night: $13, double sites $20. For reservations call 800-280-CAMP. There is a one-time reservation fee of $8.65.
Management: Eldorado National Forest, 530-644-6048.
Activities: Swimming, fishing, boating.

Crystal Basin Recreation Area

About 35 miles northeast of Placerville, off U.S. Highway 50, the Crystal Basin Recreation Area encompasses an extensive, scenic area of lakes, forested streams, and hiking trails. The area was named for the crystalline effect of snow covering the granite ridges and outcroppings of the Sierra Nevada. Three large lakes—Ice House and Union Valley Reservoirs and Loon Lake—provide the area's major attraction, water sports. They also host most of Crystal Basin's 19 campgrounds. Big Hill Lookout, south of Union Valley Reservoir, provides a panoramic view over the region.

Finding the campground: From the intersection of California Highway 49 and U.S. Highway 50 in Placerville, drive east on US 50 for 21 miles, turn left (north) onto Ice House Road, and drive 11 miles.

About the campground: Ice House is the first of three major lakes of the Crystal Basin Recreation Area north of US 50. It encompasses 650 acres at high water and provides good trout fishing. A mix of brown, rainbow, and brook trout are stocked annually. Elevation 5,500 feet. Stay limit 14 days. Open from June 1 through October 15.

8 Ice House Reservoir: Northwind

Location: 33 miles northeast of Placerville.
Sites: 10 sites for self contained RVs.
Facilities: Tables, fire rings, vault toilets. Dump station and boat ramp 1 mile west. No drinking water. The facilities are wheelchair accessible.
Fee per night: $5.
Management: Eldorado National Forest, 530-644-6048.
Activities: Swimming, fishing, boating.
Finding the campground: From the intersection of California Highway 49 and U.S. Highway 50 in Placerville, drive east on US 50 for 21 miles, turn left (north) onto Ice House Road, and drive 11 miles. From Ice House Campground (number 7), take the left fork in the road and continue 1 mile east along the north shore of the lake.

About the campground: Situated on a rise just above the lake. See Ice House Campground (number 7). Elevation 5,500 feet. Stay limit 14 days. Open from May 15 through October 31.

9 Ice House Reservoir: Strawberry Point

Location: 34 miles northeast of Placerville.
Sites: 10 sites for self contained RVs.
Facilities: Tables, fire rings, vault toilets. Dump station and boat ramp 2 miles west. No drinking water. The facilities are wheelchair accessible.
Fee per night: $5.

Management: Eldorado National Forest, 530-644-6048.
Activities: Swimming, fishing, boating.
Finding the campground: From the intersection of California Highway 49 and U.S. Highway 50 in Placerville, drive east on US 50 for 21 miles, turn left (north) onto Ice House Road, and drive 11 miles. From Ice House Campground (number 7), take the left fork in the road and continue 2 miles east along the north shore of the lake.

About the campground: See Ice House Campground (number 7). Elevation 5,500 feet. Stay limit 14 days. Open from May 15 through October 31.

10 Wrights Lake

Location: 39 miles northeast of Placerville.
Sites: 70 sites for tents and RVs, including 3 double sites and 15 equestrian sites.
Facilities: Tables, fire rings, drinking water, vault toilets.
Fee per night: $12, double sites $24. For reservations call 800-280-CAMP. There is a one-time reservation fee of $8.65. Reservations are required from July 10 to September 6.
Management: Eldorado National Forest, 530-644-6048.
Activities: Swimming, fishing, boating, horseback riding.
Finding the campground: From the intersection of California Highway 49 and U.S. Highway 50 in Placerville, drive east on US 50 for 21 miles, turn left (north) onto Ice House Road, and drive 11 miles. Take the left fork in the road and continue 5 miles east on Forest Road 32, turn left onto Wrights Lake Road (Forest Road 4), and drive 2 miles.

About the campground: Situated on the shoreline of a scenic, alpine lake that is stocked annually with brown and rainbow trout. No motorized boats are allowed on the lake. Elevation 7,000 feet. Stay limit 14 days. Open from June 15 through October 15.

11 Union Valley Reservoir: Jones Fork

Location: 33 miles northeast of Placerville.
Sites: 10 sites for tents and RVs up to 27 feet long.
Facilities: Tables, fire rings, vault toilets. Dump station and boat ramp nearby. No drinking water.
Fee per night: $5.
Management: Eldorado National Forest, 530-644-6048.
Activities: Swimming, fishing, boating.
Finding the campground: From the intersection of California Highway 49 and U.S. Highway 50 in Placerville, drive east on US 50 for 21 miles, turn left (north) onto Ice House Road, and drive about 12 miles.

About the campground: Situated on the southeastern shore of Union Valley Reservoir, a 3,000-acre lake that is well stocked annually with rainbow and brook trout. Elevation 4,900 feet. Stay limit 14 days. Open from May 15 through October 31.

12 Union Valley Reservoir: Fashoda

Location: 35 miles northeast of Placerville.
Sites: 30 sites for tents.
Facilities: Tables, fire rings, drinking water, vault toilets. The facilities are wheelchair accessible.
Fee per night: $13.
Management: Eldorado National Forest, 530-644-6048.
Activities: Swimming, fishing, boating.
Finding the campground: From the intersection of California Highway 49 and U.S. Highway 50 in Placerville, drive east on US 50 for 21 miles, turn left (north) onto Ice House Road, and drive about 12.5 miles. Turn left (west) onto Forest Road 12N35 and drive 1.5 miles.

About the campground: See Jones Fork Campground (number 11). Although listed as a walk-in campground, Fashoda has a service road for unloading camping gear.

13 Union Valley Reservoir: Sunset

Location: 35 miles northeast of Placerville.
Sites: 131 sites for tents and RVs, including 8 double sites.
Facilities: Tables, fire rings, drinking water, vault toilets. Dump station, boat ramp, and swimming beach nearby. The facilities are wheelchair accessible.
Fee per night: $13, $20 double. For reservations call 800-280-CAMP. There is a one-time reservation fee of $8.65.
Management: Eldorado National Forest, 530-644-6048.
Activities: Swimming, fishing, boating.
Finding the campground: From the intersection of California Highway 49 and U.S. Highway 50 in Placerville, drive east on US 50 for 21 miles, turn left (north) onto Ice House Road, and drive about 12.5 miles. Turn left (west) onto Forest Road 12N35 and drive 1.5 miles, just past Fashoda Campground (number 12).

About the campground: See Jones Fork Campground (number 11). Situated on a peninsula jutting out into the lake. Overflow camping is available for $5 at the Sunset Boat Ramp.

14 Union Valley Reservoir: Wench Creek

Location: 36 miles northeast of Placerville.
Sites: 100 sites for tents and RVs, plus 2 group sites for up to 50 people each.
Facilities: Tables, fire rings, drinking water, flush and vault toilets. Dump station, boat ramp, and swimming beach 2 miles away.

Fee per night: $13, $60 group. Reservations for group camp only; call 800-280-CAMP. There is a one-time reservation fee of $8.65.
Management: Eldorado National Forest, 530-644-6048.
Activities: Swimming, fishing, boating.
Finding the campground: From the intersection of California Highway 49 and U.S. Highway 50 in Placerville, drive east on US 50 for 21 miles, turn left (north) onto Ice House Road, and drive about 15 miles.

About the campground: See Jones Fork Campground (number 11).

15 Union Valley Reservoir: Yellowjacket

Location: 42 miles northeast of Placerville.
Sites: 40 sites for tents and RVs up to 23 feet long.
Facilities: Tables, fire rings, drinking water, flush and vault toilets, boat ramp. Dump station nearby.
Fee per night: $13. For reservations call 800-280-CAMP. There is a one-time reservation fee of $8.65.
Management: Eldorado National Forest, 530-644-6048.
Activities: Swimming, fishing, boating.
Finding the campground: From the intersection of California Highway 49 and U.S. Highway 50 in Placerville, drive east on US 50 for 21 miles, turn left (north) onto Ice House Road, and drive about 19 miles. Turn left (west) onto Forest Road 12N78, drive half a mile, take the left fork, and drive another 1.5 miles.

About the campground: See Jones Fork Campground (number 11).

16 Union Valley Reservoir: Wolf Creek

Location: 43 miles northeast of Placerville.
Sites: 42 sites for tents and RVs, including 4 double sites.
Facilities: Tables, fire rings, drinking water, vault toilets. The facilities are wheelchair accessible. Boat ramp and dump station nearby.
Fee per night: $13, $20 for double sites. For reservations call 800-280-CAMP. There is a one-time reservation fee of $8.65.
Management: Eldorado National Forest, 530-644-6048.
Activities: Swimming, fishing, boating.
Finding the campground: From the intersection of California Highway 49 and U.S. Highway 50 in Placerville, drive east on US 50 for 21 miles, turn left (north) onto Ice House Road, and drive about 19 miles. Turn left (west) onto Forest Road 12N78 and drive 1.5 miles.

About the campground: See Jones Fork Campground (number 11).

17 South Fork

Location: 45 miles northeast of Placerville.
Sites: 17 sites for tents and RVs.

Facilities: Tables, fire rings, vault toilets. No drinking water.
Fee per night: None.
Management: Eldorado National Forest, 530-644-6048.
Activities: Fishing.
Finding the campground: From the intersection of California Highway 49 and U.S. Highway 50 in Placerville, drive east on US 50 for 21 miles, turn left (north) onto Ice House Road, and drive about 23 miles. Turn left (west) onto Forest Road 13N28 and drive 1 mile.

About the campground: Situated near the South Fork of the Rubicon River, which provides fair trout fishing. Elevation 5,200 feet. Stay limit 14 days. Open from June 1 through October 15.

18 Gerle Creek Reservoir

Location: 50 miles northeast of Placerville.
Sites: 50 sites for tents and RVs up to 23 feet long.
Facilities: Tables, fire rings, drinking water, vault toilets, fishing pier. The facilities are wheelchair accessible.
Fee per night: $13. For reservations call 800-280-CAMP. There is a one-time reservation fee of $8.65.
Management: Eldorado National Forest, 530-644-6048.
Activities: Hiking, fishing, swimming, boating.
Finding the campground: From the intersection of California Highway 49 and U.S. Highway 50 in Placerville, drive east on US 50 for 21 miles, turn left (north) onto Ice House Road, and drive about 27 miles. Turn left onto Forest Road 33 and drive 1.5 miles. Then turn left onto the campground access road and drive half a mile.

About the campground: Situated on the shore of Gerle Creek Reservoir, a small lake covering a little more than 100 acres. The lake is not stocked, and fishing is mediocre. No motorized boats are allowed. Elevation 5,300 feet. The fishing pier and a paved trail are wheelchair-accessible. Stay limit 14 days. Open from June 1 through October 15.

19 Airport Flat

Location: 50 miles northeast of Placerville.
Sites: 16 sites for tents and RVs up to 23 feet long.
Facilities: Tables, fire rings, vault toilets. No drinking water. The facilities are wheelchair accessible.
Fee per night: None.
Management: Eldorado National Forest, 530-644-6048.
Activities: Fishing, hiking.
Finding the campground: From the intersection of California Highway 49 and U.S. Highway 50 in Placerville, drive east on US 50 for 21 miles, turn left (north) onto Ice House Road, and drive about 27 miles. Turn left onto Forest Road 33 and drive 2 miles.

About the campground: Situated on Gerle Creek, which provides mediocre trout fishing. The Summer Harvest Trail begins at the campground, highlighting plants gathered for food by American Indians. Elevation 5,300 feet. Stay limit 14 days. Open from June 1 through October 15.

20 Loon Lake: Loon Lake

Location: 51 miles northeast of Placerville.
Sites: 53 sites for tents and RVs, plus 15 sites for self-contained RVs at adjacent Loon Lake Boat Ramp.
Facilities: Tables, fire rings, drinking water, vault toilets, boat ramp, swimming beach. The facilities are wheelchair accessible.
Fee per night: $13. Reservations (except for boat ramp sites) may be made by calling 800-280-CAMP. There is a one-time reservation fee of $8.65.
Management: Eldorado National Forest, 530-644-6048.
Activities: Hiking, fishing, swimming, boating, sailboarding.
Finding the campground: From the intersection of California Highway 49 and U.S. Highway 50 in Placerville, drive east on US 50 for 21 miles, turn left (north) onto Ice House Road, and drive about 30 miles.

About the campground: Situated on the south shore of the lake, which covers about 600 acres and is well stocked annually with rainbow trout. Elevation 6,378 feet. Stay limit 14 days. Open from June 15 through September 15.

21 Loon Lake: Loon Lake Equestrian Camp

Location: 51 miles northeast of Placerville.
Sites: 9 sites for tents and RVs, plus 1 group camp for up to 25 people.
Facilities: Tables, fire rings, drinking water, vault toilets.
Fee per night: $13, group fee $50. Reservations may be made (required for group camp) by calling 800-280-CAMP. There is a one-time reservation fee of $8.65.
Management: Eldorado National Forest, 530-644-6048.
Activities: Horseback riding, hiking, fishing, swimming, boating, sailboarding.
Finding the campground: From the intersection of California Highway 49 and U.S. Highway 50 in Placerville, drive east on US 50 for 21 miles, turn left (north) onto Ice House Road, and drive about 30 miles.

About the campground: See Loon Lake Campground (number 20).

22 Loon Lake: Loon Lake Group Camp 2

Location: 51 miles northeast of Placerville.
Sites: 6 sites for tents and RVs; each holds up to 25 people.
Facilities: Tables, fire rings, drinking water, vault toilets.
Fee per night: $13. Reservations required; call 800-280-CAMP. There is a one-time reservation fee of $8.65.

Management: Eldorado National Forest, 530-644-6048.
Activities: Hiking, fishing, swimming, boating, sailboarding.
Finding the campground: From the intersection of California Highway 49 and U.S. Highway 50 in Placerville, drive east on US 50 for 21 miles, turn left (north) onto Ice House Road, and drive about 30 miles.

About the campground: See Loon Lake Campground (number 20).

23 Loon Lake: Northshore

Location: 54 miles northeast of Placerville.
Sites: 10 sites for tents and RVs.
Facilities: Tables, fire rings, vault toilets. No drinking water. The facilities are wheelchair accessible.
Fee per night: $5.
Management: Eldorado National Forest, 530-644-6048.
Activities: Hiking, fishing, swimming, boating, sailboarding.
Finding the campground: From the intersection of California Highway 49 and U.S. Highway 50 in Placerville, drive east on US 50 for 21 miles, turn left (north) onto Ice House Road, and drive about 30 miles. Turn left onto Loon Lake Road (Forest Road 13N18) and drive 3 miles.

About the campground: See Loon Lake Campground (number 20).

24 Loon Lake: Red Fir Group Camp

Location: 54 miles northeast of Placerville.
Sites: 1 site for tents and RVs, holds up to 25 people and 6 vehicles.
Facilities: Tables, fire rings, drinking water, vault toilets.
Fee per night: $35. Reservations required; call 800-280-CAMP. There is a one-time reservation fee of $8.65.
Management: Eldorado National Forest, 530-644-6048.
Activities: Hiking, fishing, swimming, boating, sailboarding.
Finding the campground: From the intersection of California Highway 49 and U.S. Highway 50 in Placerville, drive east on US 50 for 21 miles, turn left (north) onto Ice House Road, and drive about 30 miles. Turn left onto Loon Lake Road (Forest Road 13N18) and drive 3 miles, just past Northshore Campground (number 23).

About the campground: See Loon Lake Campground (number 20). Elevation 6,500 feet.

25 Capps Crossing

Location: 30 miles east of Placerville.
Sites: 11 sites for tents and RVs.
Facilities: Tables, fire rings, drinking water, vault toilets. The facilities are wheelchair accessible.

Fee per night: $11.
Management: Eldorado National Forest, 530-644-6048.
Activities: Hiking, fishing, gold panning.
Finding the campground: From the intersection of California Highway 49 and U.S. Highway 50 in Placerville, drive east on US 50 for 12 miles, take the Sly Park Road exit, and drive south 4 miles on Sly Road to Jenkinson Lake. Cross the dams onto Iron Mountain Road (Mormon Emigrant Trail) and drive east 9 miles. Turn right (south) onto North South Road (Capps Crossing Road) and drive 5 miles.

About the campground: Situated on the banks of the North Fork of the Cosumnes River, well off the beaten track for those seeking solitude. Elevation 5,200 feet. Stay limit 14 days. Open from June 15 through October 31.

26 Sand Flat

Location: 28 miles east of Placerville.
Sites: 29 sites for tents and RVs, including 1 double site.
Facilities: Tables, fire rings, drinking water, vault toilets. The facilities are wheelchair accessible.
Fee per night: $11, double site $22.
Management: Eldorado National Forest, 530-644-6048.
Activities: Fishing, swimming.
Finding the campground: From the intersection of California Highway 49 and U.S. Highway 50 in Placerville, drive east on US 50 for 28 miles.

About the campground: Situated in an attractive setting on the South Fork of the American River, adjacent to US 50. Trout fishing is mediocre to poor. Elevation 3,900 feet. Stay limit 14 days. Open from April 15 through November 15.

27 China Flat

Location: 33 miles east of Placerville.
Sites: 18 sites for tents and RVs, including 1 double site.
Facilities: Tables, fire rings, drinking water, vault toilets. The facilities are wheelchair accessible.
Fee per night: $11, double site $22.
Management: Eldorado National Forest, 530-644-6048.
Activities: Fishing, swimming, hiking, gold panning.
Finding the campground: From the intersection of California Highway 49 and U.S. Highway 50 in Placerville, drive east on US 50 for 30 miles, turn right (south) at Kyburz onto Silver Fork Road, and drive 2.6 miles.

About the campground: Situated on the Silver Fork of the American River, which offers much better trout fishing than the South Fork. The Silver Fork is stocked annually with rainbow trout. Elevation 4,800 feet. Stay limit 14 days. Open from April 25 through October 31.

28 Silver Fork

Location: 38 miles east of Placerville.
Sites: 35 sites for tents and RVs, including 4 double sites.
Facilities: Tables, fire rings, drinking water, vault toilets. The facilities are wheelchair accessible.
Fee per night: $11, double site $22.
Management: Eldorado National Forest, 530-644-6048.
Activities: Fishing, swimming, hiking, OHV driving.
Finding the campground: From the intersection of California Highway 49 and U.S. Highway 50 in Placerville, drive east on US 50 for 30 miles, turn right (south) at Kyburz onto Silver Fork Road, and drive 8 miles.

About the campground: Situated on the Silver Fork of the American River, which offers much better trout fishing than the South Fork. The Silver Fork is stocked annually with rainbow trout. Trails for off-highway driving lead eastward from the campground. Elevation 5,600 feet. Stay limit 14 days. Open from May 15 through October 31.

29 Lovers Leap

Location: 16 miles southwest of South Lake Tahoe.
Sites: 21 sites for tents.
Facilities: Tables, fire rings, drinking water, vault toilets.
Fee per night: None.
Management: Eldorado National Forest, 530-644-6048.
Activities: Hiking, fishing, rock climbing, OHV driving.
Finding the campground: From the northern intersection of California Highway 89 and U.S. Highway 50 in South Lake Tahoe, drive southwest on US 50 for 16 miles.

About the campground: Lovers Leap is a massive cliff famous for some of the best rock climbing in the Sierra Nevada, with multiple-pitch routes from novice level to expert. The campground is also used as an overnight starting point for backpackers hiking into the Desolation Wilderness. An OHV trail runs south from the campground. Horsetail Falls, just north of CA 50 at Twin Falls, is a spectacular cascade plunging into Pyramid Canyon. Elevation 5,800 feet. Stay limit 14 days. Open from May 15 through October 31.

30 Woods Lake

Location: 26 miles south of South Lake Tahoe.
Sites: 25 sites for tents, including 2 double sites.
Facilities: Tables, fire rings, drinking water (hand-pumped), vault toilets. The facilities are wheelchair accessible.
Fee per night: $10, double $18.
Management: Eldorado National Forest, 209-295-4251.

Activities: Hiking, fishing, swimming, boating.

Finding the campground: From the northern intersection of California Highway 89 and U.S. Highway 50 in South Lake Tahoe, drive south and then east on CA 89 for 15 miles, turn right (south) onto California Highway 88, and drive 10 miles. Turn left (south) at Woods Lake turnoff and drive 1 mile.

About the campground: A small, scenic lake in a secluded location, Woods is stocked annually with rainbow trout. No motors are permitted on the lake. A 3.5-mile loop trail to Round Top and Winnemucca Lakes begins at the campground. Woods Lake was described by *Sunset Magazine* as one of the 100 best campgrounds in the western United States. Elevation 8,200 feet. Stay limit 14 days. Open from July 1 through October 15.

---

31 Caples Lake

Location: 27 miles south of South Lake Tahoe.

Sites: 35 sites for tents and RVs.

Facilities: Tables, fire rings, drinking water, vault toilets. Boat ramp nearby.

Fee per night: $11.

Management: Eldorado National Forest, 209-295-4251.

Activities: Hiking, fishing, swimming, boating, OHV driving.

Finding the campground: From the northern intersection of California Highway 89 and U.S. Highway 50 in South Lake Tahoe, drive south and then east on CA 89 for 15 miles, turn right (south) onto California Highway 88 and drive 12 miles. You will pass the entrance to the Kirkwood Ski Area 1 mile before you reach the campground.

About the campground: Caples is an attractive lake on CA 88. It covers about 600 acres and offers good trout fishing in late spring and early summer. Each year the lake is stocked with a heavy mix of rainbow, brown, and brook trout—all in the 10- to 12-inch range. There is a 10-mile-per-hour speed limit for boats. An 8-mile round-trip trail leads from the campground along the southwest shore of the lake to Emigrant Lake. AN OHV trail runs north from the Kirkwood Ski Area. Elevation 7,800 feet. Stay limit 14 days. Open from June 1 through October 15.

---

32 Kirkwood Lake

Location: 30 miles south of South Lake Tahoe.

Sites: 12 sites for tents.

Facilities: Tables, fire rings, drinking water, vault toilets.

Fee per night: $10.

Management: Eldorado National Forest, 209-295-4251.

Activities: Hiking, fishing, boating.

Finding the campground: From the northern intersection of California Highway 89 and U.S. Highway 50 in South Lake Tahoe, drive south and then east on CA 89 for 15 miles, turn right (south) onto California Highway 88, and drive 15 miles.

About the campground: A small lake in a beautiful setting, Kirkwood yields only small trout. No motors are allowed on the lake. Elevation 7,600 feet. Stay limit 14 days. Open from June 16 through October 15.

33 Silver Lake East

Location: 34 miles south of South Lake Tahoe.
Sites: 62 sites for tents and RVs.
Facilities: Tables, fire rings, drinking water, vault toilets. Boat ramp and rentals nearby.
Fee per night: $11. For reservations call 800-280-CAMP. There is a one-time reservation fee of $8.65.
Management: Eldorado National Forest, 209-295-4251.
Activities: Hiking, fishing, swimming, boating, OHV driving.
Finding the campground: From the northern intersection of California Highway 89 and U.S. Highway 50 in South Lake Tahoe, drive south and then east on CA 89 for 15 miles, turn right (south) onto California Highway 88, and drive 19 miles.

About the campground: Two miles long and a mile wide at its widest point, Silver Lake enjoys a classic Sierra setting at the base of a granite cirque. It is a good place to fish for trout: each year it is stocked with a heavy mix of rainbows, brooks, and browns. The campground is on the northeast shore of the lake. An OHV trail leads east, and hiking trails run east, south, and west. Elevation 7,200 feet. Stay limit 14 days. Open from June 1 through October 15.

34 Silver Lake West

Location: 34 miles south of South Lake Tahoe.
Sites: 35 sites for tents and RVs.
Facilities: Tables, fire rings, drinking water, vault toilets. Boat ramp and rentals nearby.
Fee per night: $10.
Management: Eldorado National Forest, 209-295-4251.
Activities: Hiking, fishing, swimming, boating, OHV driving.
Finding the campground: From the northern intersection of California Highway 89 and U.S. Highway 50 in South Lake Tahoe, drive south and then east on CA 89 for 15 miles, turn right (south) onto California Highway 88, and drive 19 miles.

About the campground: See Silver Lake East Campground (number 33) for lake and area information. The campground is across the highway from the lake and Silver Lake East Campground.

35 PiPi

Location: 34 miles northeast of Jackson.
Sites: 51 sites for tents and RVs, including 3 double sites.

Facilities: Tables, fire rings, drinking water, vault toilets, fishing piers. The facilities are wheelchair accessible.
Fee per night: $10, double site $18.
Management: Eldorado National Forest, 209-295-4251.
Activities: Swimming, fishing, hiking.
Finding the campground: From the intersection of California Highways 49 and 88 in Jackson, take CA 88 northeast for 26 miles, turn left (north) onto Omo Ranch Road, and drive 1.5 miles. Turn right (north) onto North South Road (Forest Road 6) and drive 6 miles.

About the campground: Situated on the bank of the Middle Fork of the Cosumnes River, with good swimming holes nearby. A barrier-free interpretive trail highlights American Indian history and mid-1800s mining activity in the area. The fishing piers are also barrier-free. Elkins Flat, an OHV staging area about 2 miles north of PiPi, permits open camping at no cost. Except for vault toilets, there are no facilities there. Elevation 4,100 feet. Stay limit 14 days. Open from April 15 through November 15.

36 Lumberyard

Location: 37 miles northeast of Jackson.
Sites: 5 sites for tents and RVs.
Facilities: Tables, fire rings, vault toilet. No drinking water.
Fee per night: None.
Management: Eldorado National Forest, 209-295-4251.
Activities: None.
Finding the campground: From the intersection of California Highways 49 and 88 in Jackson, take CA 88 northeast for 37 miles.

About the campground: This campground is best used as an overnight stop along the Carson Pass National Scenic Byway (CA 88). Stay limit 14 days. Open from June 1 through October 15.

37 Mokelumne River

Location: 46 miles northeast of Jackson.
Sites: 8 sites for tents.
Facilities: Tables, fire rings, vault toilet. No drinking water.
Fee per night: None.
Management: Eldorado National Forest, 209-295-4251.
Activities: Fishing, swimming.
Finding the campground: From the intersection of California Highways 49 and 88 in Jackson, take CA 88 northeast for 37 miles, turn right (south) onto Ellis Road (Forest Road 92), and drive about 9 miles.

About the campground: Situated in the canyon of the North Fork of the Mokelumne River, which offers several nearby swimming holes and fishing for small trout. Elevation 3,200 feet. Stay limit 14 days. Open all year.

38 | Moore Creek

Location: 46 miles northeast of Jackson.
Sites: 8 sites for tents.
Facilities: Tables, fire rings, vault toilet. No drinking water.
Fee per night: None.
Management: Eldorado National Forest, 209-295-4251.
Activities: Fishing, swimming.
Finding the campground: From the intersection of California Highways 49 and 88 in Jackson, take CA 88 northeast for 37 miles, turn right (south) onto Ellis Road (Forest Road 92), and drive about 9 miles on a steep, narrow road to the campground, just beyond Mokelumne River Campground (number 37).

About the campground: See Mokelumne River Campground (number 37).

39 | White Azalea

Location: 47 miles northeast of Jackson.
Sites: 6 sites for tents.
Facilities: Vault toilet. No drinking water.
Fee per night: None.
Management: Eldorado National Forest, 209-295-4251.
Activities: Fishing, swimming, hiking.
Finding the campground: From the intersection of California Highways 49 and 88 in Jackson, take CA 88 northeast for 37 miles, turn right (south) onto Ellis Road (Forest Road 92), and drive about 10 miles.

About the campground: See Mokelumne River Campground (number 37). A trailhead 3 miles east of the campground leads 4 miles along the north shore of Salt Springs Reservoir to Blue Hole and Salt Springs. Elevation 3,500 feet. Stay limit 14 days. Open all year.

40 | Middle Fork Cosumnes River

Location: 42 miles northeast of Jackson.
Sites: 5 sites for tents.
Facilities: Tables, fire rings, vault toilet. No drinking water.
Fee per night: None.
Management: Eldorado National Forest, 209-295-4251.
Activities: Fishing, swimming, hiking.
Finding the campground: From the intersection of California Highways 49 and 88 in Jackson, take CA 88 northeast for 38 miles, turn left (north) onto Forest Road 8N23, and drive 3.5 miles.

About the campground: Situated on the bank of the river with a swimming hole nearby. Fishing is fair for small native trout. Elevation 6,800 feet. Stay limit 14 days. Open from June 15 through October 15.

41 | Bear River Reservoir: Sugar Pine Point

Location: 46 miles northeast of Jackson.
Sites: 8 sites for tents, plus 2 sites for RVs up to 25 feet long.
Facilities: Tables, fire rings, vault toilet. No drinking water.
Fee per night: $8.
Management: Eldorado National Forest, 209-295-4251.
Activities: Fishing, swimming, boating.
Finding the campground: From the intersection of California Highways 49 and 88 in Jackson, take CA 88 northeast for 40 miles, turn right (south) onto Bear River Reservoir Road, and drive 2.5 miles to a Y intersection. Turn left onto an unpaved road and drive 3 miles.

About the campground: About 3 miles long and up to half a mile wide, the reservoir covers 725 acres. Fishing can be very good, as the lake is well stocked with a mix of rainbow, brook, and brown trout. The campground is on the north shore of the lake. Bear River Lake Resort, a commercial campground 2 miles west of the campground (you pass it on the way here), offers a boat ramp, dump station, showers, laundry, store, restaurant, and hookup sites if the public campground is full. Elevation 6,000 feet. Stay limit 14 days. Open from June 1 through November 15.

42 | Bear River Reservoir: South Shore

Location: 44 miles northeast of Jackson.
Sites: 22 sites for tents and RVs up to 25 feet long, including 4 double sites.
Facilities: Tables, fire rings, drinking water, vault toilets. Boat ramp 2 miles northeast.
Fee per night: $11, double sites $22.
Management: Eldorado National Forest, 209-295-4251.
Activities: Fishing, swimming, boating.
Finding the campground: From the intersection of California Highways 49 and 88 in Jackson, take CA 88 northeast for 40 miles, turn right (south) onto Bear River Reservoir Road, and drive 4 miles.

About the campground: See Sugar Pine Point Campground (number 41).

43 | Bear River Reservoir: Pardoes Point

Location: 45 miles northeast of Jackson.
Sites: 10 sites for tents.
Facilities: Tables, fire rings, vault toilets. No drinking water.
Fee per night: $8.
Management: Eldorado National Forest, 209-295-4251.
Activities: Fishing, swimming, boating.
Finding the campground: From the intersection of California Highways 49 and 88 in Jackson, take CA 88 northeast for 40 miles, turn right (south) onto Bear River Reservoir Road, and drive 5 miles.

About the campground: See Sugar Pine Point Campground (number 41).

44 Bear River Reservoir: Bear River Group Camp

Location: 46 miles northeast of Jackson.
Sites: 3 group sites for tents: 2 for up to 25 people, 1 for up to 50.
Facilities: Tables, fire rings, drinking water, vault toilets.
Fee per night: $50-$100. Reservations required; call number below.
Management: Eldorado National Forest, 209-295-4251.
Activities: Fishing, swimming, boating.
Finding the campground: From the intersection of California Highways 49 and 88 in Jackson, take CA 88 northeast for 40 miles, turn right (south) onto Bear River Reservoir Road, and drive 5.5 miles.

About the campground: See Sugar Pine Point Campground (number 41).

45 Blue Lake: Lower Blue Lake

Location: 30 miles south of South Lake Tahoe.
Sites: 16 sites for tents and RVs.
Facilities: Tables, fire rings and grills, drinking water, vault toilets, boat ramp.
Fee per night: $15.
Management: PG&E, 530-386-5164.
Activities: Hiking, swimming, fishing, boating.
Finding the campground: From the northern intersection of California Highway 89 and U.S. Highway 50 in South Lake Tahoe, drive south and then east on CA 89 for 15 miles, turn right (south) onto California Highway 88, and drive 2.5 miles. Turn left (south) onto Blue Lakes Road and drive 12 miles.

About the campground: Situated on the south shore of the lake, which has good fishing for trout; catchable size rainbow and fingerling brook trout are stocked annually. Elevation 8,100 feet. Stay limit 14 days. Open from July 1 through October 15.

46 Blue Lake: Middle Creek

Location: 31 miles south of South Lake Tahoe.
Sites: 5 sites for tents and RVs.
Facilities: Tables, fire rings and grills, drinking water, vault toilets. Boat ramp nearby.
Fee per night: $15.
Management: PG&E, 530-386-5164.
Activities: Hiking, swimming, fishing, boating.
Finding the campground: From the northern intersection of California Highway 89 and U.S. Highway 50 in South Lake Tahoe, drive south and then east on CA 89 for 15 miles, turn right (south) onto California Highway 88, and drive 2.5 miles. Turn left (south) onto Blue Lakes Road and drive 12 miles. From Lower Blue Lake Campground (number 45), drive north along the lake 1.5 miles.

About the campground: See Lower Blue Lake Campground (number 45). Elevation 8,200 feet.

47 Blue Lake: Blue Lake Dam

Location: 32 miles south of South Lake Tahoe.
Sites: 25 sites for tents and RVs.
Facilities: Tables, fire rings and grills, drinking water, vault toilets. Boat ramp nearby.
Fee per night: $15.
Management: PG&E, 530-386-5164.
Activities: Hiking, swimming, fishing, boating.
Finding the campground: From the northern intersection of California Highway 89 and U.S. Highway 50 in South Lake Tahoe, drive south and then east on CA 89 for 15 miles, turn right (south) onto California Highway 88, and drive 2.5 miles. Turn left (south) onto Blue Lakes Road and drive 12 miles. From Lower Blue Lake Campground (number 45), drive north along the lake 2 miles.

About the campground: See Lower Blue Lake Campground (number 45). Elevation 8,200 feet.

48 Blue Lake: Upper Blue Lake

Location: 33 miles south of South Lake Tahoe.
Sites: 32 sites for tents and RVs.
Facilities: Tables, fire rings and grills, drinking water, vault toilets. Boat ramp nearby.
Fee per night: $15.
Management: Pacific Gas and Electric, 530-386-5164.
Activities: Hiking, swimming, fishing, boating.
Finding the campground: From the northern intersection of California Highway 89 and U.S. Highway 50 in South Lake Tahoe, drive south and then east on CA 89 for 15 miles, turn right (south) onto California Highway 88, and drive 2.5 miles. Turn left (south) onto Blue Lakes Road and drive 12 miles. From Lower Blue Lake Campground (number 45), drive north along the lake 3 miles.

About the campground: See Lower Blue Lake Campground (number 45). Elevation 8,200 feet.

49 Hope Valley

Location: 19 miles southeast of South Lake Tahoe.
Sites: 20 sites for tents and RVs, plus 1 group site.
Facilities: Tables, fire rings, drinking water, vault toilets.
Fee per night: $8, group fee $16. For reservations (required for the group site) call 800-280-CAMP. There is a one-time reservation fee of $8.65.
Management: Toiyabe National Forest, 702-882-2766.
Activities: Fishing.
Finding the campground: From the northern intersection of California Highway 89 and U.S. Highway 50 in South Lake Tahoe, drive south and then

east on CA 89 for 15 miles, turn right onto California Highway 88, and drive 2.6 miles. Turn left (south) onto Blue Lakes Road and drive 1.5 miles.

About the campground: Situated on the bank of the West Fork of the Carson River, which is well stocked annually with rainbow trout. Fishing is best in late spring and early summer. Elevation 7,300 feet. Stay limit 14 days. Open from June through September.

50 Kit Carson

Location: 16 miles southeast of South Lake Tahoe.
Sites: 12 sites for tents and RVs up to 23 feet long.
Facilities: Tables, fire rings, drinking water, vault toilets.
Fee per night: $8.
Management: Toiyabe National Forest, 702-882-2766.
Activities: Fishing.
Finding the campground: From the northern intersection of California Highway 89 and U.S. Highway 50 in South Lake Tahoe, drive south and then east on CA 89 for 15 miles, turn left onto California Highway 88/89, and drive 1.2 miles.

About the campground: Situated on the bank of the West Fork of the Carson River, which is well stocked annually with rainbow trout. Fishing is best in late spring and early summer. Elevation 6,900 feet. Stay limit 14 days. Open from June through September.

51 Snowshoe Springs

Location: 17 miles southeast of South Lake Tahoe.
Sites: 13 sites for tents.
Facilities: Tables, fire rings, drinking water, vault toilets.
Fee per night: $8.
Management: Toiyabe National Forest, 702-882-2766.
Activities: Fishing.
Finding the campground: From the northern intersection of California Highway 89 and U.S. Highway 50 in South Lake Tahoe, drive south and then east on CA 89 for 15 miles, turn left onto California Highway 88/89, and drive 1.5 miles.

About the campground: See Kit Carson Campground (number 50). Elevation 6,600 feet.

52 Crystal Springs

Location: 20 miles southeast of South Lake Tahoe.
Sites: 22 sites for tents and RVs up to 23 feet long.
Facilities: Tables, fire rings, drinking water, vault toilets.
Fee per night: $8.
Management: Toiyabe National Forest, 702-882-2766.
Activities: Fishing.

Finding the campground: From the northern intersection of California Highway 89 and U.S. Highway 50 in South Lake Tahoe, drive south and then east on CA 89 for 15 miles, turn left onto California Highway 88/89, and drive 5 miles.

About the campground: See Kit Carson Campground (number 50). Elevation 6,000 feet. Open from May through September.

53 Turtle Rock

Location: 25 miles southeast of South Lake Tahoe.
Sites: 28 sites for tents and RVs.
Facilities: Tables, grills, drinking water, vault toilets.
Fee per night: $10.
Management: Alpine County Parks Department, 916-694-2255.
Activities: None.
Finding the campground: From the northern intersection of California Highway 89 and U.S. Highway 50 in South Lake Tahoe, drive southeast on CA 89 for 25 miles.

About the campground: A wooded campground close to CA 89, best used as an overnight stop or if the campground at Grover Hot Springs (6 miles south, see below) is full. Elevation 5,500 feet. No stay limit. Open from May through October.

54 Markleeville

Location: 28 miles southeast of South Lake Tahoe.
Sites: 10 sites for tents and RVs up to 23 feet long.
Facilities: Tables, fire rings, drinking water, vault toilets.
Fee per night: $8.
Management: Toiyabe National Forest, 702-882-2766.
Activities: Fishing.
Finding the campground: From the northern intersection of California Highway 89 and U.S. Highway 50 in South Lake Tahoe, drive south on CA 89 for 28 miles.

About the campground: Situated on the banks of Markleeville Creek, which provides fishing for small trout. This campground provides an option if the campground at Grover Hot Springs (3.5 miles west, see below) is full. Elevation 5,500 feet. Stay limit 14 days. Open from May through September.

55 Grover Hot Springs State Park

Location: 32 miles southeast of South Lake Tahoe.
Sites: 76 sites for tents and RVs.
Facilities: Tables, fire grills, drinking water, showers, flush toilets, mineral springs pools. The facilities are wheelchair accessible.

Fee per night: $16, pets $1. A separate fee of $4 is charged for pool entry. For reservations call 800-444-7275. There is a one-time reservation fee of $7.50.
Agency: California Department of Parks and Recreation, 530-694-2248.
Activities: Hiking, fishing, swimming.
Finding the campground: From the northern intersection of California Highway 89 and U.S. Highway 50 in South Lake Tahoe, drive south on CA 89 for 28 miles to Markleeville, turn right (west) onto Hot Springs Road, and drive 3.5 miles.

About the campground: Selected as one of the 100 best campgrounds west of the Mississippi by *Sunset Magazine*, this camp features sites well spaced in a tall pine forest. The hot springs—one hot pool and one cold—are 0.3 mile by trail or 0.5 mile by road from the campground. The hot pool is fed by the runoff from six mineral springs; it surfaces at 148 degrees F, but cold water is added to bring it down to 104 degrees. The mountain setting is impressive, and the pools are open all year, closing only for cleaning and for the Thanksgiving, Christmas, and New Year holidays. The campground is open from May to September, but camping is permitted in winter in the day use area adjacent to the park entrance. The 20 units there have fire pits, grills, and tables, with drinking water and toilets available. Elevation 6,000 feet. Stay limit 15 days.

STANISLAUS-TOIYABE AREA

The Stanislaus National Forest and a portion of the Toiyabe National Forest make up most of this area of the High Sierra region. The Stanislaus covers almost 900,000 acres and contains 800 miles of rivers and streams, of which 29 miles of the Tuolumne and 11 miles of the Merced are designated Wild and Scenic Rivers. Nearly 500 miles of trails and 1,000 miles of abandoned roads are available for use by hikers and equestrians, while 150 miles of trails and 2,000 miles of dirt roads are open to mountain bikers. Inhabiting the forest are 325 species of wildlife and 18 of fish.

Although Toiyabe is the largest national forest in the contiguous 48 states, only a small part of it lies within California, northwest of Mono Lake. The Carson Pass Scenic Byway, considered one of the most scenic routes in the nation, runs through Woodfords Canyon over Carson Pass and ends in California's Central Valley region. Marvelous views of the Sierra Nevada and high mountain valleys unfold en route.

1 Centerville Flats

Location: 34 miles southeast of South Lake Tahoe.
Sites: Open camping for tents and RVs.
Facilities: Tables, fire rings, vault toilets. No drinking water.
Fee per night: None.
Management: Toiyabe National Forest, 702-882-2766.
Activities: Fishing.

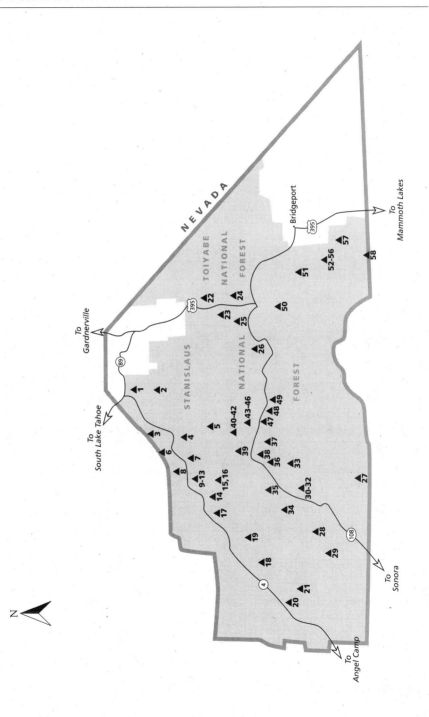

STANISLAUS-TOIYABE AREA CAMPGROUNDS

	Group sites	RV sites	Total sites	Max. RV length	Hookups	Toilets	Showers	Drinking water	Dump station	Pets	Wheelchair	Recreation	Fee ($)	Season	Can reserve	Length of stay
1 Centerville Flats		•	open			V				•		F				16
2 Wolf Creek		•	open			V				•		F				16
3 Silver Creek		•	22			V		•		•		F	8	June 14–Sept. 8	•	14
4 Bloomfield		•	open			V		•		•		F		June–October		14
5 Highland Lakes		•	35			V		•		•		SFB	5	June–October		14
6 Hermit Valley		•	open			V				•		HF		June–October		14
7 Pacific Valley		•	open			V				•		HF		June–October		14
8 Mosquito Lakes		•	9			V				•		HF		June–October		14

Lake Alpine (9–13)

	Group sites	RV sites	Total sites	Max. RV length	Hookups	Toilets	Showers	Drinking water	Dump station	Pets	Wheelchair	Recreation	Fee ($)	Season	Can reserve	Length of stay
9 Lake Alpine		•	26			F	•	•		•	•	HSF BL	13	June–October		14
10 Backpackers			6			F		•		•		HS FB	13	May–October		1
11 Pine Marten		•	33			F		•		•		HS FB	13	May–October		14
12 Silver Valley		•	25			F		•		•	•	HS FB	13	May–October		14
13 Silvertip		•	24			F		•		•		HS FB	13	mid-June–September		14
14 Stanislaus River		•	25			V		•		•		SF	5	June–September		14
15 Spicer Reservoir		•	60			V		•		•	•	SFBL	12	June–September		14
16 Spicer Reservoir Group Camp	•	•				V		•		•		SFB	90	June–September	•	14
17 Big Meadow	•	•	69			V		•		•		H	10–30	May–September	•	
18 Board's Crossing		•	open			V		•		•		F		April–September		14
19 Sourgrass		•	15	19		V		•		•		SF	5	April–September		14

Calaveras Big Trees State Park (20–21)

	Group sites	RV sites	Total sites	Max. RV length	Hookups	Toilets	Showers	Drinking water	Dump station	Pets	Wheelchair	Recreation	Fee ($)	Season	Can reserve	Length of stay
20 North Grove	•	•	75			F	•	•	•	•	•	H	12–16		•	15
21 Oak Hallow		•	54			F	•	•	•	•	•	H	12–16	April–October	•	15
22 Shingle Mill		•	90			V		•		•		F	8	May–September		14
23 Bootleg		•	63			V		•		•		F	9	May–September	•	14
24 Chris Flat		•	15			V		•		•		F	9	May–October		14
25 Sonora Bridge		•	23	30		V		•		•		F	9	May–October 14	•	14
26 Leavitt Meadows		•	16	23		V		•		•		HF	9	May–October 14		14
27 Hull Creek		•	16			V		•		•		F	5	May–September		14
28 Fraser Flat		•	38			V		•		•	•	SF	9	May–September		14
29 Sand Bar Flat		•	10			V		•		•	•	SF	7	May–September		14

Pine Crest Lake (30–32)

	Group sites	RV sites	Total sites	Max. RV length	Hookups	Toilets	Showers	Drinking water	Dump station	Pets	Wheelchair	Recreation	Fee ($)	Season	Can reserve	Length of stay
30 Meadowview		•	100			F	•	•	•			HS	12 FB	May–August		14
31 Pinecrest Lake		•	200			F	•	•	•			HSF BL	14	May–September	•	14
32 Pioneer Trail Group Camp	•	•	3			V		•		•		HS FB	50–65	May–September	•	14
33 Herring Creek Reservoir		•	26			P				•		HSF		May–October		14
34 Beardsley Reservoir		•	26			V		•		•		HS FB		May–October		14
35 Cascade Creek		•	12			V				•			5	May–September		14
36 Mill Creek		•	17			V				•			5	May–September		14
37 Niagara Creek OHV Camp		•	10			V				•		OF	5	May–September		14
38 Niagara Creek		•	10			V				•		F	5	May–September		14
39 Fence Creek		•	30			P				•		F	5	May–September		14

	Group sites	RV sites	Total sites	Max. RV length	Hookups	Toilets	Showers	Drinking water	Dump station	Pets	Wheelchair	Recreation	Fee ($)	Season	Can reserve	Length of stay
40 Clark Fork		•	88	23		F		•	•	•	•	HF	10–11	May–September		14
41 Clark Fork Horse Camp		•	14	23		V		•		•		RF	5	May–September		14
42 Sand Flat		•	68			V		•		•		F	7	May–September		14
43 Boulder Flat		•	20			V		•		•		F	10–14	May–September		14
44 Brightman Flat		•	33			V				•		F	7	May–September		14
45 Dardanelle		•	28			V		•		•		F	12–16	May–September		14
46 Pigeon Flat			7			V				•		HF	7	May–September		14
47 Eureka Valley		•	27	23		V		•		•		HF	9.50	May–September		14
48 Baker		•	44	23		V		•		•		F	9	May–October		14
49 Deadman		•	17	23		V		•		•		HF	9	May–September		14
50 Obsidian		•	14	30		V				•		HF	5	June 5–Oct. 14		14
51 Buckeye	•	•	66	30		F		•		•		HSF	9–35	May–Oct. 13	•	14
52 Honeymoon Flat		•	45	36		V		•		•		F	9	May–October	•	14
53 Robinson Creek		•	54			F		•		•		F	10	May–October	•	14
54 Paha		•	22	36		F		•		•		F	10	May–Oct. 13	•	14
55 Crags		•	27			F		•		•	•	F	10	May–Oct. 13		14
56 Lower Twin Lakes		•	15	36		F		•		•		HS FB	10	May–Oct. 13	•	14
57 Green Creek	•	•	13	23		V		•		•		HF	9–35	May 15–September	•	14
58 Trumbull Lake		•	45	36		V		•		•		HF	9	June 28–Oct. 19	•	14

Hookups: W = Water E = Electric S = Sewer
Toilets: F = Flush V = Vault P = Pit C = Chemical
Recreation: H = Hiking S = Swimming F = Fishing B = Boating L = Boat Launch O = Off-highway Driving R = Horseback Riding
Maximum Trailer/RV Length given in feet. Stay Limit given in days. Fee given in dollars.
If no entry under **Season,** campground is open all year. If no entry under **Fee,** camping is free.

Finding the campground: From the northern intersection of California Highway 89 and U.S. Highway 50 in South Lake Tahoe, drive south on CA 89 for 32 miles, turn right (south) onto California Highway 4, and drive 2 miles.

About the campground: Situated near the East Fork of the Carson River, which is well stocked annually with rainbow trout. Elevation 6,000 feet. Stay limit 16 days. Open all year.

2 Wolf Creek

Location: 39 miles southeast of South Lake Tahoe.
Sites: Open camping for tents and RVs.
Facilities: Tables, fire rings, vault toilets. No drinking water.
Fee per night: None.
Management: Toiyabe National Forest, 702-882-2766.
Activities: Fishing.
Finding the campground: From the northern intersection of California Highway 89 and U.S. Highway 50 in South Lake Tahoe, drive southeast on CA 89 for 32 miles, turn right (south) onto California Highway 4, and drive 2 miles. Turn left (southeast) onto Wolf Creek Road and drive 5 miles.

About the campground: Situated on the bank of a small creek with fair to poor fishing for small native trout. Elevation 6,400 feet. Stay limit 16 days. Open all year.

3 Silver Creek

Location: 39 miles southeast of South Lake Tahoe.
Sites: 22 sites for tents and RVs.
Facilities: Tables, fire rings, drinking water, vault toilets.
Fee per night: $8. For reservations call 800-280-CAMP. There is a one-time reservation fee of $8.65.
Management: Toiyabe National Forest, 702-882-2766.
Activities: Fishing.
Finding the campground: From the northern intersection of California Highway 89 and U.S. Highway 50 in South Lake Tahoe, drive southeast on CA 89 for 32 miles, turn right (south) onto California Highway 4, and drive 7 miles.

About the campground: Situated near Silver Creek, which provides fishing in early summer for small trout. Elevation 6,800 feet. Stay limit 14 days. Open from June 14 through September 8.

4 Bloomfield

Location: 62 miles northeast of Angels Camp.
Sites: Dispersed camping for tents and smaller RVs. Not recommended for trailers.

Facilities: 5 tables and fire rings, drinking water (hand-pumped), vault toilets.
Fee per night: None.
Management: Stanislaus National Forest, 209-795-1381.
Activities: Fishing.
Finding the campground: From the intersection of California Highways 49 and 4 in Angels Camp, drive northeast about 60 miles on CA 4 (passing Lake Alpine at milepoint 47), turn right (southeast) onto Highland Lake Road, and drive 1.5 miles.

About the campground: Situated on the bank of the North Fork of the Mokelumne River, where trout fishing is mediocre. There is little to recommend this campground except solitude. A campfire permit is required. Elevation 8,000 feet. Stay limit 14 days. Open from June through October.

5 Highland Lakes

Location: 66 miles northeast of Angels Camp.
Sites: 35 sites for tents and smaller RVs. Not recommended for trailers.
Facilities: Tables, fire rings, drinking water, vault toilets. Boat ramp 1 mile northeast.
Fee per night: $5.
Management: Stanislaus National Forest, 209-795-1381.
Activities: Fishing, swimming, boating, hiking.
Finding the campground: From the intersection of California Highways 49 and 4 in Angels Camp, drive northeast about 60 miles on CA 4 (passing Lake Alpine at milepoint 47), turn right (southeast) onto Highland Lake Road, and drive 5.5 miles.

About the campground: Situated on the shoreline of the southernmost of two small, alpine lakes in a beautiful panoramic setting. The lakes provide only mediocre fishing for small brook trout. The boat ramp is on the northernmost of the two lakes. Trails lead from the campground into the Carson-Iceberg Wilderness. A campfire permit is required. Elevation 8,000 feet. Stay limit 14 days. Open from June through October.

6 Hermit Valley

Location: 56 miles northeast of Angels Camp.
Sites: Dispersed camping for tents and RVs.
Facilities: 3 tables and fire rings, vault toilets. No drinking water.
Fee per night: None.
Management: Stanislaus National Forest, 209-795-1381.
Activities: Fishing, hiking.
Finding the campground: From the intersection of California Highways 49 and 4 in Angels Camp, drive northeast about 56 miles on CA 4.

About the campground: Situated near the confluence of Grouse Creek and the North Fork of the Mokelumne River. Trout fishing is fair to poor. A trail leads north from the campground into the Mokelumne Wilderness. A campfire permit is required. Elevation 7,500 feet. Stay limit 14 days. Open from June through October.

7 Pacific Valley

Location: 54 miles northeast of Angels Camp.
Sites: Dispersed camping for tents and RVs.
Facilities: 9 tables and fire rings, vault toilets. No drinking water.
Fee per night: None.
Management: Stanislaus National Forest, 209-795-1381.
Activities: Fishing, hiking.
Finding the campground: From the intersection of California Highways 49 and 4 in Angels Camp, drive northeast about 54 miles on CA 4.

About the campground: Situated near the bank of Pacific Creek, where trout fishing is fair to poor. A trail leads south from the campground into the Carson-Iceberg Wilderness. A campfire permit is required. Elevation 7,600 feet. Stay limit 14 days. Open from June through October.

8 Mosquito Lakes

Location: 53 miles northeast of Angels Camp.
Sites: 9 sites for tents and RVs.
Facilities: Tables, fire rings, vault toilets. No drinking water.
Fee per night: None.
Management: Stanislaus National Forest, 209-795-1381.
Activities: Fishing, hiking.
Finding the campground: From the intersection of California Highways 49 and 4 in Angels Camp, drive northeast about 53 miles on CA 4.

About the campground: Situated about a mile from a small, pretty lake that offers fair fishing for small trout. Trailheads about a mile east and west of the campground lead into the Carson-Iceberg and Mokelumne Wildernesses respectively. A campfire permit is required. Elevation 8,260 feet. Stay limit 14 days. Open from June through October.

9 Lake Alpine: Lake Alpine

Location: 47 miles northeast of Angels Camp.
Sites: 26 sites for tents and RVs.
Facilities: Tables, fire rings, drinking water, showers, flush and vault toilets, boat ramp. Store within walking distance. The facilities are wheelchair accessible.
Fee per night: $13.
Management: Stanislaus National Forest, 209-795-1381.
Activities: Fishing, swimming, boating, hiking.
Finding the campground: From the intersection of California Highways 49 and 4 in Angels Camp, drive northeast about 47 miles on CA 4.

About the campground: Located on the southwest shore of a beautiful lake that is stocked annually with rainbow trout. A 4-mile loop trail circles the lake, with an optional spur up Inspiration Point. Elevation 7,300 feet. Stay limit 14 days. Open from June through October.

10 Lake Alpine: Backpackers

Location: 48 miles northeast of Angels Camp.
Sites: 6 sites for tents.
Facilities: Tables, fire rings. Drinking water, flush toilets, and parking located across the road at Chickaree Picnic Area. Boat ramp and store 1 mile away.
Fee per night: $13.
Management: Stanislaus National Forest, 209-795-1381.
Activities: Fishing, swimming, boating, hiking.
Finding the campground: From the intersection of California Highways 49 and 4 in Angels Camp, drive northeast about 48 miles on CA 4.

About the campground: See Lake Alpine Campground (number 9) for area information. The campground is primarily for the use of backpackers hiking into the Mokelumne and Carson-Iceberg Wildernesses, but it can serve as an overnight stop if other campgrounds are full. Stay limit 1 night. Open from May through October.

11 Lake Alpine: Pine Marten

Location: 48 miles northeast of Angels Camp.
Sites: 33 sites for tents and RVs.
Facilities: Tables, fire rings, drinking water, flush toilets. Boat ramp and store 1 mile away.
Fee per night: $13.
Management: Stanislaus National Forest, 209-795-1381.
Activities: Fishing, swimming, boating, hiking.
Finding the campground: From the intersection of California Highways 49 and 4 in Angels Camp, drive northeast about 48 miles on CA 4.

About the campground: See Lake Alpine Campground (number 9) for area information.

12 Lake Alpine: Silver Valley

Location: 48 miles northeast of Angels Camp.
Sites: 25 sites for tents and RVs.
Facilities: Tables, fire rings, drinking water, flush toilets. Boat ramp and store 1 mile away. The facilities are wheelchair accessible.
Fee per night: $13.
Management: Stanislaus National Forest, 209-795-1381.
Activities: Fishing, swimming, boating, hiking.
Finding the campground: From the intersection of California Highways 49 and 4 in Angels Camp, drive northeast about 48 miles on CA 4.

About the campground: See Lake Alpine Campground (number 9) for area information. A trail from the campground leads to connecting trails in the Carson-Iceberg Wilderness.

13 Lake Alpine: Silvertip

Location: 46 miles northeast of Angels Camp.
Sites: 24 sites for tents and RVs.
Facilities: Tables, fire rings, drinking water, flush toilets. Boat ramp and store 1 mile away.
Fee per night: $13.
Management: Stanislaus National Forest, 209-795-1381.
Activities: Fishing, swimming, boating, hiking (all at Lake Alpine, 1 mile east).
Finding the campground: From the intersection of California Highways 49 and 4 in Angels Camp, drive northeast about 46 miles on CA 4.

About the campground: See Lake Alpine Campground (number 9) for area information. Silvertip can be used as an overflow area when lakeside campgrounds are full. An official overflow area, Lodgepole, is 1 mile west of Silvertip on CA 4. Elevation 7,500 feet. Stay limit 14 days. Open from mid-June through September.

14 Stanislaus River

Location: 44 miles northeast of Angels Camp.
Sites: 25 sites for tents and RVs.
Facilities: Tables, fire rings, drinking water (hand pumped), vault toilets.
Fee per night: $5.
Management: Stanislaus National Forest, 209-795-1381.
Activities: Fishing, swimming.
Finding the campground: From the intersection of California Highways 49 and 4 in Angels Camp, drive northeast about 41 miles on CA 4, turn right (east) onto Spicer Reservoir Road (Forest Road 7N01), and drive about 3 miles.

About the campground: A wooded location on the banks of the North Fork of the Stanislaus River. Elevation 6,200 feet. Stay limit 14 days. Open from June through September.

15 Spicer Reservoir

Location: 49 miles northeast of Angels Camp.
Sites: 60 sites for tents and RVs.
Facilities: Tables, fire rings, drinking water, vault toilets, boat ramp. The facilities are wheelchair accessible.
Fee per night: $12.
Management: Stanislaus National Forest, 209-795-1381.
Activities: Fishing, swimming, boating.

Finding the campground: From the intersection of California Highways 49 and 4 in Angels Camp, drive northeast about 41 miles on CA 4, turn right (east) onto Spicer Reservoir Road (Forest Road 7N01), and drive about 8 miles.

About the campground: Six miles long and up to a mile wide, Spicer Reservoir covers only about 230 acres. Fishing is fairly good for rainbow and brown trout, and the lake is being heavily stocked annually with Eagle Lake trout fingerlings. Elevation 6,300 feet. Stay limit 14 days. Open from June through September.

16 Spicer Reservoir Group Camp

Location: 50 miles northeast of Angels Camp.
Sites: Several large sites for tents and RVs.
Facilities: Tables, fire rings, drinking water, vault toilets.
Fee per night: About $90, depending upon group size. Reservations required; call number below.
Management: Stanislaus National Forest, 209-795-1381.
Activities: Fishing, swimming, boating.
Finding the campground: From the intersection of California Highways 49 and 4 in Angels Camp, drive northeast about 41 miles on CA 4, turn right (east) onto Spicer Reservoir Road (Forest Road 7N01), and drive about 9 miles.

About the campground: See Spicer Reservoir Campground (number 15).

17 Big Meadow

Location: 38 miles northeast of Angels Camp.
Sites: 68 sites for tents and RVs, plus 1 group site.
Facilities: Tables, fire rings, drinking water, vault toilets.
Fee per night: $10, group fee $30 for up to 25 people, $1 per person thereafter. For reservations call 800-280-CAMP. There is a one-time reservation fee of $8.65. Reservations required for group site.
Management: Stanislaus National Forest, 209-795-1381.
Activities: Hiking, hunting.
Finding the campground: From the intersection of California Highways 49 and 4 in Angels Camp, drive northeast about 38 miles on CA 4.

About the campground: Elevation 6,500 feet. Open in winter for camping and cross-country skiing. Group camp open from May through September. Stay limit 14 days.

18 Board's Crossing

Location: 28 miles northeast of Angels Camp.
Sites: Dispersed sites for tents and small RVs. Not recommended for trailers.
Facilities: 5 tables and fire rings, drinking water, vault toilets.
Fee per night: None.
Management: Stanislaus National Forest, 209-795-1381.

Activities: Fishing, hunting.

Finding the campground: From the intersection of California Highways 49 and 4 in Angels Camp, drive northeast about 25 miles on CA 4, turn right (east) onto Board's Crossing Road (Forest Road 52), and drive 2 miles. Turn right at the campground entrance road and drive 1 mile.

About the campground: Situated in a wooded location on the bank of the North Fork of the Stanislaus River. Elevation 3,800 feet. Stay limit 14 days. Open from April through September.

19 Sourgrass

Location: 29 miles northeast of Angels Camp.
Sites: 15 sites for tents and RVs up to 19 feet long.
Facilities: Tables, fire rings, drinking water, vault toilets.
Fee per night: $5.
Management: Stanislaus National Forest, 209-795-1381.
Activities: Fishing, swimming.
Finding the campground: From the intersection of California Highways 49 and 4 in Angels Camp, drive northeast about 25 miles on CA 4, turn right (east) onto Board's Crossing Road (Forest Road 52), and drive 4 miles.

About the campground: Situated in a wooded location on the bank of the North Fork of the Stanislaus River. Elevation 3,900 feet. Stay limit 14 days. Open from April through September.

20 Calaveras Big Trees State Park: North Grove

Location: 26 miles northeast of Angels Camp.
Sites: 74 sites for tents and RVs, plus 1 group site.
Facilities: Tables, fire rings, stone barbecues, drinking water (spigot at each site), flush toilets, showers, dump station, visitor center. The facilities are wheelchair accessible.
Fee per night: $12-$16, pets $1. For reservations call 800-444-7275. There is a one-time reservation fee of $7.50.

Calaveras Big Trees State Park

This park encompasses more than 6,000 acres and contains more than 1,000 ancient sequoia trees in two separate groves about 5 miles apart. The mile-long North Grove Loop Trail, which passes through the best known of the groves, begins in the North Grove Campground and visits, among other attractions, the Abraham Lincoln Tree. The park's second and largest stand of sequoia, the South Grove, is actually 5 miles northeast of North Grove. You can reach it via the park's Memorial Parkway. The South Grove Trail, 5.2 miles round trip, visits the Agassiz Tree, the largest in the park. Self-guiding brochures to both groves may be purchased at the visitor center.

Agency: California Department of Parks and Recreation, 209-795-2334.
Activities: Hiking.
Finding the campgrounds: From the intersection of California Highways 49 and 4 in Angels Camp, drive 26 miles northeast on CA 4.

About the campgrounds: Campsites are well spaced along intermittent Big Trees Creek, in a forest composed mainly of pines. Elevation 4,800 feet. Stay limit 15 days. Open all year.

21 Calaveras Big Trees State Park: Oak Hollow

Location: 28 miles northeast of Angels Camp.
Sites: 54 sites for tents and RVs.
Facilities: Tables, fire rings, stone barbecues, drinking water, flush toilets, showers, dump station, visitor center. The facilities are wheelchair accessible.
Fee per night: $12-$16, pets $1. For reservations call 800-444-7275. There is a one-time reservation fee of $7.50.
Agency: California Department of Parks and Recreation, 209-795-2334.
Activities: Hiking.
Finding the campgrounds: From the intersection of California Highways 49 and 4 in Angels Camp, drive 26 miles northeast on CA 4. From North Grove Campground (number 20), continue 2 miles past the entrance station on Memorial Parkway (River Road).

About the campground: See North Grove Campground (number 20). Stay limit 15 days. Open from April through October.

22 Shingle Mill

Location: 64 miles southeast of South Lake Tahoe.
Sites: 90 sites for tents and RVs.
Facilities: Tables, fire rings, drinking water, vault toilets.
Fee per night: $8.
Management: Toiyabe National Forest, 760-932-7070.
Activities: Fishing.
Finding the campground: From the northern intersection of California Highway 89 and U.S. Highway 50 in South Lake Tahoe, drive southeast on CA 89 for about 48 miles, turn right (south) onto U.S. Highway 395, and drive 16 miles.

About the campground: Situated near the bank of the West Walker River, a popular trout stream with good fishing for rainbows. Elevation 6,600 feet. Stay limit 14 days. Open from May through September.

23 Bootleg

Location: 66 miles southeast of South Lake Tahoe.
Sites: 63 sites for tents and RVs.
Facilities: Tables, fire rings, drinking water, vault toilets.

Fee per night: $9. For reservations call 800-280-CAMP. There is a one-time reservation fee of $8.65.
Management: Toiyabe National Forest, 760-932-7070.
Activities: Fishing.
Finding the campground: From the northern intersection of California Highway 89 and U.S. Highway 50 in South Lake Tahoe, drive southeast on CA 89 for about 48 miles, turn right (south) onto U.S. Highway 395, and drive 18 miles.

About the campground: Situated across the highway from the West Walker River, a popular trout stream with good fishing for rainbows. Elevation 6,600 feet. Stay limit 14 days. Open from May through September.

24 Chris Flat

Location: 68 miles southeast of South Lake Tahoe.
Sites: 15 sites for tents and RVs.
Facilities: Tables, fire rings, drinking water, vault toilets.
Fee per night: $9.
Management: Toiyabe National Forest, 760-932-7070.
Activities: Fishing.
Finding the campground: From the northern intersection of California Highway 89 and U.S. Highway 50 in South Lake Tahoe, drive south on CA 89 for about 48 miles, turn right (south) onto U.S. Highway 395, and drive 20 miles.

About the campground: Situated along the bank of the West Walker River, with easy access from the campground to this popular trout stream with good fishing for rainbows. Elevation 6,600 feet. Stay limit 14 days. Open from May through October.

25 Sonora Bridge

Location: 18 miles northwest of Bridgeport.
Sites: 23 sites for tents and RVs up to 30 feet long.
Facilities: Tables, fire rings, drinking water, vault toilets.
Fee per night: $9. For reservations call 800-280-CAMP. There is a one-time reservation fee of $8.65.
Management: Toiyabe National Forest, 760-932-7070.
Activities: Fishing.
Finding the campground: From Bridgeport, drive 16 miles northwest on U.S. Highway 395, turn left (west) onto California Highway 108, and drive 2 miles.

About the campground: Situated about a mile from the West Walker River, a popular trout stream with good fishing for rainbows. Elevation 6,800 feet. Stay limit 14 days. Open from May 1 through October 14.

26 Leavitt Meadows

Location: 22 miles northwest of Bridgeport.
Sites: 16 sites for tents and RVs up to 23 feet long.
Facilities: Tables, fire rings, drinking water, vault toilets.
Fee per night: $9.
Management: Toiyabe National Forest, 760-932-7070.
Activities: Fishing, hiking.
Finding the campground: From Bridgeport, drive 16 miles northwest on U.S. Highway 395, turn left (west) onto California Highway 108, and drive 6 miles.

About the campground: Located on the banks of the West Walker River, a good trout stream. Leavitt Falls is about a mile away, and a 2-mile trail leads from the campground to Secret Lake. Elevation 7,000 feet. Stay limit 14 days. Open from May 1 through October 14.

27 Hull Creek

Location: 28 miles northeast of Sonora.
Sites: 16 sites for tents and RVs.
Facilities: Tables, fire rings, drinking water, vault toilets.
Fee per night: $5.
Management: Stanislaus National Forest, 209-586-3234.
Activities: Fishing.
Finding the campground: From the intersection of California Highways 49 and 108 in Sonora, drive 17 miles northeast on CA 108 to Long Barn, turn right onto Hull Meadow Road (Forest Road 31), and drive 11 miles.

About the campground: Situated in a secluded spot on the banks of Hull Creek, a stream too small for good fishing. Elevation 5,600 feet. Stay limit 14 days. Open from May through September, with winter camping permitted at no cost.

28 Fraser Flat

Location: 26 miles northeast of Sonora.
Sites: 38 sites for tents and RVs.
Facilities: Tables, stoves, drinking water, vault toilets. The facilities are wheelchair accessible.
Fee per night: $9.
Management: Stanislaus National Forest, 209-586-3234.
Activities: Fishing, swimming, hunting.
Finding the campground: From the intersection of California Highways 49 and 108 in Sonora, drive 23 miles northeast on CA 108, turn left (north) onto Spring Gap Road (Forest Road 4N01), and drive 3 miles.

About the campground: Situated on the South Fork Stanislaus River, a pretty stream that is stocked annually with rainbow trout. Elevation 4,800 feet. Stay limit 14 days. Open from May through September.

29 Sand Bar Flat

Location: 33 miles northeast of Sonora.

Sites: 10 sites for tents and RVs.

Facilities: Tables, stoves, drinking water, vault toilets. The facilities are wheelchair accessible.

Fee per night: $7.

Management: Stanislaus National Forest, 209-586-3234.

Activities: Fishing, swimming, hunting.

Finding the campground: From the intersection of California Highways 49 and 108 in Sonora, drive 23 miles northeast on CA 108, turn left (north) onto Spring Gap Road (Forest Road 4N01), and drive 10 miles.

About the campground: Situated on an attractive part of the South Fork Stanislaus River, which is stocked annually with rainbow trout. Elevation 3,000 feet. Stay limit 14 days. Open from May through September.

30 Pinecrest Lake: Meadowview

Location: 27 miles northeast of Sonora.

Sites: 100 sites for tents and RVs.

Facilities: Tables, stoves, drinking water, flush toilets, dump station. Boat ramp 1 mile.

Fee per night: $12.

Management: Stanislaus National Forest, 209-965-3434.

Activities: Fishing, swimming, boating, hiking, all at Pinecrest Lake, 1 mile east.

Finding the campground: From the intersection of California Highways 49 and 108 in Sonora, drive 27 miles northeast on CA 108.

About the campground: See Pinecrest Lake Campground (number 31) for area information. Elevation 5,600 feet. Stay limit 14 days. Open from May through August.

31 Pinecrest Lake: Pinecrest Lake

Location: 28 miles northeast of Sonora.

Sites: 200 sites for tents and RVs.

Facilities: Tables, stoves, drinking water, flush toilets, dump station, boat ramp.

Fee per night: $14. Reservations may be made by calling 800-280-CAMP. There is a one-time reservation fee of $8.65.

Management: Stanislaus National Forest, 209-965-3434.

Activities: Fishing, swimming, boating, hiking.

Finding the campground: From the intersection of California Highways 49 and 108 in Sonora, drive 27 miles northeast on CA 108.

About the campground: Situated on the southwest shore of Pinecrest Lake, which is 1 mile long and half a mile wide and covers about 300 acres. There is a 20-mile-per-hour speed limit for boats on the lake. Fishing is good for small rainbow trout. A hiking trail circles the lake, and there is a 2-mile round-trip side trip to tiny Catfish Lake. Elevation 5,600 feet. Stay limit 14 days. Open from May through September. Winter camping is permitted free of charge but with fewer facilities available.

32 Pinecrest Lake: Pioneer Trail Group Camp

Location: 28 miles northeast of Sonora.
Sites: 3 group sites for tents and RVs.
Facilities: Tables, stoves, drinking water, vault toilets. Boat ramp nearby.
Fee per night: $50-$65. Reservations required; call 800-280-CAMP. There is a one-time reservation fee of $8.65.
Management: Stanislaus National Forest, 209-965-3434.
Activities: Fishing, swimming, boating, hiking.
Finding the campground: From the intersection of California Highways 49 and 108 in Sonora, drive 27 miles northeast on CA 108. Turn right at Meadowview Campground (number 30) and continue past it for 1 mile.

About the campground: Situated about half a mile from Pinecrest Lake. See Pinecrest Lake Campground (number 31) for area information. Elevation 5,700 feet. Stay limit 14 days. Open from May through September.

33 Herring Creek Reservoir: Herring Creek

Location: 36 miles northeast of Sonora.
Sites: 26 sites for tents and RVs.
Facilities: Fire grills, pit toilets. No drinking water.
Fee per night: None.
Management: Stanislaus National Forest, 209-965-3434.
Activities: Fishing, swimming, hiking.
Finding the campground: From the intersection of California Highways 49 and 108 in Sonora, drive 28 miles northeast on CA 108. About 1 mile north of Strawberry, turn right (east) onto Forest Road 4N12 and drive 7.5 miles.

About the campground: Situated on the shore of small Herring Creek Reservoir. A trail leads from the campground northeast along Herring Creek and then on into the Emigrant Wilderness. Elevation 7,350 feet. Stay limit 14 days. Open from May through October.

34 Beardsley Reservoir

Location: 40 miles northeast of Sonora.
Sites: 26 sites for tents and RVs.
Facilities: Tables, stoves, drinking water, vault toilets. Boat ramp nearby.
Fee per night: None.
Management: Stanislaus National Forest, 209-965-3434.
Activities: Fishing, swimming, boating, hiking.

Finding the campground: From the intersection of California Highways 49 and 108 in Sonora, drive 32 miles northeast on CA 108, turn left (west) on Forest Road 52 and drive 7.5 miles. After crossing the dam, the road follows the lakeshore for about half a mile; the campground is along the road.

About the campground: Situated along the west shore of Beardsley Reservoir, which is about 2 miles long and up to 1 mile wide. The lake is heavily stocked with rainbow trout annually, but it is subject to such heavy water drawdowns that the only rewarding time to fish is early spring. Elevation 3,400 feet. Stay limit 14 days. Open from May through October.

35 Cascade Creek

Location: 37 miles northeast of Sonora.
Sites: 12 sites for tents and RVs.
Facilities: Tables, fire rings, vault toilets. No drinking water.
Fee per night: $5.
Management: Stanislaus National Forest, 209-965-3434.
Activities: None.
Finding the campground: From the intersection of California Highways 49 and 108 in Sonora, drive 37 miles northeast on CA 108.

About the campground: There is little reason to stay at this campground, which offers no activities nearby. Elevation 6,000 feet. Stay limit 14 days. Open from May through September.

36 Mill Creek

Location: 40 miles northeast of Sonora.
Sites: 17 sites for tents and RVs.
Facilities: Tables, fire rings, vault toilets. No drinking water.
Fee per night: $5.
Management: Stanislaus National Forest, 209-965-3434.
Activities: None.
Finding the campground: From the intersection of California Highways 49 and 108 in Sonora, drive 40 miles northeast on CA 108.

About the campground: This campground offers little to those seeking outdoor activities, although its location on the bank of Mill Creek is attractive. Elevation 6,200 feet. Stay limit 14 days. Open from May through September.

37 Niagara Creek OHV Camp

Location: 45 miles northeast of Sonora.
Sites: 10 sites for tents and RVs.
Facilities: Tables, fire rings, vault toilets. No drinking water.
Fee per night: $5.
Management: Stanislaus National Forest, 209-965-3434.
Activities: OHV driving, fishing.

Finding the campground: From the intersection of California Highways 49 and 108 in Sonora, drive 42 miles northeast on CA 108, turn right onto Forest Road 6N24, and drive less than a quarter-mile. Turn right onto Forest Road 5N01 and drive 2.5 miles.

About the campground: Situated on the bank of small Niagara Creek, the campground has four-wheel-drive and off-highway trails and roads leading north and east. Elevation 7,000 feet. Stay limit 14 days. Open May through September.

38 Niagara Creek

Location: 43 miles northeast of Sonora.
Sites: 10 sites for tents and RVs.
Facilities: Tables, stoves, vault toilets. No drinking water.
Fee per night: $5.
Management: Stanislaus National Forest, 209-965-3434.
Activities: Fishing.
Finding the campground: From the intersection of California Highways 49 and 108 in Sonora, drive 42 miles northeast on CA 108, turn right onto Forest Road 6N24 and drive less than a mile.

About the campground: Situated on the bank of small Niagara Creek. Elevation 6,600 feet. Stay limit 14 days. Open from May through September.

39 Fence Creek

Location: 48 miles northeast of Sonora.
Sites: 30 sites for tents and RVs.
Facilities: Tables, fire rings, pit toilets. No drinking water.
Fee per night: $5.
Management: Stanislaus National Forest, 209-965-3434.
Activities: Fishing.
Finding the campground: From the intersection of California Highways 49 and 108 in Sonora, drive 47 miles northeast on CA 108, turn left onto Clark Fork Road, and drive 1 mile.

About the campground: Elevation 6,100 feet. Stay limit 14 days. Open from May through September.

40 Clark Fork

Location: 52 miles northeast of Sonora.
Sites: 88 sites for tents and RVs up to 23 feet long.
Facilities: Tables, stoves, drinking water, flush and vault toilets, dump station. The facilities are wheelchair accessible.
Fee per night: $10-$11.
Management: Stanislaus National Forest, 209-965-3434.
Activities: Hiking, fishing.

Finding the campground: From the intersection of California Highways 49 and 108 in Sonora, drive 47 miles northeast on CA 108, turn left onto Clark Fork Road, and drive 5 miles.

About the campground: Trails lead north from the campground into the Carson-Iceberg Wilderness. Elevation 6,200 feet. Stay limit 14 days. Open from May through September.

41 Clark Fork Horse Camp

Location: 53 miles northeast of Sonora.
Sites: 14 sites for tents and RVs up to 23 feet long.
Facilities: Tables, fire rings, drinking water, vault toilets. Dump station nearby.
Fee per night: $5.
Management: Stanislaus National Forest, 209-965-3434.
Activities: Horseback riding, fishing.
Finding the campground: From the intersection of California Highways 49 and 108 in Sonora, drive 47 miles northeast on CA 108, turn left onto Clark Fork Road, and drive 6 miles.

About the campground: The campground is primarily for equestrian use. Trails for equestrians and hikers lead north from near the campground into the Carson-Iceberg Wilderness. Elevation 6,200 feet. Stay limit 14 days. Open from May through September.

42 Sand Flat

Location: 53 miles northeast of Sonora.
Sites: 53 sites for RVs, plus 15 walk-in sites for tents.
Facilities: Tables, stoves, drinking water, vault toilets. Dump station nearby.
Fee per night: $7.
Management: Stanislaus National Forest, 209-965-3434.
Activities: Fishing.
Finding the campground: From the intersection of California Highways 49 and 108 in Sonora, drive 47 miles northeast on CA 108, turn left onto Clark Fork Road, and drive 6 miles.

About the campground: Trails lead north from west of the campground into the Carson-Iceberg Wilderness. Elevation 6,200 feet. Stay limit 14 days. Open from May through September.

43 Boulder Flat

Location: 48 miles northeast of Sonora.
Sites: 20 sites for tents and RVs, including some double sites.
Facilities: Tables, stoves, drinking water, vault toilets.
Fee per night: $10, double site $14.
Management: Stanislaus National Forest, 209-965-3434.
Activities: Fishing.

Finding the campground: From the intersection of California Highways 49 and 108 in Sonora, drive 48 miles northeast on CA 108.

About the campground: Situated on the bank of the Middle Fork of the Stanislaus River, which is stocked annually with rainbow trout, though heavy fishing keeps fish size small. Elevation 5,600 feet. Stay limit 14 days. Open from May through September.

44 Brightman Flat

Location: 49 miles northeast of Sonora.
Sites: 33 sites for tents and RVs.
Facilities: Tables, fire rings, vault toilets. No drinking water.
Fee per night: $7.
Management: Stanislaus National Forest, 209-965-3434.
Activities: Fishing.
Finding the campground: From the intersection of California Highways 49 and 108 in Sonora, drive 49 miles northeast on CA 108.

About the campground: See Boulder Flat Campground (number 43) for area information. Elevation 5,700 feet. Stay limit 14 days. Open from May through September.

45 Dardanelle

Location: 50 miles northeast of Sonora.
Sites: 28 sites for tents and RVs, including some double sites.
Facilities: Tables, stoves, drinking water, vault toilets.
Fee per night: $12, double sites $16.
Management: Stanislaus National Forest, 209-965-3434.
Activities: Fishing.
Finding the campground: From the intersection of California Highways 49 and 108 in Sonora, drive 50 miles northeast on CA 108.

About the campground: See Boulder Flat Campground (number 43) for area information. Elevation 5,600 feet. Stay limit 14 days. Open from May through September.

46 Pigeon Flat

Location: 51 miles northeast of Sonora.
Sites: 7 sites for tents.
Facilities: Tables, fire rings, vault toilet. No drinking water.
Fee per night: $7.
Management: Stanislaus National Forest, 209-965-3434.
Activities: Fishing, hiking.
Finding the campground: From the intersection of California Highways 49 and 108 in Sonora, drive 51 miles northeast on CA 108.

About the campground: See Boulder Flat Campground (number 43) for area information. An interpretive trail leads from the campground to the Columns of the Giants, an interesting formation of columnar basalt similar to that at Devils Postpile National Monument. Elevation 7,000 feet. Stay limit 14 days. Open from May through September.

47 Eureka Valley

Location: 51 miles northeast of Sonora.
Sites: 27 sites for tents and RVs up to 23 feet long.
Facilities: Tables, fire rings, drinking water, vault toilets.
Fee per night: $9.50.
Management: Stanislaus National Forest, 209-965-3434.
Activities: Fishing, hiking.
Finding the campground: From the intersection of California Highways 49 and 108 in Sonora, drive 51 miles northeast on CA 108.

About the campground: See Boulder Flat Campground (number 43) for area information. A trail half a mile east of the campground leads north to the Carson-Iceberg Wilderness. The campground is 1 mile east of the Columns of the Giants, an interesting formation of columnar basalt similar to that at Devils Postpile National Monument. Elevation 6,100 feet. Stay limit 14 days. Open from May through September.

48 Baker

Location: 54 miles northeast of Sonora.
Sites: 44 sites for tents and RVs up to 23 feet long.
Facilities: Tables, stoves, drinking water, vault toilets.
Fee per night: $9.
Management: Stanislaus National Forest, 209-965-3434.
Activities: Fishing.
Finding the campground: From the intersection of California Highways 49 and 108 in Sonora, drive 54 miles northeast on CA 108.

About the campground: See Boulder Flat Campground (number 43) for area information. Elevation 6,200 feet. Stay limit 14 days. Open from May through October.

49 Deadman

Location: 55 miles northeast of Sonora.
Sites: 17 sites for tents and RVs up to 23 feet long.
Facilities: Tables, stoves, drinking water, vault toilets.
Fee per night: $9.
Management: Stanislaus National Forest, 209-965-3434.
Activities: Fishing, hiking.
Finding the campground: From the intersection of California Highways 49 and 108 in Sonora, drive 55 miles northeast on CA 108.

About the campground: See Boulder Flat Campground (number 43) for area information. A trail from the campground leads south to several destinations in the Emigrant Wilderness, including Relief Reservoir (4 miles) and Kennedy Lake (7 miles). Elevation 6,200 feet. Stay limit 14 days. Open from May through September.

50 Obsidian

Location: 20 miles northwest of Bridgeport.
Sites: 14 sites for tents and RVs up to 30 feet long.
Facilities: Tables, fire rings, vault toilets. No drinking water.
Fee per night: $5.
Management: Toiyabe National Forest, 760-932-7070.
Activities: Hiking, fishing.
Finding the campground: From Bridgeport, drive northwest on U.S. Highway 395 for about 17 miles, turn left (south) onto Forest Road 066 (dirt road), and drive 3 miles.

About the campground: Situated on the bank of Molybdenite Creek. Two trails lead from the campground south to the Hoover Wilderness, one along the creek and the other through Burt Canyon. Elevation 7,800 feet. Stay limit 14 days. Open from June 5 through through October 14.

51 Buckeye

Location: 10 miles west of Bridgeport.
Sites: 65 sites for tents and RVs up to 30 feet long, plus 1 group site.
Facilities: Tables, fire rings, drinking water, flush toilets.
Fee per night: $9, group site $35. Reservations required for group site; call 800-280-CAMP. There is a one-time reservation fee of $8.65.
Management: Toiyabe National Forest, 760-932-7070.
Activities: Hiking, fishing, swimming.
Finding the campground: From the intersection of U.S. Highway 395 and County Road 420 (Twin Lakes Road) in Bridgeport, drive southwest on CR 420 about 7 miles, turn right (north) onto Forest Road 017 (Buckeye Road), and drive 3 miles.

About the campground: A natural, undeveloped hot spring is within a 2-mile walk of the campground. Nearby Buckeye Creek can be a good place to find large brown trout, and it is stocked with almost 4,000 rainbows annually. Several trails lead out from the camp. One follows Buckeye Creek southwest to the Hoover Wilderness and on into Yosemite National Park; another traces Eagle Creek southward. Elevation 7,000 feet. Stay limit 14 days. Open from May 1 through October 13.

52 Honeymoon Flat

Location: 8 miles southwest of Bridgeport.
Sites: 45 sites for tents and RVs up to 36 feet long.

Facilities: Tables, fire rings, drinking water, vault toilets.
Fee per night: $9. Reservations may be made by calling 800-280-CAMP. There is a one-time reservation fee of $8.65.
Management: Toiyabe National Forest, 760-932-7070.
Activities: Fishing.
Finding the campground: From the intersection of U.S. Highway 395 and County Road 420 (Twin Lakes Road) in Bridgeport, drive southwest on CR 420 about 8 miles.

About the campground: Situated on the banks of Robinson Creek, which is heavily stocked with rainbow trout. Elevation 7,000 feet. Stay limit 14 days. Open from May through October.

53 Robinson Creek

Location: 9 miles southwest of Bridgeport.
Sites: 54 sites for tents and RVs.
Facilities: Tables, fire rings, drinking water, flush toilets.
Fee per night: $10. Reservations may be made by calling 800-280-CAMP. There is a one-time reservation fee of $8.65.
Management: Toiyabe National Forest, 760-932-7070.
Activities: Fishing.
Finding the campground: From the intersection of U.S. Highway 395 and County Road 420 (Twin Lakes Road) in Bridgeport, drive southwest on CR 420 about 9 miles.

About the campground: Situated on the bank of Robinson Creek, which is heavily stocked with rainbow trout. Elevation 7,000 feet. Stay limit 14 days. Open from May through October.

54 Paha

Location: 10 miles southwest of Bridgeport.
Sites: 22 sites for tents and RVs up to 36 feet long.
Facilities: Tables, fire rings, drinking water, flush toilets. Boat ramp nearby.
Fee per night: $10. Reservations required; call 800-280-CAMP. There is a one-time reservation fee of $8.65.
Management: Toiyabe National Forest, 760-932-7070.
Activities: Fishing.
Finding the campground: From the intersection of U.S. Highway 395 and County Road 420 (Twin Lakes Road) in Bridgeport, drive southwest on CR 420 about 9.5 miles.

About the campground: Situated about 1.5 miles from the water activities at Lower Twin Lakes (number 56). Elevation 7,000 feet. Stay limit 14 days. Open from May 1 through October 13.

55 Crags

Location: 10 miles southwest of Bridgeport.
Sites: 27 sites for tents and RVs.
Facilities: Tables, fire rings, drinking water, flush toilets. Boat ramp nearby. The facilities are wheelchair accessible.
Fee per night: $10.
Management: Toiyabe National Forest, 760-932-7070.
Activities: Fishing.
Finding the campground: From the intersection of U.S. Highway 395 and County Road 420 (Twin Lakes Road) in Bridgeport, drive southwest on CR 420 about 10 miles.

About the campground: Situated about 1 mile from the water activities at Lower Twin Lakes (number 56). Elevation 7,000 feet. Stay limit 14 days. Open from May 1 through October 13.

56 Lower Twin Lakes

Location: 11 miles southwest of Bridgeport.
Sites: 15 sites for tents and RVs up to 36 feet long.
Facilities: Tables, fire rings, drinking water, flush toilets. Boat ramp nearby.
Fee per night: $10. Reservations required; call 800-280-CAMP. There is a one-time reservation fee of $8.65.
Management: Toiyabe National Forest, 760-932-7070.
Activities: Hiking, fishing, swimming, boating.
Finding the campground: From the intersection of U.S. Highway 395 and County Road 420 (Twin Lakes Road) in Bridgeport, drive southwest on CR 420 about 10.5 miles.

About the campground: The two largest brown trout caught in California—both over 26 pounds—were taken from Lower Twin Lake. In addition to the chance to land a large brown, you can fish for rainbows, with which the lake is heavily stocked each year. Elevation 7,000 feet. Stay limit 14 days. Open from May 1 through October 13.

57 Green Creek

Location: 11 miles south of Bridgeport.
Sites: 11 sites for tents and RVs up to 23 feet long, plus 2 group sites.
Facilities: Tables, fire rings, drinking water, vault toilets.
Fee per night: $9, group fee $35. Reservations required for group sites; call 800-280-CAMP. There is a one-time reservation fee of $8.65.
Management: Toiyabe National Forest, 760-932-7070.
Activities: Hiking, fishing.

Finding the campground: From Bridgeport, drive south on U.S. Highway 395 for about 4 miles, turn right (south) onto Green Lakes Road (dirt), and continue about 7 miles.

About the campground: Situated on the bank of Green Creek, a fairly good stream for small trout. A trail leads southwest from the campground to a series of small, secluded lakes (2 to 6 miles) and then continues on into Yosemite National Park. Elevation 7,500 feet. Stay limit 14 days. Open from May 15 through September 30.

58 | Trumbull Lake

Location: 19 miles south of Bridgeport.
Sites: 45 sites for tents and RVs up to 36 feet long.
Facilities: Tables, fire rings, drinking water, vault toilets.
Fee per night: $9. For reservations call 800-280-CAMP. There is a one-time reservation fee of $8.65.
Management: Toiyabe National Forest, 760-932-7070.
Activities: Hiking, fishing.
Finding the campground: From Bridgeport, drive south on U.S. Highway 395 for about 13 miles, turn right (west) onto Virginia Lakes Road (dirt), and drive about 6 miles.

About the campground: Trumbull Lake and the nearby Virginia Lakes are stocked annually with rainbows and offer fair fishing for small trout. A trail from the campground (4 miles round trip) visits six tiny lakes. The same trail continues a total of 9 miles to Green Creek Campground (number 57), passing more than a dozen small lakes en route. It also provides access to Yosemite National Park. Elevation 9,500 feet. Stay limit 14 days. Open June 28 through October 19.

YOSEMITE AREA

Magnificent Yosemite National Park is the centerpiece of this area of the High Sierra region. But the Sierra and Inyo National Forests also contribute deep woods, sparkling lakes, soaring mountains, and wonderful vistas to the scene. The Sierra is home to 315 different animal species and 31 species of fish and contain hundreds of miles of trails, rivers, and streams. The Sierra Vista National Scenic Byway traverses many of the most dramatic parts of Sierra National Forest, including Fresno Dome and Nelder Grove, home to 106 mature sequoia intermingled with second-growth fir and cedar.

1 | River Ranch

Location: 13 miles east of Sonora.
Sites: 55 sites for tents and RVs.
Facilities: Tables, grills, drinking water, showers, flush toilets.

YOSEMITE AREA

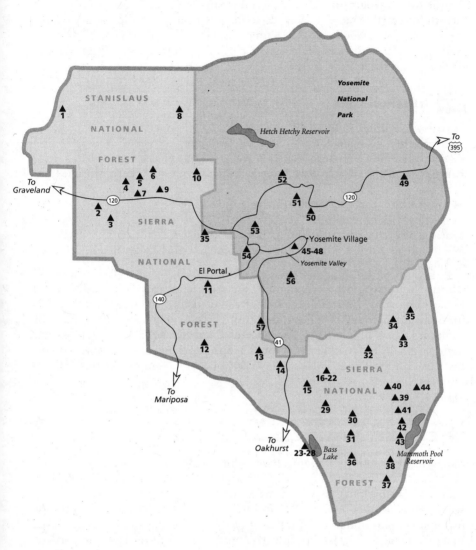

Yosemite
National
Park

Hetch Hetchy Reservoir

To
395

STANISLAUS

NATIONAL

FOREST

To
Graveland

Yosemite Village

45-48

Yosemite Valley

El Portal

To
Mariposa

To
Oakhurst

Bass
Lake

Mammoth Pool
Reservoir

SIERRA

NATIONAL

FOREST

SIERRA

NATIONAL

FOREST

N

YOSEMITE AREA CAMPGROUNDS

	Group sites	RV sites	Total sites	Max. RV length	Hookups	Toilets	Showers	Drinking water	Dump station	Pets	Wheelchair	Recreation	Fee ($)	Season	Can reserve	Length of stay
1 River Ranch		•	55			F	•	•		•		F	14	March–November	•	14
2 The Pines	•	•	13			V	•			•			9–45	May–October		14
3 Moore Creek Group Camp	•		1			V				•				May–October	•	14
4 Lumsden			11			V				•		F		April–October		14
5 South Fork			8			V				•		F		April–October		14
6 Lumsden Bridge			9			V				•		F		April–October		14
7 Lost Claim		•	10			V	•			•		F	8	May–Sept. 15		14
8 Cherry Valley		•	46	22		V	•			•		HS FB	10–20	April–October		14
9 Sweetwater		•	13	22		V	•			•		F	10	April–November		14
10 Dimond O		•	38			V	•			•	•	F	11	April–November		14
11 Indian Flat		•	18	23		V	•			•		SF	12			14
12 Jerseydale		•	10			V	•			•			10	May–November		14
13 Summit Camp			10			V	•			•		H		June–October		14
14 Summerdale		•	30			V	•			•		FS	12	May–September		14
15 Nelder Grove		•	10			V				•		H		May–September		14
16 Soquel		•	14	23		V				•		F	9	June–October		14
17 Greys Mountain		•	12	23		V				•		F	9	June–October		14
18 Texas Flat Group Camp	•	•	4	23		V				•		R		June–October	•	14
19 Kelty Meadow		•	12	23		V				•		R	9	June–October	•	14
20 Fresno Dome		•	12	23		V				•		HF	9	June–October		14
21 Little Sandy		•	10			V				•		F		June–November		14
22 Big Sandy		•	14	17		V				•		F		June–November		14

Bass Lake (23–28)

No.	Name	Group sites	RV sites	Total sites	Max. RV length	Hookups	Toilets	Showers	Drinking water	Dump station	Pets	Wheelchair	Recreation	Fee ($)	Season	Can reserve	Length of stay
23	Forks		•	31	23		F		•		•		HSF BL	15	May–September	•	14
24	Crane Valley Group Camp	•	•	7			V				•		HS FB	20–50	May–September	•	14
25	Recreation Point Youth Camp	•	•	4			F		•		•		HS FB	20–50	May–September	•	14
26	Lupine-Cedar		•	113			F		•		•		HS FB	15–30	May–September	•	14
27	Spring Cove		•	63	31		F		•		•		HS FB	15	May–September	•	14
28	Wishon Point		•	47			F		•		•		HS FBL	15–30	May–September	•	14
29	Chilkoot		•	7	23		V				•		F	9	May–September		14
30	Gaggs Camp		•	9	19		V				•		F		June–October		14
31	Whiskers		•	8			V				•		F		June–October		14
32	Upper Chiquito		•	20	23		V				•		H		June–September		14
33	Bowler Group Camp	•	•	4	23		V				•		H		June–September		14
34	Clover Meadow		•	7	19		V	•			•		H		June–September		14
35	Granite Creek		•	20			V				•		HSF		June–September		14
36	Whiskey Falls		•	14			V				•		F		May–September		14
37	Fish Creek		•	7	17		V				•		HF	10	April–October		14
38	Rock Creek		•	19	32		V	•			•		HSF	12	April–October		14
39	Soda Springs		•	16	23		V				•		SF		April–October		14
40	Lower Chiquito		•	7	23		V				•		SF	9	May–September		14
41	Placer			7			V	•			•		F	10	April–September		14
42	Sweet Water		•	10	17		V				•		SF	10	May–October		14

		Group sites	RV sites	Total sites	Max. RV length	Hookups	Toilets	Showers	Drinking water	Dump station	Pets	Wheelchair	Recreation	Fee ($)	Season	Can reserve	Length of stay
43	Mammoth Pool		•	48			V	•		•			HS FB	12	April–October		14
44	Little Jackass		•	5			V		•				F		May–October		14

Yosemite National Park (45–57)

		Group sites	RV sites	Total sites	Max. RV length	Hookups	Toilets	Showers	Drinking water	Dump station	Pets	Wheelchair	Recreation	Fee ($)	Season	Can reserve	Length of stay
45	Lower Pines	•	•	62	35		F	•				•	HS FR	15–30	March–October	•	7
46	Upper Pines		•	238	35		F	•	•	•			HS FR	15	March–October	•	7
47	North Pines		•	85	30		F	•					HS FR	15	March–October	•	7
48	Sunnyside Walk-in				35		F	•					HSF	3			7/30
49	Tuolumne Meadows	•	•	325	35		F	•	•	•			HS FR	15–35	mid-June–September	•	14
50	Porcupine Flat		•	52	35		V						H	6	July–early Sept.		14
51	Yosemite Creek		•	75			P			•			HF	6	July–early Sept.		14
52	White Wolf		•	87	35		F	•		•			HF	10	July–early Sept.		14
53	Tamarack Flat		•	52			P						H	6	June–early Sept.		14
54	Crane Flat		•	166	35		F	•		•			H	15	June–October	•	14
55	Hodgdon Meadow	•	•	109	35		F	•		•				15		•	14/30
56	Bridalveil Creek	•	•	110	35		F	•		•			HFR	10–35	June–September	•	14/30
57	Wawona	•	•	105	35		F		•	•		•	HS FR	15		•	14/30

Hookups: W = Water E = Electric S = Sewer
Toilets: F = Flush V = Vault P = Pit C = Chemical
Recreation: H = Hiking S = Swimming F = Fishing B = Boating L = Boat Launch O = Off-highway Driving R = Horseback Riding
Maximum Trailer/RV Length given in feet. Stay Limit given in days. Fee given in dollars.
If no entry under **Season,** campground is open all year. If no entry under Fee, camping is free.

Fee per night: $14. Reservations accepted; call 209-928-3708.
Management: Stanislaus National Forest, 209-586-3234.
Activities: Fishing.
Finding the campground: From the intersection of California Highways 49 and 108 in Sonora, drive 2 miles east on CA 108, turn right (southeast) onto Tuolumne Road (County Road E18), and drive 6.5 miles. Turn right onto Cottonwood Road and drive 4 miles.

About the campground: Situated in a meadow at the confluence of Basin Creek and the North Fork Tuolumne River, which is stocked with rainbow trout annually. Elevation 2,500 feet. Stay limit 14 days. Open March through November.

2 The Pines

Location: 9 miles east of Groveland.
Sites: 12 sites for tents and small RVs, plus 1 group site.
Facilities: Tables, fire rings, drinking water, vault toilets.
Fee per night: $9. Group site $45.
Management: Stanislaus National Forest, 209-962-7825.
Activities: None.
Finding the campground: From Groveland, drive 9 miles east on California Highway 120. The campground is adjacent to the Groveland Ranger District Office.

About the campground: The Pines is best used as an overnight stop or as a base from which to explore the Tuolumne Wild and Scenic River Area. The campground is 14 miles west of the Big Oak Flat Entrance to Yosemite National Park and 20 miles southwest of the Hetch Hetchy Entrance. Yosemite Valley is 28 miles to the southeast, making The Pines a good alternative camping spot if Yosemite campgrounds are full. Stay limit 14 days. Open from May through October.

3 Moore Creek Group Camp

Location: 13 miles southeast of Groveland.
Sites: 1 group site for up to 45 people.
Facilities: 2 tables, 1 grill, vault toilet. No drinking water.
Fee per night: None. Reservations required; call 209-962-7825.
Management: Stanislaus National Forest, 209-962-7825.
Activities: None.
Finding the campground: From Groveland, drive 10.5 miles east on California Highway 120, turn right onto Forest Road 20 (Moore Creek Road), and drive 2.5 miles.

About the campground: The campground is best used as an overnight stop or as a base from which to explore the Tuolumne Wild and Scenic River Area. The campground is 14 miles west of the Big Oak Flat Entrance to Yosemite National Park and 20 miles southwest of the Hetch Hetchy Entrance. Yosemite

Valley is 28 miles to the southeast, making Moore Creek a good alternative camping spot if Yosemite campgrounds are full. Stay limit 14 days. Open from May through October.

4 Lumsden

Location: 15 miles east of Groveland.
Sites: 11 tent sites.
Facilities: Tables, grills, vault toilets. No drinking water.
Fee per night: None.
Management: Stanislaus National Forest, 209-962-7825.
Activities: Fishing, rafting.
Finding the campground: From Groveland, drive 10 miles east on California Highway 120, turn left onto Ferretti Road, and drive about 1 mile. Turn right onto Lumsden Road and drive 4 miles. This is a steep, narrow, dirt road that is subject to closure in wet weather. It is not suitable for trailers or RVs larger than pickups.

About the campground: Situated close to the bank of the Tuolumne, a nationally designated Wild and Scenic River, the campground is an access point for rafting the river. The three forks of the Tuolumne receive a combined stockage of about 35,000 legal-size rainbow trout. Elevation 1,500 feet. Stay limit 14 days. Open from April through October.

5 South Fork

Location: 16 miles east of Groveland.
Sites: 8 tent sites.
Facilities: Tables, grills, vault toilets. No drinking water.
Fee per night: None.
Management: Stanislaus National Forest, 209-962-7825.
Activities: Fishing, rafting.
Finding the campground: From Groveland, drive 10 miles east on California Highway 120, turn left onto Ferretti Road, and drive about 1 mile. Turn right onto Lumsden Road and drive 4.5 miles. This is a steep, narrow, dirt road that is subject to closure in wet weather. It is not suitable for trailers or RVs larger than pickups.

About the campground: Situated near the confluence of the South Fork and the Main Fork of the Tuolumne River. See Lumsden Campground (number 4).

6 Lumsden Bridge

Location: 17 miles east of Groveland.
Sites: 9 tent sites.
Facilities: Tables, grills, vault toilets. No drinking water.
Fee per night: None.
Management: Stanislaus National Forest, 209-962-7825.

Activities: Fishing, rafting.

Finding the campground: From Groveland, drive 10 miles east on California Highway 120, turn left onto Ferretti Road, and drive about 1 mile. Turn right onto Lumsden Road and drive 5.5 miles. This is a steep, narrow, dirt road that is subject to closure in wet weather. It is not suitable for trailers or RVs larger than pickups.

About the campground: See Lumsden Campground (number 4).

7 Lost Claim

Location: 12 miles east of Groveland.

Sites: 10 sites for tents and small RVs.

Facilities: Tables, grills, well water, vault toilets.

Fee per night: $8.

Management: Stanislaus National Forest, 209-962-7825.

Activities: Fishing.

Finding the campground: From Groveland drive 12 miles east on California Highway 120.

About the campground: Situated on a small tributary of the Tuolumne, the campground is also about half a mile from the South Fork of the river. It is 11 miles west of the Big Oak Flat Entrance to Yosemite National Park and 17 miles southwest of the Hetch Hetchy Entrance. Yosemite Valley is 25 miles to the southeast, making Lost Claim a good alternative camping spot if Yosemite campgrounds are full. Elevation 3,100 feet. Stay limit 14 days. Open from May 1 through September 15.

8 Cherry Valley

Location: 35 miles northeast of Groveland.

Sites: 46 sites for tents and RVs up to 22 feet long, including some multi-family units.

Facilities: Tables, grills, drinking water, vault toilets. Boat ramp 1.3 miles south.

Fee per night: $10 single-family unit, $20 multifamily unit.

Management: Stanislaus National Forest, 209-962-7825.

Activities: Hiking, fishing, swimming, boating.

Finding the campground: From Groveland, drive east on California Highway 120 for 15 miles, turn left (north) onto Cherry Valley Road (Forest Road 1N07), and drive 20 miles.

About the campground: Situated at a scenic location on the southwest shore of Cherry Lake, which is stocked annually with 35,000 catchable-size rainbow trout. Trails from Cherry Lake Dam (1.5 miles south of the campground) lead north into the Emigrant Wilderness and east to Lake Eleanor, Hetch Hetchy, and other points in Yosemite National Park. Elevation 4,700 feet. Stay limit 14 days. Open from April through October.

9 Sweetwater

Location: 15 miles east of Groveland.
Sites: 13 sites for tents and RVs up to 22 feet long.
Facilities: Tables, grills, drinking water, vault toilets.
Fee per night: $10.
Management: Stanislaus National Forest, 209-962-7825.
Activities: Fishing.
Finding the campground: From Groveland, drive 15 miles east on California Highway 120.

About the campground: Near the South Fork of the Tuolumne River. The campground is 8 miles west of the Big Oak Flat Entrance to Yosemite National Park and 14 miles southwest of the Hetch Hetchy entrance. Yosemite Valley is 22 miles to the southeast, making Sweetwater a good alternative camping spot if Yosemite campgrounds are full. Elevation 3,000 feet. Stay limit 14 days. Open from April through November.

10 Dimond O

Location: 28 miles east of Groveland.
Sites: 38 sites for tents and small RVs.
Facilities: Tables, grills, drinking water, vault toilets. The facilities are wheelchair accessible.
Fee per night: $11.
Management: Stanislaus National Forest, 209-962-7825.
Activities: Fishing.
Finding the campground: From Groveland, drive 24 miles east on California Highway 120, turn left (north) onto Evergreen Road, and drive about 4 miles.

About the campground: Situated near the Middle Fork of the Tuolumne River, which is stocked annually with 15,000 catchable-size rainbow trout. It is 3 miles south of the Hetch Hetchy Entrance to Yosemite National Park and 5 miles north of the Big Oak Flat Entrance. Yosemite Valley is only 18 miles to the southeast, making Dimond O a good alternative camping spot if Yosemite campgrounds are full. Two former Forest Service campgrounds in this vicinity, Carlon and Middle Fork, have closed. Elevation 4,400 feet. Stay limit 14 days. Open from April through November.

11 Indian Flat

Location: 24 miles northeast of Mariposa.
Sites: 18 sites for tents and RVs up to 23 feet long.
Facilities: Tables, fire rings, drinking water, vault toilets.
Fee per night: $12.
Management: Sierra National Forest, 209-683-4665.
Activities: Swimming, fishing, rafting.

Finding the campground: From Mariposa, drive 24 miles northeast on California Highway 140.

About the campground: Situated across the highway from the scenic Merced River, which is stocked annually with rainbow trout and has deep swimming holes in the summer. Indian Flat is 4 miles west of Arch Rock, the main entrance to Yosemite National Park. Elevation 1,500 feet. Stay limit 14 days. Open all year.

12 Jerseydale

Location: 13 miles northeast of Mariposa.
Sites: 10 sites, including 2 for RVs.
Facilities: Tables, fire rings, drinking water, vault toilets.
Fee per night: $10.
Management: Sierra National Forest, 209-683-4665.
Activities: None.
Finding the campground: From Mariposa, drive 4 miles north on California Highway 140, turn right (east) onto Triangle Road, and drive 6 miles. Turn left (north) onto Jerseydale Road and drive 3 miles.

About the campground: Jerseydale is best used as an overflow camp for Yosemite National Park, whose main entrance is 24 miles to the east, or as a base from which to fish the South Fork of the Merced, 6 miles to the north. Elevation 3,600 feet. Stay limit 14 days. Open from May through November.

13 Summit Camp

Location: 19 miles north of Oakhurst.
Sites: 10 sites for tents.
Facilities: Tables, fire rings, drinking water, vault toilets.
Fee per night: None.
Management: Sierra National Forest, 209-683-4665.
Activities: Hiking.
Finding the campground: From Oakhurst, drive 12 miles north on California Highway 41, turn left onto Forest Road 5S09X, and drive 6.5 miles on a winding dirt road.

About the campground: Useful mainly as an overflow area for Yosemite, Summit Camp is 8 miles from the South Entrance and 9 miles from the Mariposa Grove of giant sequoia trees. It is possible to hike from the campground northeast 4 miles along a dirt road to the Wawona area of the park. Elevation 5,800 feet. Stay limit 14 days. Open from June through October.

14 Summerdale

Location: 15 miles north of Oakhurst.
Sites: 30 sites for tents and RVs.
Facilities: Tables, fire rings, drinking water, vault toilets.

Fee per night: $12.
Management: Sierra National Forest, 209-683-4665.
Activities: Fishing, swimming.
Finding the campground: From Oakhurst, drive 15 miles north on California Highway 41.

About the campground: An attractive location, with campsites spread along Big Creek, a tributary of the South Fork of the Merced. Summerdale is 1 mile from the South Entrance of Yosemite and 2 miles from the Mariposa Grove of giant sequoia trees. Elevation 5,000 feet. Stay limit 14 days. Open from May through September.

15 Nelder Grove

Location: 11 miles north of Oakhurst.
Sites: 7 sites for tents, plus 3 sites for RVs.
Facilities: Tables, fire rings, vault toilets. No drinking water.
Fee per night: None.
Management: Sierra National Forest, 209-683-4665.
Activities: Hiking.
Finding the campground: From Oakhurst, drive 4 miles north on California Highway 41, turn right onto Sky Ranch Road, and drive 4.5 miles. Turn left onto Forest Road 6S47Y and drive 2 miles.

About the campground: Campsites are within Nelder Grove, which contains 106 mature giant sequoia trees, including the Bull Buck Tree. The sequoias are interspersed with second-growth pine, fir, and cedar. Trails lead through the grove, which also has an interpretive display and a small museum. The campground is 15 miles from the South Entrance to Yosemite National Park. Elevation 5,300 feet. Stay limit 14 days. Open from May through September.

16 Soquel

Location: 10 miles north of Oakhurst.
Sites: 14 sites for tents and RVs up to 23 feet long.
Facilities: Tables, fire rings, vault toilets. No drinking water.
Fee per night: $9.
Management: Sierra National Forest, 209-683-4665.
Activities: Fishing.
Finding the campground: From Oakhurst, drive 4 miles north on California Highway 41, turn right onto Sky Ranch Road, and drive 5 miles. Turn right onto Forest Road 6S40 and drive 1 mile.

About the campground: Situated on the North Fork of Willow Creek, Soquel is 19 miles from the South Entrance to Yosemite. Elevation 5,400 feet. Stay limit 14 days. Open from June through October.

17 Greys Mountain

Location: 11 miles north of Oakhurst.
Sites: 12 sites for tents and RVs up to 23 feet long.
Facilities: Tables, fire rings, vault toilets. No drinking water.
Fee per night: $9.
Management: Sierra National Forest, 209-683-4665.
Activities: Fishing.
Finding the campground: From Oakhurst, drive 4 miles north on California Highway 41, turn right onto Sky Ranch Road, and drive 5 miles. Turn right onto Forest Road 6S40 and drive 2 miles.

About the campground: Situated on the North Fork of Willow Creek, Greys Mountain is 20 miles from the South Entrance to Yosemite. Elevation 5,200 feet. Stay limit 14 days. Open from June through October.

18 Texas Flat Group Camp

Location: 14 miles north of Oakhurst.
Sites: 4 group sites for tents and RVs up to 23 feet long; camp accommodates a total of 105 people.
Facilities: Tables, fire rings, vault toilets. No drinking water. Facilities for horses.
Fee per night: None, but fee charged for horses. Reservations accepted; call number below.
Management: Sierra National Forest, 209-683-4665.
Activities: Horseback riding.
Finding the campground: From Oakhurst, drive 4 miles north on California Highway 41, turn right onto Sky Ranch Road, and drive 5 miles. Turn right onto Forest Road 6S40 and drive 2 miles. From Greys Mountain Campground (number 17) drive north on Forest Road 6S08 for 1 mile, turn left onto Forest Road 6S38, and drive 2 miles.

About the campground: Primarily for equestrian use, Texas Flat is 23 miles from the South Entrance to Yosemite. Elevation 5,500 feet. Stay limit 14 days. Open from June through October.

19 Kelty Meadow

Location: 12 miles north of Oakhurst.
Sites: 12 sites for tents and RVs up to 23 feet long.
Facilities: Tables, fire rings, vault toilets. No drinking water. Facilities for horses.
Fee per night: $9. Reservations required for equestrians; call number below.
Management: Sierra National Forest, 209-683-4665.

Activities: Horseback riding.

Finding the campground: From Oakhurst, drive 4 miles north on California Highway 41, turn right onto Sky Ranch Road, and drive 8 miles.

About the campground: Kelty Meadow is used primarily by equestrians and as an overflow for Yosemite, 17 miles to the north. Elevation 5,800 feet. Stay limit 14 days. Open from June through October.

20 Fresno Dome

Location: 14 miles north of Oakhurst.

Sites: 12 sites for tents and RVs up to 23 feet long.

Facilities: Tables, fire rings, vault toilets. No drinking water.

Fee per night: $9.

Management: Sierra National Forest, 209-683-4665.

Activities: Hiking, fishing.

Finding the campground: From Oakhurst, drive 4 miles north on California Highway 41, turn right onto Sky Ranch Road, and drive 8.5 miles. Turn left onto Forest Road 6S07 and drive 1.5 miles.

About the campground: Situated in a pretty meadow adjacent to Willow Creek, the campground has an old-fashioned wishing well at its center. An easy half-mile trail leads to the top of Fresno Dome (7,540 feet). The South Entrance to Yosemite is 18 miles to the north. Elevation 6,400 feet. Stay limit 14 days. Open from June through October.

21 Little Sandy

Location: 16 miles north of Oakhurst.

Sites: 8 tent sites, 2 RV sites.

Facilities: Tables, fire rings, vault toilets. No drinking water.

Fee per night: None.

Management: Sierra National Forest, 209-683-4665.

Activities: Fishing.

Finding the campground: From Oakhurst, drive 4 miles north on California Highway 41, turn right onto Sky Ranch Road, and drive 8.5 miles. Turn left onto Forest Road 6S07 and drive 3 miles.

About the campground: Located on the bank of Big Creek, 19 miles north of the South Entrance to Yosemite. Elevation 6,100 feet. Stay limit 14 days. Open from June through November.

22 Big Sandy

Location: 17 miles north of Oakhurst.

Sites: 10 sites for tents plus 4 sites for RVs up to 17 feet long.

Facilities: Tables, fire rings, vault toilets. No drinking water.

Fee per night: $9.

Management: Sierra National Forest, 209-683-4665.

Activities: Fishing.

Finding the campground: From Oakhurst, drive 4 miles north on California Highway 41, turn right onto Sky Ranch Road, and drive 8.5 miles. Turn left onto Forest Road 6S07 and drive 4.5 miles.

About the campground: Located on the bank of Big Creek, 21 miles north of the South Entrance to Yosemite. Elevation 5,800 feet. Stay limit 14 days. Open from June through November.

23 Bass Lake: Forks

Location: 6 miles east of Oakhurst.
Sites: 25 sites for tents, plus 6 sites for tents and RVs up to 23 feet long.
Facilities: Tables, grills, drinking water, flush toilets, boat ramp.
Fee per night: $15. For reservations call 800-280-CAMP. There is a one-time reservation fee of $8.65.
Management: Sierra National Forest, 209-683-4665.
Activities: Hiking, swimming, fishing, boating, waterskiing.
Finding the campground: From Oakhurst, drive 6 miles east on County Road 426.

About the campground: Bass Lake is 4 miles long and about half a mile wide and is located in a scenic, canyonlike setting. The lake is well stocked annually with rainbow trout and kokanee fingerlings. Catches also include bass, crappie, bluegill, and catfish. The campground is on the northwest shore of the lake. A trail leads from the campground to Goat Mountain Lookout. Elevation 3,400 feet. Stay limit 14 days. Open from May through September.

24 Bass Lake: Crane Valley Group Camp

Location: 8 miles east of Oakhurst.
Sites: 7 group sites for tents and RVs; each holds 30 to 50 people.
Facilities: Tables, grills, vault toilets. Boat ramp nearby. No drinking water.
Fee per night: $20-$50. Reservations required; call 800-280-CAMP. There is a one-time reservation fee of $15.
Management: Sierra National Forest, 209-683-4665.
Activities: Hiking, swimming, fishing, boating, waterskiing.
Finding the campground: From Oakhurst, drive 6 miles east on County Road 426, turn left (north) onto Country Road 222, and drive 1.5 miles.

About the campground: See Forks Campground (number 23).

25 Bass Lake: Recreation Point Youth Camp

Location: 8 miles east of Oakhurst.
Sites: 4 group sites for tents and RVs; each holds 30 to 50 people.
Facilities: Tables, grills, drinking water, flush toilets. Boat ramp nearby.
Fee per night: $20-$50. Reservations required; call 800-280-CAMP. There is a one-time reservation fee of $15.

Management: Sierra National Forest, 209-683-4665.
Activities: Hiking, swimming, fishing, boating, waterskiing.
Finding the campground: From Oakhurst, drive 6 miles east on County Road 426, turn left (north) onto Country Road 222, and drive 1.5 miles.

About the campground: See Forks Campground (number 23).

26 Bass Lake: Lupine-Cedar

Location: 8 miles east of Oakhurst.
Sites: 113 sites for tents and RVs, including several double family sites.
Facilities: Tables, grills, drinking water, flush toilets. Boat ramp nearby.
Fee per night: $15, $30 for double sites. For reservations call 800-280-CAMP. There is a one-time reservation fee of $8.65.
Management: Sierra National Forest, 209-683-4665.
Activities: Hiking, swimming, fishing, boating, waterskiing.
Finding the campground: From Oakhurst, drive 6 miles east on County Road 426. Turn right onto CR 222 and drive 1.5 miles.

About the campground: See Forks Campground (number 23).

27 Bass Lake: Spring Cove

Location: 9 miles east of Oakhurst.
Sites: 53 sites for tents, plus 10 for RVs up to 31 feet long.
Facilities: Tables, grills, drinking water, flush toilets. Boat ramp nearby.
Fee per night: $15. For reservations call 800-280-CAMP. There is a one-time reservation fee of $8.65.
Management: Sierra National Forest, 209-683-4665.
Activities: Hiking, swimming, fishing, boating, waterskiing.
Finding the campground: From Oakhurst, drive 6 miles east on County Road 426. Turn right onto Country Road 222 and drive 2.5 miles.

About the campground: See Forks Campground (number 23).

28 Bass Lake: Wishon Point

Location: 10 miles east of Oakhurst.
Sites: 47 sites for tents and RVs, including some double family sites.
Facilities: Tables, grills, drinking water, flush toilets, boat ramp.
Fee per night: $15, $30 for double sites. For reservations call 800-280-CAMP. There is a one-time reservation fee of $8.65.
Management: Sierra National Forest, 209-683-4665.
Activities: Hiking, swimming, fishing, boating, waterskiing.
Finding the campground: From Oakhurst, drive 6 miles east on County Road 426. Turn right onto Country Road 222 and drive 3.5 miles.

About the campground: See Forks Campground (number 23).

29 Chilkoot

Location: 13 miles northeast of Oakhurst.
Sites: 7 sites for tents and RVs up to 23 feet long.
Facilities: Tables, fire rings, vault toilets. No drinking water.
Fee per night: $9.
Management: Sierra National Forest, 209-683-4665.
Activities: Fishing.
Finding the campground: From Oakhurst, drive 3.5 miles north on California Highway 41, turn right (east) onto County Road 222, and drive 5.5 miles to the town of Bass Lake. Turn left (north) onto Beasore Road (Forest Road 7) and drive 4 miles.

About the campground: Situated on the bank of Chilkoot Creek near its juncture with North Fork Willow Creek, the campground is best used as an overflow for Bass Lake (4 miles south) or Yosemite (South Entrance 20 miles). Elevation 4,600 feet. Stay limit 14 days. Open from May through September.

30 Gaggs Camp

Location: 22 miles northeast of Oakhurst.
Sites: 9 sites for tents and RVs up to 19 feet long.
Facilities: Tables, fire rings, vault toilets. No drinking water.
Fee per night: None.
Management: Sierra National Forest, 209-683-4665.
Activities: Fishing.
Finding the campground: From Oakhurst, drive 3.5 miles north on California Highway 41, turn right (east) onto County Road 222, and drive 5.5 miles to the town of Bass Lake. Turn left (north) onto Beasore Road (Forest Road 7) and drive 8 miles. Then make a hard right turn onto Forest Road 6S42 (Central Camp Road) and drive 4.5 miles. The road is gravel, narrow, and winding.

About the campground: Situated near Sand Creek, Gaggs Camp has little to recommend it except solitude. Elevation 5,700 feet. Stay limit 14 days. Open from June through October.

31 Whiskers

Location: 25 miles east of Oakhurst.
Sites: 5 sites for tents, plus 3 sites for RVs.
Facilities: Tables, fire rings, vault toilets. No drinking water.
Fee per night: None.
Management: Sierra National Forest, 209-683-4665.
Activities: Fishing.
Finding the campground: From Oakhurst, drive 3.5 miles north on California Highway 41, turn right (east) onto County Road 222, and drive 5.5 miles to the town of Bass Lake. Turn left (north) onto Beasore Road (Forest Road 7)

and drive 8 miles. Then make a hard right turn onto Forest Road 6S42 (Central Camp Road) and drive 7.5 miles. The road is gravel, narrow, and winding.

About the campground: A small stream is nearby, but there is little else to recommend camping here. Elevation 5,300 feet. Stay limit 14 days. Open from June through October.

32 Upper Chiquito

Location: 27 miles northeast of Oakhurst.
Sites: 20 sites for tents and RVs up to 23 feet long.
Facilities: Tables, fire rings, vault toilets. No drinking water.
Fee per night: None.
Management: Sierra National Forest, 209-683-4665.
Activities: Hiking.
Finding the campground: From Oakhurst, drive 3.5 miles north on California Highway 41, turn right (east) onto County Road 222, and drive 5.5 miles to the town of Bass Lake. Turn left (north) onto Beasore Road (Forest Road 7) and drive 18 miles.

About the campground: Situated on the bank of Chiquito Creek. A trail northwest of the campground leads over Chiquito Pass into Yosemite National Park (2.5 miles), connecting to several park trails. The park's South Entrance is 33 miles by vehicle. Elevation 6,800 feet. Stay limit 14 days. Open from June through September.

33 Bowler Group Camp

Location: 32 miles northeast of Oakhurst.
Sites: 4 group sites for tents and RVs up to 23 feet long; each accommodates up to 150 people.
Facilities: Tables, fire rings, vault toilets. No drinking water.
Fee per night: None.
Management: Sierra National Forest, 209-683-4665.
Activities: Hiking.
Finding the campground: From Oakhurst, drive 3.5 miles north on California Highway 41, turn right (east) onto County Road 222, and drive 5.5 miles to the town of Bass Lake. Turn left (north) onto Beasore Road (Forest Road 7) and drive 23 miles.

About the campground: The trailhead parking for a 4-mile round trip hike to Jackass Lakes is located about 0.8 mile west of the campground on Beasore Road. Elevation 7,000 feet. Stay limit 14 days. Open from June through September.

34 Clover Meadow

Location: 36 miles northeast of Oakhurst.
Sites: 7 sites for tents and RVs up to 19 feet long.
Facilities: Tables, fire rings, drinking water, vault toilets.

Fee per night: None.
Management: Sierra National Forest, 209-683-4665.
Activities: Hiking.
Finding the campground: From Oakhurst, drive 3.5 miles north on California Highway 41, turn right (east) onto County Road 222, and drive 5.5 miles to the town of Bass Lake. Turn left (north) onto Beasore Road (Forest Road 7) and drive 25 miles. Then turn left onto Forest Road 4S60 and drive 1.5 miles. The campground is next to the Clover Meadow Ranger Station.

About the campground: Trails lead west from the campground to several lakes and north into the Ansel Adams Wilderness. Elevation 7,000 feet. Stay limit 14 days. Open from June through September.

35 Granite Creek

Location: 37 miles northeast of Oakhurst.
Sites: 15 tent sites, 5 RV sites.
Facilities: Tables, fire rings, vault toilets. No drinking water.
Fee per night: None.
Management: Sierra National Forest, 209-683-4665.
Activities: Hiking, fishing, swimming.
Finding the campground: From Oakhurst, drive 3.5 miles north on California Highway 41, turn right (east) onto County Road 222, and drive 5.5 miles to the town of Bass Lake. Turn left (north) onto Beasore Road (Forest Road 7) and drive 25 miles. Then turn left onto Forest Road 4S60 and drive 3 miles.

About the campground: Trails lead west from the campground to several different lakes and north and east into the Ansel Adams Wilderness. Elevation 7,000 feet. Stay limit 14 days. Open from June through September.

36 Whiskey Falls

Location: 10 miles northeast of North Fork
Sites: 14 sites for tents and RVs.
Facilities: Tables, fire rings, vault toilets. No drinking water.
Fee per night: None.
Management: Sierra National Forest, 209-683-4665.
Activities: Fishing.
Finding the campground: From North Fork (south of Bass Lake), drive 3 miles east on County Road 233, turn left onto Forest Road 8S09, and proceed 6 miles. Turn right onto Forest Road 8S70 and drive 1 mile.

About the campground: Elevation 5,800 feet. Stay limit 14 days. Open from May through September.

37 Fish Creek

Location: 18 miles east of North Fork.
Sites: 7 sites for tents and RVs up to 17 feet long.

Facilities: Tables, fire rings, vault toilets. No drinking water.
Fee per night: $10.
Management: Sierra National Forest, 209-683-4665.
Activities: Hiking, fishing.
Finding the campground: From North Fork, drive east and then south 3 miles on County Road 225, turn left onto Minarets Road (Forest Road 81), and drive 15 miles.

About the campground: Situated on the bank of a small creek containing small, wild trout. A trail from the campground leads 6 miles north to Mammoth Pool. Elevation 4,600 feet. Stay limit 14 days. Open from April through October.

38 Rock Creek

Location: 21 miles northeast of North Fork.
Sites: 19 sites for tents and RVs up to 32 feet long.
Facilities: Tables, fire rings, drinking water, vault toilets.
Fee per night: $12.
Management: Sierra National Forest, 209-683-4665.
Activities: Hiking, fishing, swimming.
Finding the campground: From North Fork, drive east and then south 3 miles on County Road 225, turn left onto Minarets Road (Forest Road 81) and drive 18 miles.

About the campground: Situated on the bank of Rock Creek, which provides good swimming in spring and early summer, and fishing for small, wild trout. A dirt road leads southeast from the campground and connects to a trail to Mammoth Pool. Elevation 4,300 feet. Stay limit 14 days. Open from April through October.

39 Soda Springs

Location: 31 miles northeast of North Fork.
Sites: 16 sites for tents and RVs up to 23 feet long.
Facilities: Tables, fire rings, vault toilets. No drinking water.
Fee per night: None.
Management: Sierra National Forest, 209-683-4665.
Activities: Fishing, swimming.
Finding the campground: From North Fork, drive east and then south 3 miles on County Road 225, turn left onto Minarets Road (Forest Road 81), and drive 28 miles.

About the campground: Situated on the bank of Chiquito Creek, which provides swimming in spring and early summer, and fishing for small, wild trout. The campground also serves as an overflow for Mammoth Pool, 7 miles to the southeast. Elevation 4,400 feet. Stay limit 14 days. Open from April through October.

40 Lower Chiquito

Location: 36 miles northeast of North Fork.
Sites: 7 sites for tents and RVs up to 23 feet long.
Facilities: Tables, fire rings, vault toilets. No drinking water.
Fee per night: $9.
Management: Sierra National Forest, 209-683-4665.
Activities: Fishing, swimming.
Finding the campground: From North Fork, drive east and then south 3 miles on County Road 225, turn left onto Minarets Road (Forest Road 81), and drive 29 miles. Turn left onto Forest Road 6S71 and drive 3.5 miles.

About the campground: Situated on the bank of Chiquito Creek, which provides swimming in spring and early summer, and fishing for small, wild trout. The campground also serves as an overflow for Mammoth Pool, 9 miles southeast. Elevation 4,900 feet. Stay limit 14 days. Open from May through September.

41 Placer

Location: 35 miles northeast of North Fork.
Sites: 7 sites for tents.
Facilities: Tables, fire rings, drinking water, vault toilets.
Fee per night: $10.
Management: Sierra National Forest, 209-683-4665.
Activities: Fishing.
Finding the campground: From North Fork, drive east and then south 3 miles on County Road 225, turn left onto Minarets Road (Forest Road 81), and drive 31 miles. Turn left onto Mammoth Pool Road (Forest Road 6S71) then drive 0.7 mile.

About the campground: Situated on the bank of Chiquito Creek, which provides fishing for small, wild trout. The campground also serves as an overflow for Mammoth Pool, 3 miles southeast. Elevation 4,100 feet. Stay limit 14 days. Open from April through September.

42 Sweet Water

Location: 36 miles northeast of North Fork.
Sites: 5 sites for tents, plus 5 sites for RVs up to 17 feet long.
Facilities: Tables, fire rings, vault toilets. No drinking water.
Fee per night: $10.
Management: Sierra National Forest, 209-683-4665.
Activities: Fishing, swimming.
Finding the campground: From North Fork, drive east and then south 3 miles on County Road 225, turn left onto Minarets Road (Forest Road 81), and

drive 31 miles. Turn left onto Mammoth Pool Road (Forest Road 6S71) and drive 1.5 miles.

About the campground: Situated on the bank of Chiquito Creek, which provides spring and summer swimming, and fishing for small, wild trout. The campground also serves as an overflow for Mammoth Pool, 2 miles south. Elevation 3,800 feet. Stay limit 14 days. Open from May through October.

43 Mammoth Pool

Location: 38 miles northeast of North Fork.
Sites: 18 sites for tents, plus 30 sites for tents or RVs, including 5 multi-family sites.
Facilities: Tables, fire rings, drinking water, vault toilets. Boat ramp and grocery store nearby.
Fee per night: $12.
Management: Sierra National Forest, 209-683-4665.
Activities: Fishing, swimming, boating, waterskiing, hiking.
Finding the campground: From North Fork, drive east and then south 3 miles on County Road 225, turn left onto Minarets Road (Forest Road 81), and drive 31 miles. Turn left onto Mammoth Pool Road (Forest Road 6S71) then drive 4 miles.

About the campground: Mammoth Pool is a steep-sided reservoir in the San Joaquin River gorge. It is 5 miles long and about three-quarters of a mile at its widest point. It is well stocked annually with rainbow trout. The lake is subject to heavy drawdowns of water in late summer and fall. A trail leads north from the campground into the Ansel Adams Wilderness and south to Fish Creek. Elevation 3,500 feet. Stay limit 14 days. Open from April through October.

44 Little Jackass

Location: 37 miles northeast of North Fork.
Sites: 5 sites for tents and RVs.
Facilities: Tables, fire rings, vault toilets. No drinking water.
Fee per night: None.
Management: Sierra National Forest, 209-683-4665.
Activities: Fishing.
Finding the campground: From North Fork, drive east and then south 3 miles on County Road 225, turn left onto Minarets Road (Forest Road 81), and drive 33 miles. Turn right onto Forest Road 6S22 and drive half a mile.

About the campground: Located on the bank of the West Fork of Jackass Creek, the campground can be used as overflow for Mammoth Pool, 6 miles to the south. Elevation 4,800 feet. Stay limit 14 days. Open from May through October.

Yosemite National Park

"No temple wrought with hands can compare to Yosemite," wrote John Muir, the famed Western naturalist whose efforts led to the establishment of the park in 1890. This magnificent park encompasses three-quarter of a million acres and offers so much that it would take a lifetime to experience it all.

Yosemite is a series of very different regions, all linked together by roads, valleys, and trails. Yosemite Valley is one such region, with its stunning scenery. It attracts 90 percent of the visitors. Tuolumne Meadows-Tioga Pass is another. Its high plateau is accessible only from May to November. The Hetch Hetchy Wilderness and the Grand Canyon of the Tuolumne are two more. Little Yosemite Valley might qualify, and Wawona certainly does.

Just as Yosemite is different parks, it is also different experiences. Tourists in Yosemite Valley ride the shuttle bus to restaurants and souvenir shops. The affluent stay in the elegant Ahwahnee Hotel, the less so in RVs in the campgrounds. At a high-country camp, backpackers cook their meals on a camp stove and crawl into sleeping bags. Who is having more fun? There is no pat answer. Certainly those who take to the trails see magnificent scenery to reward their efforts. But a rider of the shuttle bus in the valley also enjoys a marvelous panorama of unparalleled views without leaving his seat. Yosemite has something for everyone.

For most visitors, Yosemite Valley is Yosemite. After all, Yosemite Falls, Bridalveil Fall, El Capitan, and Half Dome are all here, plus other breathtaking sights. However, this popularity has its price. From spring through fall, campgrounds are often full, and in summer the valley roads are choked with traffic. Fortunately, campers need not add their cars and RVs to the crush. A free shuttle bus service connects the campgrounds with most valley attractions, including Yosemite Village (visitor center, store, post office, museum, restaurants), Housekeeping Camp (showers, laundry), Yosemite Falls, lodges, the Ahwahnee Hotel, and various trailheads.

Premier hikes from the valley include Upper Yosemite Falls (7.2 miles round trip, elevation gain 2,700 feet), Four-Mile-Trail to Glacier Point (3,200-foot elevation gain), top of Vernal Fall and Nevada Fall (3 miles and 7 miles round trip respectively, with trailheads within walking distance of the campgrounds), and a cable-assisted climb of Half Dome (17 miles round trip, 4,800-foot elevation gain). A great way to climb Half Dome is to combine a horseback trip to the base of the dome with the climb. For information, call Yosemite Valley Stables, 209-372-8348. Another world-class hike is to take the bus to Glacier Point and hike down the magnificently scenic Panorama Trail to the valley floor (8.5 miles, descending 3,200 feet, via Illilouette, Nevada, and Vernal Falls).

In January 1997, three campgrounds in Yosemite Valley were destroyed by floods (Upper and Lower River Campgrounds and Group Camp). Some of these campsites may be restored at other locations in the valley in the future. Check with the park for the latest information. Three of the remaining campgrounds are clustered close together in "The Pines," near the western end of the valley, close to the base of Half Dome, which towers over the campsites (although mostly obscured by the trees). Sites are closer together than usual, impinging somewhat on privacy. However, the valley's attractions more than make up for the inconvenience, and there is too much to see and do to spend much time in the campground.

Half Dome, a rare geological phenomenon, may well be the most recognizable feature in all of Yosemite National Park.

45 Yosemite National Park: Yosemite Valley (Lower Pines)

Location: East end of Yosemite Valley.
Sites: 60 sites for tents and RVs up to 35 feet long, plus several double sites, reservable wheelchair-accessible sites, and 2 group sites, each for up to 12 people.
Facilities: Tables, grills/fire rings, drinking water, flush toilets, bear-proof food lockers. Dump station at Upper Pines Campground (number 46).
Fee per night: $15, double and group sites $30. Reservations required; call 800-436-PARK or reserve online at http://reservations.nps.gov.
Management: Yosemite National Park, 209-372-0265.
Activities: Hiking, fishing, swimming, rafting, cycling, horseback riding.
Finding the campground: Enter Yosemite Valley from California Highway 120, 140, or 41, and follow Southside Drive (one-way into the valley) and signs for "Yosemite Valley Destinations," and "Pines Campgrounds."

About the campground: As the name indicates, the campsites are situated along several loops in a forest of tall pines. No pets allowed. Elevation 4,000 feet. Stay limit 7 days. Open from March through October.

46 Yosemite National Park: Yosemite Valley (Upper Pines)

Location: East end of Yosemite Valley.
Sites: 238 sites for tents and RVs up to 35 feet long.

Facilities: Tables, grills/fire rings, drinking water, flush toilets, bear-proof food lockers, dump station.

Fee per night: $15. Reservations required; call 800-436-PARK or reserve on-line at http://reservations.nps.gov.

Management: Yosemite National Park, 209-372-0265.

Activities: Hiking, fishing, swimming, rafting, cycling, horseback riding.

Finding the campground: Enter Yosemite Valley from California Highway 120, 140, or 41, and follow Southside Drive (one-way into the valley) and signs for "Yosemite Valley Destinations," and "Pines Campgrounds."

About the campground: The setting is similar to Lower Pines (number 45), but the campground is much larger and thus more spread out. Upper Pines is the closest campground to the trail system leading to Vernal and Nevada Falls, Half Dome, and the Panorama Trail to Glacier Point. Elevation 4,000 feet. Stay limit 7 days. Open from March through October.

47 Yosemite National Park: Yosemite Valley (North Pines)

Location: East end of Yosemite Valley.

Sites: 85 sites for tents and RVs up to 30 feet long.

Facilities: Tables, grills/fire rings, drinking water, flush toilets, bear-proof food lockers, dump station at Upper Pines Campground (number 46).

Fee per night: $15. Reservations required; call 800-436-PARK or reserve on-line at http://reservations.nps.gov.

Management: Yosemite National Park, 209-372-0265.

Activities: Hiking, fishing, swimming, rafting, cycling, horseback riding.

Finding the campground: Enter Yosemite Valley from California Highway 120, 140, or 41, and follow Southside Drive (one-way into the valley) and signs for "Yosemite Valley Destinations," and "Pines Campgrounds."

About the campground: See the "Pines" campgrounds (numbers 45, 46). No pets allowed. Elevation 4,000 feet. Stay limit 7 days. Open from March through October.

48 Yosemite National Park: Yosemite Valley (Sunnyside Walk-in)

Location: 1 mile west of Yosemite Village.

Sites: 35 sites for tents.

Facilities: Tables, grills, drinking water, flush toilets.

Fee per night: $3 per person.

Agency: Yosemite National Park, 209-372-0265.

Activities: Hiking, swimming, fishing.

Finding the campground: From Yosemite Village, drive west 1 mile, just past Yosemite Lodge.

About the campground: Although technically a walk-in campground, Sunnyside's campsites begin within 50 feet of its parking lot, making it an option

For many visitors, the breathtaking Yosemite Valley, shown here with Half Dome in the distance, is their definitive image of Yosemite National Park.

for tent campers who find other valley campgrounds full or who do not have reservations at one of them. Sites are rented on a "per person basis," meaning that six people will be placed in each campsite regardless of the number of people in your own party. Sunnyside often fills before 9 A.M. daily from May through September. The Upper Yosemite Falls Trailhead begins at the campground, and Lower Yosemite Falls is within easy walking distance. Elevation 4,000 feet. Stay limit 7 days from May 1 through September 15, 30 days the rest of the year. Open all year. No pets allowed.

49 Yosemite National Park: Tuolumne Meadows

Location: 7 miles west of Tioga Pass Entrance (East Entrance).

Sites: 314 sites for tents and RVs up to 35 feet long, plus 7 group sites for up to 30 people each and 4 equestrian sites for up to 6 people each.

Facilities: Tables, grills, drinking water, flush toilets, dump station, store, gas station, restaurant. Showers at Tuolumne Lodge, 0.5 mile away.

Fee per night: $15, equestrian sites $20, group sites $35. Reservations accepted; call 800-436-PARK or reserve online at http://reservations.nps.gov. Reservations required for group and equestrian sites.

Agency: Yosemite National Park, 209-372-0265.

Activities: Hiking, swimming, fishing, horseback riding.

Finding the campground: From the Tioga Pass Entrance, drive west 7 miles on California Highway 120 (Tioga Pass Road).

The Tuolumne River winds through Tuolumne Meadows, a beautiful spot in upcountry Yosemite.

About the campground: Tuolumne Meadows is a beautiful spot in upcountry Yosemite. Surrounding peaks, such as Unicorn and Cathedral, make a perfect frame for the green meadows and the small streams that flow through them, feeding into the Tuolumne River. The campground is shaded by a forest of medium-sized mixed pines, and it is laid out in several loops. Many attractive day hikes are possible from the campground, including a climb to the top of Lembert Dome (9,450 feet, 3 miles round trip), a hike to Dog Lake (3.5 miles), a hike to Elizabeth Lake (4.5 miles), and an easy, scenic, 1.5-mile stroll around the meadow to Soda Springs and Parsons Lodge. No pets are allowed in the horse camp. Elevation 8,600 feet. Stay limit 14 days. Open from mid-June through late September.

50 Yosemite National Park: Porcupine Flat

Location: 21 miles west of Tioga Pass Entrance (East Entrance).
Sites: 52 sites for tents, including limited space for RVs up to 35 feet long.
Facilities: Tables, grills, vault toilets. No drinking water.
Fee per night: $6.
Agency: Yosemite National Park, 209-372-0265.
Activities: Hiking.
Finding the campground: From the Tioga Pass Entrance, drive west 21 miles on California Highway 120.

About the campground: RVs only have access to the front section of the campground. A trail leads east from the campground, connecting to another trail leading to North Dome, which overlooks Yosemite Valley (6 miles one way). Elevation 8,100 feet. Stay limit 14 days. Open from July through early September. No pets allowed.

51 Yosemite National Park: Yosemite Creek

Location: 35 miles north of Yosemite Village.
Sites: 75 sites for tents or small RVs.
Facilities: Tables, grills, pit toilets. No drinking water.
Fee per night: $6.
Agency: Yosemite National Park, 209-372-0265.
Activities: Hiking, fishing.
Finding the campground: From Yosemite Village, drive west on Northside Drive for 6 miles, bear right at a fork onto Big Oak Flat Road, and drive 9 miles to the intersection with California Highway 120 (Tioga Pass Road). Continue on Tioga Pass Road for 15 miles, turn right at the Yosemite Creek access road, and drive 5 miles. The access road is winding, steep, and narrow and not suitable for large RVs or trailers.

About the campground: A trail leads south from the campground to the top of Upper Yosemite Falls and to the summit of El Capitan. Elevation 7,660 feet. Stay limit 14 days. Open from July through early September.

52 Yosemite National Park: White Wolf

Location: 30 miles north of Yosemite Village.
Sites: 87 sites for tents and RVs up to 35 feet long.
Facilities: Tables, grills, drinking water, flush toilets.
Fee per night: $10.
Agency: Yosemite National Park, 209-372-0265.
Activities: Hiking, fishing.
Finding the campground: From Yosemite Village, drive west on Northside Drive for 6 miles, bear right at a fork onto Big Oak Flat Road, and drive 9 miles to the intersection with California Highway 120 (Tioga Pass Road). Continue on Tioga Pass Road for 14 miles, turn left onto the campground access road, and drive 1 mile.

About the campground: Trails from the campground lead east to Lukens Lake (4 miles) and north to Harden Lake and the Grand Canyon of the Tuolumne (5 miles). Elevation 8,000 feet. Stay limit 14 days. Open from July through early September.

53 Yosemite National Park: Tamarack Flat

Location: 21 miles west of Yosemite Village.
Sites: 52 sites for tents or small RVs.

A trail leads from Yosemite Creek Campground to the summit of El Capitan, perhaps the largest exposed granite monolith in the world.

Facilities: Tables, grills, pit toilets. No drinking water.
Fee per night: $6.
Agency: Yosemite National Park, 209-372-0265.
Activities: Hiking.
Finding the campground: From Yosemite Village, drive west on Northside Drive for 6 miles, bear right at a fork onto Big Oak Flat Road, and drive 9 miles to the intersection with California Highway 120 (Tioga Pass Road). Continue on Tioga Pass Road for 3 miles, turn left onto the campground access road, and drive 3 miles. The dirt access road to the campground is not suitable for large RVs or trailers.

About the campground: A trail leads north from the campground to Aspen Valley and east to the summit of El Capitan. Elevation 6,300 feet. Stay limit 14 days. Open from June through early September. No pets allowed.

54 Yosemite National Park: Crane Flat

Location: 16 miles west of Yosemite Village.
Sites: 166 sites for tents and RVs up to 35 feet long.
Facilities: Tables, grills, drinking water, flush toilets.
Fee per night: $15. Reservations required; call 800-436-PARK or reserve online at http://reservations.nps.gov.
Agency: Yosemite National Park, 209-372-0265.
Activities: Hiking.
Finding the campground: From Yosemite Village, drive west on Northside Drive for 6 miles, bear right at a fork onto Big Oak Flat Road, and drive 10 miles.

About the campground: The campground is within a few minutes drive of Merced Grove and Tuolumne Grove, both of which contain giant, old-growth sequoia trees. Elevation 6,200 feet. Stay limit 14 days. Open from June through October.

55 Yosemite National Park: Hodgdon Meadow

Location: 22 miles northwest of Yosemite Valley.
Sites: 105 sites for tents and RVs up to 35 feet long, plus 4 group sites for up to 30 people each.
Facilities: Tables, grills, drinking water, flush toilets.
Fee per night: $15. Reservations are required from May through October for individual sites, year-round for group sites. Call 800-436-PARK or reserve online at http://reservations.nps.gov.
Agency: Yosemite National Park, 209-372-0265.
Activities: None.
Finding the campground: From Yosemite Village, drive west on Northside Drive for 6 miles, bear right at a fork onto Big Oak Flat Road, and drive 16 miles.

Bridalveil Fall plunges 620 feet from a hanging valley just below Cathedral Rocks.

About the campground: Elevation 4,872 feet. Stay limit 14 days from May 1 through September 15, 30 days the rest of the year. Open all year.

56 Yosemite National Park: Bridalveil Creek

Location: 23 miles south of Yosemite Village.

Sites: 110 sites for tents and RVs up to 35 feet long, plus several group sites for tents only (up to 30 people each) and several equestrian sites (up to 6 people and 2 horses each).

Facilities: Tables, grills, drinking water, flush toilets.

Fee per night: $10, group sites $35, equestrian sites $20. Reservations required for group and equestrian sites; call 800-436-PARK or reserve online at http://reservations.nps.gov.

Agency: Yosemite National Park, 209-372-0265.

Activities: Hiking, fishing, horseback riding.

Finding the campground: From Yosemite Village, drive west on Northside Drive for 5 miles, turn left onto California Highway 41, and drive 9 miles. Turn left onto Glacier Point Road and drive 9 miles.

About the campground: Situated in a wooded grove along Bridalveil Creek. Several excellent trails are located within walking distance of the campground. McGurk Meadow Trail begins 0.2 mile west of the campground turnoff and leads 2 miles downhill to an attractive meadow and an old cabin that belonged to one of the original Yosemite pioneers. The Ostrander Lake Trail (12.7 miles round trip) begins 1.3 miles east of the campground turnoff and leads to a beautiful alpine lake, offering views of Mount Starr King, the Yosemite Valley

Overflow Camping near Yosemite National Park

Every year, thousands of campers are turned away from Yosemite campgrounds because they are full, especially during the summer months and on holiday weekends. The best way to avoid this disappointment is to travel during off-peak periods, reserve campground space when possible, and arrive at campgrounds early in the day. For those who find themselves without a space inside the park itself, the following campgrounds are within a reasonable driving distance. All are described in this book and are listed in the index.

Big Oak Flat and Hetch Hetchy Entrances: Dimond O, Sweetwater, Lost Claim, The Pines, Moore Creek.

Arch Rock Entrance (El Portal): Indian Flat, Merced River Recreation Area.

South Entrance (Wawona): Summerdale, Summit, Big Sandy, Little Sandy, Fresno Dome, Soquel, Greys Mountain, Nelder Grove, Crane Valley, Forks, Lupine-Cedar, Spring Cove, Wishon Point.

East Entrance (Tioga Pass): Tioga Lake, Ellery Lake, Junction, Saddlebag Lake, Lower Lee Vining, Cattleguard, Moraine, Boulder, Aspen, Big Bend.

The humongous California Tunnel Tree in Mariposa Grove strains the incredulity and the neck muscles of a visitor.

domes, and the peaks of the Clark Range en route. The Mono Meadow Trail (3 miles round trip) provides magnificent views of Half Dome, the Clark Range, and Mount Starr King from the eastern end of the meadow. It begins 2.5 miles east of the campground turnoff.

Six miles east of the campground is the parking lot for the 2.2-mile round trip to the top of Sentinel Dome, with its panoramic view over the park. From the same parking area, a 2.2-mile trail leads to the spectacular cliffs and fissures of Taft Point. This campground is also the closest one to the magnificent overlook at Glacier Point (6 miles northeast). Elevation 7,200 feet. Stay limit 14 days. Open from June through September.

57 Yosemite National Park: Wawona

Location: 25 miles southwest of Yosemite Village.
Sites: 100 sites for tents and RVs up to 35 feet long, plus 1 group site for up to 30 people and 4 equestrian sites for up to 6 people each.
Facilities: Tables, fire grills/rings, drinking water, flush toilets, dump station. At Wawona, half a mile from the campground, are a store, post office, gas station, and 9-hole golf course.
Fee per night: $15. Reservations required for individual sites from May through October, year-round for group and equestrian camps. Call 800-436-PARK or reserve online at http://reservations.nps.gov.
Agency: Yosemite National Park, 209-372-0265.
Activities: Hiking, swimming, fishing, horseback riding.

Finding the campground: From Yosemite Village, drive west on Northside Drive for 5 miles, turn left onto California 41 and drive 20 miles.

About the campground: Spread out laterally in several loops along the banks of the South Fork of the Merced River, the campground provides swimming holes and fishing sites at many campsites. The Mariposa Grove of giant sequoia trees can be reached by a 6-mile trail from Wawona, by car, or by a free shuttle bus, which leaves from the post office. The grove contains many mature trees, including the Grizzly Giant, estimated to be more than 2,700 years old, and a tunnel tree, with a passage cut through its base.

A fine hike, little known among the more famous (and crowded) waterfall hikes, is the trail to Chilnaulna Falls. From Wawona, this scenic route gradually climbs 2,400 feet in 4.2 miles. A lovely basin is formed by the upper falls, with water flowing through five small, attractive pools before plunging over the main falls. Elevation 4,000 feet. Stay limit 14 days from May 1 through September 15, 30 days the rest of the year. Open all year.

MAMMOTH BASIN

Most of the undeveloped land in this area lies within the Inyo National Forest and in two of its wilderness areas: Ansel Adams and John Muir. Central to the area is the community of Mammoth Lakes, one of California's major summer and winter outdoor playgrounds. Mammoth Mountain, which towers over the town, hosts skiers in the winter and hikers and mountain bikers from spring through fall. Devils Postpile National Monument and Rainbow Falls are two of the attractions of Reds Meadow, west of the town. Jewel-like lakes at the base of snowcapped mountains beckon swimmers, anglers, and boaters.

The Lee Vining Canyon Scenic Byway leads to the East Entrance of Yosemite National Park, the highest vehicle crossing of the Sierra Nevada. Beginning at California Highway 395 about a half-mile south of Lee Vining, the route climbs 12 miles through spectacular Lee Vining Canyon to Tioga Pass (9,945 feet). Only the artificial border of the national park separates the upper portions of the canyon and its beautiful alpine lakes from the geologically similar Yosemite high country it adjoins.

1 Lundy Canyon

Location: 12 miles northwest of Lee Vining.
Sites: 50 sites for tents and RVs up to 23 feet long.
Facilities: Vault toilets, boat launch. No drinking water.
Fee per night: $7.
Management: Mono County Building and Parks Department, 760-932-5231.
Activities: Hiking, fishing, boating.
Finding the campground: From Lee Vining, drive north 7 miles on U.S. Highway 395, turn left (west) onto Lundy Lake Road, and drive 5 miles.

About the campground: Situated on Lundy Creek near Lundy Lake, which is well stocked annually with rainbow trout and brown trout fingerlings. Lundy

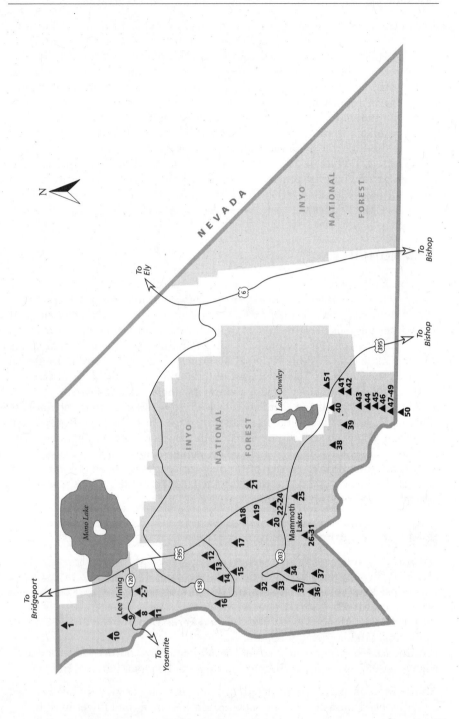

Mammoth Basin Campgrounds

	Group sites	RV sites	Total sites	Max. RV length	Hookups	Toilets	Showers	Drinking water	Dump station	Pets	Wheelchair	Recreation	Fee ($)	Season	Can reserve	Length of stay
1 Lundy Canyon		•	50	23		V				•		HF BL	7	May–October		
2 Lower Lee Vining		•	59			P				•		F	7	May–October		
3 Cattleguard		•	16			P				•		F	7	May–October		
4 Moraine		•	30			P				•		F	7	May–October		
5 Boulder		•	22			P				•		F	7	May–October		
6 Aspen		•	58			P	•			•		F	7	May–October		14
7 Big Bend		•	17	27		V	•		•	•	•	F	11	April 25–Oct. 15		14
8 Ellery Lake		•	15			F	•		•	•	•	F	11	June–Oct. 15		14
9 Junction		•	13			V				•		F	6	June–Oct. 15		14
10 Saddlebag Lake	•	•	21			V	•		•	•	•	HF BL	11–30	June–Oct. 15	•	14
11 Tioga Lake		•	13			V	•		•	•	•	F	11	June–Oct. 15		14

June Lake Loop (12–16)

	Group sites	RV sites	Total sites	Max. RV length	Hookups	Toilets	Showers	Drinking water	Dump station	Pets	Wheelchair	Recreation	Fee ($)	Season	Can reserve	Length of stay
12 Oh! Ridge		•	148	32		F	•			•		SF	12	April 23–October	•	14
13 June Lake		•	28	23		F	•			•		HS FBL	12	April 23–October	•	14
14 Gull Lake		•	11	23		F	•			•		HS FBL	12	April 23–October		14
15 Reversed Creek		•	17	23		F	•			•		F	12	May 15–Oct. 15		14
16 Silver Lake		•	63			F	•			•		HF BLR	12	April 23–October		14
17 Hartley Springs		•	20			V				•		H		June–Sept. 15		14
18 Glass Creek		•	50			V				•		HF		May 15–October		21
19 Obsidian Flat Group Camp	•	•	1			V				•		F	20	June–Oct. 15	•	14

	Group sites	RV sites	Total sites	Max. RV length	Hookups	Toilets	Showers	Drinking water	Dump station	Pets	Wheelchair	Recreation	Fee ($)	Season	Can reserve	Length of stay
20 Deadman		•	30			V				•		F		June–Oct. 15		14
21 Big Springs		•	26			V				•		F		April 25–October		21
Mammoth Lakes Basin (22–31)																
22 New Shady Rest		•	95			F	•	•		•		HOR	12	April 20–Oct. 13		14
23 Old Shady Rest		•	61			F	•	•		•		HR	12	June–Sept. 9		14
24 Pine Glen	•	•	17			F	•	•		•		HR	12–50	May 20–Sept. 27	•	14
25 Sherwin Creek		•	87			F	•	•		•		HOR	12	May 22–Sept. 13	•	21
26 Twin Lakes		•	94			F	•			•	•	HSF BLR	13	June 10–October		7
27 Pine City		•	10			F	•			•	•	HR	13	mid-June–mid-Sept.		14
28 Coldwater		•	77			F	•			•		HFR	13	mid-June–mid-Sept.		14
29 Lake George		•	16	23		F	•			•		HSF BLR	13	June 24–Sept. 13		7
30 Lake Mary		•	48	30		F	•			•		SF BLR	13	June 18–Sept. 13		14
31 Horseshoe Lake Group Camp	•	•	4			F	•			•		HS FBR	28–60	June 25–Sept. 14	•	14
Reds Meadow (32–37)																
32 Agnew Meadows	•	•	25			C	•			•		HFR	12–30	June 26–Oct. 4	•	14
33 Upper Soda Springs		•	29			F	•			•		HFR	12	June 26–Sept. 20		14
34 Pumice Flat	•	•	21			F	•			•		HFR	12–100	June 26–Sept. 20	•	14
35 Minaret Falls		•	27			C	•			•		HFR	12	June 26–Sept. 20		14
36 Devils Postpile National Monument		•	21			F	•			•		HFR	12	June 26–Snow		14
37 Reds Meadow		•	56	30		F	•	•		•		HR	12	June 26–Oct. 27		14
38 Convict Lake		•	88			F	•	•		•		HF BL	13	April 22–October		7

	Group sites	RV sites	Total sites	Max. RV length	Hookups	Toilets	Showers	Drinking water	Dump station	Pets	Wheelchair	Recreation	Fee ($)	Season	Can reserve	Length of stay
39 McGee Creek		•	28	23		F		•		•	•	HFR	12	April 24–Sept.	•	14
40 Crowley Lake		•	47			P				•				April 20–October		14
41 French Camp		•	86	23		F	•	•	•	•		F	12	April 24–October	•	21
42 Holiday		•	35	23		V	•			•		F	12	as needed		14
43 Aspen Group Camp	•	•	1	23		F	•			•		F	40	mid-May–mid-Oct.	•	14
44 Iris Meadow		•	14	23		F	•			•		F	12	June 26–October		7
45 Big Meadow		•	11	23		F	•			•		F	12	June 26–October		7
46 Palisade		•	5	23		F	•			•		F	12	June 26–October		7
47 East Fork		•	133			F	•			•		F	12	May 22–September	•	14
48 Pine Grove		•	11	23		F	•			•		F	12	May 22–Oct. 16		7
49 Upper Pine Grove		•	8	23		F	•			•	•	FR	12	May 22–Oct. 16		7
50 Rock Creek Lake	•	•	29	23		F	•			•		HFR	12–40	May 22–October	•	7
51 Tuff		•	34			F	•			•			12	April 24–Oct. 23	•	21

Hookups: W = Water E = Electric S = Sewer
Toilets: F = Flush V = Vault P = Pit C = Chemical
Recreation: H = Hiking S = Swimming F = Fishing B = Boating L = Boat Launch O = Off-highway Driving R = Horseback Riding
Maximum Trailer/RV Length given in feet. Stay Limit given in days. Fee given in dollars.
If no entry under **Season,** campground is open all year. If no entry under Fee, camping is free.

Tufa towers crowd the shores of Mono Lake, an oasis at the transition point between the Sierra Nevada and the Great Basin Desert.

Lake is also famous for large Alpers trout. A trail leads southwest from the campground to a series of small lakes in the Hoover Wilderness and to Saddlebag Lake (number 10). Elevation 7,800 feet. Open from May through October.

2 Lower Lee Vining

Location: 3 miles west of the town of Lee Vining.
Sites: 59 sites for tents and RVs.
Facilities: Tables, some stone fire rings, pit toilets. No drinking water.
Fee per night: $7.
Agency: Mono County Building and Parks Department, 760-932-5231.
Activities: Fishing.
Finding the campground: From Lee Vining, drive south on U.S. Highway 395 for 0.5 mile, turn right onto California Highway 120, and drive 2.5 miles.

About the campgrounds: Four campgrounds are spread closely along 2 miles of Lee Vining Creek, a beautiful stream with good fishing for rainbow trout. Campsites are in everything from large open fields to wooded areas, with some located right on the banks of the stream. The campgrounds (see also Cattleguard, Moraine, Boulder, Aspen, and Big Bend, numbers 3-7) also provide a base for exploring Mono Lake and basin. They are located within 5 miles of the Mono Basin Scenic Area Visitor Center and about 15 miles from the South Tufa and Navy Beach tufa viewing areas. The campgrounds also serve as an overflow area for Yosemite National Park, 8 miles to the west. Elevation 7,600 to 8,000 feet. Open from May through October.

3 Cattleguard

Location: 4 miles west of Lee Vining.
Sites: 16 sites for tents and RVs.
Facilities: Tables, some stone fire rings, pit toilets. No drinking water.
Fee per night: $7.
Agency: Mono County Building and Parks Department, 760-932-5231.
Activities: Fishing.
Finding the campground: From Lee Vining, drive south on U.S. Highway 395 for 0.5 mile, turn right onto California Highway 120, and drive 3 miles.

About the campground: See Lower Lee Vining Campground (number 2).

4 Moraine

Location: 4 miles west of Lee Vining.
Sites: 30 sites for tents and RVs.
Facilities: Tables, some stone fire rings, pit toilets. No drinking water.
Fee per night: $7.
Agency: Mono County Building and Parks Department, 760-932-5231.
Activities: Fishing.
Finding the campground: From Lee Vining, drive south on U.S. Highway 395 for 0.5 mile, turn right onto California Highway 120, and drive 3 miles. Turn left onto Poole Power Plant Road, and then turn left again. The road dead-ends at the campground, in about 200 yards.

About the campground: See Lower Lee Vining Campground (number 2).

5 Boulder

Location: 4 miles west of Lee Vining.
Sites: 22 sites for tents and RVs.
Facilities: Tables, some stone fire rings, pit toilets. No drinking water.
Fee per night: $7.
Agency: Mono County Building and Parks Department, 760-932-5231.
Activities: Fishing.
Finding the campground: From Lee Vining, drive south on U.S. Highway 395 for 0.5 mile, turn right onto California Highway 120, and drive 3 miles. Turn left onto Poole Power Plant Road, then make the first right turn and drive 0.5 mile.

About the campground: See Lower Lee Vining Campground (number 2).

6 Aspen

Location: 6 miles west of Lee Vining.
Sites: 58 sites for tents and RVs.
Facilities: Tables, some stone fire rings, drinking water, pit toilets.
Fee per night: $7.
Agency: Mono County Building and Parks Department, 760-932-5231.
Activities: Fishing.
Finding the campground: From Lee Vining, drive south on U.S. Highway 395 for 0.5 mile, turn right onto California Highway 120, and drive 4 miles. Turn left and then right, and follow the gravel road for 1.7 miles.

About the campground: Located on an attractive section of Lee Vining Creek (see Lower Lee Vining Campground, above). Many campsites are right on the banks of the stream, among both tall pines and smaller aspen, affording both heavily wooded and more open sites. The campground also serves as an overflow area for Yosemite National Park, 8 miles to the west. Elevation 8,000 feet. Stay limit 14 days. Open from May through October.

7 Big Bend

Location: 7 miles west of Lee Vining.
Sites: 17 sites for tents and RVs up to 27 feet long.
Facilities: Tables, fire rings, drinking water, vault toilets. The facilities are wheelchair accessible.
Fee per night: $11.
Agency: Inyo National Forest, 760-924-5500.
Activities: Fishing.
Finding the campground: From Lee Vining, drive south on U.S. Highway 395 for 0.5 mile, turn right onto California Highway 120, and drive 4 miles. Turn left and then right, and follow the gravel road for 2.7 miles.

About the campground: A heavily shaded campground with some smaller sites on the banks of Lee Vining Creek. Fishing is similar to Aspen Campground (number 6). The campground also serves as an overflow area for Yosemite National Park, 8 miles to the west. Elevation 7,800 feet. Stay limit 14 days. Open from April 25 through October 15.

8 Ellery Lake

Location: 10 miles west of Lee Vining.
Sites: 15 sites for tents and RVs.
Facilities: Tables, fire rings, drinking water, flush toilets. The facilities are wheelchair accessible.
Fee per night: $11.
Agency: Inyo National Forest, Mammoth Ranger District, 760-924-5500.

Activities: Fishing.

Finding the campground: From Lee Vining, drive south on U.S. Highway 395 for 0.5 mile, turn right onto California Highway 120, and drive 9 miles.

About the campground: Situated in a dramatic setting on the shore of a beautiful, blue, alpine lake, the campground is only 2 miles east of the western entrance to Yosemite. It is an excellent alternative to camping in the park at Tuolumne Meadows. The lake is stocked annually with rainbow trout. Elevation 9,500 feet. Stay limit 14 days. Open from June 1 through October 15.

9 Junction

Location: 10 miles west of Lee Vining.
Sites: 13 sites for tents and RVs.
Facilities: Tables, fire rings, vault toilets. No drinking water.
Fee per night: $6.
Agency: Inyo National Forest, Mammoth Ranger District, 760-924-5500.
Activities: Fishing.
Finding the campground: From Lee Vining, drive south on U.S. Highway 395 for 0.5 mile, turn right onto California Highway 120, and drive 9 miles. Across the highway from Ellery Lake Campground (number 8).

About the campground: Junction shares with Ellery Lake Campground (number 8) a dramatic setting and easy accessibility to Yosemite National Park. Elevation 9,600 feet. Stay limit 14 days. Open from June 1 through October 15.

10 Saddlebag Lake

Location: 12 miles west of Lee Vining.
Sites: 20 sites for tents and RVs, plus 1 group site for up to 40 people.
Facilities: Tables, fire rings, drinking water, vault toilets, store, boat ramp and rentals. The facilities are wheelchair accessible.
Fee per night: $11, group site $30. Reservations required for group site; call 800-280-CAMP. There is a one-time reservation fee of $15.
Agency: Inyo National Forest, Mammoth Ranger District, 760-924-5500.
Activities: Hiking, fishing, boating.
Finding the campground: From Lee Vining, drive south on U.S. Highway 395 for 0.5 mile, turn right on California Highway 120, and drive 9 miles. Turn right (north) onto Forest Road 04 and drive 2 miles.

About the campground: Saddlebag Lake is the highest lake accessible by car in California. It occupies a spectacular if stark setting well above treeline. The campground is within a quarter-mile of the lakeshore. The lake is well stocked annually with rainbow trout. A 4-mile trail circles the lake, another leads northwest to a series of smaller lakes, and a third leads north and then west to Lundy Canyon and Lundy Lake. The western entrance to Yosemite is 4 miles to the south. Elevation 10,087 feet. Stay limit 14 days. Open from June 1 through October 15.

11 Tioga Lake

Location: 11 miles west of Lee Vining.
Sites: 13 sites for tents and RVs.
Facilities: Tables, fire rings, drinking water, vault toilets. The facilities are wheelchair accessible.
Fee per night: $11.
Agency: Inyo National Forest, Mammoth Ranger District, 760-924-5500.
Activities: Fishing.
Finding the campground: From Lee Vining, drive south on U.S. Highway 395 for 0.5 mile, turn right (west) onto California Highway 120, and drive 10 miles.

About the campground: Situated in a spectacular setting beside a beautiful alpine lake, which is stocked annually with rainbow trout. The campground is an excellent alternative to Yosemite's Tuolumne Campground, and the park's eastern entrance is only 1 mile south. Elevation 9,700 feet. Stay limit 14 days. Open from June 1 through October 15.

12 June Lake Loop: Oh! Ridge

Location: 17 miles northwest of the community of Mammoth Lakes.
Sites: 148 sites for tents and RVs up to 32 feet long.
Facilities: Tables, fire rings, drinking water, flush toilets, playground. Boat ramp 2 miles south.

Sweeping views of the Sierra Nevada are typical of most campsites at Oh! Ridge Campground, northwest of the community of Mammoth Lakes.

Fee per night: $12. For reservations call 800-280-CAMP. There is a one-time reservation fee of $8.65.

Management: Inyo National Forest, 760-647-3000.

Activities: Swimming, fishing.

Finding the campground: From the Mammoth Lakes exit on U.S. Highway 395, drive northwest 15 miles on US 395, turn left (west) onto California Highway 158 (June Lake Loop), and drive 1.2 miles. Turn right (north) onto Oh! Ridge Road and drive half a mile.

About the campground: The June Lake Loop Road (CA 158) traverses a beautiful horseshoe-shaped glacial canyon with streams, waterfalls, forests, alpine meadows, and high desert. Spectacular mountain scenery greets you at almost every turn in the road. There are four lakes along the loop, with public campgrounds on three of them and a private campground on the fourth (Grant Lake).

The exclamation point in Oh! Ridge is well deserved. Overlooking June Lake and the snowcapped peaks of the Sierra Nevada beyond, this campground has one of the most magnificent views of any in this book, and many campsites are located to take advantage of it. There is no direct access to the lake, but June Lake Beach is less than 0.5 mile away. Elevation 7,600 feet. Stay limit 14 days. Open from April 23 through October 31.

13 June Lake Loop: June Lake

Location: 17 miles northwest of the community of Mammoth Lakes.

Sites: 28 sites for tents and RVs up to about 23 feet long.

Facilities: Tables, fire rings, drinking water, flush toilets, boat ramp.

Fee per night: $12. For reservations call 800-280-CAMP. There is a one-time reservation fee of $8.65.

Management: Inyo National Forest, 760-647-3000.

Activities: Swimming, fishing, boating, hiking.

Finding the campground: From the Mammoth Lakes exit on U.S. Highway 395, drive northwest 15 miles on US 395, turn left (west) onto California Highway 158 (June Lake Loop), and drive 2 miles.

About the campground: Although the campground is directly on the lake, the water is not visible from most campsites, nor are the surrounding mountains. Campers seeking a view should camp at Oh! Ridge Campground (number 12). June Lake is heavily stocked annually with rainbow trout. A trail leads southwest from the campground to tiny Yost Lake and on to Glass Creek Meadow. See Oh! Ridge Campground for more area information. Elevation 7,600 feet. Stay limit 14 days. Open from April 23 through October 31.

14 June Lake Loop: Gull Lake

Location: 18 miles northwest of the community of Mammoth Lakes.

Sites: 11 sites for tents and RVs up to about 23 feet long.

Facilities: Tables, fire rings, drinking water, flush toilets, boat ramp.

Fee per night: $12.
Management: Inyo National Forest, 760-647-3000.
Activities: Swimming, fishing, boating, hiking.
Finding the campground: From the Mammoth Lakes exit on U.S. Highway 395, drive northwest 15 miles on US 395, turn left (west) onto California Highway 158 (June Lake Loop), and drive 3 miles.

About the campground: For its small size (a little over 60 acres), Gull Lake is heavily stocked with fish—more than 35,000 catchable-size rainbow trout and 10,000 cutthroat trout fingerlings annually. A trail leads west 2 miles from the campground to Silver Lake and north 3 miles to Reversed Peak (9,473 feet). See Oh! Ridge Campground (number 12) for area information. Elevation 7,600 feet. Stay limit 14 days. Open from April 23 through October 31.

15 June Lake Loop: Reversed Creek

Location: 18 miles northwest of the community of Mammoth Lakes.
Sites: 17 sites for tents and RVs up to about 23 feet long.
Facilities: Tables, fire rings, drinking water, flush toilets. Boat ramp at June Lake, 1 mile north.
Fee per night: $12.
Management: Inyo National Forest, 760-647-3000.
Activities: Fishing.
Finding the campground: From the Mammoth Lakes exit on U.S. Highway 395, drive northwest 15 miles on US 395, turn left (west) onto California Highway 158 (June Lake Loop), and drive 3 miles. The campground is across the highway from Gull Lake Campground (number 14).

About the campground: Being the only stream in the area flowing toward rather than away from the mountains gave Reversed Creek its name. Situated across the highway from Gull Lake in a stand of tall pines, the campground is the most shaded and heavily wooded of those along June Lake Loop. Reversed Creek is stocked annually with a modest number of rainbow trout. See Oh! Ridge Campground (number 12) for more area information. Elevation 7,600 feet. Stay limit 14 days. Open from May 15 through October 15.

16 June Lake Loop: Silver Lake

Location: 21 miles northwest of the community of Mammoth Lakes.
Sites: 63 sites for tents and RVs.
Facilities: Tables, fire rings, drinking water, flush toilets, boat ramp.
Fee per night: $12.
Management: Inyo National Forest, 760-647-3000.
Activities: Fishing, boating, hiking, horseback riding.
Finding the campground: From the Mammoth Lakes exit on U.S. Highway 395, drive northwest 15 miles on US 395, turn left (west) onto California Highway 158 (June Lake Loop), and drive 6 miles.

About the campground: Located at the north end of Silver Lake, the campground occupies an open field with great views of the surrounding mountains. Only a few sites are near the water's edge, but all enjoy the view. If the campground is full, a large private campground is located across the highway. The lake is heavily stocked annually with rainbow trout. A trail leads from the south end of the lake to Agnew Lake (1 mile) and then divides into 2 trails (1 east, 1 south), each leading to a different series of lakes in the Ansel Adams Wilderness. Elevation 7,200 feet. Stay limit 14 days. Open April 23 through October 31.

17 Hartley Springs

Location: 13 miles northwest of the community of Mammoth Lakes.
Sites: 20 sites for tents and RVs.
Facilities: Tables, fire rings, vault toilets. No drinking water.
Fee per night: None.
Management: Inyo National Forest, 760-647-3000.
Activities: Hiking.
Finding the campground: From the Mammoth Lakes exit on U.S. Highway 395, drive northwest 11 miles on US 395, turn left (west) onto Forest Road 2S10, and drive 1 mile. Turn right onto Forest Road 2S48 and drive about 1 mile.

About the campground: Situated 2 miles north of Obsidian Dome, a volcanic "glass" flow of interest because of its unusual formation. Elevation 8,400 feet. Stay limit 14 days. Open from June 1 through September 15.

18 Glass Creek

Location: 10 miles northwest of the community of Mammoth Lakes.
Sites: 50 sites for tents and RVs.
Facilities: Tables, fire rings, vault toilets. No drinking water.
Fee per night: None.
Management: Inyo National Forest, 760-647-3000.
Activities: Hiking, fishing.
Finding the campground: From the Mammoth Lakes exit on U.S. Highway 395, drive northwest 9 miles on US 395, turn left (west) onto Glass Creek Road, and drive about 1 mile. It may be necessary to drive past this turnoff to find an authorized U-turn area, to gain access to the west side of US 395.

About the campground: A trail from the campground leads west along Glass Creek and the southern edge of Obsidian Dome, a volcanic "glass" flow of unusual formation. Fishing in Glass Creek usually results in mediocre catches of small trout; the stream is only minimally stocked. Elevation 7,600 feet. Stay limit 21 days. Open from May 15 through October 31.

19 Obsidian Flat Group Camp

Location: 10 miles northwest of the community of Mammoth Lakes.
Sites: 1 group site for tents and RVs.
Facilities: Tables, fire rings, vault toilets. No drinking water.
Fee per night: $20. For reservations call 800-280-CAMP. There is a one-time reservation fee of $15.
Management: Inyo National Forest, 760-647-3000.
Activities: Fishing.
Finding the campground: From the Mammoth Lakes exit on U.S. Highway 395, drive northwest 8 miles on US 395, turn left (west) onto Deadman Creek Road (Forest Road 2S05), and drive about 2 miles.

About the campground: Situated near Deadman Creek, where catches of small rainbow and native trout are possible. Elevation 7,800 feet. Stay limit 14 days. Open from June 1 through October 15.

20 Deadman

Location: 10 miles northwest of Mammoth Lakes.
Sites: 30 sites for tents and RVs.
Facilities: Tables, fire rings, vault toilets. No drinking water.
Fee per night: None.
Management: Inyo National Forest, 760-647-3000.
Activities: Fishing.
Finding the campground: From the Mammoth Lakes exit on U.S. Highway 395, drive northwest 8 miles on US 395, turn left (west) onto Deadman Creek Road (Forest Road 2S05), and drive about 2 miles. The campground is adjacent to Obsidian Flat Group Camp.

About the campground: Situated on Deadman Creek, where catches of small rainbow and native trout are possible. Elevation 7,800 feet. Stay limit 14 days. Open from June 1 through October 15.

21 Big Springs

Location: 9 miles north of Mammoth Lakes.
Sites: 26 sites for tents and RVs.
Facilities: Tables, fire rings, vault toilets. No drinking water.
Fee per night: None.
Management: Inyo National Forest, 760-647-3000.
Activities: Fishing.
Finding the campground: From the Mammoth Lakes exit on U.S. Highway 395, drive northwest 7 miles on US 395, turn right (northeast) onto Owens River Road, and drive about 2 miles. Bear left at the fork and drive a quarter-mile.

About the campground: Situated on Deadman Creek, where catches of small rainbow and native trout are possible. Elevation 7,800 feet. Stay limit 21 days. Open from April 25 through October 31.

22 Mammoth Lakes Basin: New Shady Rest

Location: In the town of Mammoth Lakes.
Sites: 95 sites for tents and RVs.
Facilities: Tables, fire rings, drinking water, flush toilets, dump station, playground.
Fee per night: $12.
Agency: Inyo National Forest, 619-924-5500.
Activities: Hiking, horseback riding, biking, OHV driving.
Finding the campgrounds: Heading west on California Highway 203 in Mammoth Lakes, turn right immediately after passing the Forest Service visitor center.

About the campground: Situated in an attractive Jeffrey pine forest within the town of Mammoth Lakes, New Shady Rest is best suited as a base for exploring the Mammoth Basin area and for overnighting when the lakeside campgrounds are full. It is within easy walking distance of the Forest Service visitor center and restaurants and shopping facilities in town. Hiking, biking, and OHV trails are nearby. Horses may be rented at an adjacent riding stable. Elevation 7,800 feet. Stay limit 14 days. Open from April 20 through October 13. Some sites remain open in winter for tent camping only.

23 Mammoth Lakes Basin: Old Shady Rest

Location: In the town of Mammoth Lakes.
Sites: 61 sites for tents and RVs.

Mammoth Lakes Basin

Famous for its world-class skiing, Mammoth Lakes Basin is also a year-round recreational area offering a magnificent setting for many other outdoor activities. When the skiing season ends, mountain bikers hurtle down the Kamikaze Trail on 11,000-foot-high Mammoth Mountain, while hikers and equestrians take to miles of trails of their own. Just southwest of the community of Mammoth Lakes are five wonderfully scenic lakes that are accessible by vehicle and eight more accessible by trail. Fishing is good in most of them.

There are nine campgrounds in the area: three in town and six along Lake Mary Road. Those in town, New and Old Shady Rest and Pine Glen, serve mainly as bases from which to explore the surrounding area and as overflow areas for the lake campgrounds. Elevations range from 7,800 feet in town to between 8,700 and 9,000 feet at lake sites.

Facilities: Tables, fire rings, drinking water, flush toilets, dump station, playground.
Fee per night: $12.
Agency: Inyo National Forest, 619-924-5500.
Activities: Hiking, horseback riding.
Finding the campgrounds: Heading west on California Highway 203 in Mammoth Lakes, turn right immediately after passing the Forest Service visitor center.

About the campground: See New Shady Rest (number 22). Stay limit 14 days. Open from June 1 through September 9.

24 Mammoth Lakes Basin: Pine Glen

Location: In the town of Mammoth Lakes.
Sites: 11 family sites, plus 6 group sites for tents and RVs.
Facilities: Tables, fire rings, drinking water, flush toilets, dump station, playground.
Fee per night: $12. Group sites $35-$50. Reservations required for group sites; call 800-280-CAMP. There is a one-time reservation fee of $15.
Agency: Inyo National Forest, 619-924-5500.
Activities: Hiking, horseback riding.
Finding the campgrounds: Heading west on California Highway 203 in Mammoth Lakes, turn right immediately after passing the Forest Service visitor center.

About the campground: See New Shady Rest (number 22). Stay limit 14 days. Open from May 20 through September 27.

25 Mammoth Lakes Basin: Sherwin Creek

Location: 3 miles southeast of the town of Mammoth Lakes.
Sites: 87 sites for tents and RVs.
Facilities: Tables, fire rings, drinking water, flush toilets, dump station, playground.
Fee per night: $12. For reservations call 800-280-CAMP. There is a one-time reservation fee of $8.65.
Agency: Inyo National Forest, 619-924-5500.
Activities: Hiking, OHV driving, horseback riding nearby.
Finding the campgrounds: From the Forest Service visitor center in Mammoth Lakes, take California Highway 203 west for 0.3 mile, turn left (south) onto Old Mammoth Road, and drive 1 mile. Bear left onto Forest Road 4S08 and drive 2 miles.

About the campground: Situated in an open pine forest on Sherwin Creek. A mile-long road from the campground leads to a trail that rises steeply to Sherwin Lakes (2 miles) and continues on to Valentine Lake (5 miles). Sherwin Lakes provide good fishing. A motocross track is located 1 mile southwest of camp. Stay limit 21 days. Open from May 22 through September 13.

26 Mammoth Lakes Basin: Twin Lakes

Location: 3 miles southwest of the town of Mammoth Lakes.
Sites: 94 sites for tents and RVs.
Facilities: Tables, fire rings, drinking water, flush toilets, boat ramp, store. The facilities are wheelchair accessible.
Fee per night: $13.
Agency: Inyo National Forest, 619-924-5500.
Activities: Hiking, fishing, boating, swimming, horseback riding.
Finding the campgrounds: From the Forest Service visitor center in Mammoth Lakes, take California Highway 203 west for 1 mile, bear left (southwest) onto Lake Mary Road, and drive 2.3 miles.

About the campground: The campground is divided into two sections, one on the east shore and the other on the west shore of the lakes. The setting of the lakes is beautiful and is enhanced by Twin Falls, which spills into the upper lake from Lake Mamie. Many campsites are on the water, with great views of Twin Falls and the surrounding mountains. Twin Lakes are well stocked annually with rainbow trout, and both are heavily fished by anglers in boats and float tubes.

A trail leads northeast from the campground, past sites of historic interest, to Panorama Dome (1.5-mile loop via Valley View Point), which provides excellent views of the surrounding area. The Mammoth Mountain Summit Trail leads northwest from campsite 30 of the west loop of the campground. It reaches the peak in 4 miles, with an elevation gain of 2,500 feet. Mammoth Rock Trail, an equestrian and hiker trail, begins about half a mile east of the campground on Old Mammoth Road (3 miles, one way). Mammoth Pack Station is nearby for horse rental and equestrian tours. Elevation 8,600 feet. Stay limit 7 days. Open from June 10 through October 31.

27 Mammoth Lakes Basin: Pine City

Location: 5 miles south of Mammoth Lakes.
Sites: 10 sites for tents and RVs.
Facilities: Tables, fire rings, drinking water, flush toilets. The facilities are wheelchair accessible.
Fee per night: $13.
Agency: Inyo National Forest, 619-924-5500.
Activities: Hiking, horseback riding.
Finding the campgrounds: From the Forest Service visitor center in Mammoth Lakes, take California Highway 203 west for 1 mile, bear left (southwest) onto Lake Mary Road, and drive 3.2 miles. Bear left onto Forest Road 4S09 and drive 0.3 mile.

About the campground: Situated in a pine forest across the road from Lake Mary, the campground has no direct lake access. Mammoth Pack Station is nearby for horse rental and equestrian tours. Elevation 8,900 feet. Stay limit 14 days. Open from mid-June to mid-September.

From Twin Falls, the view of Twin Lakes Campground is spectacular. The views from the camp-sites, many of them on the lakeshore, are equally outstanding.

28 | Mammoth Lakes Basin: Coldwater

Location: 5 miles south of Mammoth Lakes.
Sites: 77 sites for tents and RVs.
Facilities: Tables, fire rings, drinking water, flush toilets.
Fee per night: $13.
Agency: Inyo National Forest, 619-924-5500.
Activities: Hiking, fishing, horseback riding.
Finding the campgrounds: From the Forest Service visitor center in Mammoth Lakes, take California Highway 203 west for 1 mile, bear left (southwest) onto Lake Mary Road, and drive 3.2 miles. Bear left onto Forest Road 4S09 and drive 0.5 mile. Then turn left onto Forest Road 4S25 and drive 0.3 mile.

About the campground: Situated on Coldwater Creek, 0.3 mile from Lake Mary. There is no view of the lake or direct access. A trail from the campground leads to Emerald Lake (0.75 mile) and Sky Meadows (2 miles); both trails offer fine views of the surrounding Sierra peaks. Mammoth Pack Station is nearby for horse rental and equestrian tours. Elevation 8,900 feet. Stay limit 14 days. Open from mid-June to mid-September.

29 | Mammoth Lakes Basin: Lake George

Location: 6 miles southwest of the town of Mammoth Lakes.
Sites: 16 sites for tents and RVs up to 23 feet long.
Facilities: Tables, fire rings, drinking water, flush toilets, boat ramp.
Fee per night: $13.
Agency: Inyo National Forest, 619-924-5500.
Activities: Hiking, fishing, swimming, boating, horseback riding.
Finding the campgrounds: From the Forest Service visitor center in Mammoth Lakes, take California Highway 203 west for 1 mile, bear left (southwest) onto Lake Mary Road, and drive 3.2 miles. Bear left onto Forest Road 4S09 and drive 1.5 miles.

About the campground: The lake is in a marvelously scenic setting in a deep rock basin at the base of 10,377-foot Crystal Crag. From the campground there is direct access to the lake, which is well stocked annually with rainbow trout. The Barrett Lake/T.J. Lake Trail, a 1-mile round trip from the campground, affords a maximum display of mountain scenery for minimum effort. The Crystal Lake/Mammoth Crest Trail, 6 miles round trip, provides even more spectacular scenery. Mammoth Pack Station is nearby for horse rental and equestrian tours. Elevation 9,000 feet. Stay limit 7 days. Open from June 24 through September 13.

30 | Mammoth Lakes Basin: Lake Mary

Location: 6 miles south of the town of Mammoth Lakes.
Sites: 48 sites for tents and RVs up to 30 feet long.
Facilities: Tables, fire rings, drinking water, flush toilets, boat launch and rentals, pier.

Fee per night: $13.
Agency: Inyo National Forest, 619-924-5500.
Activities: Fishing, swimming, boating, horseback riding.
Finding the campgrounds: From the Forest Service visitor center in Mammoth Lakes, take California Highway 203 west for 1 mile, bear left (southwest) onto Lake Mary Road, and drive 3.2 miles. Bear left onto Forest Road 4S09 and drive 1.5 miles.

About the campground: Lake Mary was selected by *Sunset Magazine* as one of the 100 best campgrounds in the western United States. The campsites are on a rise overlooking the lake and offer direct access to the water. Scenery at the lakeside is beautiful. The lake is heavily stocked annually with rainbow trout, and fishing is usually good from a trolling boat and fair from shore. Mammoth Pack Station is nearby for horse rental and equestrian tours. Elevation 8,900 feet. Stay limit 14 days. Open from June 18 through September 13.

31 Mammoth Lakes Basin: Horseshoe Lake Group Camp

Location: 6 miles south of the town of Mammoth Lakes.
Sites: 4 group sites for tents and RVs.
Facilities: Tables, fire rings, drinking water, flush toilets, swimming beach.
Fee per night: $28-$60. Reservations required; call 800-280-CAMP. There is a one-time reservation fee of $15.
Agency: Inyo National Forest, 619-924-5500.
Activities: Fishing, hiking, swimming, boating, horseback riding.
Finding the campgrounds: From the Forest Service visitor center in Mammoth Lakes, take California Highway 203 west for 1 mile, bear left (southwest) onto Lake Mary Road, and drive 5 miles to the end of the road.

About the campground: Although the campground is situated in a secluded setting on a scenic lake, the ambiance is somewhat marred by a large section of standing dead trees along the shoreline in the vicinity of the parking lot. Fishing is only fair; a small rainbow trout population exists. A trail leads from the parking lot to McLeod Lake (0.5 mile) and over Mammoth Pass to Reds Meadow (4 miles) and Devils Postpile (6 miles). Mammoth Pack Station is nearby for horse rental and equestrian tours. Elevation 8,900 feet. Stay limit 14 days. Open from June 25 through September 14.

32 Reds Meadow: Agnew Meadows

Location: 10 miles northwest of the town of Mammoth Lakes.
Sites: 21 sites for tents and RVs, plus 4 group sites.
Facilities: Tables, fire rings, drinking water, chemical toilets.
Fee per night: $12. Group fee $15-$30. Reservations required for group camp; call 800-280-CAMP. There is a one-time reservation fee of $15.
Management: Inyo National Forest, 619-924-5500.
Activities: Hiking, fishing, horseback riding.
Finding the campground: From the Forest Service visitor center in Mammoth Lakes, drive west on California Highway 203 for 6 miles to the Reds

Reds Meadow

Reds Meadow is a forested canyon through which flows the Middle Fork of the San Joaquin River. It is accessible via a narrow road that drops 2,000 feet from the Mammoth Lakes area. The road begins at Minaret Vista, a spectacular lookout over The Minarets, Mount Ritter, and other snow-covered, jagged peaks of the Sierra Nevada. Several trails, two small lakes, and two impressive waterfalls are located along the valley floor, as is Devils Postpile National Monument, an unusual geological formation of basalt rock columns.

Fishing for rainbow trout is good in the Upper San Joaquin River, particular north of Agnew Meadows. Swimming is permitted in Starkweather and Sotcher Lakes, and horseback riding and equestrian tours are available from two pack stations. In the summer, Minaret Summit Road is closed to private vehicle traffic, and visitors are required to ride a shuttle bus to and from the valley. An exception is made for campers staying in one of the six campgrounds on the valley floor: Agnew Meadows, Upper Soda Springs, Pumice Flat, Minaret Falls, Devils Postpile National Monument, and Reds Meadow.

Meadow entrance station. Check in and request a permit to use the road for camping purposes. Continue on what is now Minaret Summit Road for about 3 miles, descending on a paved but narrow and sometimes one-way route. Turn right onto the campground entry road and drive half a mile.

About the campground: Situated along the bank of a feeder stream of the Middle Fork of the San Joaquin River, which provides good fishing for small trout. The Pacific Crest Trail passes the campground, offering a fine hike along the river to Soda Springs (3 miles), Devils Postpile (7 miles), Reds Meadow (9 miles), and Rainbow Falls (10 miles). In the summer, you can make the return trip on the park shuttle bus. You can also take the trail northward to Emerald and Thousand Island Lakes (6 miles), two beautiful spots in the shadow of two of the Minaret peaks. A pack station is located near the beginning of the campground entry road. Elevation 8,400 feet. Stay limit 14 days. Open from June 26 through October 4.

33 Reds Meadow: Upper Soda Springs

Location: 11 miles west of the town of Mammoth Lakes.
Sites: 29 sites for tents and RVs.
Facilities: Tables, fire rings, drinking water, flush toilets.
Fee per night: $12.
Management: Inyo National Forest, 619-924-5500.
Activities: Hiking, fishing, horseback riding.
Finding the campground: From the Forest Service visitor center in Mammoth Lakes, drive west on California Highway 203 for 6 miles to the Reds Meadow entrance station. Check in and request a permit to use the road for

The Minarets take a bite out of the sky along the narrow road to Reds Meadow.

camping purposes. Continue on what is now Minaret Summit Road for about 5 miles, descending on a paved but narrow and sometimes one-way route to the valley floor.

About the campground: Situated near the bank of the Middle Fork of the San Joaquin River, at a point where the Pacific Crest Trail crosses the river (see Agnew Meadows Campground, number 32). The river is stocked annually with trout from a place near the campground. Swimming is permitted at Starkweather Lake, about a mile north. A pack station is 2 miles north for horse rental and equestrian tours. Elevation 7,700 feet. Stay limit 14 days. Open from June 26 through September 20.

34 Reds Meadow: Pumice Flat

Location: 12 miles west of the town of Mammoth Lakes.
Sites: 17 family sites, plus 4 group sites for tents and RVs.
Facilities: Tables, fire rings, drinking water, flush toilets.
Fee per night: $12. Group sites $40-$100. Reservations required for group sites; call 800-280-CAMP. There is a one-time reservation fee of $15.
Management: Inyo National Forest, 619-924-5500.
Activities: Hiking, fishing, horseback riding.
Finding the campground: From the Forest Service visitor center in Mammoth Lakes, drive west on California Highway 203 for 6 miles to the Reds Meadow entrance station. Check in and request a permit to use the road for camping purposes. Continue on what is now Minaret Summit Road for about 6 miles, descending on a paved but narrow and sometimes one-way route to the valley floor.

About the campground: See Agnew Meadows Campground (number 32) for fishing information. Swimming is permitted in Starkweather Lake, about 1 mile north, and Sotcher Lake, about 2 miles south. A pack station is located at Reds Meadow, about 2 miles south. Elevation 7,700 feet. Stay limit 14 days. Open from June 26 through September 20.

35 Reds Meadow: Minaret Falls

Location: 14 miles west of the town of Mammoth Lakes.
Sites: 27 sites for tents and RVs.
Facilities: Tables, fire rings, drinking water, chemical toilets.
Fee per night: $12.
Management: Inyo National Forest, 619-924-5500.
Activities: Hiking, fishing, horseback riding.
Finding the campground: From the Forest Service visitor center in Mammoth Lakes, drive west on California Highway 203 for 6 miles to the Reds Meadow entrance station. Check in and request a permit to use the road for camping purposes. Continue on what is now Minaret Summit Road for about 7 miles, descending on a paved but narrow and sometimes one-way route to the valley floor. Turn right onto the campground access road and drive half a mile.

About the campground: Situated in a beautiful setting, with Minaret Falls just across the San Joaquin River. A mile-long trail leads from the campground to Devils Postpile. See Agnew Meadows Campground (number 32) for fishing information. Swimming is permitted in Sotcher Lake, about 1 mile south. A pack station is located at Reds Meadow, about 2 miles south. Elevation 7,600 feet. Stay limit 14 days. Open from June 26 through September 20.

36 Reds Meadow: Devils Postpile National Monument

Location: 14 miles west of the town of Mammoth Lakes.
Sites: 21 sites for tents and RVs.
Facilities: Tables, fire rings, drinking water, flush toilets.
Fee per night: $12.
Management: Devils Postpile National Monument, 760-934-2289.
Activities: Hiking, fishing, horseback riding.
Finding the campground: From the Forest Service visitor center in Mammoth Lakes, drive west on California Highway 203 for 6 miles to the Reds Meadow entrance station. Check in and request a permit to use the road for camping purposes. Continue on what is now Minaret Summit Road for about 8 miles, descending on a paved but narrow and sometimes one-way route to the valley floor.

About the campground: Devils Postpile is an unusual columnar-jointed basalt, formed when lava erupting from the river valley cooled and cracked into postlike columns. The campground is near the bank of the Middle Fork of the San Joaquin River, about half a mile north of the actual "postpile" on an

An unusual formation of basalt rock column, formed when a lava eruption cooled, is the highlight of Devil's Postpile National Monument in the Mammoth Lakes area.

easy trail. The same trail continues for 2.5 more miles to Rainbow Falls. Swimming is permitted in Sotcher Lake, about 1 mile south. A pack station is located at Reds Meadow, about 2 miles south. The combined Pacific Crest/John Muir Trail passes through the monument, offering hiking opportunities north and south. Elevation 7,600 feet. Stay limit 14 days. Open from June 26 until snowfall.

37 Reds Meadow: Reds Meadow

Location: 15 miles west of the town of Mammoth Lakes.
Sites: 56 sites for tents and RVs up to 30 feet long.
Facilities: Tables, fire rings, drinking water, flush toilets, hot springs showers and tubs.
Fee per night: $12.
Management: Inyo National Forest, 619-924-5500.
Activities: Hiking, horseback riding.
Finding the campground: From the Forest Service visitor center in Mammoth Lakes, drive west on California Highway 203 for 6 miles to the Reds Meadow entrance station. Check in and request a permit to use the road for camping purposes. Continue on what is now Minaret Summit Road for about 9 miles, descending on a paved but narrow and sometimes one-way route to the valley floor.

About the campground: Situated in a sloping meadow dotted with trees, the campground at Reds Meadow features a rustic bathhouse with six separate rooms, each with a shower and a large tub. Hot water is supplied from a nearby natural hot spring. There is no charge, but donations are encouraged. Trails lead from the campground to Devils Postpile (1 mile), Sotcher Lake (half a mile), and Red Cones, a series of small, volcanically formed cinder cones (6.5 mile loop). Swimming is permitted at Sotcher Lake, and horse rentals and equestrian tours are available at Reds Meadow Pack Station. Elevation 7,600 feet. Stay limit 14 days. Open from June 26 through October 27.

38 Convict Lake

Location: 9 miles southeast of the town of Mammoth Lakes.
Sites: 88 sites for tents and RVs.
Facilities: Tables, fire rings and grills, drinking water, flush toilets, dump station, boat ramp and rentals.
Fee per night: $13.
Agency: Inyo National Forest, 619-924-5500.
Activities: Fishing, boating, hiking.
Finding the campground: From Mammoth Lakes, drive east on California Highway 203 for 3 miles, turn right onto U.S. Highway 395, and drive 4 miles. Turn right onto Forest Road 07 and drive 2 miles.

About the campground: Convict Lake has one of the most spectacular settings in the Sierra Nevada. The sheer sides of Mount Morrison and Laurel Mountain plunge directly down to the shoreline. The campsites are not directly on the lake, but they enjoy the full mountain panorama from open sites in a brush and grass field. The lake is heavily stocked with rainbow trout annually. A 2-mile trail circles the lake and also leads through Convict Creek Canyon to Mildred Lake (5 miles) and Lake Dorothy (6 miles). Elevation 7,600 feet. Stay limit 7 days. Open from April 22 through October 31.

39 McGee Creek

Location: 13 miles southeast of the town of Mammoth Lakes.
Sites: 28 sites for tents and RVs up to 23 feet long.
Facilities: Tables, fire rings, drinking water, flush toilets. The facilities are wheelchair accessible.
Fee per night: $12. For reservations call 800-280-CAMP. There is a one-time reservation fee of $8.65.
Management: Inyo National Forest, 760-873-2500.
Activities: Hiking, fishing, horseback riding.
Finding the campground: From Mammoth Lakes, drive east on California Highway 203 for 3 miles, turn right onto U.S. Highway 395, and drive 7 miles southeast. Turn off to the right onto the frontage road paralleling the freeway and drive 1.5 miles. Turn right onto McGee Creek Road and drive 1.5 miles.

About the campground: Situated in an attractive meadow, adjacent to McGee Creek, which is stocked annually with rainbow trout. From the steep road leading to the campground, you get great views of the Sierra Nevada and Owen Valley. Sites are paved and level. There are no large trees, but ramadas shade the picnic tables. A hiker and equestrian trail about a mile southwest of the campground leads to Horsetail Falls and several small lakes. Elevation 7,600 feet. Stay limit 14 days. Open from April 24 through September 30.

40 Crowley Lake

Location: 13 miles southeast of the town of Mammoth Lakes.
Sites: 47 sites for tents and RVs, plus a group parking area.
Facilities: Tables, fire rings, pit toilets. No drinking water.
Fee per night: None.
Management: Bureau of Land Management, 760-872-4881.
Activities: Fishing, boating, swimming at Crowley Lake (3 miles away).
Finding the campground: From Mammoth Lakes, drive east 3 miles on California Highway 203, turn right onto U.S. Highway 395, and drive 7 miles southeast. Turn off to the right onto the frontage road paralleling the freeway and drive 2.5 miles.

About the campground: This campground is located in open high-desert country, where there are no trees and the wind can often be strong. The area looks out over Crowley Lake, about 3 miles away. There is a boat ramp at South Landing. The lake is stocked annually with 40,000 rainbow trout and more than 300,000 Eagle Lake and rainbow fingerlings. Sacramento perch are also stocked. Elevation 7,000 feet. Stay limit 14 days. Open from April 20 through October 31.

41 French Camp

Location: 18 miles southeast of the town of Mammoth Lakes.
Sites: 86 sites for tents and RVs up to 23 feet long.
Facilities: Tables, fire rings, drinking water, flush toilets, dump station.
Fee per night: $12. For reservations call 800-280-CAMP. There is a one-time reservation fee of $8.65.
Management: Inyo National Forest, 760-873-2500.
Activities: Fishing.
Finding the campground: From Mammoth Lakes, drive 3 miles east on California Highway 203, turn right onto U.S. Highway 395, and drive 14.5 miles southeast. Turn right (south) at Tom's Place exit onto Rock Creek Road (Forest Road 12) and drive 0.25 mile.

About the campground: Situated on Rock Creek near the entrance to Rock Creek Canyon, the campground is used as a base for activities at Crowley Lake, 3 miles to the northwest. The creek offers fair fishing for small trout. Elevation 7,500 feet. Stay limit 21 days. Open from April 24 through October 31.

42 Holiday

Location: 18 miles southeast of the town of Mammoth Lakes.
Sites: 35 sites for tents and RVs up to 23 feet long.
Facilities: Tables, fire rings, drinking water, vault toilets.
Fee per night: $12.
Management: Inyo National Forest, 760-873-2500.
Activities: Fishing.
Finding the campground: From Mammoth Lakes, drive 3 miles east on California Highway 203, turn right onto U.S. Highway 395, and drive 14.5 miles southeast. Turn right (south) at the Tom's Place exit onto Rock Creek Road (Forest Road 12) and drive 0.5 mile.

About the campground: Situated near the entrance to Rock Creek Canyon. Elevation 7,500 feet. Stay limit 14 days. The campground serves as an overflow area and is open as needed.

43 Aspen Group Camp

Location: 21 miles southeast of the town of Mammoth Lakes.
Sites: 1 group site for tents and RVs up to 23 feet long.
Facilities: Tables, fire rings, drinking water, flush toilets.
Fee per night: $40. Reservations required; call 800-280-CAMP. There is a one-time reservation fee of $15.
Management: Inyo National Forest, 760-873-2500.
Activities: Fishing.
Finding the campground: From Mammoth Lakes, drive 3 miles east on California Highway 203, turn right onto U.S. Highway 395, and drive 14.5 miles southeast. Turn right (south) at Tom's Place exit onto Rock Creek Road (Forest Road 12) and drive a little over 3 miles.

About the campground: Situated on Rock Creek, with fishing for small trout. Elevation 8,100 feet. Stay limit 14 days. Open from mid-May through mid-October.

44 Iris Meadow

Location: 21 miles southeast of Mammoth Lakes.
Sites: 14 sites for tents and RVs up to 23 feet long.
Facilities: Tables, fire rings, drinking water, flush toilets.
Fee per night: $12.
Management: Inyo National Forest, 760-873-2500.
Activities: Fishing.
Finding the campground: From Mammoth Lakes, drive 3 miles east on California Highway 203, turn right onto U.S. Highway 395, and drive 14.5 miles southeast. Turn right (south) at Tom's Place exit onto Rock Creek Road (Forest Road 12) and drive 3.75 miles.

About the campground: Situated on Rock Creek, with fishing for small trout. Elevation 8,300 feet. Stay limit 7 days. Open from June 26 through October 31.

45 Big Meadow

Location: 22 miles southeast of the town of Mammoth Lakes.
Sites: 11 sites for tents and RVs up to 23 feet long.
Facilities: Tables, fire rings, drinking water, flush toilets.
Fee per night: $12.
Management: Inyo National Forest, 760-873-2500.
Activities: Fishing.
Finding the campground: From Mammoth Lakes, drive 3 miles east on California Highway 203, turn right onto U.S. Highway 395, and drive 14.5 miles southeast. Turn right (south) at Tom's Place exit onto Rock Creek Road (Forest Road 12) and drive 4.75 miles.

About the campground: Situated on Rock Creek, with fishing for small trout. Elevation 8,600 feet. Stay limit 7 days. Open from June 26 through October 31.

46 Palisade

Location: 23 miles southeast of the town of Mammoth Lakes.
Sites: 5 sites for tents and RVs up to 23 feet long.
Facilities: Tables, fire rings, drinking water, flush toilets.
Fee per night: $12.
Management: Inyo National Forest, 760-873-2500.
Activities: Fishing.
Finding the campground: From Mammoth Lakes, drive 3 miles east on California Highway 203, turn right onto U.S. Highway 395, and drive 14.5 miles southeast. Turn right (south) at Tom's Place exit onto Rock Creek Road (Forest Road 12) and drive 5.75 miles.

About the campground: Situated on Rock Creek, with fishing for small trout. Elevation 8,600 feet. Stay limit 7 days. Open from June 26 through October 31.

47 East Fork

Location: 24 miles southeast of the town of Mammoth Lakes.
Sites: 133 sites for tents and RVs.
Facilities: Tables, fire rings, drinking water, flush toilets.
Fee per night: $12. For reservations call 800-280-CAMP. There is a one-time reservation fee of $8.65.
Management: Inyo National Forest, 760-873-2500.
Activities: Fishing.

Finding the campground: From Mammoth Lakes, drive 3 miles east on California Highway 203, turn right onto U.S. Highway 395, and drive 14.5 miles southeast. Turn right (south) at Tom's Place exit onto Rock Creek Road (Forest Road 12) and drive 6.75 miles.

About the campground: Situated on Rock Creek, with fishing for small trout. Elevation 9,000 feet. Stay limit 14 days. Open from May 22 through September 30.

48 Pine Grove

Location: 25 miles southeast of the town of Mammoth Lakes.
Sites: 11 sites for tents and RVs up to 23 feet long.
Facilities: Tables, fire rings, drinking water, flush toilets.
Fee per night: $12.
Management: Inyo National Forest, 760-873-2500.
Activities: Fishing.
Finding the campground: From Mammoth Lakes, drive 3 miles east on California Highway 203, turn right onto U.S. Highway 395, and drive 14.5 miles southeast. Turn right (south) at Tom's Place exit onto Rock Creek Road (Forest Road 12) and drive 7.75 miles.

About the campground: Situated on Rock Creek, with fishing for small trout. A pack station is nearby offering horse rentals and trips. Elevation 9,300 feet. Stay limit 7 days. Open from May 22 through October 16.

49 Upper Pine Grove

Location: 26 miles southeast of the town of Mammoth Lakes.
Sites: 8 sites for tents and RVs up to 23 feet long.
Facilities: Tables, fire rings, drinking water, flush toilets. The facilities are wheelchair accessible.
Fee per night: $12.
Management: Inyo National Forest, 760-873-2500.
Activities: Fishing, horseback riding.
Finding the campground: From Mammoth Lakes, drive 3 miles east on California Highway 203, turn right onto U.S. Highway 395, and drive 14.5 miles southeast. Turn right (south) at Tom's Place exit onto Rock Creek Road (Forest Road 12) and drive about 8 miles.

About the campground: Situated on Rock Creek, with fishing for small trout. A pack station is nearby offering horse rentals and trips. Elevation 9,400 feet. Stay limit 7 days. Open from May 22 through October 16.

50 Rock Creek Lake

Location: 28 miles southeast of the town of Mammoth Lakes.
Sites: 28 sites, plus 1 group site for tents and RVs up to 23 feet long.
Facilities: Tables, fire rings, drinking water, flush toilets.

Fee per night: $12. Group site $40. Reservations required for the group site; call 800-280-CAMP. There is a one-time reservation fee of $15.
Management: Inyo National Forest, 760-873-2500.
Activities: Fishing, hiking, horseback riding.
Finding the campground: From Mammoth Lakes, drive 3 miles east on California Highway 203, turn right onto U.S. Highway 395, and drive 14.5 miles southeast. Turn right (south) at Tom's Place exit onto Rock Creek Road (Forest Road 12) and drive about 10 miles.

About the campground: Selected by *Sunset Magazine* as one of the 100 best in the west, the campground is situated on small but beautiful Rock Creek Lake, which is well stocked annually with rainbow trout. A trail leads north from the campground to Hilton Creek Lakes, and another trail 1.5 miles south of the camp leads to Little Lakes Valley, which holds more than a dozen small lakes. A nearby pack station offers horse rentals and trips. Elevation 9,700 feet. Stay limit 7 days. Open from May 22 through October 31.

51 Tuff

Location: 15 miles southeast of Mammoth Lakes.
Sites: 34 sites for tents and RVs.
Facilities: Tables, fire rings, drinking water, flush toilets.
Fee per night: $12. For reservations call 800-280-CAMP. There is a one-time reservation fee of $8.65.
Management: Inyo National Forest, 760-873-2500.
Activities: None. Fishing, boating, and swimming at Crowley Lake, 4 miles west.
Finding the campground: From the intersection of California Highway 203 and U.S. Highway 395 (the Mammoth Lakes exit), drive east 15 miles on US 395.

About the campground: Campsites are organized in three separate loops along a small but attractive stocked trout stream. Tuff can be used as a base for those wanting to fish at Crowley Lake or explore the nearby Owens River Gorge. Elevation 7,000 feet. Stay limit 21 days. Open from April 24 through October 23.

Index

D

E

F

N

About the Author

Richard McMahon lives in Kahuku, Hawaii, but spends his summers in an RV traveling California. He has written numerous articles for magazines and newspapers and writes a weekly outdoor column for *The Advertiser*, Honolulu's largest daily paper. After retiring from the U.S. Army, he led hiking and backpacking trips worldwide for Mountain Travel and REI Adventures. In addition to this book, he is the author of *Camping Southern California, Adventuring in Hawaii, Camping Hawaii,* and *Scenic Driving Hawaii.*